1870

This book belongs to

_____

_____

_____

_____

1917

AMERICAN CAKE

ANNE BYRN

AMERICAN CAKE

FROM COLONIAL GINGERBREAD
TO CLASSIC LAYER,
THE STORIES AND RECIPES
BEHIND MORE THAN 125
OF OUR BEST-LOVED CAKES

RODALE

RODALE
wellness

Live happy. Be healthy. Get inspired.

Sign up today to get exclusive access to our authors, exclusive bonuses,
and the most authoritative, useful, and cutting-edge information on health,
wellness, fitness, and living your life to the fullest.

Visit us online at RodaleWellness.com
Join us at RodaleWellness.com/join

© 2016 by Anne Byrn

Photographs © 2016 by Rodale Inc.

Bake-Off is a registered trademark of the Pillsbury Company.

Printed in the United States of America
Rodale Inc. makes every effort to use acid-free ♾, recycled paper ♺.

Front cover recipes: (*top*) Pink Champagne Cake (*page 218*) and (*bottom left to bottom right*) Harriott Horry's Water Cake (*page 31*); Lady Baltimore Cake (*page 110*); and The Doberge Torte (*page 241*)

Back cover recipes (*top left to top right*): Coconut Layer Cake (*page 55*); Boston Cream Pie (*page 46*); and Chocolate Stout Cake (*page 288*)

Spine recipe: 1–2–3–4 Cake (*page 96*)

The credits are on page 329.

Book design by Amy C. King
Photographs by Mitch Mandel / Rodale Images
Food Styling by Paul Grimes
Prop styling by Carla Gonzalez-Hart

Library of Congress Cataloging-in-Publication Data is on file with the publisher.

ISBN 978–1–62336–543–1   hardcover

4   6   8   10   9   7   5   3   hardcover

Follow us @RodaleBooks on 🐦 📘 📌 📷

We inspire health, healing, happiness, and love in the world.
Starting with you.

As ever,
for John,
Kathleen,
Litton,
and
John

Contents

Remember, men love Swans Down cakes (and the girls who bake them!).
—GENERAL FOODS, 1955

Cakes were the pride and joy of many a cook, and at times almost an insignia of status.... Everyone in the neighborhood knew who made the best caramel or coconut or chocolate cake, and at community dinners those prized creations were the first to disappear.
—JOHN EGERTON, Southern Food, 1987

In early America the question was, "Who gets to eat cake." ... It separates the haves from the have-nots.
—LENI SORENSEN, 2015

When I think of American cake, it is a layer cake, two or three, with cream or jam between the layers and some frosting. That is very American.
—JANICE LONGONE, 2015

Cakes from every land have been introduced to America—but none is as glamorous as the typically American cake developed in this country—the gorgeous concoction of richly tender layers, crowned with luscious creamy icing.
—BETTY CROCKER, 1942

Cake was love, femininity, happiness, and a man around the house.
—LAURA SHAPIRO, Something from the Oven, 2004

That most wonderful object of domestic art called trifle . . . with its charming confusion of cream and cake and almonds and jam and jelly and wine and cinnamon and froth.
—OLIVER WENDELL HOLMES SR., 1861

Sometimes my mother baked cakes in the fireplace. She put the whole cake inside a big iron pot that sat on the edge of the hearth. The lid of the pot had a rim large enough to hold pieces of coal from the fireplace and so with the fire surrounding the pot and the hot coals on top of it the cake baked quite evenly. Mother was able to tell when the cake was done by some extra sense: she just knew.
—EDNA LEWIS, In Pursuit of Flavor, 1988

Introduction

THE HISTORY OF CAKE IN AMERICA

THE FIRST AMERICAN CAKE wasn't sweet, wasn't frosted, wasn't grand. It was more like a johnny-cake or hoe cake, based on cornmeal and cooked on a griddle. What a far cry that seems from the grand cakes of today—the triple-tiered, chocolate-frosted, and candle-covered confections we look forward to on birthdays and other celebrations.

Cakes have become an icon of American culture and a window to understanding ourselves. Be they vanilla, lemon, ginger, chocolate, cinnamon, boozy, Bundt, layered, marbled, even topped with meringue—they are etched in our psyche. Cakes relate to our lives, heritage, and hometowns.

But why cake? And what role does cake baking play in our country's history? These are questions I have wondered all my life as cake has been my passion, obsession, and occupation. I have baked cakes for my family and friends ever since I was tall enough to reach the box of Hershey's cocoa. I baked the classic French genoise and dainty madeleines at cooking school in Paris. And as a newspaper journalist, I have researched the best flours for baking, the best methods for mixing the batter, and the best frosting recipes because these were things that helped my readers bake better cakes.

I have wondered why devil's food cake is not red in color, how the Southern delicacy known as Japanese Fruit Cake (page 128) could be so named when there appears to be nothing Japanese about the recipe, and how Depression-era cooks managed to bake cakes without eggs, milk, and butter. Who invented the flourless chocolate cake, the St. Louis Gooey Butter Cake (page 184), the Tunnel of Fudge Cake (page 226)? Were these now-legendary recipe mishaps the result of a lapse of memory, frugality, or being too lazy to run to the store for more flour?

I could taste the lemon and almond in Mashula's Coconut Cake as I read Eudora Welty's *Delta Wedding*

and smell the bourbon-filled Lane Cake (page 113) in *To Kill a Mockingbird*. These American cakes are a product of our history, culture, creativity, sensibility, new inventions, local ingredients, and sheer whimsy. The key cake ingredients—butter, eggs, sugar, and flour—have not changed over the course of American history. But our taste in cake has changed since the first immigrants came to this country and brought European ideas like meringue; ingredients such as honey, yeast, and spices; and culinary know-how. The African slaves brought a natural creativity to baking and a deft hand with new ingredients like coconut. And more recently, Hispanic immigrants share relatively new additions to the American cake collection— Chocoflan (page 297) and Tres Leches Cake (page 300).

The recipe for American cake looks something like this—one part technique and history from a homeland, one part available ingredients, and one part American spirit. According to historian Daniel Boorstin, what made Americans who they were "was not what they sought but what they accomplished." America accomplished much as a young nation, and in the American kitchen, the cooks—be they Pennsylvania Dutch, French, English, African, Irish, Polish, Russian, Italian, or Scandinavian— contributed the ideas, techniques, inventions, spark, spirit, and history that crumb by crumb made American cake. The beautifully diverse and resourceful community of cooks who first baked American cake worked off-script, improvising their family recipes with ingredients at hand. But in regions of diversity, such as North Carolina, Texas, Kentucky, and Pennsylvania, a blending of cultures and styles of baking occurred. Neighborliness and community building were key components of survival in early America. It went well beyond borrowing a cup of sugar. If you didn't help out your neighbor, hard weather or attacks by Indians or animals threatened your existence. People were dependent on each other, which reinforced a generosity of spirit, and that spirit was evident at quilting bees, barn raisings, church socials, and other good excuses to share cake, coffee, and a recipe.

With the founding of the new country came patriotism, the mother in the home, the great migration west, emigration from Europe, the rise of the middle class, better ingredients, appliances, cooking schools, and inventions like baking powder that made baking cake faster and less expensive, needing fewer eggs. But war and depression resulted in lean years and also a new creativity on how to bake with limited resources. Postwar years brought the baby boom, Bake-Offs,® Tupperware, women in the workforce, the rise of commercial bakeries, and an eye on convenience. And yet cake never left the spotlight. According to historian Laura Shapiro, "cake had a grip on the heart that bread simply couldn't match."

Cake has certainly had a hold on America. Today's American cake is still baked, frosted, and decorated at home. We might be baking with eggs from our backyard hens, and our cakes are more natural, possibly organic, maybe flourless or gluten-free, or an update of a classic cake, such as a red velvet cake, but calling for beets to tint it red. We've come a long way.

And what a delicious coast-to-coast journey it has been. Through this book, you will travel with me and savor our nation's history of cake baking through contemporary eyes. From the dark, moist gingerbread of New England, to the elegant English-style pound cake of Virginia, to the hardscrabble apple stack cake of Appalachia (page 136), to the slow-drawl, Deep South caramel (page 208), to Hawaii's Chantilly Cake (page 273) and Alaska's rhubarb (page 283), to the more modern California cakes of almond or orange. For today in midwestern kitchens a caramel icing is still stirred over the stove and poured onto hearty cakes of applesauce or mincemeat. And in the upper Midwest and Pacific Northwest, families still bake the Bundt cakes, German meringue cakes, and Scandinavian coffee cakes passed down from their ancestors.

American cake lets us look into the world from which we came and the one we inhabit today. It is synonymous with celebrations and happy times, just as it was when our nation was young. So crack the eggs, sift the flour, and set the oven. The diverse, delicious, and fascinating story of cake in America begins.

Enjoy!
Anne Byrn

CAKE VS. PIE

AS OPPOSED TO PIE, which was eaten out of the hand by field laborers, cake took a higher level of skill in the kitchen to prepare. Historian William Woys Weaver said that in the Pennsylvania Dutch community, people belonged to either pie or cake families, and baking cake elevated your social status. The word "cake" comes from the Middle English "kake" and borrowed from Old Norse. It is similar to the Swedish word for cake, which is "*kaka,*" and the German "*kuchen,*" according to Oxford University Press.

Wooden Spoons, Wood Fires, and Chipped Teacups

BAKING THE EARLY AMERICAN CAKES

BAKING A CAKE may seem like a simple task. It uses butter, eggs, sugar, and flour—ingredients found in most every kitchen. And yet, to bake well you need these ingredients and the know-how to pull them together. This has been true since the first Americans baked cakes in wood-fired ovens, and it remains true today.

Before we embark on the journey into the kitchens of the past and see these classic cakes through contemporary eyes, let's envision a wooden spoon creaming butter, a teacup measuring flour, and a crude oven with no modern thermostat baking a cake. It helps to understand the ingredients, ovens, and equipment before we even think about recipes.

So much has changed in American ingredients since the first cake was baked. The flour was less refined. Eggs varied in size. Methods, too, have changed dramatically. There were no KitchenAids on the counter, so cakes were laborious to make. You beat butter with a wooden spoon and then added the sugar gradually until the mixture lightened. You added the yolks of eggs—saving the whites for beating and folding in for leavening. And flour was measured with what you had—a teacup.

Butter, Eggs, Sugar, Flour

REGIONAL RAW INGREDIENTS

CAKE INGREDIENTS haven't changed, but they look a little different today than they used to look.

BUTTER

It's been a staple ingredient ever since the first dairy cows were raised on American land. Europeans were accustomed to cooking with butter, and they knew how to make butter.

Harriott Pinckney Horry of 18th-century South Carolina carefully details "Making Butter" in her diary, preserved in the book *A Colonial Plantation Cookbook*, edited by the late Richard J. Hooker. The process begins with the regular milking of cows and ends with the proper storage of butter so that it remains sweet in flavor.

What resulted after churning was a mass of fresh butter, salted and stored in the cellar or springhouse, or if you were selling the butter, shaped into blocks and packaged for sale at the market. Salt was a preservative and added flavor, and it was rinsed off the butter before baking. The liquid left after churning was aptly called buttermilk, and it was a beverage as well as a valuable addition to cakes and breads.

In early cake recipes, you often see the measure, "butter the size of an egg." That equals 2 ounces, or 4 tablespoons.

EGGS

When you look at older cake recipes, the number of eggs looks excessive. But eggs back then were smaller than today. A pound of eggs used in the earliest pound cakes equaled 12 to 16 eggs. So important were eggs in baking and cooking that families raised hens, and if they didn't they swapped goods with their neighbors for eggs, or they bought fresh eggs at market.

Early cakes were dependent on eggs for leavening as well as for tenderness and color. So great care went into the beating of egg yolks and whites to create a perfect cake. For example, old recipes advised you to beat egg yolks for an hour with a hickory rod or small peach branch on an oval platter. The Dover, or hand-crank, eggbeater was invented about 1870, and it made whipping egg whites for layer cakes, angel food cakes, and meringues much easier.

SUGAR

You could sweeten a cake with honey, maple syrup, molasses, sorghum, and cane syrup in early America, and plenty of people did out of necessity. These sweeteners were local and less expensive. But if you had the money to spend on the best ingredients for your cakes, the one ingredient that would improve your social status and produce the nicest cakes was refined sugar.

Also known as "slave sugar" by abolitionists because sugarcane production was dependent on slaves, refined cane sugar was the best sweetener you could buy. Early Americans paid dearly for it. Before it was produced in the Caribbean, the best sugar came from Madeira in small loaves. But by the 1640s, sugar production had began in Barbados and later in Jamaica. Most of the sugar went to kings, governors, and wealthy landowners. Molasses—the by-product of sugar refining, what drained out when sugar was compacted into molds—was sold to American colonists.

American sugar production ramped up in 1810 with sugar produced along the Georgia coast and in Louisiana. As a result, sugar prices fell, and sugar became more accessible to the middle class. But the lack of sugar during the War of 1812 got people thinking of other sources for sweetening. Corn sugar (syrup) was introduced in 1836, then sorghum in 1854, and beet sugar in the 1880s. The Southern sugar industry came to a halt during the Civil War, and the refineries moved north to New York City and Brooklyn. The port, the railroads, and the banks to finance the industry made sugar big business in New York until World War I. Granulated sugar as we know it was introduced at a Boston refinery in the 1850s.

Sugar has been rationed in times of war. It has been used as a medicine. It has been coveted and despised. It has been too costly to afford, and now in our modern world it seems to be everywhere. But early Americans knew what today's baker knows—sugar is a necessary ingredient in baking a cake because it provides tenderness and flavor.

FLOUR

Flour varied from region to region in America, depending on where the wheat was grown, harvested, and milled. Early flour was oatmeal-like in color when compared with the white bleached flour of today. It was rough in texture, too, and it wasn't until the late 1800s that machinery was developed to remove the bran from the wheat, making white flour possible.

Every region had a miller, for flour truly was the staff of life. People baked their own bread, and one of the most important commodities at local groceries that crisscrossed America was bread flour.

But bread flour wasn't the best flour for making cakes. It was too high in protein and gluten. People figured out ways to modify their local flour, adding cornstarch or potato flour, to soften it. These early homemade attempts were the beginnings of cake flour. In 1856 the Ingleheart brothers of Evansville, Indiana, created a way to grind and sift flour many more times than regular all-purpose flour required. It was called Swans Down.

A decade later, a large flour mill opened in Minneapolis along the banks of the Mississippi River. Using the bounty of spring wheat from midwestern farms and the river for transportation, the Washburn-Crosby Company, later General Mills, was born. Three years later, Charles Pillsbury opened a similar large flour mill. Washburn-Crosby's Gold Medal all-purpose flour was so named because it won awards at an international milling competition. Both companies bleached flour to make a white flour that performed well in cake baking, and the bleaching process had been patented by 1845. Regional flour mills such as the Knoxville Milling Company and its White Lily brand made from soft red winter wheat were also popular, and they produced a light bleached flour beloved by Southern bakers.

But even at the turn of the 20th century, not everyone was a fan of the new bleached white flour. In the 1912 best-selling cookbook *The Neighborhood Cook Book*, published by the Council of Jewish Women in Portland, Oregon, an advertisement for Crown unbleached flour was ahead of its time when it read: "Purity and Flavor Not Sacrificed for Artificial Color."

And purity was something the early American kitchen lacked. If the bugs weren't in the flour, then they were in the kitchen. An 1895 Montgomery Ward & Co. catalog advertised flour bins with this message: "The flour saved pays the cost. Keep your flour in the Columbia Flour Bin, secure from moisture, dust, dirt, and vermin."

Today there is a renewed interest in unbleached, regional flours. There is worry that our flour has lost its flavor and the original varieties of flour have lost their prominence. David Shields, author of *Southern Provisions*, says heirloom wheat varieties like Purple Straw are making a comeback. Purple Straw was still cultivated in some Southern states until the 1970s. It is a high-protein but low-gluten soft winter wheat that produces cakes that rise high in the pan but are also tender and spongy.

OTHER AMERICAN SWEETENERS

MOLASSES. A key secret ingredient in New England gingerbread, baked beans, and rum, molasses has a unique place in American food history. It was the most commonly used sweetener in early American cooking up until the 1880s, when domestic sugar production increased. Cheap and available, molasses was the sweetener of the masses and was the by-product of the refined white sugar produced and shipped to the wealthy. Psychologically and economically, molasses was a revolutionary ingredient.

John Adams writes in a letter to Judge William Tudor on August 11, 1818, that molasses helped usher in American independence:

Witts may laugh at our fondness for Molasses & we ought all join in the laugh with as much good humour always asserted & proved that Virginians loved Molasses as well as New Englandmen did. I know not why we should blush to confess that Molasses was an essential ingredient in American Independence. Many great Events have proceeded from much smaller causes.

According to the Massachusetts Historical Society, the sugar islands (Barbados and Jamaica) experienced a huge demand for sugar from European colonizers. Sugar was profitable, but so was molasses, which could be distilled into rum. And this glut of molasses helped form the triangular trade exchange—New England rum to West Africa and Europe, West African slaves to the sugar islands, then the sugar islands' molasses to New England rum distilleries.

When French molasses from Martinique became less expensive for American colonists to purchase, England could not compete and sought a molasses monopoly. It imposed a tax on molasses coming from foreign colonies with the Molasses Act of 1733. The act created fear in the colonies that relied on the rum trade and those colonists accustomed to drinking all the rum they liked. It is estimated that just before the Revolutionary War, the average colonist consumed 4 gallons of rum per year.

At first the colonists protested and then ignored the Molasses Act, smuggling in French and Spanish molasses to avoid taxation. But the Sugar Act of 1764 imposed new duties on sugar and molasses from non-British colonies, and it gave permission to seize the cargo of violators. Taxation without representation

(continued)

became the plight of the colonists and created the beginnings of the American Revolution.

Native Americans collecting sap and cooking maple syrup in pots, North America, ca. 1724

MAPLE SYRUP. Slashing sugar maple trees for the sap and boiling this down over a fire into a sweet syrup is an old ritual in the Northeast and upper Midwest. Colonists learned from the Native Americans how to extract the sap from the maple tree and make the oldest American sugar, produced and sold since the 1790s. Historians are not sure if the method of cooking down and evaporating the water from the sap was an Indian technique or one learned from

French explorers. But what is known is that maple syrup was preferred to white sugar by Quakers and abolitionists, who boycotted West Indies slave sugar. And most maple syrup was made by dairy farmers who relied on the off-season extra income it provided.

HONEY. An old and naturally occurring sweetener, honey was popular in Europe, and beekeeping was woman's work in early America. Bees were imported from Europe in the early 1600s, and families raised a colony of bees near their house for honey. Or wild honey was foraged from fields and forests. The first honey that runs through the comb was considered the best, and when all the honey was pressed out, the comb was boiled down to extract the natural beeswax for candles. Honey gave moisture to cakes and breads, and it made them better keepers.

CANE SYRUP. Found in warm southern climates where sugarcane grew, cane syrup was the juice pressed from the canes and cooked down into a syrup. Many years ago, people might grow their own sugarcane to extract the juice and boil it down into syrup. But today most cane syrup is bought, and the favorite longtime brand is Steen's, sold in the yellow can and the foundation of Louisiana syrup cake.

SORGHUM or sorghum molasses, as it was often called, was the cheapest sweetener in the South in the years leading up to the Civil War and during Reconstruction. A grass indigenous to Asia and Africa, sorghum was grown experimentally by the 1850s from Minnesota south to Georgia. It tolerated cold and was good feed for cattle.

Unable to get Louisiana and Georgia sugar during and after the Civil War, cooks turned to sorghum. They baked cakes, made fruit preserves, and sweetened their coffee with it.

Leavening
THE ROAD TO BAKING POWDER

LEAVENINGS ARE ingredients used to lighten a cake batter and make it rise. The earliest American cake leavening agent was yeast. It was called "emptins," a leftover from beer and cider fermentation.

Another early natural leavening agent was beaten egg or egg white. For angel food cakes, egg whites were beaten until stiff peaks formed, and then the light mixture was folded gently into the batter. Air was incorporated into the whites as they were beaten, and it expanded in the hot oven, causing the cake to rise.

Air also was beaten into butter and sugar, and into a dozen eggs, in making pound cakes. Without the aid of the modern electric mixer, this process took muscle and patience. But not everyone had the skill needed to make pound cake. So there became a need for an easy, inexpensive, foolproof leavening in America.

The first of the chemical leavenings was a late-18th-century ingredient called potash—the ash from cleared and burned hardwood trees in the Hudson River Valley and other woodsy areas. Land was being cleared for farms and to establish new towns and cities in America, and women would take the burned hardwood ash, run water through it to produce lye water for use in cleaning, and dry what was left into potash.

Pearlash was a purified form of this potash; in the cake batter, when blended with an acidic ingredient like molasses, buttermilk, sour milk, or lemon juice, it produced carbon dioxide that lightened the batter and helped the cake rise. Pearlash changed the way America baked a cake, requiring fewer eggs and a lot less beating by hand. By 1792 the United States was exporting 8 tons of pearlash to Europe a year. Four recipes in the first American cookbook—Amelia Simmons's *American Cookery,* published in 1796—contained pearlash. You dissolved it in water or milk before adding it to the rest of the ingredients. But because of its bitter aftertaste, pearlash was most palatable in highly spiced cakes like gingerbread, which masked the flavor.

Meanwhile, the Europeans didn't have hardwood trees to spare to burn into ash, and the French government offered a monetary prize for a way to turn salt into soda ash—and sodium bicarbonate was born. It was expensive to buy this new French leavening, so potassium bicarbonate, or saleratus, was invented for use in America. Saleratus meant "aerated salt," was less bitter than pearlash, and was used in Mary Randolph's *Virginia House-wife* recipes. But bicarbonate of soda—baking soda—was deemed the better leavening agent because it produced carbon dioxide more quickly. American baking soda production began in 1867, and Arm & Hammer was the largest producer. A lesser-known leavening called cream of tartar had been around for decades and was the acidic salt found on the inside of wine barrels after fermentation.

For baking powder to be invented, it took the combination of baking soda and cream of tartar to be successful. First invented in England in the 1840s, baking powder was developed in America a decade later. In 1859 the Rumford Company introduced the first calcium phosphate baking powder with cornstarch added to make it moisture resistant and help keep the ingredients from reacting in the container.

After Rumford there was Royal baking powder, then came double-acting baking powder sold under the Calumet and Clabber Girl brands.

The baking powder companies printed cookbooks and recipe brochures and became one of the largest sources of cake recipes in the early 20th century. The road to baking powder wasn't a straight path, but each invention, whether in Europe or America, seemed to fuel the next invention. As a result, baking powder made baking a cake less cumbersome and less time consuming, and gave cakes the light texture characteristic of our modern American cake.

The American Oven

WOOD, COAL, GAS, AND ELECTRIC

ALONG WITH the right ingredients, America's cakes needed ovens in which to bake. The earliest cakes were baked over a wood fire, either at the hearth in cast iron or in wood-fired ovens.

Cooking by fire was time consuming, hard work, and dangerous. Fire was the second-leading cause of death for young women after childbirth in Colonial times. In wealthy homes, brick was the material of choice for fireplaces, hearths, and chimneys. And kitchens were built separate from the rest of the house to prevent fires. But in more modest homes, the early fireplaces and chimneys were made of stone found nearby. Once the family could afford to add another room to their home, that new room became the living space and the older part with chimney and hearth became the kitchen.

Cooking and baking over the hearth was done with heavy cast-iron pots and pans of all sizes, both flat bottomed and rounded, and with legs to keep them off the hearth. The early fireplace was quite large, as it needed to heat the room and also fuel the cooking. An iron bar was built into the back of the fireplace, and from it hung pots and pans at different distances from the fire. Ovens were built into the side of a fireplace, and they were just a simple brick or stone chamber that could be heated with hot wood coals; then the coals were removed and breads and cakes went into the oven to bake.

Thomas Jefferson's Monticello had a state-of-the-art kitchen for its time. In 1796 the kitchen contained two Dutch ovens, according to records at Monticello. Later it had a French-style stew-hole stove, gleaned from enslaved cook James Hemings's cooking in Paris, where coals from the fire were placed into a cast-iron grate, like a long stove. On the grates sat copper pots and pans of soups and sauces simmering, and they could be stirred and monitored by a cook who did not have to lean over the blazing fire on the hearth.

When the wood-fire and coal cast-iron cookstoves came along after the Civil War, it is no wonder people lined up to buy them. They were not only a huge improvement over cooking over an open fire, but they were beautiful pieces of equipment. Sold directly to the customer, the Home Comfort ranges from the Wrought Iron Range Company of St. Louis were known for beautiful style and handy features: a soot door for ash removal plus a lower warming drawer, graceful legs, and a space below the oven itself for ventilation and cleaning.

How to tell if a wood-fire oven was ready for baking? According to Harva Hachten and Terese Allen in *The Flavor of Wisconsin,* you could hold your hand in the oven for a count of 20. Or place a white sheet of paper on the floor of the oven. The paper burned if the oven was too hot. It turned yellow or buff in color, on the other hand, if the oven was ready for baking. Some cooks threw flour on the floor of the oven, and if the flour caught fire, the oven was too hot. If the flour browned after a few seconds, it was just right for baking a cake.

But the women of the First Congregational Church of Marysville, Ohio, published a cookbook called *The Centennial Buckeye Cook Book* in 1876, and they expressed their frustration over an oven that wasn't automatically regulated. And they added that cooks everywhere would "hail the day when some enterprising Yankee or Buckeye girl shall invent a stove or range with a thermometer attached to the oven, so that the heat may be regulated accurately."

After coal ovens came gas ovens, and after gas came electric. It would take nearly 40 years for the oven thermostat to be invented. Even then the early oven temperature settings weren't precise, offering only "slow," "moderate," and "hot." By the end of the 1940s, after World War II, the temperatures—350°F or 375°F as we know them—were added.

Setting the oven, timing the cake, watching for signs of doneness, all these were possible once electricity came along. General Electric brought the self-cleaning oven to market in 1963. Baking a cake got to be less of a chore and more of a pleasure.

Measurements
A BLEND OF ART AND SCIENCE

THE LATE HISTORIAN Karen Hess wrote that the American habit of measuring with a cup originated in frontier life when a cup was always at hand.

Anyone who has ever baked a cake by an old recipe knows that measuring is subjective. A pinch of salt, a dash of cinnamon, a scant cup flour, a rounded teaspoon baking powder? Those were colloquial measures given from one cook to another, from a cook comfortable with baking and with using the same ingredients over time.

But when teaching others to bake a cake through classes and through cookbooks, the measurements have to be more precise. Removing the element of surprise and uncertainty gives a greater chance for continued success. Modern pastry cooks will affirm the most consistent way to bake is through weights rather than measures. With a scale, there is no subjectivity. Even if flours change, an ounce is an ounce.

Our ancestors knew this. To bake a sponge or pound cake, they weighed the eggs first, and depending on the weight of those eggs, they then used the corresponding amount of butter, sugar, and flour. Scales have been around since the 18th century, although they weren't considered important in the kitchen until the 1860s, when cookbook authors such as England's Isabella Beeton called them essential. The prestigious cooking schools of Boston and Philadelphia opened their doors around the end of the 19th century and gave America measuring guides—not with scales, but with cups and tablespoons.

Here are some of the more popular measures of the 17th and 18th centuries and the equivalents today:

A GILL = 4 FLUID OUNCES

WINEGLASS = 2 FLUID OUNCES

BUTTER THE SIZE OF AN EGG = 2 OUNCES, OR 4 TABLESPOONS

Decoding measures in old recipes has been the passion of historians such as the late Karen Hess, who explained Mary Randolph's system of measurements in a foreword to a new edition of *The Virginia Housewife*. Thanks to these historians, and a good bit of trial and error, I have been able to unlock the door on the cakes of the past.

CAKE PANS: FROM LOAVES TO TUBES TO JELLY ROLLS TO BUNDTS

Old recipes didn't always specify the size of the pan to use like they do today. Very old cookbooks just say that the cake goes into an "oven" as opposed to being baked on the hearth. The size of a pan had a lot to do with the size of the oven in which the cake was placed to bake. With the invention of the modern electric oven, and with baking powder allowing cakes to bake up light and fluffy in all sizes of pans, the pan possibilities increased over the years. And resourceful Americans found multiple uses for the same pan. But before baking powder and big ovens, it all started with a loaf.

LOAF PAN. An efficient pan in which to bake cake, bread, or meat, the loaf pan could fit into small ovens. The resulting baked goods sliced easily and kept well, and cakes needed no icing. Loaves have continued to be popular pans. The most common size is the 9" × 5" × 3" pan. "Loaf cakes" hit their stride in the 1950s. Mini loaf pans boomed in the 1970s.

KUGELHOPF. The fluted cake pan of Scandinavia, Germany, and eastern Europe that led to the development of the Bundt pan, it held coffee cakes and celebratory cakes served during the holidays.

TUBE OR TUBED PAN. Popular with the Pennsylvania Dutch, the tube or tubed pans, as they were often called, were used to bake angel food cakes. They were advertised in the early 1800s.

LAYER. Early Americans baked stiff yeast fruitcakes in layers by baking the cakes in springformlike pans. And they baked layers of sponge cake using hoops on a baking sheet. These hoops were adjustable and made of wood, metal, and often paper. Sets of metal layer pans were sold in the 1890s, and the word "tin" referring to the metal comes into our jargon and is often used as a replacement for the word "pan."

SMALL CAKES OR MUFFINS. Different from the cupcakelike muffins we know today, these were more like round English muffins. Hoops were placed on baking tins, and the cake batter would be poured into the hoops and baked for small cakes.

MUFFINS AND CUPCAKES. What we call cupcakes or muffins used to be called "gems." Nathaniel Waterman of Boston designed a gem pan in 1859 and patented it for the gem, which was a small, healthy bread made with whole wheat flour. Later, cakelike muffins were gaining in popularity. Influenced by the French, according to a *Brooklyn Daily Eagle* food story in 1870, these muffins created a need for a muffin pan in 1873. Bakeries were also making cupcakes in similar pans in the late 1800s. By 1910 food writers were suggesting you bake your cupcakes in gem pans or "cupcake tins."

SPRINGFORM PAN. An old pan used to bake the first cheesecakes, the springform has a detachable side that allows tender-crumbed cakes to unmold easily. It came back into vogue in the 1980s when cheesecakes and tortes were in fashion.

DRIPPING PAN OR JELLY ROLL. The American jelly roll was first baked in a dripping pan—recipes told you to use the dripping pan as early as 1872.

13" × 9" PAN. Looking through old newspaper recipes, you find that rectangular pan sizes don't appear with any regularity until the 1950s. Why this size? Possibly it was the cake mix manufacturers placing instructions for baking the cake in this pan on the box. Or it was the popularity of the Rice Krispies treats that called for this pan or, as historian Darra Goldstein surmises, it was a busy America on the move. This pan was convenient to bake a cake, grab it, and go.

BUNDT. A spin-off of the old Kugelhopf pan, the Bundt was invented by Nordic Ware in 1950. Years later, with the nationwide popularity of the 1966 Pillsbury Bake-Off® second-place-winning Tunnel of Fudge Cake (page 226), the Bundt became an overnight success.

SHEET PANS AND RESTAURANT-INFLUENCED PANS. Often confused with the 13" × 9", sheet pans are a larger version of the shallow jelly roll pan. When 1950s commercial bakeries popularized the long, flat decorated sheet cakes, the words were added to our vocabulary. But a baking "sheet" is an old phrase, referring to the thin sheet of tin used to make it. A sheet of cake meant a "slab" of cake. The Texas sheet cake—or sheath cake, as it is called by many locals—is a slab of chocolate cake covered in fudge frosting. Half sheet pans and larger "hotel" pans are widely used in the restaurant industry, and with restaurant recipes influencing home cooking, cooks today use the same culinary lingo. Recipes calling for sheet pans often refer to them as "rimmed baking sheets." You can buy sheet pans along with other restaurant bakeware at cooking and restaurant supply stores.

How to Use This Book

INGREDIENTS, OVENS, cooking equipment, methods, and measurements have changed through American cake history. But the cakes baked then and the cakes baked now are similar.

Each recipe in this book has been baked in a modern kitchen. Historic recipes such as the Martha Washington Great Cake (page 35) had to be scaled back to fit into today's smaller pan. And some ingredients such as hickory nuts were difficult to track down locally so, thanks to the Internet, I ordered them from Wisconsin. Ditto the huckleberries, which came from Washington State. Our eggs are larger, so I had to reduce the number of eggs in older recipes. Butter now comes salted or unsalted, so I used unsalted in old recipes calling for the butter to be rinsed (of salt) before baking. And flour really differed over time. In older recipes, I used unbleached flour. In mid-20th-century recipes, I used bleached all-purpose flour. Some recipes called for cake flour. Others left a whole lot to the imagination, so I tried to be as historically correct as possible but also create a cake that works today. When I measured flour into cups, I spooned flour into measuring cups then leveled the top with a knife.

Those old recipes void of method that left you wondering which way to proceed were frustrating but also enlightening. It was a place in time when baking was a skill to learn from someone else. You needed to shadow your mother or apprentice with a baker to fully learn how to bake a cake. And the cookbook writers felt that way, too, because they weren't instructional. So I relied on my gut baking skills in those recipes, or I asked an expert.

Another thing has changed over time, and it has nothing to do with wars, depressions, good times, stock market upticks, westward migration, or any of the cultural factors that influenced what cakes we used to bake. Our tastes have changed. Cakes of early America were less sweet, less soft, and less perfect. Cakes of the mid–20th century seem the sweetest of all. Today's restaurant cakes seem oddly similar to the early American cakes, using local ingredients, such as locally produced stout. They call for cornmeal along with unbleached flour, and they are often baked in cast-iron pans. This has much to do with a desire for back-to-basics baking after so many decades of processed foods and convenience-driven products.

As you bake your way through the pages of this book, stop to soak in the history and try not to judge the recipes with your modern eyes. The early pound cake was heavy, yes, but delicious. You can imagine it sliced and served with tea. Cakes might be unfrosted for a reason—the high price of sugar at the time. Or the cake was topped with a modest meringue, typical in the hardscrabble 1930s. You will not only gather some outstanding recipes in this book but also gain an appreciation for how cake mirrors its cultural time.

The following recipes come from home cooks, pastry chefs, old cookbooks, state fair winners, family recipe files, home demonstration agents, back of the box, cookbook authors, bakeries, breweries, newspapers, magazines, cooking teachers, hotels, historians, restaurants, tearooms, recipe contests, farmers, government brochures, and historic homes and museums. A few are from my recipe files. They exhibit the true American spirit and show the rich and valuable history of cake in this country.

1650 *to* 1799

Baking Cakes *in* Early America

~~~

FROM THE PURITANS who settled in New England to the Dutch in New York, Quakers in Philadelphia, Germans in much of Southeastern Pennsylvania, and British on down the coastline to Charleston, people came to America to build a new life. Once home kitchens and bake ovens were established, and once a source of sweetener was available—whether it was local honey, maple syrup, molasses, or the more expensive white sugar—cake baking in America began.

The first true cakes baked at home on American soil were sweet, yeasty, breadlike cakes and fruitcakes, British pound cakes, cheesecakes, sponge cakes, and a molasses ginger cake. They were leavened with yeast cultures brought with the settlers from Europe or made from the foamy barm skimmed from fermented beverages like beer. The Moravian Sugar Cake (page 25) and the New Orleans King Cake (page 18), for instance, were both based on yeast. Other cakes were rich with eggs, such as the early cheesecakes and British-style pound cake. A different twist was found in the English and French style of light sponge cakes containing a high ratio of eggs and sugar but no butter. Served with fresh berries, they suited the warmer climates and the plantation lifestyles of Virginia and South Carolina.

The colonists baked gingerbread, too, and their recipes were both English and German in origin. But it was not until the wood ash leavening called potash was produced by burning cleared trees in the Hudson River Valley that American gingerbread benefited from this leavening and became soft and more cake-like in texture. Potash, or pearlash as it was known, was an alkali and a forerunner of baking soda. When combined in a gingerbread batter with sour milk or molasses, which were both acidic, it produced carbon dioxide bubbles that helped raise the cake in the oven.

Cakes in the early colonies were baked for the same reasons they are today—to celebrate a birthday, a wedding, a houseguest, a holiday. They were baked for everyday meals (gingerbread, sponge cake) as well as important events (Fraunces Tavern Carrot Tea Cake, page 32, for George Washington on British Evacuation Day in New York). Knowing how to bake a cake was a skill passed on from mother to daughter. Recipes, called receipts, were carefully handwritten in journals, and over the generations more recipes, notes, and thoughts were added.

Colonists relied on cookbooks, initially mostly English, and later on American cookbooks written by authors such as Amelia Simmons with her *American Cookery*. In this first cookbook published in America, in 1796, Simmons adapted well-known British cooking methods to American ingredients.

But clearly, cakes were baked by the wealthy, who could afford the ingredients. Compared with pies, cakes were more expensive to bake and required more skill and time to pull off. If you want to understand cakes in the colonies, says Virginia historian and author Leni Sorensen, just look at the ingredients. White sugar was imported and expensive.

"The ability to make cake separated the haves from the have-nots," says Sorensen. "The poor didn't eat sweets. They wanted fat meat like pork for sustenance. They made do with field peas. And they couldn't afford sugar, currants, brandy, and spices."

In the Northeast, the Puritans of the 17th-century Massachusetts Bay Colony baked cakes as soon as they were able, says Sorensen. The cakes they prepared were often sweetened with molasses instead of white sugar. At the turn of the 19th century, when African slaves were crucial to white sugar production in the West Indies, abolitionists in New England avoided white sugar because they viewed it as slave sugar.

By contrast, where the weather wasn't as severe as in the North and where affluent plantation life influenced the cooking, cooks prepared British loaf cakes with ingredients at hand as well as with their supply of imported foods. There was no need to embellish recipes as there might have been in England, according to Katharine Harbury in her *Colonial Virginia's Cooking Dynasty* cookbook. Virginia cooks needed to do little to local apples, fresh butter, and abundant wild fruit to make a cake delicious. Plus, the tobacco farmers of Virginia loved to entertain and took great effort to serve the best food to their guests. Food needed to be "memorable enough to spark admiration," says Harbury.

Leni Sorensen adds that cake baking in Virginia increased after the influx of young, marriageable Englishwomen. They bought the white sugar needed to bake pound cakes, sponge cakes, and fruitcakes.

In the 18th century, while American men were founding the new republic, American women were in the kitchen not only baking or supervising the baking of cakes but educating children and instilling a respect for the country. Historians call this the "republican motherhood," which laid the groundwork for the future of America. And after the Revolution, women's role in the kitchen remained important but expanded outside the home.

All cakes didn't look the same in early America. They were small or grand, studded with dried fruit or as plain and simple as a sponge cake. They were dense and breadlike, sweet and yeasty, baked atop pastry, sweetened with cooked carrots or local honey, or baked with the most expensive refined white sugar money could buy. They were different and yet they were similar, using American ingredients, an American cookbook, and American ingenuity to adapt the new to the old to bake an American cake.

AMERICAN GINGERBREAD

MAKES: 8 SERVINGS

PREP: 15 MINUTES

BAKE: 35 TO 40 MINUTES

Butter for prepping the pan, at room temperature

1 teaspoon baking soda

1 cup boiling water

1 cup molasses

2 large eggs

½ cup (1 stick) unsalted butter, at room temperature

½ cup granulated sugar

2 cups all-purpose flour

1½ teaspoons ground ginger

1 teaspoon ground cinnamon

¼ teaspoon ground allspice

Amelia Simmons wrote the first American cookbook in 1796. It wasn't well edited and later would be plagiarized by authors who followed her, but *American Cookery* contained recipes for simple fare—roasts, soups, breads, and desserts such as gingerbread. Simmons included 7 versions of gingerbread in her book. Her cakey Gingerbread No. 2 contained white sugar, butter, and eggs, a departure from the stiff, traditional gingerbread dough rolled and cut into cookies. If you bake any of these old recipes verbatim today, you will not have much success. So the following recipe is an adaptation of several of her recipes to create a uniquely American gingerbread recipe that works today.

1. Place a rack in the center of the oven, and preheat the oven to 375°F. Brush an 8″ or a 9″ square baking pan with a little soft butter. In a small bowl, stir the baking soda into the boiling water until the soda is dissolved. Set aside.

2. Place the molasses and eggs in a large bowl, and stir with a wooden spoon to combine and break up the egg yolks. Add the ½ cup butter, sugar, flour, ginger, cinnamon, and allspice, and stir well until the mixture is smooth, 40 strokes. Stir the baking soda and water mixture into the batter until it is smooth, 1 minute.

3. Pour the batter into the prepared pan, and place the pan in the oven. Bake until the gingerbread rises and the top springs back when lightly pressed with a finger, 35 to 40 minutes. Remove the pan from the oven. Let the gingerbread rest in the pan for 20 minutes before slicing. Serve warm with a pour of cream.

GINGERBREAD was a stomach settler in the 17th century. In Benjamin Franklin's autobiography, he writes of buying gingerbread before a long sea voyage. Stephen Schmidt, New York food historian, says bakers would set up shop along the wharves and docks to sell gingerbread to sailors. At the time, people assumed it was the treacle, or molasses, in the gingerbread that made them feel less queasy onboard, but it may have been the ginger. Long thought to aid digestion, ginger was first a medicine, said the late historian Karen Hess, before it was used as a baking ingredient.

LONG BEFORE COLONISTS LANDED on American soil, gingerbread was baked across Europe. Evan Jones wrote in his book *American Food* that early settlers from Moravia, Switzerland, and parts of the old Austro-Hungarian regions inherited the knack of cooking with spices from generations past. Essentially a honey cake with fragrant spices, gingerbread was easily adapted to less expensive molasses in America and was often called "molasses gingerbread." It was soft and more cakelike in consistency than the hard, crisp gingerbread rolled and cut into shapes. Gingerbread would turn out to be the perennial favorite in early American kitchens. Its heavy spices overrode the bitter aftertaste of crude leavening agents.

MARY BALL WASHINGTON GINGERBREAD

MAKES: 16 TO 20 SERVINGS

PREP: 25 MINUTES

BAKE: 35 TO 40 MINUTES

Butter for prepping the pan

3 cups all-purpose flour

2 tablespoons ground ginger

1 teaspoon cream of tartar

1 teaspoon baking soda

1 teaspoon ground cinnamon

¼ teaspoon ground nutmeg

⅛ teaspoon ground mace

1 large orange

½ cup (1 stick) lightly salted butter, at room temperature

½ cup light brown sugar, firmly packed

1 cup molasses

½ cup warm milk

1 wineglass (2 ounces) brandy or coffee

3 large eggs, beaten

1 cup seedless golden raisins

FOR A MODERN VANILLA SAUCE: Place 1 cup sugar and 2 tablespoons cornstarch in a small saucepan. Stir in 2 cups boiling water, and place over medium heat. Stir and let lightly boil until thickened, 1 minute. Remove the pan from the heat and stir in 4 tablespoons butter and 2 teaspoons vanilla extract. Serve warm over gingerbread.

Once sold for 10 cents a copy and now a priceless artifact, this gingerbread recipe has had several names. One was Lafayette Gingerbread, because Mary Ball Washington, mother of George Washington and his sister Betty Washington Lewis, would serve the aromatic cake to guests, including the Marquis de Lafayette during a visit to their home in the late 1780s. Betty would continue her mother's legacy by baking the cake at her home, now known as Kenmore Plantation, in Fredericksburg, Virginia. But time marched on, and the family gingerbread recipe was forgotten—that is until 1922, when Kenmore was deteriorating and the Kenmore Association and Daughters of the American Revolution (DAR) had to find $30,000 for its repairs and restoration. While sorting through boxes in the attic, Emily Fleming and her daughter Annie Smith found a handwritten diary that contained Mary Washington's gingerbread recipe. They typed and sold copies of the Kenmore Gingerbread recipe to visitors for 10 cents each and negotiated a sweeter deal by selling the recipe to the Hills Brothers Company of New York for $100. Hills Brothers packaged the ingredients as Dromedary Gingerbread Mix, selling it in US supermarkets and providing it at a discount to DAR chapters that sold it to benefit Kenmore. To taste the cake that saved the house, here is the recipe. It is also referred to as Mary Ball Washington Gingerbread, after its creator.

1. Place a rack in the center of the oven, and preheat the oven to 350°F. Lightly grease a 13" × 9" metal baking pan with butter and set it aside.

2. Sift the flour into a large mixing bowl. Stir in the ginger, cream of tartar, baking soda, cinnamon, nutmeg, and mace, and set the bowl aside.

3. Grate the orange zest and set aside. Cut the orange in half and squeeze the juice to yield 4 tablespoons. Add it to the zest in a small bowl.

4. Place the butter in a large bowl, and beat with a wooden spoon until creamy. Add the brown sugar and molasses, and beat until smooth, 1 to 2 minutes. Fold in the flour mixture along with the milk, brandy, eggs, and the reserved orange juice and zest. Beat until smooth, 2 minutes. Fold in the raisins.

5. Turn the batter into the prepared pan, and place the pan in the oven. Bake until the top springs back when lightly pressed with a finger, 35 to 40 minutes. Remove from the oven. Let cool in the pan for 15 minutes, then slice and serve with Vanilla Sauce, if desired.

NEW ORLEANS KING CAKE

(GÂTEAU DES ROIS)

MAKES: 12 TO 18 SERVINGS

PREP: 2½ TO 3 HOURS

BAKE: 25 TO 30 MINUTES

DOUGH

¼ cup warm water (105° to 115°F)

1 package (¼ ounce) active dry yeast

¼ cup warm whole milk (105° to 115°F)

½ cup (1 stick) unsalted butter, at room temperature

2 tablespoons granulated sugar

½ teaspoon ground nutmeg

½ teaspoon salt

3 cups bread flour, plus 2 tablespoons for kneading the dough

2 large eggs, lightly beaten

FILLING

6 tablespoons unsalted butter, melted

1 cup light brown sugar, firmly packed

2 teaspoons ground cinnamon

CAKE NOTES: Adapt this wonderful coffee cake to flavors you love. Roll up raisins or cranberries, chopped pecans or sliced almonds, even orange or lemon zest along with the cinnamon and sugar. This cake needs no glaze at all, but if you want to gild the lily, add a sprinkling of confectioners' sugar or the modern glaze on page 20.

When most of us think of Colonial America, we think of the 13 colonies along the East Coast. But down on the Gulf of Mexico at the mouth of the Mississippi River, colonization of a different sort was going on in what would become the city of New Orleans. French, Spanish, Basque, and Haitian food traditions fused in a wonderful way, forming the legacy of today's Creole and Cajun cuisines. The cake most associated with New Orleans is the King Cake, enjoyed throughout the Mardi Gras carnival season but originally baked just for Epiphany, the 12th night after Christmas. It is different from the more modern French King Cake, which uses puff pastry dough. According to Liz Williams, food authority and director of the Southern Food and Beverage Museum in New Orleans, the first King Cake in town was a cinnamon-swirled, brioche-style cake brought to New Orleans by the Basque settlers in 1718. Here is this cake, based on a recipe from the *Times-Picayune* in *Cooking Up a Storm*, edited by Judy Walker and Marcelle Bienvenu. It is a beautiful ring-shaped coffee cake in which you can place a toy baby, or fève, once it is baked; or garnish it with the festive purple, yellow, and green sprinkles or icing now associated with Mardi Gras; or do as the early settlers did and simply bake it and serve it warm with good coffee on Epiphany, Mardi Gras, or most any holiday of the year.

1. For the dough, pour the warm water into a large, warmed bowl. Sprinkle in the yeast and stir until it dissolves. Stir in the warm milk, butter, sugar, nutmeg, and salt. Add 1 cup of the flour and blend well. Stir in the eggs and the remaining 2 cups flour to make a soft dough. At the end of the blending, you may need to use your hands to work in all of the flour.

2. Lightly flour a work surface and turn out the dough. Knead until it is smooth and elastic, about 5 minutes. Add a little more flour if needed if the dough sticks. Place the dough in a large bowl lightly rubbed with soft butter. Turn the dough to grease the top of the dough. Cover the bowl with a kitchen towel or plastic wrap and put in a warm place until the dough doubles in size, about 1 hour.

3. For the filling, punch down the dough with your hands. Transfer it to a lightly floured work surface and, with a floured rolling pin, roll the

continued

dough to a 26″ × 9″ rectangle. Brush with the melted butter. Combine the brown sugar and cinnamon in a small bowl and sprinkle this mixture evenly over the butter to within ¹⁄₂″ of the edges.

4. Beginning at the long end, roll the dough up tightly, as for a jelly roll. Lightly blot the seam with water so that the dough edges stick together, and pinch them together well. Carefully pick up the rolled dough and place it, seam side down, on a large baking sheet lined with parchment paper. Bring together the 2 ends to make a 12″ circle, seal the ends with a little water, and pinch the ends together. If desired, use a sharp knife to slice open the middle of the circle all the way around, cutting through the layers and almost to the bottom of the dough. Cover the dough with a kitchen towel and put in a warm place to rise and double in size, about 40 minutes.

5. Preheat the oven to 350°F. When preheated, uncover the dough and place the pan in the oven. Bake the cake until it is lightly browned all over, 25 to 30 minutes. Remove the cake from the baking sheet with a metal spatula to cool for 15 minutes on a wire rack. (If you want to insert "la fève" or a plastic baby figurine, push it into the underside of the cake now.)

6. Slice and serve.

THE KING CAKE tradition includes placing something in the cake to represent the baby Jesus. It used to be a porcelain collectible trinket called "la fève," the French word for broad bean. A dried bean itself was often used. The fève was inserted in the cake before baking. Nowadays people insert "la fève" after the cake has baked, and it might be a plastic baby, a porcelain figurine, or simply a pecan half. The person who finds "la fève" in his or her slice makes next year's King Cake.

A Modern Mardi Gras Glaze

1½ cups confectioners' sugar, sifted

2 to 3 tablespoons whole milk

¼ teaspoon almond extract

Purple, green, and yellow food coloring to tint the glaze

Place the sugar in a medium bowl, and whisk in enough milk to make a smooth glaze. Add the extract. Divide the glaze into thirds and tint each third either purple, green, or yellow. Spoon each color over a third of the cooled cake and allow 20 minutes for the glaze to set before serving.

POUND CAKE

THE VENERABLE POUND CAKE is old, stodgy, and simply wonderful. With its tight, dense crumb and crusty top, it is a cake that needs no frosting, no refrigeration, no fuss. Constructed of 1 pound each of a handful of ingredients—flour, sugar, butter, eggs—the pound cake is a timeless English recipe that now has an American flavor all its own.

In her book *American Cookery* in 1796, author Amelia Simmons shares the first pound cake recipe printed in America, a pound cake with rosewater. Mary Randolph in her 1824 *The Virginia House-wife* cookbook bakes a pound cake that calls for "some grated lemon peel, a nutmeg, and a gill of brandy."

In the days before electric mixers, when the careful creaming of butter and sugar ensured the pound cake would rise, blending with a slotted wooden spoon or paddle was hard work. The ingredients were heavy. The kitchen was hot from the wood-fueled stove. If the ingredients were not creamed properly, the cake would not rise. Ingredients would be wasted. Knowing how to bake a pound cake was a skill passed along from one cook to another.

Pound cake batter could be a blueprint for bigger and flashier cakes, too. Adding currants, candied citrus peel, citron, almonds, and sherry, Mary Harris Frazer in her *Kentucky Receipt Book* of 1903 turned the simple pound cake into a near fruitcake worthy of a special occasion.

As cooks experimented with the basic pound cake recipe, veering from the easy-to-remember formula, they found that deviations were often successful. The addition of liquids made a more tender crumb, and acidic liquids like sour cream and buttermilk tenderized the cake. Heavy cream is an old and popular addition, whether the cream was just poured in or whipped first and folded into the batter before baking.

Once baking powder was found in American kitchen cupboards, the pound cake would change even more, becoming what is called a "composition cake" and not a true pound cake, says cookbook author and baking expert Greg Patent. It was lighter in texture but lost the characteristic dense, firm texture of real pound cake.

Pound cake variations in more recent years have included add-ins such as brown sugar, cocoa, candy bars, cake mixes, 7Up, coconut, Meyer lemon, and lavender.

When making pound cakes and all cakes containing butter, be sure the butter is soft but not too soft before you begin beating it. Patent says the optimum temperature is 70°F. You can stick a thermometer in the butter or guess that the butter is ready when it is able to bend but not melt.

Beat the butter with an electric mixer until it is creamy in texture—thus the verb "to cream" the butter. Then beat the sugar gradually into the butter until the mixture is pale yellow in color. This aerates the batter, whipping in pockets of air that will expand during baking and lighten the cake.

Eggs need to be at room temperature for a pound cake. Take them out of the refrigerator about 20 minutes before you plan to bake, or place them in a bowl of warm water for 5 minutes. Add them one at a time to the batter to ensure that each egg has been well incorporated. Most pound cake recipes call for 6 to 8 eggs. Old recipes call for 12 eggs because eggs were smaller than they are today. If in doubt, weigh your eggs. A true pound cake needs 16 ounces of eggs, and large eggs are about 2 ounces each in the shell.

The type of flour you use is personal taste. Some purists such as the late Edna Lewis call for unbleached flour. Patent recommends cake flour. Weigh out 1 pound of flour and then sift it for a lighter cake. Sifting is an age-old process to remove impurities in flour, but cooks have found through time that it improves the crumb of the cake.

Indian Pound Cake

If there was one cake of the early 1800s that placed American baking on the map, it was Indian Pound Cake. Most associated with Eliza Leslie, the cookbook author who was the first to publish the recipe in 1828, it is really the creation of Elizabeth Goodfellow, the Philadelphia Quaker cooking school teacher who taught Leslie to cook. This cake was a part of Mrs. Goodfellow's recipe collection and contained cornmeal, which back then was known as "Indian meal." At the time, it was a way to incorporate the most American ingredient into a classic British recipe. In 1846 Leslie includes the recipe in another book, *The Indian Meal Book*, published in London about the time of Ireland's potato famine. She wrote the book to introduce cornmeal to the Irish and English, who were searching for baking alternatives to expensive wheat flour.

17TH-CENTURY CHEESECAKE

MAKES: 12 TO 16 SERVINGS

PREP: 25 TO 30 MINUTES

BAKE: 1 HOUR 5 TO 10 MINUTES

CRUST

⅔ cup unbleached flour, plus
3 tablespoons for rolling the crust

⅔ cup whole wheat flour

¼ teaspoon salt

10 tablespoons unsalted butter, chilled

1 large egg white

¼ to ⅓ cup very cold water

FILLING

¼ cup whole almonds, finely ground (to yield ⅓ cup)

¼ cup (4 tablespoons) unsalted butter, at room temperature

¼ cup granulated sugar

¼ teaspoon ground nutmeg

¼ teaspoon salt

1 large egg yolk

1 pound ricotta cheese

½ cup heavy cream

½ cup currants

THE CREAMY TEXTURE of cheesecake is universally loved. That texture is what the colonists came to know as "cheese," and they gave that name to desserts that might not contain cheese at all—such as a lemon "cheese" cake, also called jelly cake, of Virginia that contained no cheese but had a lemon curd filling between the sponge cake layers.

It might come as a surprise that one of America's oldest desserts is the cheesecake. Cheesecake is an "ancient" recipe, according to food historian Jan Longone. Made by the Romans and Greeks (although they didn't call it cheesecake), this dessert is adaptable to different soft cheeses, flavorings, and baking methods. When the early American colonists baked cheesecake, they made it with fresh cheese curds similar to our cottage or ricotta cheese. Philadelphia was something of a cheesecake hub, according to historian William Woys Weaver. The first inn serving cheesecake was situated in a cherry orchard, so it is very possible that the first cheesecake was a cherry cheesecake. Soon interest for cheesecake spread outside Philadelphia. In 1758 the Sun Inn, run by Moravians in Bethlehem, Pennsylvania, placed cheesecake on the menu. Nowadays there are myriad cheesecake possibilities, but if we step back in time and envision what the Pilgrims might have baked in Plymouth Colony, it would be a cheesecake with those fresh curds. Today, Plimoth Plantation is a living history museum in Plymouth, Massachusetts, that researches the history of the colony and reenacts daily life for visitors. Their historians discovered this recipe and updated it for modern use. Ricotta cheese is the most similar to the early cheese curds.

1. For the crust, place the flours and salt in a large bowl and stir to combine. Cut the butter into tablespoon-size pieces and distribute on top of the flours. With a pastry blender or two sharp paring knives, cut the butter into the flour until the mixture is the size of small peas. Add the egg white and the ¼ cup cold water, and stir with a fork until the dough comes together. Add more water if needed. The dough will be wet. Wrap the dough in parchment paper and chill for 30 minutes.

2. Meanwhile, make the filling. Place the almonds on a large cutting board, and with a large, heavy knife, chop the nuts into tiny pieces until they resemble fine meal. Set aside.

3. Place the butter and sugar in a large mixing bowl, and cream with a wooden spoon for 60 strokes. Work in the nutmeg, salt, egg yolk, ricotta, and cream, and blend until smooth. Fold in the ground almonds and currants. Set aside.

continued

4. Place a rack in the center of the oven, and preheat the oven to 350°F. Set aside an ungreased 9″ springform pan or deep pie plate.

5. Scatter the 3 tablespoons flour over a work surface and rolling pin, and remove the dough from the refrigerator. Roll out the dough to about ¼″ thickness in a 12″ circle. Slide a thin metal spatula under the dough and wrap it onto the rolling pin, using the rolling pin to transfer the dough to the prepared pan. Press the dough into the pan and up the edges about 1½″. Pour the filling into the crust, and spread to smooth the top. Place the pan in the oven.

6. Bake the cake until the filling is just set but a little jiggly in the center, 1 hour 5 to 10 minutes. Remove the pan from the oven to a wire rack to cool 1 hour. Unfasten the collar of the springform pan, if using, and transfer the cake to a serving plate. Or, if using a pie pan, slice the cake from the pan while still a little warm.

A NOTE TO THE MODERN COOK: The crust and filling can be made in a food processor fitted with a steel blade. Place the flours and salt in the processor and pulse. Cut the cold butter into tablespoons and distribute around the processor. Process until the mixture is the size of small peas, 10 to 15 seconds. Add the egg white and ¼ cup cold water. Pulse until the dough holds together. Add more water if needed. The dough will be wet. Wrap the ball of dough in plastic wrap and chill for 30 minutes. The filling can be made in the same food processor. Wipe it out, add the almonds, and pulse until the nuts are well ground, like fine meal, about 45 seconds. Turn the almonds into a large bowl and set aside. Place the butter, sugar, nutmeg, salt, egg yolk, ricotta, and cream in the processor and blend until smooth. Fold in the almonds and currants to finish the filling and proceed with step 4 of the recipe. Flavor the filling with ½ teaspoon vanilla extract, if desired.

FIRST AMERICAN COOKBOOK

THE EARLY AMERICAN COOK had at her fingertips plenty of English cookbooks, but they didn't speak to the new American culture. She might have relied on her own handwritten collection of family recipes, too. But as 18th-century American cooking evolved, there was no cookbook written using distinctly American ingredients until 1796, when Amelia Simmons had her simple, down-to-earth recipes published in a modest, 47-page, paperbound book called *American Cookery*.

"It was a noteworthy event," said Mary Tolford Wilson in her 1958 essay explaining the significance of Simmons's work. Simmons was the first to use the word "shortening"—meaning a mixture of lard and butter—in a recipe book. She also shared the first Election Cake recipe. Most important, this cookbook was the first to document the initial step on the road to baking powder. American cooks had been using potash, which they called "pearlash," to launder clothes. Amelia Simmons included four recipes calling for pearlash, and the rest is history.

Simmons was an orphan, and some historians believe she was illiterate. But they do not discount her cooking skills. Her book was reprinted and much plagiarized over the years. Her greatest legacy was being the first to recognize and document what was uniquely American in the kitchen and turning it into a book "written by an American, for Americans," said the late historian Karen Hess. And that made her the mother of American cookbooks.

MORAVIAN SUGAR CAKE

MAKES: 12 TO 16 SERVINGS

PREP: 4 TO 5 HOURS

BAKE: 25 TO 30 MINUTES

1 medium-size baking potato, peeled and cut into 1" pieces

1 package (¼ ounce) active dry yeast

½ teaspoon plus 1 cup granulated sugar

¼ cup + 2 tablespoons warm potato water (100° to 110°F)

½ cup vegetable shortening

¼ cup (4 tablespoons) unsalted butter, at room temperature

1 teaspoon salt

2 large eggs, beaten, at room temperature

3 cups all-purpose flour, plus up to ½ cup flour for kneading

1 cup (2 sticks) unsalted butter, cut into ⅛" slices

1 cup light brown sugar, firmly packed

2 teaspoons ground cinnamon

One of the earliest American coffee cakes was literally passed along from mother to daughter. Moravian brides in the 1700s baked a rich potato cake with a starter yeast given to them by their mothers or neighbors. From this starter, they made their own yeast by reserving a bit of the dough to be the starter for the next round of baking. What makes a Moravian Sugar Cake distinctive is not only the mashed potatoes in the dough but also the dimples or "puddles" on top, which collect brown sugar, butter, and cinnamon as the cake bakes. This cake has been served on Easter morning following sunrise church service for generations. Moravians settled in the Winston-Salem area of North Carolina in 1753, and today at Old Salem, a living history village, you can taste the cake like it used to be prepared—pulled from the wood-fired oven at Winkler Bakery. This recipe is adapted from one shared by North Carolina food writer Sheri Castle. It originally belonged to Beth Tartan, who was the food editor of the *Winston-Salem Journal* for many years. The early Moravians would not have used vegetable shortening. They would have baked with a mixture of butter and lard.

1. Place the potato in a small saucepan, cover with water to a depth of 1", and simmer, covered, until tender, 10 to 15 minutes. Drain well, reserving the cooking water. Force the potato through a ricer into a small bowl or mash as smooth as possible with a fork. Measure out 1 cup of gently packed potatoes into a small bowl, and stir in 2 tablespoons of the reserved cooking water. Cover and keep warm.

2. In a glass measuring cup, dissolve the yeast and ½ teaspoon of the sugar in ¼ cup of the reserved potato water. Let stand until the mixture bubbles up, 5 minutes.

3. Combine the potatoes, the remaining 1 cup sugar, the shortening, ¼ cup butter, and salt in a large mixing bowl, and beat with an electric mixer on medium speed until the shortening melts, 2 minutes. Stir in the yeast mixture and beat on low speed for 30 seconds. Cover with a kitchen towel and let rise in a warm place (80° to 85°F), free from drafts, until spongy, 1½ hours.

4. Stir in the eggs and flour to make a soft dough. Shape the dough into a

continued

ball. Place in a greased bowl, turning to grease the top. Cover with plastic wrap and let rise in a warm place, free from drafts, for 2 hours. The dough will increase in size by one half.

5. Turn the dough out onto a lightly floured surface and knead until it is smooth and elastic, 5 minutes. Pat the dough evenly into a greased 13″ × 9″ baking pan. Cover with plastic wrap and let rise in a warm place, free from drafts, 45 minutes to an hour.

6. Place a rack in the center of the oven, and preheat the oven to 375°F. With your thumb or the end of a wooden spoon, deeply dimple the dough. Tuck the slices of butter into the dimples and over the top of the dough. Place the brown sugar and cinnamon in a small bowl and stir to combine; sprinkle this evenly over the dough and down into the dimples.

7. Place the pan in the oven, and bake until the cake is well browned and cooked through, 25 to 30 minutes. Let cool for 30 minutes in the pan before serving.

The Moravians

Thought to be one of the oldest Protestant denominations, the Moravian Church was founded in what is now the Czech Republic. Refugees fled to Germany in 1722 for religious freedom, and they first attempted settlement in the American colony of Georgia with General James Oglethorpe in 1735. That attempt was unsuccessful, but what followed on Christmas Eve in 1740 in Bethlehem, Pennsylvania, would not only be a success but would establish the rich Moravian culture in America. A people dedicated to their church, community, schools, and trades, the Moravians were well-known for their baking. They staged "love feasts" in church, passing warm yeast buns and sweetened coffee around the congregation.

THE PENNSYLVANIA DUTCH

WE CAN THANK THE BRITISH for the fruitcake, pound cake, and sponge cake legacy in America, but we need to recognize the Germans who settled in Pennsylvania for the culinary contributions they provided. Called the Pennsylvania Dutch, this large group of people first sailed for America from Germany and Switzerland in 1683 and landed in Philadelphia. Farmers, they followed the rivers until they found the fertile areas where black walnut trees grew.

They were Lutheran, Reformed, Brethren, Mennonite, Moravian, Amish, and more and had left their homeland to find religious freedom in America. They were not Dutch, but the early English settlers took their German "Deutsch" to be "Dutch." And because they settled in Pennsylvania, they became known as the Pennsylvania Dutch.

These hardworking people brought with them the German love of cake baking, if they could afford it. If not, they baked pie. With large families and growing communities, their lifestyle centered around faith and family and allowed many occasions where cakes might be served.

The great American cakes that undoubtedly came from Pennsylvania Dutch kitchens are the applesauce cake, crumb coffee cake, molasses coffee cake (Shoofly Pie, page 73), Moravian Sugar Cake (page 25), chocolate cakes, angel food cake, and black walnut cake.

CLASSIC POUND CAKE

MAKES: 16 TO 18 SERVINGS

PREP: 20 MINUTES

BAKE: 1 HOUR 20 TO 25 MINUTES

Butter and flour for prepping the pan

2 cups (4 sticks; 1 pound) unsalted butter, at room temperature

2¼ cups (1 pound) granulated sugar

6 large eggs, at room temperature

4 cups sifted all-purpose flour (see Cake Notes)

½ teaspoon salt

1 teaspoon grated lemon zest, almond extract, or vanilla extract, if desired

CAKE NOTES: Many purists insist on using unbleached flour in pound cake. It would be more similar to the flour available to the early American colonists. Pound cakes are good keepers. When cooled and wrapped in aluminum foil, they improve in flavor and texture the day after baking, and they stay fresh on the kitchen counter for up to a week. Well wrapped, they freeze for up to 6 months.

Don't Be Sad

Should your pound cake develop what is known as a sad streak— that circular dip around the top center of the cake—don't fret. It is likely caused by slight underbaking, although some people will say you overmixed the batter and still others say the recipe contains too many eggs. It is considered good luck in the South.

Think how hot it must have been in the kitchen making pound cake on humid summer days in early Virginia. However, pound cake is one of the most cherished American cakes, brought to the United States from England. The earliest written mention of pound cake in America is a recipe dated 1754 from Wicomico Church, Virginia. In the colonies, pound cake was baked everywhere but became synonymous with Virginia and the gentrified tobacco plantation owners who lived there. Mary Randolph in *The Virginia House-wife,* written in 1824, first washes the salt from the butter and rubs the butter with a wooden paddle until "it is soft as cream." She adds "powdered" sugar, which would have been sugar finely ground with a mortar and pestle, and she beats her eggs first to a "froth" before adding them to the batter. Through the decades, pound cake has gotten easier to prepare thanks to the electric mixer. Simple, unadulterated, without frosting or fuss, the classic pound cake is made from just what its name suggests—a pound each of sugar, butter, eggs, and flour. It is oddly similar to the French *quatre quarts* (four quarters).

1. Place an oven rack in the center of the oven, and preheat the oven to 325°F. Lightly grease and flour a 10″ tube pan and set aside.

2. Place the butter in a large mixing bowl, and beat with an electric mixer on low speed until the butter is lightly creamed, 30 seconds. With the mixer running on low, gradually add the sugar, beating until the mixture is well creamed and fluffy, 2 minutes. Turn off the mixer and scrape down the sides of the bowl with a rubber spatula.

3. Add the eggs to the sugar and butter mixture, one at a time, beating well after each addition. In a separate bowl, combine the flour and the salt, then add to the creamed mixture in thirds, beating on low during each addition. Fold in the lemon zest, almond extract, or vanilla, if desired.

4. Pour the batter into the prepared pan, smooth the top, and place the pan in the oven. Bake until the top of the cake is golden brown and firm to the touch, 1 hour 20 to 25 minutes.

5. Remove the pan from the oven, and place on a wire rack to cool for 20 minutes. Run a knife around the edges of the pan, and invert the cake once and then again so it rests right side up. Let cool on the rack completely, 1 hour, before slicing.

HARRIOTT HORRY'S WATER CAKE

MAKES: 8 SERVINGS

PREP: 25 MINUTES

BAKE: 28 TO 32 MINUTES

12 ounces (about 1½ cups) granulated sugar

4 ounces (½ cup) water

5 whole large eggs

2 large egg yolks

6 ounces (1½ cups) unbleached flour

Sponge Cake Pan Prep

Sponge cakes are like angel food cakes in that they should be baked in ungreased pans. This allows the cake to cling to the sides of the pan as it bakes. Angel food cakes benefit from cooling upside down in the pan so that the fragile foam of eggs that has set during baking will not be disturbed as the cake cools. But sponge cakes can be cooled in the pan right side up.

Harriott Pinckney Horry of South Carolina managed a large rice plantation during the Revolutionary War and again during widowhood. She did what most well-to-do women of that period did—she wrote down her "receipts" in a book. Much can be learned about her tastes, social status, and life events by reading her diary, which she began in 1770, some 26 years before the publication of the first American cookbook. According to Richard J. Hooker, who translated the diary into the book *A Colonial Plantation Cookbook* in 1984, Harriott was the daughter of Eliza Lucas Pinckney, a strong woman herself who pioneered indigo cultivation in South Carolina. Harriott housed Revolutionary War refugees when the British occupied nearby Charleston. After the war, she entertained General Washington at her home and traveled, writing about her journeys, meals, and discoveries, such as learning of refrigeration at Mary Randolph's boardinghouse in Virginia. This is Harriott's recipe for an early American sponge cake called a "water cake." Sugar from the West Indies was sold by the loaf to plantations. Cooks would break off a chunk and grind it into granules for cooking, or they might do as this recipe suggests and dissolve the loaf sugar in water first.

1. Place a rack in the center of the oven, and preheat the oven to 350°F. Line the bottom of a 10″ springform pan with parchment paper. Set aside.

2. Place the sugar and water in a medium-size saucepan over medium-low heat. Stir and cook until the sugar has dissolved, 5 to 6 minutes. Turn off the heat and let the sugar syrup rest until it is cool to the touch.

3. Place the whole eggs and egg yolks in a large mixing bowl, and whisk by hand until combined. Gradually pour in the sugar syrup and whisk until the egg and sugar mixture has doubled in volume and is frothy, 3 to 4 minutes. Sift the flour over the top of the egg and sugar mixture and fold it in with a wooden spoon or a rubber spatula. Turn the batter into the prepared pan, smoothing the top. Place the pan in the oven.

4. Bake until the cake is golden brown on top and springs back when lightly pressed in the center, 28 to 32 minutes. Remove the pan from the oven, and let it cool on a rack for 15 minutes. Run a knife around the edges of the pan, and unfasten the collar of the springform pan. Let the cake cool completely, 1 hour. To serve, run a serrated knife under the cake to free it from the bottom of the pan. Serve with fresh berries.

FRAUNCES TAVERN CARROT TEA CAKE

MAKES: 12 TO 16 SERVINGS

PREP: 20 TO 25 MINUTES

BAKE: 40 TO 45 MINUTES

4 medium carrots, trimmed and peeled

Butter and flour for prepping the pan

¾ cup (1½ sticks) unsalted butter, at room temperature

2 cups granulated sugar

4 large eggs

2 cups all-purpose flour

1 tablespoon ground cinnamon

1 teaspoon ground nutmeg

½ teaspoon salt

Whipped cream for serving

CAKE NOTE: You can cook the carrots until soft and then mash and strain them of juice as would have been done in the old days. Or you can cook the carrots until they just begin to soften, let them cool, and grate them using a cheese grater to get streaks of carrot throughout the cake.

This recipe may be one of the earliest carrot cake recipes in America. Throughout Europe, cooked mashed carrots had been added to puddings and confections since medieval times because cooked carrots were an inexpensive sweetener to use instead of costly sugar. The early Americans did the same. Without the vegetable graters we have today, they cooked carrots first, then mashed and strained them through a sieve to make them fine enough to fold into desserts. This cake, a cousin of the pound cake, was on the dessert menu at the Fraunces Tavern in New York on November 25, 1783. That was British Evacuation Day, when the British finally left New York and General George Washington rode his horse triumphantly down Broadway to the tavern, where a great feast was staged in his honor. Washington would give a symbolic 13 toasts at that meal, with the last one being "May the remembrance of this day be a lesson to princes." This carrot cake recipe has been shared by other authors but in a modern form, incorporating vegetable oil and baking soda, two ingredients that would not have been available to the tavern proprietor and cook Fraunces. So I am sharing a closer idea of what could have been baked that day. The butter and sugar would have been creamed by hand, and the oven was wood fired. The cake was served for dessert. You may top it with sweetened whipped cream or a more modern topping—ice cream or confectioners' sugar. Interestingly, Fraunces would go on to be Washington's steward at the first presidential residence in New York and travel with him to Philadelphia when Washington set up residence there. Fraunces was reported to be a fine cook, but Washington dismissed him twice for spending too much money on ingredients for meals.

1. Place the peeled carrots in a saucepan with 1″ of water. Bring to a boil over medium-high heat and, when boiling, reduce the heat to medium and let the carrots simmer until they begin to soften, 5 minutes. Remove the pan from the heat and drain off the water. Let the carrots cool in the pan.

2. Place a rack in the center of the oven, and preheat the oven to 350°F. Grease and flour a 10″ springform pan, shake out the excess flour, and set the pan aside.

continued

3. Place the butter and sugar in a large mixing bowl, and beat until creamy, about 1 minute. Add the eggs, one at a time, until they are smooth and satiny, 4 to 5 minutes of beating in total. In a separate bowl, sift together the flour, cinnamon, nutmeg, and salt, and fold into the batter with a wooden spoon. Set aside.

4. Grate the cooled carrots to yield 2 cups. Fold the carrots into the batter. Turn the batter into the prepared pan, and place the pan in the oven.

5. Bake the cake until it is golden brown and a toothpick inserted in the center comes out clean, 40 to 45 minutes. Remove the pan from the oven to a wire rack to cool for 20 minutes. Run a knife around the edges of the pan, and unfasten the collar of the springform pan. Run a knife underneath the cake to free it from the bottom of the pan, and place it on a serving platter. Slice and serve warm with the whipped cream.

ODE TO AMERICAN FRUITCAKE

ONE OF THE GRAND CAKES of early America, the fruitcake was packed with imported dried fruit and nuts, redolent with spices, soaked in brandy, and leavened with yeast. It was a majestic cake—something to celebrate. It was baked to commemorate occasions—weddings, birthdays, homecomings, and elections. Large, grand, and showy, it is no wonder fruitcakes were called "great cakes."

Early fruitcakes were pound cakes with the addition of dried fruit, spices, and alcohol. Often they contained a yeast called barm, the foam from fermented alcoholic beverages. These cakes were extravagant not only because the ingredients were expensive and had to be shipped in from around the world but also because they were so large. You had to have the oven and a sizable mold in which to bake them. And you had to be wealthy enough to afford the Wiesbaden candied cherries, the candied citron and pineapple, the best blanched almonds, Malaga raisins . . . the list could go on. Only the wealthy could buy the makings for a fruitcake.

The Hartford Election Cake and the Martha Washington Great Cake were both large fruitcakes intended to feed a crowd. Deep in regional pockets and in recipe boxes of America, you find even more types of fruitcakes designed to feed a family. In Pennsylvania the dark fruitcakes with heavy spice and molasses were called "black cake." These fruitcakes were made with brown sugar, spices, and dark dried fruit and brandy. On the other hand, white fruitcakes were made as white as possible by using just egg whites and almonds. They went by names like "lady cake" and "bride cake." One white fruitcake beloved in the Carolinas is the Sally White, made with almonds, coconut, and citron. It was first baked by a bakery in Wilmington, North Carolina.

Alcohol was needed to flavor and preserve fruitcake. The longer the fruitcake was marinated in brandy or rum, the more potent and moist it became. And obviously more delicious! Fruitcakes were in fashion for a long time, and they haven't gone out of favor in some homes, where the family fruitcake is made for Christmas.

MARTHA WASHINGTON GREAT CAKE

MAKES: 12 SERVINGS

PREP: 2½ TO 3 HOURS

BAKE: 2¼ TO 2½ HOURS

1 pound currants (about 3 cups)

¾ cup white wine

Butter and flour for prepping the pan

1 cup granulated sugar

1 cup (2 sticks) unsalted butter, at room temperature

4 large eggs, at room temperature

2 cups all-purpose flour

½ teaspoon salt

1 teaspoon ground cinnamon

1 teaspoon ground nutmeg

1 teaspoon ground mace

George Washington and his wife, Martha, fed family and visitors at their home, Mount Vernon, situated along the Potomac River south of what is now Washington, DC. In 1797 Washington returned to Mount Vernon after refusing to serve a third term as president. He was just in time for Christmas. Martha arranged for a large fruitcake called a "great cake" to be baked in his honor and served as dessert on the 12 days of Christmas. It was common for wealthy colonists such as the Washingtons to bake great cakes. According to the historians at Mount Vernon, the cake held a vast quantity of dried fruit and spices, was dense, and would have been baked in a large, round mold. It would have looked like an Italian panettone but would have been much heavier and contained more fruit. The following recipe for today's kitchen is adapted from *The Martha Washington Cook Book*, by Marie Kimball. While many great cakes included the yeast from barm—the foam that rises to the top of fermented liquor—as an ingredient, this cake needs no yeast. It is baked in a large loaf pan and is flavored with white wine. If you want your cake to be even more like Martha Washington's cake, use half wine and half brandy. And like all fruitcakes and great cakes, the flavors meld and improve several days after baking.

1. Place the currants in a medium-size bowl, and pour the wine over them. Stir to distribute the wine. Cover the bowl and put in a warm place for 2 hours so the currants plump up and absorb some of the wine.

2. Place a rack in the center of the oven, and preheat the oven to 250°F. Generously grease and flour a 10½″ × 5½″ × 3″ loaf pan. Shake out the excess flour, and set the pan aside.

3. Drain the currants well, reserving the wine. You should have about 3 ounces of wine. Set it and the currants aside.

4. Place the sugar and butter in a large bowl, and beat with an electric mixer on medium-high speed until light and fluffy, 3 to 4 minutes. Add the eggs, one at a time, beating well after each addition. Scrape down the sides of the bowl with a rubber spatula.

continued

5. Sift the flour, salt, cinnamon, nutmeg, and mace into a medium-size bowl. Alternately add the flour mixture and the wine to the batter, beginning and ending with the flour mixture, beating on low speed until just combined. Fold in the currants until well distributed. Turn the batter into the prepared pan, and place the pan in the oven.

6. Bake the cake until a toothpick inserted in the center comes out clean, $2^{1}/_{4}$ to $2^{1}/_{2}$ hours. Place the pan on a wire rack to cool for 15 minutes. Run a knife around the edges of the pan, gently shake the pan to loosen the cake, and invert the cake once and then again so the cake cools right side up on the rack for at least 30 minutes before slicing. The cake will slice better after it is completely cooled, 2 hours. Store as you would a fruitcake, wrapped in cheesecloth in a tightly sealed tin or wrapped in plastic.

THE ELECTION CAKE

AFTER THE REVOLU- TIONARY WAR, when American voters cast their ballots in elections, an Election Day celebration was quite an event. It was filled with patriotic pride for the new country, and people celebrated with a festive meal, drink, and cake.

A massive Election Cake, a yeasty great cake filled with spices and dried fruits, was baked to feed the town. Often confectioners sold tickets to the event. On one such Election Day in 1841 in Montpelier, Vermont, the bakery advertised that with a 50-cent ticket you would receive a pound-size serving of cake and the chance of a ring inside.

Historians have disagreed about the antecedents of the Election Cake. Some feel it is unique to America, and others insist this same type of fruitcake was baked in England—it just wasn't known as Election Cake. The cake has been linked to Hartford, Connecticut, and called the Hartford Election Cake. But the late historian Karen Hess said Election Cakes were baked throughout New England, not just in Hartford. When her book *American Cookery* was first printed in Hartford in 1796,

Amelia Simmons did not share an Election Cake recipe.

No doubt Election Cakes were served from New England down to the South, but nowhere do they have such a rich heritage as in Connecticut. Historian Stephen Schmidt, a Connecticut native who researched the cake, explains that Election Day was a big deal in Connecticut and Rhode Island during Colonial times because people there had the right to elect their own governors, unlike the residents of other colonies. Election Day became a holiday in Connecticut because Puritans selected secular holidays to replace the traditional "red letter days," or religious holidays. On Election Day, in addition to voting, Connecticut colonists attended a service in the meetinghouse where they heard a sermon, followed by meals at homes and then, at night, Election Day "drinkings" where the cake was served. Women baked the cakes, but they were not allowed to vote.

Over time the election process changed. A national election in the fall took prominence, and local elections didn't have the fanfare they once did. Election Cake, Hartford Election Cake, Independence Cake, Franklin Gingerbread, and Democratic Tea Cakes—these patriotic cakes became cakes of the past.

1800 *to* 1869

New Cakes & New Directions

❀❀❀

THE ELECTION CAKES baked after America won her independence helped instill national pride, and the cakes baked in the first half of the 19th century, such as the Washington Cake, continued this patriotic theme. America's consummate hostess, Dolley Madison, was First Lady in the White House, and she embodied the female initiative: Be strong and manage the home.

In the early 1800s, cakes were made from regional and imported ingredients and were influenced by America's westward expansion across the continent. The wheat Europeans brought to America and grew in the Hudson River Valley and in Pennsylvania during the Colonial period went west after the War of 1812. Indiana and Illinois became the new breadbasket of the United States. This was greatly influenced by their proximity to rivers with steamboats transporting wheat to market. In the westward frontier life, cooks used Dutch ovens to simmer meals and bake cakes such as the Cowboy Cake (page 45), an eggless cake that could be baked over an open fire.

Cooks in the early 1830s welcomed bicarbonate of soda—baking soda—as a better-tasting replacement for pearlash and saleratus to leaven their cakes. Two decades later, baking powder and the gas stove were invented, and this revolutionized cake baking.

These chemical leavenings, baking soda and baking powder, allowed the busy middle class to bake lighter cakes quickly into shortcakes. Washington Irving wrote in "The Legend of Sleepy Hollow" (1819) of a table set with "sweet cakes and short cakes, ginger cakes and crumbling cruller and the whole family of cakes." And the nation fell in love with strawberry shortcake (page 61), a favorite wherever strawberries grew wild, and they grew wild across much of the eastern part of the country. Other local foods like hickory nuts, black walnuts, blueberries, and cornmeal were folded into pound cakes, layer cakes, and shortcakes. And until railroads shipped food cross country toward the end of the 1800s, regional foods stayed in the region.

Local blackberries made into jam were the key ingredient in the German-inspired jam cake of Pennsylvania and Ohio that came south into Kentucky, Tennessee, northern Alabama, and east to the Carolinas (page 52). It was made with baking soda, blackberry jam you put up over the summer, and lots of spices. These jam cakes were holiday perennials, good keepers, and longtime family favorites.

Away from small-town life and westward expansion, German men baked professionally in the big cities and would begin a legacy of German bakeries that still exists today. Americans dined in grand hotels and restaurants, unlike the taverns and inns of the 18th century. American cooks got inspiration from the chef-created desserts, as well as from cookbooks and magazines. A popular "pie" of the time that more resembled cake was the Boston cream pie (page 46). It was baked in pie tins, contained a custard filling, and often was covered with a chocolate glaze. America's first taste of chocolate with cake was in glazes, fillings, and frostings. At the end of the 19th century, chocolate was folded into the cake batter itself.

Down South where cotton was king, cake baking became a part of the antebellum way of life. Sugar production moved into Louisiana after its statehood in 1812. Both New Orleans and Charleston were busy ports where imports of coconuts, spices, almonds, and chocolate came into the market. Charleston was the strawberry capital of the United States in the 1800s and a food hub with not only availability of ingredients but fine confectioners' shops to buy candies and cakes. Philadelphia, too, was a food center, not only for exotic imports but also for the Quaker cooking schools that trained future cooks and writers.

African American cooks played an important role in creating the cakes of these shops and at home in the Deep South. In the decades leading up to the Civil War, the fine food of the plantations would not have been possible without the creativity, hard work, and skill of enslaved cooks who cracked coconuts, caramelized sugar, sifted flour, ground sugar, and whipped egg whites without the modern conveniences we have today. The country was dividing between the industrialized North and the southern slave states at midcentury.

New American cookbook authors emerged, writing the "housewife" books of Virginia, Kentucky, and South Carolina. They would use classic cooking techniques, incorporate the local foods of their regions, and present it all in a cosmopolitan way. And they were joined by New England household primers offering women advice on managing their homes and lives. This was the birth of women's magazines, such as *Godey's Lady's Book*, published in Philadelphia, with the largest circulation of any magazine prior to the Civil War. Its editor, Sarah Josepha Hale, preached domesticity as a virtue and exposed American women to new ideas and recipes. And while its articles and recipes were published during the Civil War, the war was not mentioned in its commentary.

Outside of the country, America's eyes were on England's Queen Victoria, who wed in white in 1840. This was the beginning of the Victorian age, which would influence fashion, food, and etiquette for the next 60 years. Cakes in America had changed. The new American cake was easier to prepare and lighter in texture, contained more accessible ingredients, and was welcomed by all.

LEMON AND MOLASSES SPICE MARBLE CAKE

MAKES: 12 TO 16 SERVINGS
PREP: 40 TO 45 MINUTES
BAKE: 50 TO 55 MINUTES

MOLASSES BATTER

Butter and flour for prepping the pan
(see tip on page 42)

6 tablespoons unsalted butter, at room
temperature

¼ cup plus 2 tablespoons light brown
sugar, firmly packed

3 large egg yolks, at room temperature

¾ cup unsulfured molasses

1⅔ cups all-purpose flour

½ teaspoon baking soda

½ teaspoon cream of tartar

½ teaspoon ground cinnamon

¼ teaspoon ground mace

¼ teaspoon ground nutmeg

¼ teaspoon ground cloves

¼ cup plus 2 tablespoons buttermilk,
at room temperature

LEMON BATTER

6 tablespoons unsalted butter, at room
temperature

1 cup granulated sugar

2 teaspoons grated lemon zest
(from 2 medium lemons)

1 tablespoon fresh lemon juice

1⅔ cups all-purpose flour

½ teaspoon baking soda

½ teaspoon cream of tartar

¾ cup buttermilk, at room temperature

3 large egg whites, at room
temperature

⅛ teaspoon salt

GARNISH

Lemon Glaze, if desired (see page 42)

A s new American bakers became more proficient at baking cakes, they added flourishes and touches to make their cakes dazzling to the eye. Swirling batters of different hues, called marbling, was a technique used in Europe. It appeared in American cakes in the mid-1800s, most likely a gift from German bakers. The first newspaper advertisements for "Marble Cake" were from bakeries, and it did not take long for home cooks to figure out how to "dye" part of their batter with a little molasses and spices to make it darker. Or they might make 2 cake batters, one light and one dark, and alternate spoonfuls of them in a baking pan. They were already experimenting with alternating dark and light baked layers in the Jenny Lind Cake and the Dolly Varden Cake. This was taking that creativity one step further. Toward the end of the 19th century, chocolate was added to the dark part of the batter, and chocolate marble cakes were born. In this recipe, adapted from Richard Sax's book *Classic Home Desserts*, both a molasses and a lemon batter are alternately dolloped and swirled in a tube pan and, when sliced, reveal a stunning marble pattern. The yolks from the 3 eggs are used in the molasses batter, and the whites are used in the lemon batter. For the modern cook, I added a quick lemon glaze to keep the cake moist and accentuate the lemon flavor.

1. Place a rack in the center of the oven, and preheat the oven to 350°F. Generously butter and flour a 10" tube pan, and shake out the excess flour. Set the pan aside.

2. For the molasses batter, place the butter and sugar in a large mixing bowl, and beat with an electric mixer on medium speed until fluffy and lighter in color, about 3 minutes. Beat in the egg yolks, one at a time, just until combined. Scrape down the sides of the bowl with a rubber spatula. Beat in the molasses on medium speed just until combined.

3. Place the flour, soda, cream of tartar, cinnamon, mace, nutmeg, and cloves in a small bowl and sift together. Add to the batter in 3 additions, alternately with the buttermilk in 2 additions. Beat on medium speed, just until each is combined. Scrape the bowl often and set aside.

4. For the lemon batter, place the butter, sugar, and lemon zest in a large mixing bowl, and beat on medium speed until fluffy and lighter in color,

continued

about 3 minutes. Scrape down the sides of the bowl and add the lemon juice. Beat just until combined.

5. Place the flour, soda, and cream of tartar in a small bowl and sift together. Add to the batter in 3 additions, alternately with the buttermilk in 2 additions, beating on medium speed just until each is combined. Scrape the bowl often and set aside.

6. Beat the egg whites and salt in a clean medium-size bowl with clean beaters on high speed until soft peaks form, 3 to 4 minutes. With the spatula, gently fold about a quarter of the whites into the lemon batter, just until combined. Fold in the remaining whites, just until combined.

7. Dollop the batters into the bottom of the prepared pan, alternating each flavor 3 times. Gently rap the pan once against the countertop to settle the batters. With a butter knife, swirl the batter together a couple of times, but don't overdo it. Place the pan in the oven.

8. Bake until the cake is golden brown and a toothpick inserted near the center emerges clean, 50 to 55 minutes.

9. Cool the cake in the pan on a wire rack for 10 to 15 minutes. Run the tip of the knife around the cake to loosen it from the sides and tube; invert once and then again so the cake is right side up on the rack. Cool completely, 1 hour. If desired, serve with the modern Lemon Glaze. Slice and serve.

TIP: If you want to use a Bundt pan, the baking time will be 42 to 47 minutes.

> **LEMON GLAZE:** *Whisk together 1$\frac{1}{2}$ cups confectioners' sugar and 2 to 3 tablespoons fresh lemon juice until smooth. Poke holes in the top of the cooled cake with a fork, and spoon the glaze over the top of the cake.*

Marble Cakes and American Government

If you study American government, talk will turn to cake. The terms "layer cake" and "marble cake" have been used to describe two different ways of governing our country. The layer cake, or dual federalism, was set up by the founders of this country, who feared a strong central government and instead promoted states' rights. It is much like a layer cake, with state government on one level and the federal government on another. However, after the Great Depression, the federal government had to establish more control to bring about a national recovery. Marble cake federalism, or cooperative federalism, is the sharing of authority between states and the federal government. Like the decorative swirls in the cake, the state and federal government authority overlap.

JENNY LIND CAKE

DAZZLED BY THE CELEBRITY of Swedish opera singer Jenny Lind, Americans would name a cake for her in the 1850s. It was a three-layer cake with the bottom and top layers either white or yellow but the center layer darker and filled with dried fruit and spice. Americans had not been introduced to chocolate cake yet, but they were fascinated by the contrast of light and dark when stacking cakes. Jenny Lind was something of an idol, called the "Swedish nightingale" because of her sweet soprano voice. Across Europe, crowds packed the streets when Jenny Lind was in town, and when she toured America in the 1850s, she became a household name. America, as we know, has always loved celebrities. This same cake would also be known as the Dolly Varden Cake, after a Charles Dickens character and a colorful women's fashion style of the 1870s.

THE HOUSEWIFE COOKBOOKS

BEFORE HOUSEWIVES were the stars of modern television, they were the target audience for early 1800s cookbooks that instructed them how to cook and entertain well. Here are three of the most famous of those cookbooks.

The Virginia House-wife, by Mary Randolph, 1824

Born into privilege with family ties to both Thomas Jefferson and George Washington, Mary Randolph was the consummate Virginia hostess. Her husband, David, was appointed US Marshall of Virginia. They were an early power couple, and dinner at their elegant Richmond home was a coveted invitation. But her husband's Federalist views conflicted with those of President Jefferson, and Jefferson fired David Randolph. To make ends meet, the Randolphs sold their home and tobacco plantations, and Mary opened a Richmond boardinghouse. For the next 11 years, she prepared fine food with local ingredients and elevated Virginia cooking to an art form. Broiling shad, frying strawberry fritters, baking pound cake, making vanilla ice cream: These were some of her skills and delicacies. An inventive and resourceful woman, she designed one of the first refrigerators to keep food cold in summer heat. On better financial footing than they had been a decade earlier, the Randolphs moved to Washington, DC, to live with their son, and here Mary wrote her famous cookbook. It is a collection of sage advice mingled with down-home and sophisticated recipes. *The Virginia House-wife* might not have been the first American cookbook, but historians believe it was the most important cookbook of the 19th century. Mary's rule of running a household still works today: "Let everything be done at the proper time, keep everything in its proper place, and put everything to its proper use."

The Kentucky Housewife, by Lettice Bryan, 1839

Little is known about Lettice Bryan other than she lived in Kentucky, her ancestors came from Virginia, and she was the wife of a Louisville physician. Her book, which instructs how to supervise people and get food to the table, speaks to the plantation mistress who managed slaves. Her tone is friendly and precise, advising anyone baking a cake to prepare the fruits and seasonings the day before—to first dust raisins with flour before folding them into a cake batter, to rinse butter twice in cold water because it was heavily salted. Bryan was clearly influenced by Mary Randolph, whose book had been published 15 years earlier. In addition to making your own French mustard, she advises you to soak cucumbers in vinegar, toss strawberries with sugar and pile them with whipped cream into "a pyramidic heap," and cook local foods like pokeweed. But her 1,300 recipes are clearly all over the place, from West India gumbo—stewed okra (ochra) with butter—to pear ice cream, Dutch doughnuts, Italian creams, and cupcakes. She experiments with early food colorings, too, dyeing foods green with the puree of spinach. Kentucky was a slave state, but it did not secede from the Union. After the Civil War, enslaved women and men who worked in the kitchens of the large farms left. Bryan's recipes using hearth cooking and slave labor reflected a prewar style of cooking, and it fell out of favor once woodstoves became popular.

The Carolina Housewife, by Sarah Rutledge, 1847

Like Mary Randolph, Sarah Rutledge came from a prestigious family. Her father, Edward Rutledge, was one of the signers of the Declaration of Independence. Her book, which she wrote under the name "Lady of Charleston," featured the cuisine of the Low Country—Charleston and the surrounding coastal area. Until her book, few outside the region had prepared the unique foods of the Low Country, and Rutledge fashioned the foods she knew into their own regional cuisine. From the plentiful oyster and rice recipes to the tea cakes of sponge, pound, and ginger, this book is a celebration and a tutorial on how to cook food from the coast. It shares mullet recipes and turtle soup and describes how to make a French omelet as well as a cheesecake in which you fold groundnuts (peanuts). Breads and cakes are quick to prepare, reflecting the warmer climate of South Carolina.

It also has nuances of the city of brotherly love because Rutledge had taken cooking classes with the esteemed Elizabeth Goodfellow in Philadelphia. Rutledge shares one of the first mentions of the "composition cake," a spinoff of the pound cake containing sour milk and pearlash.

But America didn't have the only "housewife" books. English housewife books were published as early as 1596—*The Good Housewife's Jewel*. Then there was *The British Housewife* (1756) by Mrs. Martha Bradley and *The Frugal Housewife* by Susannah Carter in 1803. Carter's books were published in America and contained American recipes like Indian pudding and buckwheat cakes.

COWBOY CAKE

MAKES: 8 TO 10 SERVINGS

PREP: 40 TO 45 MINUTES

BAKE: 25 TO 30 MINUTES

1 cup raisins (see Cake Note)

3 cups water

1 tablespoon vegetable shortening

1 teaspoon baking soda

1 cup granulated sugar

1 teaspoon ground cinnamon

½ teaspoon ground nutmeg

Pinch of salt

2 cups all-purpose flour

TOPPING

Reserved raisin cooking liquid

1 cup granulated sugar

1 tablespoon vegetable shortening

Mock Whipped Cream

Canned evaporated milk was an easy stand-in for real cream in frontier kitchens. Cooks would get it as cold as possible and then whip and sweeten. It didn't have the stability of real whipped cream, but it was a soft, creamy topping to Dutch oven cakes.

As America expanded west of the Mississippi River with the 1803 Louisiana Purchase, "make-do" cakes that could be baked on the move suited those challenging times. One such cake was the Cowboy Cake, similar to a boiled raisin cake baked during the Civil War and World War I. It was made by simmering raisins in water; adding shortening, baking soda, sugar, spices, and flour; and baking the batter in a Dutch oven. The big plus was that pioneers traveling west or prospectors hoping to strike it rich in the 1849 gold rush didn't need to add eggs, butter, or milk to this cake. This crowd-pleasing recipe comes from Luann Sewell Waters of Wynnewood, Oklahoma, who teaches Dutch oven cooking today and has researched the old recipes of the West.

1. Place the raisins and water in a 10″ Dutch oven over medium-high heat. Let the water come to a simmer, then reduce the heat and let the raisins simmer uncovered until they turn a caramel-brown color and soften, 15 to 20 minutes. Drain the raisins and set aside, reserving all the cooking liquid. Measure out 1 cup of the reserved liquid and place this in the Dutch oven.

2. Place a rack in the center of the oven and preheat the oven to 350°F. To the 1 cup warm liquid, add the shortening and stir to melt. Let this cool. Stir in the baking soda, sugar, cinnamon, nutmeg, salt, and flour until smooth. Stir in the reserved raisins. Set aside.

3. For the topping, place the remaining cooking liquid in a medium-size pan with the sugar and shortening over medium-high heat. Bring to a boil and cook, stirring, until the mixture thickens and is syrupy, 10 to 15 minutes. If you have a candy thermometer, bring the mixture to 220°F. Stir well and pour carefully onto the top of the cake batter. Cover the Dutch oven, and place the pan in the oven.

4. Bake the cake until it springs back when lightly pressed in the center, 25 to 30 minutes. Serve warm.

CAKE NOTE: Instead of raisins, you can use chopped dried peaches or apricots.

BOSTON CREAM PIE

MAKES: 12 TO 16 SERVINGS

PREP: 55 TO 60 MINUTES;
5 HOURS TO CHILL FILLING

BAKE: 18 TO 22 MINUTES

FILLING

1½ cups whole milk, divided use

⅓ cup granulated sugar

½ heaping teaspoon unflavored gelatin

Dash of salt

2 large egg yolks

1½ tablespoons cornstarch

1½ tablespoons unsalted butter

1 teaspoon vanilla extract (see Cake Notes on page 48)

CAKE

Butter and flour for prepping the pans

1½ cups sifted cake flour

2 teaspoons baking powder

¼ teaspoon salt

⅓ cup unsalted butter, at room temperature

1 teaspoon vanilla extract

¾ cup granulated sugar

2 large eggs, at room temperature

½ cup whole milk, at room temperature

CHOCOLATE GLAZE

¾ cup chopped semisweet chocolate

3 tablespoons heavy cream

1 tablespoon light corn syrup

½ teaspoon vanilla extract
(see Cake Notes on page 48)

With its thick custard filling and simple butter cake, the Boston cream pie is an iconic American dessert with a much-discussed past. The most famous story of its origin was that a pastry chef named Sanzian invented this dessert for Boston's Parker House Hotel opening in October 1856, and he called his dessert the "Chocolate Cream Pie." The words "pie" and "cake" were briefly interchangeable because they were baked in the same-size pan. But historians say the dessert was simply a popular "custard cake" fashioned after a jelly-filled Washington Pie (Cake). As early as 1864 in a short story called "The Gulf Between Them," by Mrs. Ann S. Stephens, the luncheon tray contained cold sliced chicken, apricot jelly, and "custard-cake." In 1866 *Godey's Lady's Book* shares a recipe for Almond Custard Cake, and in 1869 a Tennessee newspaper recipe for a "Very Nice Custard Cake" resembles the Boston cream pie, but without the chocolate glaze. The late historian Gil Marks researched the Boston cream pie and found no mention of it being served at the Parker House Hotel opening; instead the first reference to it was in the 1872 *Methodist Almanac.* By then custard cakes, cream pies, and chocolate cream pies were all cakes filled with custard. Baking chocolate was making its appearance in glazes and frostings about this time, so cooks would have created a simple chocolate coating for the custard cake. If the Parker House pastry chef had prepared the dessert, it was no doubt a popular choice on the menu. He added a little rum to the filling and pressed toasted sliced almonds onto the sides of the cake, both nice touches. Today Boston cream pie is the state cake of Massachusetts. This cake recipe is adapted from *The American Heritage Cookbook,* and the filling and glaze recipes are adapted from *Yankee* magazine. For all the disagreement about its origin, you cannot dispute that Boston cream pie is one of the most universally loved and recognized American cakes.

1. For the filling, place 1¼ cups of the milk and the sugar, gelatin, and salt in a large saucepan over medium heat. Whisk and bring barely to a simmer, whisking to dissolve the sugar and gelatin completely, 2 to 3 minutes. Meanwhile, in a medium-size bowl, whisk together the egg yolks, cornstarch, and the remaining ¼ cup of milk. Off the heat, pour 1 cup of

continued

the hot milk mixture into the egg mixture and whisk to combine, then strain this mixture back into the saucepan with the remaining hot milk. Over medium heat, whisk the mixture continuously until it is thickened and bubbling in the center, 4 to 5 minutes.

2. Remove the pan from the heat and strain the mixture again into a medium-size bowl. Stir in the butter and vanilla. Whisk until smooth, then cover with plastic wrap, pressing the wrap directly onto the surface. Chill the filling for at least 5 hours, preferably overnight.

3. For the cake, place a rack in the center of the oven, and preheat the oven to 375°F. Lightly grease and flour the bottoms of two 8″ cake pans.

4. Sift together the flour, baking powder, and salt in a medium-size bowl. Set aside.

5. Place the butter and vanilla in a large mixing bowl, and beat with an electric mixer on low speed until combined, 1 minute. Slowly add the sugar, beating well on medium-high speed until the mixture is creamy and light, 2 to 3 minutes. Scrape down the sides of the bowl with a rubber spatula. Add the eggs, beating in one at a time. Scrape down the sides of the bowl again. Alternately add the flour mixture and the milk to the butter and sugar mixture, beginning and ending with the flour. Beat until smooth. Divide the batter between the 2 pans. Place the pans in the oven.

6. Bake the cakes until they are lightly golden brown and begin to pull away from the sides of the pan, 18 to 22 minutes. Place the pans on wire racks to cool for 10 minutes. Run a knife around the edges of the cakes, give them a gentle shake, then invert onto the racks to cool completely, right side up, about 45 minutes.

7. To assemble the cake, place 1 cake layer on a cake plate. Spoon the filling onto the center of the cake and spread until it barely reaches the edge of the cake. Place the second layer on top of the filling. Place the filled cake in the refrigerator while you make the glaze.

8. For the glaze, place the chocolate, cream, and corn syrup in a medium-size saucepan over medium-low heat. Whisk until smooth, 3 to 4 minutes. When the chocolate has melted, pull the pan from the heat, add the vanilla, and stir until smooth. Remove the cake from the refrigerator and spoon the glaze over the top of the cake and let it drip down the sides. Let the cake stand for 10 minutes before slicing. If not serving the cake immediately, chill it until time to serve.

CAKE NOTES: For the flavor of the Parker House version of Boston cream pie, use ½ teaspoon vanilla extract and 1 tablespoon rum in the filling. Press toasted sliced almonds onto the sides of the cake after spooning over the chocolate glaze.

AMERICA'S NATIVE NUTS

NUTS AND BAKING just seem to go together. Whether walnut, pecan, hickory, hazelnut, almond, pistachio, or peanut, they pick up the flavor of a cookie, bread, or cake. They fold into the batter, adding moistness and texture, and they sprinkle easily on top, adding crunch.

Resourceful American bakers in the early 1800s baked with the nuts harvested nearby. We call it foraging today, but in those early times it was second nature to pick up and use the foods nature offered. Across America, wild hickory, black walnut, and pecan trees thrived and offered an edible nut perfect for baking. In the South, peanuts, a legume, were grown from Virginia south and west to Texas.

BLACK WALNUTS are native to America and have grown prolifically in limestone-rich soil across the eastern United States. Their nuts are messy to harvest, even tougher to crack, but have a sweet-bitter flavor that melds well with chocolate.

ENGLISH WALNUTS, on the other hand, named after English merchants who brought them to Europe from what is now Iran, have been grown in California since the 1770s. They were first planted in missions by Franciscan monks.

HICKORY NUTS, still found wild across the eastern United States, come from a number of different varieties of hickory trees. The most common is shagbark, distinguished by the long pieces of bark that hang from the tree, shaggy in appearance. They are harvested in the fall and also tough to crack. You peel off the outer husk, boil the inside nuts, and crack the nut to expose the nut meat used in cooking. Unless you harvest hickory nuts from your land, you might be able to find them during the fall at a local farmers' market if the trees grow in the area. You can also buy them online.

The buttery rich and sweet flavor of hickory nuts is similar to that of **PECANS,** their distant cousin. Pecans grow across much of the Southeast and are native to North America. The first wild pecan trees were noticed along the coasts of Louisiana and Texas. Based on Native American research, pecans have been consumed here for more than 6,000 years. Native Americans not only ate them out of the shell but pounded them into a paste and used this as a thickener in cooking. During the American Revolution, the French in Lou-isiana added pecans to their praline candies. But it wasn't until the early 1800s in Texas that cooks started baking with pecans. By the late 1800s, pecans were being grown commercially.

PEANUTS, called groundnuts by locals in the early Carolinas and Georgia, have a mild flavor like peas when they are raw. But once the peanuts are roasted, they become deeper in color and flavor and develop that "peanut" taste. Sarah Rutledge, author of *The Carolina Housewife* (1847), shared one of the first recipes with peanuts—a peanut soup—in her book. Street vendors in Charleston, South Carolina, sold what they called "groundnut cakes," an early peanut candy. But George Washington Carver of the Tuskegee Institute in Alabama brought the peanut to the forefront when he researched peanuts after the turn of the 20th century and found 300 uses for them. After the boll weevil destroyed the cotton crop, Southern farmers turned to growing peanuts.

Here are three other nuts, not native to America but grown commercially and a part of the American cake story.

HAZELNUTS, OR FILBERTS—Grown in the Willamette Valley of Oregon, these nuts were introduced from Europe around 1847 when European farmers came to the West in hopes of striking it rich from the gold rush. Although one species of hazelnuts is native to the Pacific Northwest, it is not the species grown commercially today.

ALMONDS—An old nut beloved in Europe when ground into marzipan, it is believed to have originated in southwest Asia. Almonds came to California in 1853, but they were not the commercial crop they are today until the mid-20th century, when ramped-up marketing efforts increased demand for them.

PISTACHIOS—Also an old nut, pistachios came later, in the 1930s, to the American West, where they grow today in the dry climates of California, New Mexico, and Arizona.

The nut story isn't over. Before the blight of 1904, American **CHESTNUT** trees grew from Maine south to the Gulf of Mexico. The trees yielded kernels that were sweeter and smaller than the European chestnuts. They were most often roasted, cooked into puddings, or ground into flour.

SARAH POLK'S HICKORY NUT CAKE

MAKES: 12 TO 16 SERVINGS
....
PREP: 20 TO 25 MINUTES
....
BAKE: 55 TO 60 MINUTES
....

Butter and flour for prepping the pan

1 cup (2 sticks) unsalted butter, at room temperature

2 cups granulated sugar

4 large eggs, separated

3 cups all-purpose flour

2 teaspoons baking powder

½ teaspoon salt

1 teaspoon fresh lemon juice

1 cup whole milk or half-and-half

1 cup chopped hickory nuts (see Cake Note)

½ teaspoon pure almond extract, if desired

½ teaspoon vanilla extract, if desired (see Cake Note)

CAKE NOTE: Although vanilla extract was available after 1847, it still might have been a rare ingredient for the home baker. And almond extract would have been extravagant. Therefore, this cake would have been baked without them in the mid- to late 1800s. Extracts are a nice addition today, however, as just a little almond extract brings out the nuttiness in the hickory nuts. Do not use more than ½ teaspoon or it will overpower the delicacy of the rare hickory nuts, which can be purchased online or at farmers' markets.

When hickory trees populated America, people would rush to gather the sweet, buttery nuts in the fall before the animals did. Carol Meeks of Indianapolis said that in 1838 her great-great-grandparents purchased Indiana farmland with an abundance of shagbark hickory trees. Gathering the nuts became a generations-old tradition, and the nuts were laid under beds in the old farmhouse to dry, before cracking, shelling, and folding the nut meat into cakes and cookies for the holidays. Smooth, ivory-colored hickory nuts are one of the few indigenous American nuts, and Native Americans ate them raw. They are a lot like the pecan, only smaller, harder to obtain, and more labor intensive to shell. Hickory wood is known for its strength and durability, used for tool handles and fence posts in addition to firewood. This pound cake with chopped hickory nuts folded into the batter was popular during the 1800s and is adapted from *The First Ladies Cook Book* by Margaret Brown Klapthor. It was a favorite recipe of Sarah Polk, wife of former U.S. president James K. Polk.

1. Place a rack in the center of the oven, and preheat the oven to 350°F. Lightly butter and flour a 10″ tube pan, and shake out the excess flour. Set the pan aside.

2. Place the butter in a large mixing bowl, and beat with an electric mixer on medium speed until creamy, 1 minute. Add the sugar, a couple of tablespoons at a time, beating on medium until light and creamy, 2 minutes. Add the egg yolks, one at a time, beating until combined. Set aside.

3. Place the flour, baking powder, and salt in a large mixing bowl and sift to combine. Set aside. Place the egg whites in a large mixing bowl and, with clean beaters, beat on high speed until stiff peaks form, about 4 minutes. Set aside. Stir the lemon juice into the milk. Alternately add the flour mixture and milk to the butter mixture in 3 additions, beating on low speed just to combine. Beat in the hickory nuts and extracts, if desired, on low speed until combined. By hand, fold the beaten egg whites into the batter, just until combined. Turn the batter into the prepared pan, smooth the top, and place the pan in the oven.

4. Bake the cake until it is golden brown and begins to pull away from the sides of the pan, 55 to 60 minutes. Remove the cake from the oven, and place the pan on a wire rack to cool for 20 minutes. Run a knife around the edges of the pan, give the pan a gentle shake, then invert the cake onto the rack to cool, right side up, for 30 minutes. Slice and serve.

GRANNY KELLETT'S JAM CAKE

MAKES: 12 TO 16 SERVINGS
PREP: 45 TO 50 MINUTES
BAKE: 38 TO 42 MINUTES

CAKE

Flour and butter for greasing the pans

1 cup finely chopped pecans, walnuts, or black walnuts (see Cake Notes on page 54)

1 cup (2 sticks) unsalted butter, at room temperature

2 cups granulated sugar

4 large eggs, at room temperature

1 cup blackberry jam (see Cake Notes on page 54)

2¼ cups all-purpose flour

1 teaspoon ground cinnamon

1 teaspoon ground nutmeg

1 teaspoon ground allspice

1 teaspoon ground ginger

½ teaspoon salt

1 teaspoon baking soda

1 cup buttermilk

1 cup raisins

CARAMEL FROSTING

½ cup (1 stick) unsalted butter

1½ cups light brown sugar, firmly packed

⅓ cup heavy cream

1 teaspoon vanilla extract

Pinch of salt

1½ cups confectioners' sugar, sifted

Amanda (Granny) Kellett was known for her jam cake. Amanda baked it after the Civil War, when wild blackberries were easy to find, just as they still are in many rural parts of America. Amanda's great-granddaughter, Marion Hurley of Nashville, still makes Granny's Jam Cake and has all her life. "We would go out as children with a bucket and pick enough berries for jam," she says. "They were delicious, wild, and wonderful." Marion says the story of Granny Kellett's jam cake is retold each time her family makes the treasured cake. The story goes that Joe Kellett was wounded badly in the Civil War but was able to crawl away from battle and hide in the brush. When the battle quieted, Joe crawled to a nearby farm, and the family took him in and treated his wounds. Joe fell in love with the family's daughter—Amanda—and after the war, he finished school and came back for Amanda's hand in marriage. They would marry, raise seven children together, and run a boardinghouse where Amanda was known for her jam cake. The family continues to bake this cake on Thanksgiving, Christmas, Easter, Sundays, and birthdays—as often as possible. Marion remembers her mother's jam cakes being stored in the china cabinet. "As a child I would open up that cabinet and it smelled so good." The Kellett family bakes their cake in a tube pan for about 1 hour at 350°F. I love this cake baked in layers with a traditional caramel frosting, as they prepare it in Kentucky and Tennessee. The Caramel Frosting recipe is from Kentucky, adapted from a cookbook called *LaRue County Kitchens of Kentucky*.

1. For the cake, place a rack in the center of the oven, and preheat the oven to 350°F. Grease two 9″ round cake pans with vegetable shortening or soft butter and dust with flour. Shake out the excess flour, and set the pans aside.

2. While the oven preheats, place the nuts on a baking sheet in the oven, and let the nuts toast until just beginning to brown, 4 to 5 minutes. Remove the pan from the oven, and let the nuts cool.

3. Place the butter and sugar in a large mixing bowl, and beat with an electric mixer on high speed until creamy, 3 minutes. Turn off the mixer, and scrape down the sides of the bowl with a rubber spatula. Add the eggs, one at a time, beating well on medium speed until each egg is combined. Add the jam, and blend on low until combined. Scrape down the sides of the bowl.

continued

4. Remove 1 tablespoon of the flour and set aside. In a separate medium-size bowl, sift together the remaining flour, cinnamon, nutmeg, allspice, ginger, and salt. Set aside. In a small bowl, stir the baking soda into the buttermilk until dissolved. Add a third of the flour mixture to the egg batter, and blend on low until just incorporated. Pour in half of the buttermilk, and blend until incorporated. Repeat with the second third of the flour, the rest of the buttermilk, and the last of the flour mixture. Place the toasted nuts, raisins, and the remaining 1 tablespoon flour in a large bowl and toss to coat the nuts and raisins with flour. Fold these into the batter with the rubber spatula. Divide the batter between the prepared pans and smooth the tops. Place the pans in the oven.

5. Bake the cakes until they just begin to pull back from the edges of the pan and the top springs back when lightly pressed, 38 to 42 minutes. Remove the pans to wire racks to cool for 10 minutes. Run a knife around the edges, give the pans a gentle shake, and invert the layers once and then again so they cool right side up on the racks. Let cool completely, 30 to 40 minutes, before frosting.

6. For the frosting, place the butter, brown sugar, cream, vanilla, and salt in a medium-size saucepan over medium heat, and cook, stirring, until the mixture boils, about 2 minutes. Remove the pan from the heat and whisk in the confectioners' sugar until smooth. Use at once.

7. To assemble the cake, place 1 cake layer on a cake stand or serving plate. Spoon about a third of the warm caramel frosting over the top, and spread to smooth out. Place the second layer on top, and spoon the remaining frosting over the top and let it trickle down the sides of the cake. Let the cake rest for at least 20 minutes, then slice and serve.

CAKE NOTES: Use what blackberry jam you have on hand. If you are buying the jam, look for a 10-ounce jar. If you don't like blackberry seeds, buy seedless jam. You can substitute black raspberry, strawberry, or plum jam in this cake. Instead of toasted pecans, you can use untoasted black walnuts.

Jam Cake

The words "Kentucky jam cake" seem to roll off the tongue as easily as other Bluegrass State terms—like "bourbon" and "the Derby." Blackberries are the official state fruit of Kentucky and have been since 2004. And yet, adding blackberry jam to cake batter isn't unique to one state. Jam cakes existed in Europe and came to America with German immigrants who would put up jam from local berries and use this jam in spice cakes at holiday times. The cake traveled as people relocated into Kentucky, Tennessee, Alabama, and the Carolinas. Across the country in Oregon, a state where huckleberries, blackberries, and blueberries grow, berries have long been turned into jam cake. Food historian Betty Fussell writes of early jam cakes in her book *I Hear America Cooking*. The Gitxsan Indians of Canada would dry berries to concentrate their natural sugars and thus preserve them. As early as 1913, the *Portland Woman's Exchange Cook Book* included berry jam in the spice cake batter and also in the buttercream frosting, which turned pink from the jam. But, in Kentucky, the cake is revered. The Heitzman Bakery of Louisville has been baking jam cakes and placing them in signature pink boxes since 1891.

Jam Cake Ingredients

A proper jam cake is moist and dense and is best made with homemade blackberry jam. An old wives' tale goes something like this: If you don't use homemade jam in your jam cake, the jam will fall to the bottom of the cake. When jam cake originated in the 1800s, you couldn't go out and buy a jar of jam to put in it. The cake made use of your own homemade jam, put up from the summer crop of blackberries. The jam was measured by the teacup into the cake batter, and making aromatic jam cake cleaned out the spice cabinet. Leavened by soda and often containing buttermilk, jam cake features the nuts of the region. Black walnuts, pecans, and English walnuts all work well in jam cake. Dredge the nuts and raisins, if using, with a little flour before folding them into the recipe.

COCONUT LAYER CAKE

MAKES: 12 TO 16 SERVINGS

PREP: 60 TO 75 MINUTES

BAKE: 22 TO 25 MINUTES

Butter and flour for prepping the pans

1 cup (2 sticks) unsalted butter, at room temperature

2 cups granulated sugar

5 large eggs, separated

2 teaspoons vanilla extract

2 cups all-purpose flour

1 teaspoon baking soda

1 cup buttermilk, at room temperature

Seven-Minute Frosting (page 317)

2 to 3 cups grated fresh or packaged unsweetened coconut

A Coconut Ambrosia Cake

Ambrosia is a fruit dessert of fresh oranges and coconut served in a giant punchbowl in the South. The successful combination of those flavors is used in baking cakes, too. To impart the fresh flavor of orange in coconut cake, William Deas, a famous Charleston cook and butler in the early 1900s, would squeeze fresh orange juice over baked cake layers and then cover them with whipped cream and sprinkle on coconut.

Stacked high with fluffy white frosting and mounds of grated coconut, the coconut cake has no equal. It isn't just another pound cake, it is a coconut cake, by golly. And a bite brings back history and good memories, whether it was the cake your grandmother baked or the cake always served at Christmas. Coconut cakes have long been associated with the South, and they were baked in New Orleans and Charleston in the early 1800s. But they were also baked wherever Caribbean "cocoa nuts" arrived, for coconuts were just days away from ports such as Philadelphia and others along the Atlantic and Gulf coasts. Coconuts were good travelers because they were hard to break. Coconut was first used in candy making by French and Dutch confectioners in the 18th century before it was piled atop cake. Old Charleston records show that a pastry chef by the name of Catherine Joor had 400 pounds of coconut in her possession at her death in 1773. Coconut was a key ingredient in sponge cake (Mrs. Lettice Bryan, *The Kentucky Housewife,* 1839) and the Sally White fruitcake, a white fruitcake popular in North Carolina in the mid-1800s. Toward the end of the 19th century, coconut would be found in all sorts of cakes—sponge cakes, silver cakes made with egg whites, and a New Orleans Creole coconut pound cake with the freshly shelled coconut dried in the skillet before grating. Once baking powder was on hand in the American kitchen, and once cakes transitioned out of the tube pan and into layers, coconut cake became more of the cake we think of today.

1. Place a rack in the center of the oven, and set one rack above it if needed for the third pan. Preheat the oven to 325°F. Grease three 8" or 9" round cake pans with butter, then dust with flour, and shake out the excess flour. Set the pans aside.

2. Place the butter and sugar in a large mixing bowl, and with an electric mixer on medium speed, cream until light, 1 minute. Add the egg yolks, one at a time, and beat each until just combined. Add the vanilla.

3. Sift together the flour and baking soda in a medium-size bowl, and add this in thirds to the egg mixture, alternately with the buttermilk. Blend on medium-low until smooth.

continued

4. Place the egg whites in a large bowl and beat with an electric mixer on high speed until stiff peaks form, 4 minutes. Fold the whites into the batter with a rubber spatula until the whites are just combined. Divide the batter between the 3 pans. Place the pans in the oven, with 2 pans on the center rack and 1 pan on the rack above.

5. Bake the cake layers until they are golden brown and just pull away from the pan, 22 to 25 minutes for 9″ pans, and slightly more for 8″ pans. Let the cakes cool in the pans set on wire racks for 10 minutes. Then run a knife around the edges, give them a gentle shake to loosen from the pans, and invert them once and then again to cool right side up on the racks for at least 30 minutes before frosting.

6. While the cake is baking, make the frosting.

7. To assemble the cake, place 1 layer on a serving plate or platter. Cover with a large ladle of frosting and spread until smooth. Sprinkle on ¹/₂ cup of coconut. Add a second cake layer, cover with a ladle of frosting, then sprinkle on ¹/₂ cup of coconut. Place the final layer on top. Spread the top and sides of the cake generously with the remaining frosting. Pack 1 cup of coconut onto the sides of the cake using clean hands. If desired, sprinkle another 1 cup of coconut on the top of the cake. Decorate the top and sides with pieces of dried coconut, if desired. Slice and serve.

Flour-for-Coconuts Swap

In 1895 Philadelphia's Franklin Baker, a miller, received a shipload of coconuts as payment for flour Baker had shipped to Cuba. Baker was unable to sell the coconut, so he invested in a factory to crack, shred, and dry the coconut meat. Baker left the flour business and devoted his career to coconut, devising canned shredded coconut by 1917 and setting up a plant in the Philippines in the 1920s. In the early 1900s, coconut was the flavor of the moment, not only in coconut cake but also coconut cream pie and coconut cookies.

Baking with Fresh Coconut

Fresh coconut not only yields a bit of coconut milk, which you add to this cake filling, but the meat is more flavorful. If you want to use fresh coconut in this cake and other cakes, you will love the flavor. But be prepared for a little work.

1. Preheat the oven to 375°F. Hammer a nail into the three "eyes" of the coconut. Remove the nail to create three holes. Pour the coconut milk into a small bowl, straining it to remove any bits of husk. Set aside.

2. Place the coconut on a baking pan in the oven, and bake until it cracks, 15 to 20 minutes. It may not split all the way open. Remove the pan and coconut from the oven, and with pot holders or oven mitts, take the coconut to a hard surface, such as a cement porch or your driveway. Give it a hard whack with a rolling pin or hammer and crack the coconut open completely. Take the pieces back to the kitchen and let them cool completely.

3. Using a sharp knife, pry the meat away from the hard shell, and with a smaller paring knife, peel away the thin, dark skin. Rinse the coconut of husk and allow to dry.

4. Drop similar-size pieces into a food processor fitted with a steel blade. Pulse until it is finely grated, 1¹/₂ to 2 minutes. Repeat until all the coconut has been grated.

ROBERT E. LEE CAKE

MAKES: 12 TO 16 SERVINGS

PREP: 3 TO 4 HOURS

BAKE: 18 TO 22 MINUTES FOR 4 LAYERS; 25 TO 30 MINUTES FOR 2 LARGE LAYERS

LEMON FILLING

½ cup (1 stick) unsalted butter, melted and slightly cooled

2 large lemons (to yield ½ cup lemon juice and 1 tablespoon grated lemon zest)

6 large egg yolks, at room temperature

2 cups granulated sugar

CAKE

Butter and flour for prepping the pans

2 cups sifted all-purpose flour

1½ teaspoons baking powder

Dash of salt

8 large eggs, separated, at room temperature

2 cups granulated sugar

1 large lemon (to yield 1 heaping teaspoon grated lemon zest and scant ¼ cup lemon juice)

½ teaspoon cream of tartar

ORANGE AND LEMON ICING

¼ cup (4 tablespoons) unsalted butter, at room temperature

1 large pasteurized egg yolk (see Cake Note on page 60)

6 cups confectioners' sugar, sifted

1 medium lemon (to yield 2 tablespoons lemon juice and 1 heaping teaspoon grated lemon zest)

1 large orange (to yield 4 tablespoons orange juice and 1 heaping tablespoon grated orange zest)

Thin lemon and orange slices for garnish, if desired

Robert E. Lee, the Confederate general of the Civil War, is said to have proposed to his wife, Mary Custis, while Mary served him a slice of cake. Historians have no idea if the cake was this well-known orange and lemon cake recipe. But this recipe is the one Mary Custis Lee passed along to her daughter in a family recipe collection discovered in Virginia in the 1950s. It has been called the Lee Cake and the Lemon Jelly Cake, and it is a flavorful lemon sponge cake with a little baking powder, a novel ingredient in the 1850s. Filled with lemon curd—called "lemon jelly" at the time—and frosted with an orange and lemon icing, this cake is served today at the Beaumont Inn in Harrodsburg, Kentucky. If the icing sounds too sweet, frost it with lightly sweetened whipped cream flavored with lemon and orange zest.

1. For the filling, whisk together the melted butter, lemon juice, zest, egg yolks, and sugar in a medium-size bowl until smooth and combined. Pour this mixture into the top pan of a double boiler, and set it over a saucepan of simmering water. Cook the mixture, stirring, until it is thick and smooth, 35 to 40 minutes. Remove the pan from the heat, and continue to stir the filling for 2 more minutes so it has a chance to cool down. Pour the filling into a heatproof glass bowl, cover with plastic wrap, and chill in the refrigerator for at least 2 hours.

2. For the cake, place a rack in the center of the oven, and preheat the oven to 325°F. Lightly grease and flour four 9″ round pans. Set aside. (If you don't have 4 pans, you can stagger the baking, baking 2 at a time and cooling the pans between baking, or you can bake two 9″ layers and, once cooled, split them in half horizontally to make 4 layers.)

3. Sift the flour, baking powder, and salt into a medium-size bowl, and set the bowl aside.

4. Place the egg yolks in a large mixing bowl, and beat with an electric mixer on medium-high speed until combined, about 3 minutes. Add the sugar, 2 tablespoons at a time, and beat until the mixture is smooth and pale yellow in color. Add the lemon zest and juice, and beat on low speed until combined. Set aside.

5. Place the egg whites and cream of tartar in a large mixing bowl, and beat with clean beaters on high speed until stiff peaks form, about 5 minutes.

continued

Alternately fold the flour mixture and the beaten egg whites into the egg yolk mixture until just combined and smooth. Divide the cake between the cake pans, and smooth the tops. Place the pans in the oven.

6. Bake the layers until the cake is lightly golden and just begins to pull away from the edges, 18 to 22 minutes if baking 4 layers, 25 to 30 minutes if baking 2 large layers. Place the pans on wire racks to cool for 5 minutes. Run a sharp knife around the edges of the pans, give the pans a gentle shake to release the cakes, and invert them once and then again on the racks to cool completely, 30 minutes.

7. To assemble the cake, remove the filling from the refrigerator. Place 1 layer on a cake plate and spread a third of the chilled filling over the top, almost to the sides. Repeat with the remaining cake layers, leaving the top of the cake bare. Place the cake with filling in the refrigerator to set while you make the icing.

8. For the icing, place the butter in a large mixing bowl, and beat with an electric mixer on medium-high speed until creamy, 1 minute. Add the egg yolk and beat well. Add the confectioners' sugar in 3 additions, alternating it with the lemon and orange juices and zest, beating well after each addition and until the icing is creamy.

9. To finish, remove the cake from the refrigerator. To support the cake while frosting it, place 3 long toothpicks down into the cake. Spread the top and sides of the cake generously with icing. Garnish the top with the lemon and orange slices, if desired. Remove toothpicks before slicing.

CAKE NOTE: Use pasteurized egg in the icing recipe because the egg is not cooked.

How to Steady a Tall Cake

If you are frosting a three- to four-layer cake that has filling, you need to steady it while frosting or the cake layers may slide. Place three evenly spaced 6" toothpicks down into the top of the cake. Leave ¼" of each toothpick sticking out from the top. Frost the top and sides of the cake, then carefully remove the picks before slicing and serving.

Lemons and Oranges in Early America

Lemons and oranges have been grown along the southern Atlantic coast since the 1750s. The early settlers to South Carolina and Georgia found a sour Seville orange growing when they arrived. It was most likely a product of the early Spanish orange tree plantings in Florida, and Native Americans might have transported the orange trees north from St. Augustine to the unique microclimate of the Georgia barrier islands where citrus flourished, according to David Shields, Low Country historian. The hard freeze of 1835 devastated the coastal orange crops, but work was done in later years to come to replant those groves. Most citrus in the early 1800s was imported unless you lived near growing regions. Citrus has long been a prized ingredient in baking and an upper-class statement of wealth and importance. Citrus has never been as easy to obtain in America as it is today. But many families in all areas of the country recall how citrus was once rare and expensive, reserved for special times, and so it appears in birthday cakes or as a whole orange traditionally added to the Christmas stocking in remembrance of holidays past.

STRAWBERRY SHORTCAKE

MAKES: 8 TO 12 SERVINGS

PREP: 25 TO 30 MINUTES

BAKE: 12 TO 15 MINUTES

6 cups fresh ripe strawberries

⅓ cup granulated sugar, or more to taste

3 cups all-purpose flour, plus extra for dusting the countertop

⅓ cup granulated sugar

2 teaspoons baking powder

1 teaspoon salt

¾ cup (1½ sticks) unsalted butter, a little soft

1 large egg

1 cup heavy cream

2 tablespoons butter for buttering the shortcakes, if desired

1½ cups whipped cream, sweetened with 1 to 2 tablespoons confectioners' sugar

When the first American settlers arrived here, they found wild strawberries. For the strawberry grew across the eastern United States, and if the berries grew near you, then you learned how to put them up into syrups, cordials, jellies, and jams. One of the earliest ways to serve strawberries as a dessert was strawberry shortcake. Malinda Russell shares her recipe in her 1866 book, *A Domestic Cook Book: Containing a Careful Selection of Useful Receipts for the Kitchen*. Strawberry shortcake recipes appeared before the Civil War and were based on a biscuit dough that at first was unleavened, then leavened with baking soda, a little cream of tartar, and later with baking powder. Shortcakes without strawberries had been baked and were simply called "biscuits" by cookbook authors Harriott Pinckney Horry in 1770 and Amelia Simmons in 1796. When combined with fruit, those biscuits became shortcakes, so named because the butter or lard in the recipe made the dough short, or flaky, and also because they baked quickly. *The Weekly Standard* in Raleigh, North Carolina, in 1839 described shortcake as a "hastily baked" cake that baked in a short amount of time. But *Godey's Lady's Book* of December 1835 warned about its unhealthiness: "Shortcakes, whether hot or cold, should be banished from our tables." Fortunately they weren't. By 1857 shortcake "spread with butter and a layer of fresh strawberries and sugar" was considered "a luxury," according to the *Brooklyn Eagle*. And by 1870, *American Agriculturalist* magazine had declared the strawberry shortcake "an American institution" benefiting from the new railroads that shipped the fragile local berries from farm to market. The following easy shortcake recipe is adapted from John Martin Taylor's book *The New Southern Cook*. I have made only a few adjustments. As this recipe makes a lot of shortcake, go ahead and bake them all, then wrap them in aluminum foil and reheat uncovered on day 2 with more fresh berries and cream.

1. An hour before you will serve this dessert, hull the berries and slice all but 8, and save those for garnish, if desired. Toss the halved berries with ¹⁄₃ cup sugar (or more to taste) and set aside at room temperature.

2. Place a rack in the center of the oven, and preheat the oven to 425°F.

continued

3. Place the flour, $\frac{1}{3}$ cup sugar, the baking powder, and salt in a large mixing bowl and stir until well combined. Cut the $\frac{3}{4}$ cup butter into tablespoons and distribute over the top of the dry ingredients. With 2 sharp paring knives or a pastry blender, cut the butter into the dry ingredients until the mixture looks like uniformly sized peas. Crack the egg into a measuring cup with the cream and stir with a fork to break up the yolk. Pour this into the dough mixture and stir together with a wooden spoon or rubber spatula until the liquid is just combined.

4. Scatter flour on a work surface and turn the dough out. With floured hands, pat it to a generous 1" thickness. Flour 2" to 3" round cutters and cut the dough into 8 to 12 rounds. Place these on a baking sheet, and place the pan in the oven.

5. Bake the shortcakes until they are golden brown around the edges, 12 to 15 minutes. Remove the pan from the oven and let the shortcakes cool a few minutes, then split open the shortcakes with a fork and butter lightly with the 2 tablespoons butter, if desired.

6. To serve, place the bottom half of a shortcake in a serving bowl. Spoon sweetened berries and juice on top, then place the top half over the berries, and spoon more berries and juice on top. Spoon whipped cream over the berries and garnish with 1 fresh strawberry, if desired. Repeat with the remaining shortcakes. Drizzle any remaining juice in the bowl over the shortcakes before serving.

THE ICEBOX

BEFORE ELECTRICITY and refrigeration as we know it, cooks tried anything they could to keep food from spoiling in the summertime. They placed bottles of milk in a cold running stream, and they created their own icehouses. With long saws, farmers would harvest ice from frozen ponds and lakes and then pile it into icehouses. The first domestic iceboxes were just that—boxes. One wooden box was placed inside another wooden box, and in between went some kind of insulation—charcoal, ashes, etc. Ice would last about a day in these boxes. By 1830 ice was being harvested from larger ponds—the Great Lakes and the Erie Canal. It was shipped south and on to the West Indies. The biggest customer was New Orleans and its growing restaurant culture. On the West Coast, to supply the newly rich miners with chilled beverages and cold pats of butter, Alaskan glaciers were leased and chunks of ice were shipped to San Francisco iceboxes. A home icebox would become much needed, or as *Godey's Lady's Book* said in 1850, "a necessity of life." But consumers had to wait 60 years to get a home refrigerator in 1911 and 20 more years to get one that made ice. Commercial refrigerator production ramped up after World War II.

MALINDA RUSSELL'S WASHINGTON CAKE

MAKES: 12 TO 16 SERVINGS

PREP: 20 TO 25 MINUTES

BAKE: 1 HOUR 15 TO 20 MINUTES

Butter and flour for prepping the pan

1 cup (2 sticks) unsalted butter, at room temperature

3 cups granulated sugar

Pinch of salt, if desired

6 large eggs

1 teaspoon baking soda

1 cup sour milk or buttermilk (see Cake Note on page 66)

3 cups unbleached flour

1 teaspoon cream of tartar

1 small lemon (to yield 1 tablespoon lemon juice and 1 teaspoon grated lemon zest)

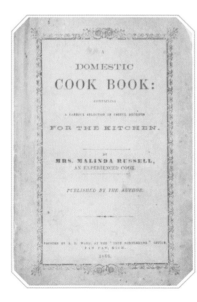

When antique cookbook collector and historian Jan Longone received a phone call from a West Coast rare book dealer asking if Longone knew anything about a pamphlet called *A Domestic Cook Book,* the answer was no. And yes. Longone didn't know the work, but she *did* know she wanted to purchase what could possibly be an unknown piece of American culinary history from the collection of the late Helen Evans Brown. *A Domestic Cook Book* is a 39-page, bittersweet first-person story, with recipes, of a free woman of color named Malinda Russell, published in 1866. It is the first cookbook authored by an African American woman, according to Longone, curator of American culinary history at the William L. Clements Library at the University of Michigan. "Mrs. Russell" was born and raised in east Tennessee, taught to cook by a Virginia slave named Fanny Steward, and ran both a boardinghouse and pastry shop during her life. In contrast to the "soul food" style of cooking most associated with African American cooks, she developed a distinctive cosmopolitan Southern/European style exhibited in her book. She flavors food with brandy, rosewater, spices, and almonds. This is one of Mrs. Russell's pound cakes, a cake very English in style that might once have been called a Queen's Cake, but that after the Revolutionary War was renamed after General George Washington by a patriotic America.

1. Place a rack in the center of the oven, and preheat the oven to 325°F. Lightly grease and flour a 10″ tube pan, and shake out the excess flour. Set the pan aside.

2. Place the butter in a large mixing bowl, and beat with an electric mixer on low speed until creamy, 1 minute. While the mixer is running, gradually add the sugar, and beat until light and creamy, 2 minutes. Scrape the sides of the bowl with a rubber spatula. Add the pinch of salt, if desired, and add the eggs, one at a time, beating on low speed until each egg is incorporated, about 15 seconds each. Turn off the mixer.

3. Stir the baking soda into the cup of sour milk. Place the flour in a large mixing bowl, and stir in the cream of tartar. Alternately add the flour

continued

and milk to the egg mixture, beginning and ending with the flour and mixing on low speed until smooth. Fold the lemon juice and zest into the batter. Turn the batter into the prepared pan, and place the pan in the oven.

4. Bake the cake until the top is golden brown and a toothpick inserted in the center comes out clean, 1 hour 15 to 20 minutes. Remove the pan from the oven, and place the pan on a wire rack to cool for 20 minutes. Run a knife around the edges of the pan, give the pan a gentle shake, then invert the cake once and then again onto the rack to cool completely, 1 hour. Slice and serve.

CAKE NOTE: Sour milk is made by adding 1 teaspoon vinegar or lemon juice to 1 cup of milk. Let it rest for about 30 minutes, or until it looks a little curdled. Or you can use buttermilk.

A NOTE TO THE MODERN COOK: *Many old cookbooks contain recipe ingredients but no method. Mrs. Russell provided a little method, but she also left much to the imagination. Would the cream of tartar be stirred into the flour or were the eggs separated and the cream of tartar added to the whites and beaten, then folded into the cake before baking? Should the baking soda be stirred into the sour milk? After studying other recipes in Mrs. Russell's book where she instructs whites to be beaten to a foam, I decided she intended whole eggs to be added to this batter. The recipe produces a tall and light pound cake, best eaten the day it is baked.*

Popularity of Washington Cakes

Mark Zanger was researching his book *The American History Cookbook* and found that of all the cakes named for elected officials, one-third were named for George Washington. Most of these recipes were a pound cake or like the Queen's Cake, which he guesses was "part of the renaming process that started right after the Revolution in which roads called 'King's Highway' were often renamed 'Washington Street.'" Washington Cakes are similar in that they are all pound cakes at heart. Most contain lemon and currants. Some contained saleratus, the forerunner to baking soda, and others were made with yeast. They were often flavored with nutmeg and brandy. They were a cake that would continue to be baked throughout the 19th century and served with great festivity on Washington's birthday in February. In the 1895 *Atlanta Exposition Cookbook*, the Washington Cake was indeed festive and complicated, containing raisins as well as currants, citron, cinnamon, nutmeg, wine, brandy, and even a caramel filling.

COMPOSITION CAKE

BY THE 1850S, America's cooks were moving away from the heavier, expensive cakes toward cakes of thrifty and simple ingredients. These cakes—composition cakes—contained less butter and fewer eggs, a shorter beating time, and the help of chemical leavening. They were the cakes that brought cake baking to the growing middle class.

THE FAMILY TREE OF AMERICAN CAKE: MEET THE MOTHER CAKES

MANY OF OUR modern cakes can be traced to cakes baked by our ancestors.

POUND CAKE. Originally leavened only by eggs, it later became the "combination cakes" that contained some baking powder. Today pound cakes are still baked and may contain sour cream or cream cheese, and are often flavored with chocolate. Recipes may be divided in half for one-loaf half-pound cakes for smaller families.

FRUITCAKE. An old cake originating in 17th-century England, the first fruitcake was leavened with yeast. Dried fruit and alcohol such as rum not only flavored but preserved the cake. Fruitcakes were good keepers, lasting a month or more. But somewhere along the way, commercial fruitcakes and their shortcuts, absence of butter, and cheap candied fruit robbed us of the flavor of real heirloom fruitcake. But it is making a comeback during the holidays in homes. Packed with apricots, peaches, prunes, cherries, and other interesting dried fruit, as well as a generous dousing of bourbon or rum, the fruitcake of today has authentic flavor.

SPICE CAKE. The gingerbread, or the cake that pairs an acid (molasses) with an alkali (baking soda) to produce a light cake with big flavor—this cake opened the door to man-made chemically leavened cakes, such as the baking powder layer cakes still baked today.

SPONGE CAKE. With ties to England and France, the sponge cake is a light cake, based on eggs. The eggs are separated, the yolks are beaten with sugar, and the whites are beaten stiff and folded into the batter. For a French style of genoise, butter is added, or hot water or milk may be added for more texture. The chiffon was an offshoot of the sponge cake and is the cake that changed the way America baked. It uses vegetable oil for moistness and beaten egg whites for volume and lightness. The chiffon is the best of both worlds—light and moist. And that's fitting for a country that loves to have it all.

ANGEL FOOD CAKE. An old American classic cake with roots in the 1830s, angel food is a sponge cake made without egg yolks, only a lot of beaten egg whites. The angel food cake was loved by cooks who used the egg yolks for mayonnaise or noodle making. And through the years it has had many variations, from chocolate, to crushed pineapple, to orange marbled.

1870 to 1899

A Scientific Approach:
Baking Powder & Fannie Farmer

———— ᕯᕯ ————

THE OLD-GUARD AMERICAN CAKES—fruitcakes, pound cakes, and yeast cakes laden with expensive ingredients—were special-occasion cakes by the end of the 19th century. Newer, lighter, faster, and whiter cakes like the jelly roll and the 1-2-3-4 Cake emerged, products of changing tastes and the convenience of baking powder. These cakes needed fewer eggs and less butter, which made them especially popular in winter months when eggs were scarce. And they were baked by a new national audience, thanks to railroads.

On May 10, 1869, the Union Pacific and the Central Pacific railroad companies joined their tracks to link the East and West Coasts of America. Called the Transcontinental Railroad, it was 3,000 miles long and allowed faster travel from New York to California. Accompanying those tracks, the telegraph pole was a natural pairing along that right-of-way. Throughout the 1800s, communication facilitated by the railroads and telegraph transformed cooking. People were traveling and exposed to new places, foods, and thoughts. Recipes with catchy names would spread overnight, such as the three-layer Minnehaha Cake—from the Native American princess in Henry Wadsworth Longfellow's poem "Song of Hiawatha."

World's fairs in Philadelphia and Chicago reinforced these new ideas. Here many people had their first taste of a banana as well as chocolate. The manufacturing of chocolate for baking was a growing field, and entrepreneur Milton Hershey came to the World's Columbian Exposition in Chicago to learn of new equipment so he could make chocolate caramels. Although chocolate had been produced since Colonial times around Boston, it took off in the second half of the 19th century with the growth of Baker Chocolate Co. in Massachusetts, Hershey in Pennsylvania, and Ghirardelli in San Francisco. America got its first taste of true chocolate cake in 1886.

Cake ingredients, once grown and purchased locally, were now easily shipped across the country. Railcars filled with ice shipped perishable products in the summer months. New towns and cities developed along the railways. Hotels and restaurants emerged to feed the travelers. And the recipes in magazines and cookbooks reached every kitchen in America, telling of the newest trend, the newest pan. An 1897 Sears, Roebuck and Co. catalog first mentioned a candy called the "brownie," and the jelly roll pans and tube pans for sale popularized cakes such as the jelly roll (page 92) as well as the angel food cake (page 76) and Sunshine Cake (page 79).

Average people could now order a pan and bake a cake. It was a time of great progress and entrepreneurial energy. Cooking innovations such as cake pans, baking powder, and new cookstoves, according to historian William Woys Weaver, were until their time "not in the grasp of average people."

Regional recipes that until then might have been undiscovered outside the local area now enjoyed the national spotlight—the Pennsylvania Dutch Shoofly Pie (page 73), Scripture Cake (page 74), and Chocolate Sauerkraut Cake (page 84), for example. And Mary Lincoln's White Almond Cake (page 70) from Lexington, Kentucky, would remain popular after President Abraham Lincoln's assassination and was served at military banquets in his honor.

At the close of the 19th century, American cooking was entering the age of science. The Boston Cooking School opened its doors in 1879, led by Mary Johnson Lincoln and then her star pupil, Fannie Farmer. They changed the way recipes were written, using standard-ized, level measurements, and they listed ingredients in their order of use in the recipe. They preached caution and precision, and they tested chocolate recipes for the ingredient's supposed link to good health. According to writer and historian Laura Shapiro, American cooking moved from the home kitchen to the laboratory where "creativity was discouraged." But theirs was a different time. A new century was dawning. The lightbulb was invented in the 1870s and replaced gas lamps. "Electricity is evidently to be the hope and dependence of the coming housekeeper," reported the *New York Times* on April 7, 1895, calling electricity "a veritable fairy godmother." It was going to get a lot easier to bake a cake.

MARY LINCOLN'S WHITE ALMOND CAKE

MAKES: 12 TO 16 SERVINGS

PREP: 25 TO 30 MINUTES

BAKE: 57 TO 62 MINUTES

Butter and flour for prepping the pan

2 cups granulated sugar

1 cup (2 sticks) unsalted butter, at room temperature

3 cups all-purpose flour

1 tablespoon baking powder

1 cup whole milk, at room temperature

1 cup (4 ounces) blanched almond slivers, very finely chopped

1½ teaspoons vanilla extract

6 large egg whites, at room temperature

½ teaspoon salt

FROSTING NOTE: To serve the cake as Mary Lincoln might have served it, make the Seven-Minute Frosting (page 317). Frost the top and sides of the cake. Garnish with chopped dried sugared pineapple or toasted slivered almonds.

Mary Todd Lincoln was raised in a wealthy Lexington, Kentucky, family and partial to the finer things in life like this white almond cake. The Todd family requested the recipe from the Lexington caterer who first made it, and it is said that Mary baked the cake for Abraham Lincoln when they courted, after they were married, and when she was First Lady. The recipe is a part of the culinary history of Kentucky and has been printed in *Godey's Lady's Book,* newspapers, and cookbooks. An avid baker, Mary was said to have purchased 13 pounds of sugar for baking in 1 week of 1849. Unlike Mary, Abe Lincoln was from log-cabin Kentucky frontier roots. A successful and skilled courtroom attorney, Lincoln helped bring an end to slavery and the Civil War. His assassination on April 14, 1865, as he was barely in his second term, shocked the country. This almond cake became a symbol of Lincoln afterward and was found on inaugural and military banquet menus in the 1870s. This recipe is adapted from the book *A Culinary History of Kentucky.*

1. Place a rack in the center of the oven, and preheat the oven to 350°F. Lightly grease and flour a 10″ tube pan with butter and flour. Shake out the excess flour, and set the pan aside.

2. Place the sugar and butter in a large bowl, and beat with an electric mixer on medium until light and fluffy, 3 minutes. Set the bowl aside.

3. Sift the flour and baking powder into a large bowl, and sift 2 more times. Add the flour mixture to the creamed butter and sugar in 3 additions, alternating with the milk. Beat on medium speed until the mixture is just blended. Scrape down the sides of the bowl with a rubber spatula, and fold in the almonds and vanilla. Set the bowl aside.

4. In a large mixing bowl, beat the egg whites and salt with clean beaters on high speed until stiff peaks form, 4 to 5 minutes. Fold about a quarter of the beaten whites into the batter, just until combined. Fold the remaining whites into the batter, just until combined. Pour the batter evenly into the prepared pan, and place the pan in the oven.

5. Bake the cake until it is golden brown and a toothpick inserted in the center comes out clean, 57 to 62 minutes. Remove the pan from the oven and place on a wire rack to cool for 15 minutes. Run a knife around the edges, give the pan a gentle shake, and invert the cake onto the rack to cool, right side up, 1 hour. Slice and serve.

SHOOFLY PIE

MAKES: 8 TO 12 SERVINGS

PREP: 35 TO 40 MINUTES

BAKE: 40 TO 45 MINUTES

1 (9") unbaked piecrust

1½ cups all-purpose flour

½ cup granulated sugar

½ cup light brown sugar, lightly packed

2 teaspoons ground cinnamon

1 teaspoon ground nutmeg

1 teaspoon baking powder

¼ teaspoon salt

3 tablespoons unsalted butter, cold

½ cup warm strong brewed coffee

½ cup molasses

½ teaspoon baking soda

Baking with the Seasons

The absence of eggs and the presence of molasses tell historians this was a wintertime dessert. Hens did not lay eggs in the cooler weather. And molasses would ferment in the summer heat without refrigeration. So this pie was perfect for cold-weather baking, needing no eggs and using molasses.

Shoofly Obsession

America was obsessed with the ditty from the 1830s, "Shoo, fly, don't bodder me . . ." It may well have been how the boxing mule got his name, which named the molasses, which named this dessert.

Placing food in pie pastry is a centuries-old tradition that allows you to eat with your hands and take food with you. The Pennsylvania Dutch placed molasses crumb cake in a piecrust and called it Shoofly Pie in the 1880s. With the spongy texture of cake and the crust of pie, this dessert is the most beloved of the Southeastern Pennsylvania region where it was born. According to historian William Woys Weaver, Shoofly Pie began as Centennial Cake in 1876, baked in a pan without a crust. The crust was later added so people could eat the cake with their hands over their morning coffee. Weaver says the name "Shoofly" comes from Shoofly the Boxing Mule, a popular circus animal at the time, and the Shoofly name was branded onto foods like Shoofly molasses, a key ingredient in this dessert. The combination of molasses, coffee, and spices in the batter bakes into an almost chocolate-like taste, and this pie/cake is incredibly delicious warm with coffee or tea. This recipe is adapted slightly from Weaver's book *As American as Shoofly Pie: The Foodlore and Fakelore of Pennsylvania Dutch Cuisine.*

1. Place a rack in the center of the oven, and preheat the oven to 350°F. Place the piecrust in a 10" metal pie pan. Crimp the edges, and place the pan in the refrigerator to stay chilled.

2. Place the flour, sugars, cinnamon, nutmeg, baking powder, and salt in the bowl of a food processor fitted with a steel blade. Or place in a large mixing bowl. Pulse or stir until well combined. Cut the butter into 12 pieces and distribute around the bowl. Pulse or cut in with 2 sharp knives or a pastry blender until the mixture is crumbly. Reserve ¼ cup of the crumbs and set aside.

3. In a large mixing bowl, stir together the coffee and molasses until combined. Stir in the baking soda. Add the dry ingredients and stir until smooth. Or, if using a food processor, pour the molasses mixture into the food processor with the dry ingredients and pulse until smooth. Remove the pie pan from the refrigerator and pour in the batter. Scatter the reserved crumbs over the top. Place the pan in the oven.

4. Bake until the center is set when lightly pressed with a finger, 40 to 45 minutes. Remove the pan from the oven, and let it rest for 15 minutes. Slice and serve warm.

SCRIPTURE CAKE

MAKES: 12 TO 16 SERVINGS

PREP: 30 TO 35 MINUTES

BAKE: 52 TO 57 MINUTES

Butter and flour to prep the pans

1 cup (2 sticks) unsalted butter, at room temperature (Judges 5:25)

2 cups granulated sugar (Jeremiah 6:20)

4 large eggs, at room temperature (Isaiah 10:14)

1 tablespoon honey (Exodus 16:31)

2½ cups all-purpose flour, divided use (1 Kings 4:22)

2 teaspoons baking powder

2 teaspoons ground cinnamon (1 Kings 10:2)

1 teaspoon ground nutmeg (1 Kings 10:2)

½ teaspoon ground cloves (1 Kings 10:2)

½ teaspoon ground allspice (1 Kings 10:2)

½ teaspoon salt (Leviticus 2:13)

2 cups chopped dried figs, about 10 ounces (1 Samuel 30:12)

1 cup chopped raisins (1 Samuel 30:12)

1 cup water (Genesis 24:20)

1 cup finely chopped almonds (Numbers 17:8)

The popular cake baked for church suppers in the 1880s and '90s was a spiced fruitcake called Scripture Cake, Scriptural Cake, or Bible Cake. Written in Sunday School fashion to teach Bible verses and baking skills, the cake was baked coast to coast. Ingredients were written like a puzzle, so you had to look up the Bible verse to know what went in the cake. Often women of the church baked Scripture Cakes and sold raffle tickets for slices at fund-raising church festivals like the Catholic Church Fair in Leavenworth, Kansas, in 1882. There doesn't seem to be one single denomination associated with these cakes, as they were baked by Presbyterians, Methodists, German Lutherans, and many more. This recipe is adapted from one printed in the *Atlanta Constitution* in 1897. It has no biblical reference for the chemical leavening baking powder, an invention of the mid-1800s, which leads us to believe the recipe is older. Some historians think the recipe might have originated in England in the late 1700s.

1. Place a rack in the center of the oven, and preheat the oven to 325°F. Grease and flour two 9″ loaf pans, shake out the excess flour, and set the pans aside.

2. Place the butter and sugar in a large mixing bowl, and beat with an electric mixer on medium-low speed until fluffy, 2 to 3 minutes. Add the eggs, one at a time, beating until well blended. Scrape down the sides of the bowl with a rubber spatula. Blend in the honey, and set aside.

3. Sift 2¼ cups of flour, the baking powder, cinnamon, nutmeg, cloves, allspice, and salt into a medium-size bowl, and set aside. Dredge the figs and raisins in the remaining ¼ cup flour. Set aside.

4. Stir the flour mixture into the butter mixture alternately with the water, beginning and ending with the flour. Fold in the figs, raisins, and almonds. Divide the batter between the prepared pans, and place the pans in the oven.

5. Bake the cakes until they are golden brown and a toothpick inserted in the center comes out clean, 52 to 57 minutes. Remove the loaves to a wire rack to cool for 10 minutes. Run a knife around the edges of the pans, shake the loaves gently, and invert them onto the rack to cool, right side up, 1 hour. Slice and serve.

ANGEL FOOD CAKE

MAKES: 12 TO 16 SERVINGS

PREP: 25 TO 30 MINUTES

BAKE: 30 TO 35 MINUTES

1 cup all-purpose flour

1 teaspoon cream of tartar

11 large egg whites (1½ cups), at room temperature

1½ cups granulated sugar

2 teaspoons vanilla extract

⅛ teaspoon salt

Any Way You Slice It . . .

After you've worked so hard incorporating air into the egg whites, carefully sifted the flour and folded it into the batter without disturbing the egg whites, and let the cake cool upside down so it doesn't deflate, you don't want to slice the cake with the wrong knife. Use a serrated knife with gentle back and forth sawing motions, or use a special angel food cake comb with tines that burrow into the cake and separate slices from the cake. For crowds and thin slicing, freeze the cake first, and while frozen, slice it using a long serrated knife.

So light in texture you must let it cool upside down in the pan inverted, the delicate and beloved angel food is a timeless American cake. It is based on stiffly beaten egg whites that trap air and become a natural leavening that causes the cake to rise. The late Evan Jones, in his book *American Food,* said the first angel food cakes were made by frugal, hardworking Pennsylvania Dutch cooks who saved egg whites on noodle-making days. These thrifty cooks could not fathom cracking a dozen eggs and discarding the whites. Another theory on where the cake originated is that Linus W. Dexter,

> *Through the years, methods for making angel food cake varied in the number of egg whites, when to add the sugar, whether to use cream of tartar or lemon juice, and how long to bake the cake. All recipes agree that angel food belongs in an ungreased pan so that the cake clings to the side as it bakes high.*
>
> *Early Prohibitionists approved of the angel food cake because it did not contain yeast, which makes alcohol when heated. One of its biggest fans was Lucy Webb Hayes, wife of US president Rutherford B. Hayes. "Lemonade Lucy," as she was called because she did not drink alcohol, served angel food cake and lemonade at the White House while her husband was in office from 1877 to 1881.*

a baking entrepreneur with bakeries in New York, Philadelphia, Baltimore, and Boston, created it. His 1899 obituary lauds the creator of the "angel cake." Before cakes were named "angel food," they were baked with just egg whites but went by different names—Silver Cakes, Lady Cakes, and White Sponge Cakes, the latter appearing in 1839 in *The Kentucky Housewife.* The cakes were prized for their white color, high volume, and delicate texture. But beating the egg whites to stiff peaks was no easy task. Cooks often used a fork, whisk, or even a tree branch, sometimes hickory and other times peach, which the Shakers thought imparted a peach flavor to the cake. By the time Malinda Russell shared a recipe for "Old Maids Cakes" leavened with beaten egg whites in her 1866 cookbook, *A Domestic Cook Book,* the rotary hand eggbeater—or Dover beater—had been invented. And in 1884 the "Angel Cake" is included in the *Boston Cooking School Cook Book* by Mrs. D. A. Lincoln. This recipe comes from the *Atlanta Exposition*

continued

Cookbook, published in 1895 and issued at the 1895 Atlanta Cotton States and International Exposition. From the recipe files of Mrs. Thomas Morgan of Atlanta, this cake is simple in its preparation and has been only slightly adapted for the modern kitchen.

1. Place a rack in the center of the oven, and preheat the oven to 350°F. Set aside an ungreased 10″ tube or angel food pan.

2. Sift the flour 4 times in a large mixing bowl. The last time, sift the cream of tartar along with the flour. Set this mixture aside.

3. Place the egg whites in a large mixing bowl, and beat with an electric mixer on high speed until they are a stiff froth, 4 to 5 minutes. Add the sugar, 2 tablespoons at a time, while beating for 4 to 5 minutes more, until stiff and glossy. Beat in the vanilla and salt. Gently fold in the flour mixture with a rubber spatula, just until combined. Turn the batter into the reserved pan. Smooth the top with the spatula, and place the pan in the oven.

4. Bake the cake until it is lightly browned and springs back when lightly pressed, 30 to 35 minutes. Remove the cake from the oven and immediately turn it upside down on a wire rack so the cake cools upside down for 1 hour.

5. When ready to serve, turn the pan right side up and run a long, sharp knife around the edges. Give the cake a gentle shake to loosen it from the pan. Invert it onto a plate or rack, then invert again so the cake is right side up. Slice and serve.

MOCK ANGEL FOOD CAKE

Bess, or Bessie, Gant was a Pittsburgh, Pennsylvania, newspaper columnist and caterer to celebrities who made her culinary mark in the 1920s and '30s. Her book, *Bess Gant's Cook Book*, held 400 of her best recipes. Gant baked a faster, more economical version of an angel food cake called a Mock Angel Food Cake. Mock angel cakes appeared as early as 1907 and were made with just three eggs. Gant's cake contained no butter and just a little water, so it was a cost cutter at a time when economy was key.

Angel Food Cake and the Amish

Phyllis Pellman Good, author of *The Best of Amish Cooking*, said angel food cakes were commonplace "on a farm where eggs are plentiful." On Amish farms, angel food purists still insist the egg whites be beaten by hand. If they are beaten too quickly with an electric mixer, Good says, the foam goes away, and the cake doesn't rise as high as it should. As the angel food requires a special tube pan, which allows the cake to bake evenly and quickly so as not to let those egg whites deflate, the pan predated the cake. If you search old newspaper archives, you will find early-1800s advertisements for the "tubed" pan in Southeastern Pennsylvania, home of the Pennsylvania Dutch. Historian William Woys Weaver said this cake would have to have been baked in the summertime when eggs were available, as hens back then didn't lay eggs in the winter.

MILWAUKEE SUNSHINE CAKE

MAKES: 8 TO 10 SERVINGS

PREP: 80 TO 90 MINUTES

BAKE: 32 TO 38 MINUTES

CUSTARD FILLING

4 large egg yolks (save 3 whites for the icing)

¾ cup sifted confectioners' sugar

¾ cup whole milk

1 teaspoon vanilla extract

1 cup (2 sticks) unsalted butter, at room temperature

Pinch of salt

CAKE

9 large eggs, separated, at room temperature

¼ cup water

1 cup granulated sugar, divided use

1 cup cake flour, sifted 3 times

1 teaspoon vanilla extract

¼ teaspoon cream of tartar

¼ teaspoon salt

BOILED WHITE ICING

1⅓ cups granulated sugar

½ cup water

3 large egg whites

Pinch of salt

1 teaspoon vanilla extract

Grated zest of 1 orange for garnish

Sunshine Cakes were baked across America in the late 1800s, but the most famous Sunshine Cake of all was baked a little later, in 1901, in Wisconsin. The Cook sisters opened a tearoom called the Cook Tea Shop in downtown Milwaukee, and their specialty was a lemon sponge cake with custard filling, a seven-minute frosting, and grated orange zest on top. When the luxury retailer George Watts moved to Milwaukee and opened a store, the Cook sisters relocated their tearoom to the second floor of Watts' new building. Their recipe is still served today at The Watts Tea Shop, and the cake with a tiny orchid garnish is a favorite of all generations.

1. For the filling, combine the egg yolks, confectioners' sugar, and milk in a large mixing bowl, and blend with an electric mixer on low speed until combined, 1 minute. Pour the mixture into the top of a double boiler.

2. Bring 1″ to 2″ water in the bottom of the double boiler to a boil, then reduce the heat to medium. Place the top of the double boiler over the water. Whisk and let cook until the custard has thickened, 8 to 10 minutes. Pour into a clean large bowl, and stir in the vanilla. Set the bowl aside.

3. Place the butter and salt in a medium-size mixing bowl, and blend with the mixer on low speed until well creamed, 1 minute. Slowly pour the cooled custard mixture into the butter, and blend on low speed until combined and smooth. Set aside.

4. For the cake, place the egg yolks, water, and ½ cup of the sugar in a large mixing bowl, and beat with the electric mixer on medium speed until light, about 2 minutes. Add the flour gradually, in 4 additions, beating for about 20 seconds on medium speed for each addition. Blend in the vanilla and set aside.

5. Place a rack in the center of the oven, and preheat the oven to 350°F. Set aside an ungreased 10″ tube pan.

6. Place the egg whites, cream of tartar, and salt in a large mixing bowl, and beat with clean beaters on high speed until soft peaks form, 2 to 3 minutes. Gradually add the remaining ½ cup sugar and beat until stiff peaks form, 2 minutes more. Fold the egg whites into the batter until just combined. Pour the batter into the prepared pan, and place the pan in the oven.

continued

7. Bake the cake until it is lightly browned and springs back when lightly pressed, 32 to 38 minutes. Remove the pan from the oven, and place it on a wire rack to cool upside down in the pan.

8. Meanwhile, make the icing. Place the sugar and water in a medium-size saucepan, and bring to a boil, stirring with a wooden spoon. Cook on medium-low heat until the sugar melts and the syrup spins a thread when you drop it from the spoon. It needs to reach 220°F on a candy thermometer, which takes 6 to 8 minutes.

9. While the sugar is cooking, beat the egg whites and salt in an electric mixer on high speed until soft peaks form, 2 to 3 minutes. Very slowly drizzle the hot sugar syrup into the beaten egg whites at medium speed. Beat constantly until the frosting stands in stiff peaks and is of spreading consistency. Add the vanilla and beat well for 20 seconds more.

10. To assemble, run a knife around the edges of the cake pan, give the pan a good shake, and invert the cake onto the rack. Slice the cake horizontally into thirds. Carefully remove the top 2 layers and set them aside. Place the bottom layer on a cake plate. Spread half of the filling over this layer, just to the edges. Place the middle layer on top. Spread the remaining filling over it, just to the edges. Place the top cake layer over the filling. Generously frost the sides and top of the cake, including down into the hole in the center. Garnish the top with the orange zest. Slice and serve.

Moonshine Cake

No sooner had America been introduced to the Sunshine Cake than a Moonshine Cake was baked in Missouri, calling for a hint of almond extract in the batter and no orange zest on top.

THE DOVER BEATER

DON'T THINK for a minute that cakes like the angel food and the Sunshine could take off and win national appeal without the invention of the eggbeater. Sure, good cooks knew how to whip egg whites on a large platter to stiff-peak perfection, but not everyone had the patience or the biceps to do so. Whipping 12 to 18 egg whites by hand was a hefty task, made a little lighter work once the manual eggbeater was born.

Called the Dover eggbeater, a hand-cranked eggbeater produced by Dover Stamping Company, this gadget beat egg whites and helped bake a generation of angel food cakes. First patented in the late 1850s, the beater would be modernized through the turn of the 20th century and lead to the electric hand mixers popular today.

American Chocolate Cake Is Born

WHEN CHOCOLATE STARTED APPEARING in cake batter before the close of the 19th century, it was a subtle addition with little fanfare. Chocolate was an unknown and expensive baking ingredient. Eliza Leslie had grated chocolate into a spice cake and shared that recipe in her 1847 cookbook. But Sarah Rorer, a dietitian, *Ladies' Home Journal* columnist, and director of the Philadelphia Cooking School, was the first to take the giant leap and stir melted chocolate into cake batter. The daughter of a chemist, Rorer had been experimenting and found chocolate melted best when combined with boiling water. Her chocolate cake recipe would be the first published, in 1886, in *Mrs. Rorer's Philadelphia Cook Book.* Cooking school teachers in Boston as well as Philadelphia were fascinated with chocolate. They taught precise measurements and preached kitchen prudence. And they also believed chocolate was good for you, that it "nourishes the body while it also stimulates the brain," according to Maria Parloa of Boston. They tested recipes for chocolate companies and lectured on chocolate's positive health benefits. Chocolate was about to become an important baking ingredient, and chocolate cake would become an American classic.

The most famous chocolate cake baked in this period was the devil's food cake. Early devil's food cakes didn't follow a particular recipe. They were made with either sour milk and baking soda or sweet (regular) milk and baking powder, and either white sugar or brown. They often called for sour cream. They might contain spices, and cooks often added leftover mashed potatoes. They were frosted with a white boiled icing or possibly fudge frosting. But they had one thing in common—more chocolate than ever before was used in the cake. Their appearance was deep and dark, contrasted to the popular pure white angel food cake.

Chocolate cakes went by different names— Black Joe Cake, Black John, Morganza, Oxblood, Hoosier, and eventually a Red Devil, which preceded today's red velvet cake. Many historians believe the cake was named "devil's" because of the reddish hue caused by the combination of cocoa and baking soda.

Turn-of-the-20th-century cookbooks offered many devil's food recipes, and none are alike. In the 1904 *Blue Grass Cook Book,* by Minnie C. Fox, a Miss Bashford of Paris, Kentucky, shares a devil's food recipe with a staggering 4 ounces chocolate in the batter, which was a lot for the time. It was crowned with a soft white icing filled with nuts and figs.

Even before 1900, A&P supermarket advertisements offered a 1-pound "wavy-iced" devil's food cake for 28 cents. Some newspaper articles weren't so favorable, calling it the cake with the "horribly suggestive name." But devil's food cake, the chocolate cake with the catchy name, was adored from the 1880s onward.

CHOCOLATE SAUERKRAUT CAKE

MAKES: 12 TO 16 SERVINGS

PREP: 45 TO 50 MINUTES

BAKE: 25 TO 30 MINUTES

Butter and flour for prepping the pans

2 cups sauerkraut (see Cake Note)

½ cup (1 stick) unsalted butter, at room temperature

1½ cups granulated sugar

3 large eggs, at room temperature

1 teaspoon vanilla extract

2 cups sifted all-purpose flour

½ cup unsweetened cocoa powder

1½ teaspoons baking soda

¼ teaspoon cream of tartar

¼ teaspoon salt

1 cup water

Chocolate Sour Cream Frosting (page 310)

CAKE NOTE: You can use any sauerkraut in this recipe. We used a 14.5-ounce can. Make sure it is well drained, rinsed, and chopped before adding to the batter.

To the Pennsylvania Dutch settlers, sauerkraut, or chopped and fermented cabbage, was a ready ingredient. And some clever cook must have figured out that no one would know sauerkraut was in a chocolate cake, plus it would add moisture to the cake, much like mashed potatoes do. Lovers of chocolate, the Pennsylvania Dutch excelled at chocolate cake baking, and recipes such as this fill their cookbooks and home recipe boxes. This recipe is adapted from one in *The Thirteen Colonies Cookbook,* by Mary Donovan, Amy Hatrak, Frances Mills, and Elizabeth Shull. It comes from the Keim Homestead historic property of West Lobachsville, Pennsylvania, where in the late 1700s Magdalena Hoch Keim fermented sauerkraut, made wine, preserved foods for the long winter ahead, and relied on her traditional recipes of Germany. But you don't have to live in Pennsylvania Dutch country to know about it. Chef Christine Ilarraza of Fort Worth, Texas, was raised in Kansas, and her German neighbors frequently made this cake. Charlie Klebenow of Montana has memories of his German grandmother baking this cake.

1. Place a rack in the center of the oven, and preheat the oven to 350°F. Lightly grease and flour two 9″ round cake pans. Set the pans aside.

2. Drain the liquid from the sauerkraut. Place it in a colander or sieve and rinse it very well under running cold water. With your hands or a wooden spoon, push excess liquid out of the sauerkraut and let it rest in the sieve or colander set over the sink.

3. Place the butter and sugar in a large mixing bowl, and blend with an electric mixer on medium speed until creamy, 2 minutes. Add the eggs, one at a time, beating well after each addition. Scrape down the bowl with a rubber spatula and fold in the vanilla.

4. Sift together the flour, cocoa, soda, cream of tartar, and salt in a medium-size bowl. Add to the creamed mixture alternately with the water, beginning and ending with the flour, beating on low speed with the mixer.

5. Remove the sauerkraut from the colander and either chop it with a knife on a cutting board or pulse 20 times in the food processor fitted with a steel blade. You want to break up the pieces but not puree them. Fold

the sauerkraut into the batter until just combined. Divide the batter between the prepared pans and smooth the tops with the spatula. Place the pans in the oven.

6. Bake the cake until it just pulls away from the edges and the top springs back when lightly pressed in the center, 25 to 30 minutes. Remove the pans from the oven and place on wire racks to cool for 10 minutes. Run a sharp knife around the edges of the pans, give them a gentle shake, and invert them once and then again so they cool right side up on the rack. Cool for 30 minutes before frosting.

7. To assemble, place 1 layer on a serving plate and spread about ⅔ cup of the frosting smoothly over the top. Place the second layer on top and spread the remaining frosting on the top and sides of the cake. Store in the refrigerator for up to 5 days.

How to Make Devil's Food Cake

To make a simple Devil's Food Cake, follow the recipe for Chocolate Sauerkraut Cake, and then omit the sauerkraut. Use ½ cup light brown sugar plus 1 cup granulated sugar. Follow the recipe directions, and bake in 9-inch layers for 25 to 30 minutes as the recipe directs. Frost with your choice of the Modern Buttercream Frosting on page 309, the Chocolate Pan Frosting on page 310, or the Ganache on page 270.

MAHOGANY CAKE WITH SEVEN-MINUTE FROSTING

MAKES: 12 TO 16 SERVINGS
PREP: 20 TO 25 MINUTES
BAKE: 18 TO 20 MINUTES

Butter and flour for prepping the pans

¾ cup (1½ sticks) unsalted butter, at room temperature

½ cup granulated sugar

1½ cups light brown sugar, lightly packed

2 large eggs, at room temperature

2 large egg yolks, at room temperature (save whites for the icing)

1 teaspoon vanilla extract

1½ cups all-purpose flour

½ teaspoon baking powder

½ teaspoon baking soda

¾ cup buttermilk, at room temperature

½ cup hot water

4 ounces unsweetened chocolate, melted and cooled

Seven-Minute Frosting (page 317)

Compared with today's deep, dark cakes that scream chocolate, the first chocolate cakes were almost apologetic. These cakes contained a modest amount of chocolate—only 2 ounces. With so little chocolate, the cake was pale in color and would be best described as Mahogany Cake, that is, nearly chocolate. This Mahogany Cake, adapted from Sarah Rorer's recipe in her 1886 cookbook, is a stepping-stone to America's devil's food cake. It uses white and brown sugar and is typically frosted with Seven-Minute Frosting, handy because you used the yolks in the cake and saved the whites for the frosting. For best results, use cake flour in this recipe.

1. Place a rack in the center of the oven, and preheat the oven to 350°F. Lightly grease and flour the bottoms of three 9″ round pans. Shake out the excess flour, and set the pans aside.

2. Place the butter in a large mixing bowl, and beat with an electric mixer on low speed until creamy, 30 seconds. Gradually add the sugars, beating on medium speed until combined and creamy. Add the whole eggs and the yolks, one at a time, beating on medium until incorporated. Beat in the vanilla, and set the batter aside.

3. Sift the flour, baking powder, and soda into a medium-size bowl. Add a third of the flour mixture to the batter, blending on low speed just until incorporated. Scrape down the sides of the bowl with a rubber spatula. Add the buttermilk and blend, then add another third of the flour. Add the hot water and blend, then add the remaining flour, beating on medium speed just until combined. Fold in the melted chocolate until smooth. Divide the batter evenly between the prepared pans, and place the pans in the oven.

4. Bake the cakes until the top springs back when lightly pressed in the center, 18 to 20 minutes. Remove the pans from the oven, and place them on a wire rack to cool for 5 minutes. Run a knife around the edges of the pans, give the pans a gentle shake, then invert onto the rack and then again so they cool right side up. Let cool completely before assembling, 30 to 40 minutes.

5. Meanwhile, make the Seven-Minute Frosting.

6. To assemble the cake, place 1 layer on a cake plate or platter. Spread with a generous ½ cup of frosting and smooth to the edges. Add the second layer and repeat with the frosting. Add the top layer, and frost the top and sides of the cake. Slice and serve.

BANGOR BROWNIES

MAKES: 8 TO 12 SERVINGS

PREP: 15 MINUTES

BAKE: 18 TO 22 MINUTES

Butter and flour for prepping the pan

2 ounces unsweetened chocolate

½ cup (1 stick) unsalted butter

1 cup granulated sugar

2 large eggs

½ cup cake flour (see Cake Notes)

Pinch of salt

½ cup chopped walnuts

CAKE NOTES: The cookbook's ingredient list calls for pastry flour; I substituted cake flour. Also, you can use the microwave for melting the chocolate. If you melt on high power in a glass bowl, microwave in 15-second increments, stirring between times to melt the chocolate. It will take from 45 seconds to 1 minute.

For more than 100 years, Bangor, Maine, and brownies have been closely associated. Cookbook author Jean Anderson writes of the Bangor housewife who forgot to add the baking powder to her chocolate cake, and the brownie was born. (She must have been incredibly forgetful because she would have had to skimp on flour and omit the milk, too, if you believe this story.) And then there is the story that one of Fannie Farmer's colleagues, Maria Howard, who worked at the Walter Lowney Chocolate Company in 1907, added an extra egg and more chocolate to Farmer's recipe, and renamed it the Bangor Brownie. Walter Lowney himself was from Bangor, so maybe she was trying to please her boss. At a competing chocolate company, Maria Parloa added an egg and baking powder to Farmer's recipe and developed the Bangor Brownie for the Baker Chocolate Co. And Bangor isn't the only place in Maine associated with brownies—so is Machias, a coastal town. The *Machias Cook Book*, published in 1899, contained a recipe for Brownie's Food, which was a dense layer cake and frosting. But the following recipe, shared in *The Service Club Cook Book* of Chicago in 1904, is one of the oldest recipes for what we now know as chocolate brownies. Fannie Farmer published a brownie in her 1896 book, but the recipe contained only molasses and no chocolate. The Service Club of Chicago is a long-running philanthropic organization founded in 1890 to improve the lives of Chicago's immigrants and their children. The cookbook cost $1 then and featured recipes from the members, including this wonderful brownie recipe.

1. Place a rack in the center of the oven, and preheat the oven to 350°F. Lightly grease and flour an 8″ square baking pan and shake out the excess flour. Set the pan aside.

2. Chop the chocolate coarsely and place in a saucepan over very low heat, stirring constantly, until the chocolate melts, 1 to 2 minutes. Set the chocolate aside to cool.

3. Place the butter and sugar in a large mixing bowl, and cream with a wooden spoon until light and fluffy, 2 minutes. Add the eggs, one at a time, beating with the spoon until the mixture is smooth. Fold in the

continued

cooled chocolate until just combined. Fold in the flour and salt until just combined. Then fold in the nuts. Turn the batter into the prepared pan and smooth the top with a rubber spatula. Place the pan in the oven.

4. Bake the brownies until the top has set and is crusty but the middle is still a little soft, 18 to 22 minutes. Remove the pan from the oven, and let the brownies rest for 20 minutes, then slice and serve.

How the American Brownie Was Named

Brownies.

¼ cup butter.
¼ cup powdered sugar.
¼ cup Porto Rico molasses.

1 egg well beaten. .
⅔ cup bread flour.
1 cup pecan meat cut in pieces.

Mix ingredients in order given. Bake in small, shallow fancy cake tins, garnishing top of each cake with one-half pecan.

One of the most beloved cakes in American history is the simple brownie. Thought to be named after the little people written about in Palmer Cox's cartoons and poems of the 1880s, the brownie has evolved into a simple, dense chocolate butter cake, often containing nuts and cut into squares. First mentioned as a candy for sale in a Sears, Roebuck and Co. catalog in 1897, brownies contained no chocolate when Fannie Farmer included them in her landmark 1896 book. They were baked in little molds made "brown" by the generous amount of molasses and chopped nuts. In the 1905 revision, Fannie Farmer would put chocolate in her recipe, but by then chocolatey brownies were popping up in cookbooks and chocolate company recipe brochures. Two 1904 cookbooks—*The Service Club Cook Book* of Chicago and *Home Cookery* of Laconia, New Hampshire—shared nearly the same recipe for Bangor Brownies, calling for 2 ounces unsweetened chocolate and what would become the formula for brownie perfection—twice as much sugar as flour. It's important to note that in 1893, at the World's Columbian Exposition in Chicago, the Palmer House Hotel chefs created a chocolate cake that could be cut into squares for ladies' box lunches. Bertha Palmer, the wealthy wife of hotel owner Potter Palmer, was president of the ladies' board for the exposition and requested this ladies' dessert. The hotel's intensely chocolate and buttery cakelike confection resembled a brownie and was covered in apricot jam, but the recipe was never printed. You can order the Palmer House Brownie if you visit the hotel today.

FANNIE FARMER, MARY LINCOLN, AND THE BOSTON COOKING SCHOOL

"WHILE THE FACT IS TO be recognized that there are some born cooks, the large majority need teaching and training," said Fannie Merritt Farmer in 1904. She was the author of six cookbooks, including the revolutionary *The Boston Cooking-School Cook Book,* published in 1896 and still in print today.

When you open a cookbook and see recipes written in cup measures, with the ingredients listed first and the method following, you can thank Fannie Farmer, who not only took a scientific approach to cooking but also encouraged American women to take cooking seriously. Farmer was a formidable food force at the turn of the 20th century, an instructor and later principal of the esteemed Boston Cooking School.

But a lesser-known woman at the Boston school laid the groundwork for Farmer's fame. Mary Johnson Lincoln, the first head of the school, wrote five cookbooks, beginning with *Mrs. Lincoln's Boston Cook Book,* in 1884. A self-taught cook with an eye for health and thrift, Lincoln said cooking schools offered cooks the chance to learn by observation and that women needed to be taught domestic science. She knew this firsthand: Her father died when she was 7 and she helped supplement the household income, and her husband was ill 4 years into their marriage and she had to join the workforce. Lincoln was the true mother of standardized measurements, although Farmer got the credit. Before Lincoln's cookbook, American recipes called for random amounts like butter "the size of an egg" and a "gill" of brandy, "teacup" of milk, "soup spoon" of cream. Lincoln listed ingredients in the order they were used in the recipe and explained cooking to women who didn't have the luxury of servants to prepare the meals. Most women at the time did their own cooking, so "these receipts are arranged as so to require the attention of but one person."

The Boston Cooking School was established by the Women's Education Association of Boston in 1879. The group was committed to domestic science and wanted to elevate the role of women in society. With culinary training, women could teach other women to cook, not only meeting the dietary needs of their families but learning a skill should they need to enter the workforce. In addition to Lincoln and Fannie Farmer, the school had celebrity cooks like Maria Parloa, who traveled the country leading cooking classes and working with food companies to develop recipes.

But it was Fannie Farmer, who followed Lincoln as school leader, who would be most famous. Farmer had been the victim of a paralytic stroke at the age of 16, was bedridden for months, and could not attend college. She learned to walk again, but with a limp, and when she was 31 she enrolled in the Boston Cooking School. An exemplary student, Farmer was asked to serve as assistant director after graduation. Two years later, she was appointed director. After her book was published, Farmer left the Boston Cooking School and opened Miss Farmer's School of Cookery in 1902. It offered a class on "sickroom cookery" for convalescents in addition to the standard home cooking classes. Without Farmer at the helm, the Boston Cooking School closed within the year.

The publishers of her book, Little Brown & Company, didn't think the book would do well. They printed a limited 3,000 copies and required Farmer to cover the cost. Fortunately for Farmer, she retained the rights to the book, which featured everything from housekeeping tips to nutritional information to the latest recipes being served in New York restaurants. The cookbook was an instant bestseller. Over the next 6 decades, the book would go through 13 editions and sell more than 4 million copies. Her book was retitled *The Fannie Farmer Cookbook* in 1965.

AMERICAN JELLY ROLL

MAKES: 8 TO 10 SERVINGS

PREP: 40 TO 45 MINUTES

BAKE: 10 TO 12 MINUTES

Parchment paper and butter for prepping the pan

¼ cup confectioners' sugar

3 large eggs, at room temperature

1 cup granulated sugar

1½ teaspoons milk

1 cup all-purpose flour

1 teaspoon baking powder

¼ teaspoon salt

1 tablespoon unsalted butter, melted

10 ounces red currant or raspberry jelly, slightly warmed

1 teaspoon confectioners' sugar for garnish

Before there were custom pans in which to bake your choice of cake, cooks were pretty resourceful. Some of our classic American cakes come out of this ingenuity. Take the jelly roll, for example. You didn't need a jelly roll pan to bake the jelly roll cake because you just poured the batter into a shallow roasting pan called a dripping pan. Mark Zanger, author of *The American History Cookbook*, says jelly rolls evolved out of jelly cakes: flat cake layers with jelly in between them. In the 1880s, cooks began making jelly cake in 1 large pan. This was a good size for serving a large family or feeding the workers on your farm. And someone got creative and transformed that flat cake into something a little more interesting, a cake roll. Dusted with confectioners' sugar and sliced, this jelly roll showcased homemade red currant or raspberry jelly inside. It's possible the cooks who baked jelly rolls were quilters, because a "jelly roll" is the quilting term for a rolled-up assortment of precut fabrics. After the Civil War, jelly roll made its appearance on hotel and banquet menus and in newspapers. By 1880 the dessert had clearly taken off, baked from Pennsylvania west to Kansas. Fannie Farmer includes a jelly roll recipe in her 1896 book, and it is baked in a dripping pan. Appealing to cooks who wanted to make something out of simple pantry ingredients, the jelly roll was thrifty and homespun, yet had a cosmopolitan flair. Here is a slight adaptation of Fannie Farmer's recipe. You can bake it in a 1″-deep shallow roasting pan or half sheet pan.

1. Place a rack in the center of the oven, and preheat the oven to 350°F. Line the bottom of a 1″ deep pan measuring 17″ × 12″ or 18″ × 12″ with the parchment paper. Butter the parchment paper and the sides of the pan, and set it aside.

2. Sift the ¼ cup confectioners' sugar onto a lint-free cotton or linen dish towel. Set aside.

3. Place the eggs in a large mixing bowl, and with an electric mixer on medium speed, beat the eggs until light in color and slightly thickened, 2 minutes. Gradually beat in the sugar while the mixer is running, beating until the mixture is pale yellow and smooth, 2 minutes more. Add the milk, just to combine. Turn off the mixer and scrape down the sides of the bowl with a rubber spatula.

continued

4. Sift the flour, baking powder, and salt into a small bowl to combine. Spoon into the egg mixture, and blend on low to combine. Add the butter and blend on low until just combined. Pour the batter into the prepared pan, and place the pan in the oven.

5. Bake the cake until the edges just begin to brown, 10 to 12 minutes. Remove the pan from the oven, and quickly run a knife around the edges of the pan. Flip the pan onto the towel dusted with confectioners' sugar, and cut off the rough edges with a serrated knife. Quickly spread the warm jelly evenly over the cake to within ½″ of the edges.

6. Immediately roll up the cake beginning at the shorter end. Keep the towel over the roll to hold it in place. The seam will be on the bottom of the roll. After 8 to 10 minutes, remove the jelly roll from the towel and place it on a serving plate. Dust with the 1 teaspoon confectioners' sugar. Slice and serve warm or at room temperature. Store tightly covered.

CAKEWALKS

IN THE LATE 1800s, cakewalks had more to do with the walk (or dance) and less to do with the cake, which was the prize. The dance was part of a minstrel show begun before the Civil War on plantations where slaves dressed up and mimicked the high-stepping way their white owners walked and danced. Cakewalks became competitive. The couple who most easily showed their finesse and likeness to white people on the dance floor would win first prize—an elaborately decorated cake—and often money.

Thus the word "cakewalk" came to mean an easy task. Yet the dancers were so accomplished at these cakewalks, they made it look easy even when it wasn't.

Cakewalks continued after the Civil War and became a big part of late-19th-century entertainment. At Chutes Park in Denver in 1898, cakewalks were staged with both black performers and black spectators. As many as 3,000 attended.

Madison Square Garden in New York hosted a national cakewalk championship in 1897. And 2 years later a cakewalk was performed at the Paris World's Fair.

The Jelly Roll Keeps Rolling . . .

After the turn of the 20th century, the jelly roll hit the road as a recipe often presented by home demonstration agents and cooking teachers. Its appeal was not only that it had a dazzling presentation but that it served as an emergency dessert. Some recipes contained only two eggs—a convenience when eggs were scarce. A 1910 recipe boasted that the jelly roll would keep fresh for a week. Baking powder companies heralded the jelly roll as a miracle cake, and they sponsored cooking schools where the jelly roll was prepared. Cooking teachers unlocked the mystery of the jelly roll, too, telling cooks to work quickly, rolling the cake while it is still warm to prevent cracking. By the late 1930s, special jelly roll pans were used and would become standardized, measuring 15" × 10" and about 1" deep. But you can still bake a jelly roll in a roasting pan or a more modern half sheet pan. Now the words "jelly roll" are a cooking term meaning to roll up anything with a filling inside. Often the word "jelly" is dropped and desserts go by just "roll." The French word "roulade," meaning "roll," had crept into the jelly roll lexicon by the 1980s. A pumpkin "roulade" with cream cheese filling was a popular dessert in this period.

PRESIDENTIAL FAVORITE CAKES

IF THERE'S ONE THING that American presidents have in common, it is that they like to eat something sweet every now and then. Abraham Lincoln hankered for honey. Ronald Reagan was partial to jelly beans. Dwight D. Eisenhower had a passion for prune whip, a popular dessert at the time. And many of our former presidents favored cake:

THE CAKE TAKERS

George Washington
*Martha Washington
Great Cake
(page 35)*

Thomas Jefferson
*Biscuit de Savoye,
a light, orange-flavored
sponge cake*

James Madison
*Dolley Madison's seed
cake, a pound cake filled
with caraway seeds*

Andrew Jackson
*Blackberry jam cake
(Find a recipe on
page 52.)*

James K. Polk
Fruitcake at Christmas

Zachary Taylor
*Cajun calas tous
chauds, sweet fried
rice dumplings*

Rutherford B. Hayes
Cornmeal cakes

Chester Arthur
Devil's food cake

Grover Cleveland
*White cake with
white frosting*

Benjamin Harrison
Fig pudding

Theodore Roosevelt
*Clove cake, a
molasses spice cake
redolent of clove*

Franklin D. Roosevelt
Fruitcake

Harry Truman
*Ozark pudding
(similar to the
Huguenot Torte,
page 181)*

Lyndon B. Johnson
*Summer fruitcake
(similar to the Cowboy
Cake, page 45)*

Richard Nixon
Baked Alaska

Jimmy Carter
*The Lane Cake
(page 113), served in
the Carter home
during his childhood*

Bill Clinton
*Carrot cake (Find a
similar recipe on
page 252.)*

Some of our presidents have favored pie.

THE PIE GUYS

- **John Adams:** *Apple Pan Dowdy*
- **Martin Van Buren:** *Brandied mincemeat pie*
- **John Tyler:** *Tyler Pudding Pie, a creamy coconut pie*

- **Franklin Pierce:** *New Hampshire-style fried apple pies*
- **James Buchanan:** *Muscadine pie*
- **Abraham Lincoln:** *Peach pie*
- **Andrew Johnson:** *Sweet potato pie*

- **James Garfield:** *Apple pie*
- **William McKinley:** *Cherry pie*
- **Calvin Coolidge:** *Pork apple pie*
- **Barack Obama:** *Nectarine pie*

1-2-3-4 CAKE

MAKES: 12 SERVINGS

PREP: 20 TO 25 MINUTES

BAKE: 25 TO 30 MINUTES

Butter and flour for prepping the pan

1 cup (2 sticks) unsalted butter, at room temperature

2 cups granulated sugar

4 large eggs, at room temperature (see Cake Notes)

3 cups cake flour (see Cake Notes)

2½ teaspoons baking powder

½ teaspoon salt

1 cup milk

1 teaspoon vanilla extract

Chocolate Pan Frosting (page 310)

CAKE NOTES: The flour is the deal breaker in this cake. Choose cake flour for a lighter crumb. If you use all-purpose flour, sift it once before measuring. For slightly more volume, separate the eggs and blend the egg yolks with the creamed butter and sugar mixture. After adding the flour alternately with the milk, fold in the beaten egg whites and vanilla.

This is one of the simplest and best-known cakes in the land, based on the idea that a basic yellow cake can be made with 1 cup butter, 2 cups sugar, 3 cups flour, and 4 eggs, plus a little leavening and liquid if you wish. Who came up with the idea of a 1-2-3-4 Cake is uncertain. The recipe itself looks like it was jotted down in the margin of a cookbook or on a homemade recipe card. And you didn't need to read to bake this cake. The earliest mention might be an 1870 *St. Joseph Herald* newspaper recipe from St. Joseph, Michigan. It calls for sour milk and baking soda, which indicates the recipe was used before baking powder was in every cupboard in America. But *Sarah Rorer's Philadelphia Cook Book* also contains a 1-2-3-4 Cake, with just butter, sugar, flour, eggs, and no liquid or baking powder. She calls the addition of liquid and baking powder a "cup cake." You will find Grandmother's 1-2-3-4 Cake in *The Rumford Complete Cook Book* of 1908, and many variations on the basic recipe would follow. When *The Joy of Cooking* by Irma Rombauer was published in 1931, it offered a "modernized" lighter cake by calling for cake flour and less of it—2⅔ cups. However the 1-2-3-4 was made and passed down through generations, this cake was and still is the standard by which people measure a layer cake. When frosted with chocolate icing, it is the embodiment of American cake.

1. Place a rack in the center of the oven, and preheat the oven to 350°F. Grease two 9″ round cake pans with butter and dust with flour. Shake out the excess flour, and set the pans aside.

2. Place the butter and sugar in a large mixing bowl, and blend with an electric mixer on medium speed until light and fluffy, 1 to 2 minutes. Add the eggs, one at a time, beating until each is well incorporated. Scrape down the sides of the bowl. Set aside.

3. Stir together the flour, baking powder, and salt in a medium-size bowl. Add a third of the flour mixture to the butter and sugar, beating on low speed until incorporated. Add half of the milk, and blend, then another third of the flour mixture, then the rest of the milk, and finally the remaining flour mixture and vanilla and blend until combined and smooth, 30 seconds.

continued

4. Divide the batter between the 2 prepared pans, and smooth the tops. Place the pans in the oven, and bake until they are lightly browned on top and the cake springs back when lightly pressed in the center, 25 to 30 minutes.

5. Place the pans on wire racks to cool for 10 minutes. Run a knife around the edges of the pans and give the pans a gentle shake to release the cake. Invert the layers once and then again so they rest right side up on the racks to completely cool, 30 minutes.

6. To assemble, place 1 layer on a cake plate or platter. Spoon about $^2/_3$ cup of frosting over the top. Place the second layer on top, and frost the top and sides of the cake with the remaining frosting. Slice and serve.

VANILLA EXTRACT

VANILLA MAY BE a world-favorite flavor, but it took its time getting into American cake batter. In fact it made its first US appearance in chocolates and tobacco, then fragrances, and finally ice cream in the early 1800s and later in cakes from the 1860s forward. Native to Mexico and naturally pollinated by *Melipona* bees and hummingbirds, the vanilla plant is related to the orchid and now grows in Madagascar, Tahiti, India, and other tropical climates. The long pods of the vanilla are cured in the sun or in ovens after picking, and the flavor of vanilla comes from the seeds and the liquid that surrounds them in the pod. The cooks of Thomas Jefferson, America's first epicure, used vanilla beans in the preparation of ice cream, which was served while Jefferson was in the White House from 1801 to 1809. But vanilla's presence in America predated Jefferson, according to Virginia food historian Leni Sorensen. "Vanillas" were on the British merchant ships with indigo and cocoa in the early 1700s. Until 1847, cooking with vanilla meant extracting the seeds from the pods. But when a wealthy customer entered Boston pharmacist Joseph Burnett's store and wanted him to create a vanilla flavor she could use to re-create the desserts she had enjoyed in Paris, the world of cooking changed forever. Burnett traveled to New York and bought the best vanilla beans he could find. He brought them back to his store laboratory and created the first vanilla extract.

BAKED ALASKA

THE CONTRAST OF a warm, lightly browned meringue outside and cold ice cream inside may create the drama in Baked Alaska, but the dessert wouldn't be the same without cake on the bottom.

To commemorate the US purchase of Alaska in 1867, the frozen dessert is said to have been created at Delmonico's restaurant in New York City. It was originally called an "Alaska Florida," with banana ice cream underneath the decorative Italian meringue.

But author Judith Choate and James Canora, Del-monico's chef, who researched the history of Delmonico's and coauthored *Dining at Delmonico's,* said the French pastry chef at the time, Charles Ranhofer, called this dessert by its classic French name, an *omelette à la Norvégienne.*

Nevertheless, the restaurant had to have enjoyed the publicity once the dining public knew the dessert as Baked Alaska and came to order this once-in-a-lifetime confection. An 1891 Philadelphia publication called *Quaker City Notes* advised readers should they travel to New York and eat this dessert, they should do so in a hurry so it doesn't burn their mouth. Or better yet, "spread the inside on the outside."

To make a Baked Alaska, cut a round of sponge, pound, or chiffon cake, place a scoop of ice cream on top of the cake, and freeze. Before you are ready to serve, spoon Italian meringue, made by whipping a hot sugar syrup into egg whites, over the ice cream and immediately bake at 500°F until browned, or brown the meringue using a small blowtorch.

(3538). ALASKA, FLORIDA (Alaska, Florida).

Prepare a very fine vanilla-flavored Savoy biscuit paste (No. 3231). Butter some plain molds two and three-quarters inches in diameter by one and a half inches in depth; dip them in fecula or flour, and fill two-thirds full with the paste. Cook, turn them out and make an incision all around the bottom; hollow out the cakes, and mask the empty space with apricot marmalade (No. 3675). Have some ice cream molds shaped as shown in Fig. 667, fill them half with uncooked banana ice cream (No. 3541), and half with uncooked vanilla ice cream (No. 3466); freeze, unmold and lay them in the hollow of the prepared biscuits; keep in a freezing box or cave. Prepare also a meringue with twelve egg-whites and one pound of sugar. A few moments before serving place each biscuit with its ice on a small lace paper, and cover one after the other with the meringue pushed through a pocket furnished with a channeled socket, beginning at the bottom and diminishing the thickness until the top is reached; color this meringue for two minutes in a hot oven, and when a light golden brown remove and serve at once.

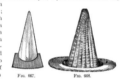

Fig. 667. Fig. 668.

1900 *to* 1916

Birth *of the* American Layer Cake

——— ⌇ ———

THE EARLY 20TH CENTURY brought dramatic changes to how Americans baked a cake—the gas cookstove, electric stand mixer, new food products like Crisco, and celebrity cooking teachers, as well as 15 million new immigrants settling here from around the world.

Until now, cakes had been baked in wood- and coal-fired ovens. Much preparation went into getting the oven to the right temperature to evenly bake a cake, and for that reason baking was not only an art but a significant time investment. Gas cookstoves introduced in 1910 became the new norm. And with gas ranges came the industry that supported them—the appliance dealers, utility companies, and home economists who taught America to bake.

Recipes like Japanese Fruit Cake (page 128), also known as Mikado Cake, the brainstorm of Kate Brew Vaughn, were highly touted in newspaper articles. People packed by the hundreds into auditoriums to see Vaughn and others like her perform their culinary magic. The Checkerboard Cake was another thriller recipe all wanted to see sliced before their very eyes. Food as art was a fascination, and cakes were crafted and decorated to look like flowers, such as the daffodil and crocus.

New regional products like Steen's cane syrup in Louisiana became the backbone of easy cakes for busy families. Karo corn syrup was born, as was Wesson oil and Snowdrift shortening and, later, Crisco, a cheap alternative to lard. Americans became more comfortable with chocolate, making a new devil's food cake and creating the timeless New England favorite called Wellesley Fudge Cake (page 118). It originated in a tearoom in Wellesley, Massachusetts, and the cake was popularized on the back of the Baker's Chocolate box.

On the West Coast in California and Oregon, the fledgling date and prune industries designed traveling marketing campaigns to get their products in the hands of consumers and into new American cakes. If you had a product to sell, you took the show on the road. And if you could afford it, you put the recipe on the back of the box and hired traveling celebrity teachers. The scientific age and agricultural opportunities were nothing without the power of advertising.

And the written word of another sort—the American novel—would bring to life a famous Charleston cake, the Lady Baltimore (page 110). In Owen Wister's 1906 book of the same name as the cake, a three-layer white butter cake, filled and frosted with boiled icing, figs, raisins, and lemon, is the centerpiece of the romantic tale set in fictional Kings Port. You didn't have to live in Charleston to fall in love with the Lady Baltimore or, for that matter, any of the new American layer cakes.

Layer cakes had been present before—Boston cream pie and jelly cakes of the late 1800s. But these showy new special-occasion layers were of a different ilk and were, as the late chef and cookbook author Bill Neal said so well, "Edwardian dessert extravaganzas" with "rich fruit and nut fillings hidden under mounds of fluffy white icing."

Yet the American layer cake could be practical, too, and it became a way for resourceful cooks to use what they had on hand, such as potatoes mashed and added to chocolate batter to keep the cake moist. Mincemeat cakes used the homemade mincemeat put up from end-of-the-season green tomatoes on the farm. Caramel made its entrance in the kitchen through burnt sugar syrups, which cooks created from nothing—just sugar and water. They used the syrup to flavor icings as well as the caramel-flavored Burnt Leather Cake (page 102).

Not all of America had the skill to caramelize sugar or the time to bake layer cakes. Fortunately there was a new style of cake, baked in one pan and run back under the broiler with an easy topping—the Lazy Daisy (page 115). And there were quick breakfast cakes like Cinnamon Flop (page 120), leavened with baking powder and served right from the pan. They spoke to a new American cook who wanted to get a cake on the table fast.

The faster cakes also resonated with America's growing immigrant population. These new Americans brought recipes, ingredients, traditions, and preferences from their Hungarian, Scandinavian, Polish, German, and Russian kitchens. They were often taught to bake in US cities by middle-class American women feeling the charitable need to help newcomers assimilate into the community. They baked the first coffee cakes, swirled with cinnamon, packed with chopped prunes, and layered with fresh cherries. They shared the cake over coffee with friends and relatives. And they helped shape a tradition—the coffee hour—that is very much a part of the American way of life.

BURNT LEATHER CAKE

MAKES: 12 TO 16 SERVINGS

PREP: 1¼ TO 1½ HOURS

BAKE: 25 TO 30 MINUTES

BURNT SUGAR SYRUP

1½ cups granulated sugar

½ cup boiling water

CAKE

Butter and flour for prepping the pans

1 cup (2 sticks) unsalted butter, at room temperature

1½ cups granulated sugar

4 large eggs, separated

2½ cups all-purpose flour

2½ teaspoons baking powder

½ teaspoon salt

¾ cup milk

½ cup reserved Burnt Sugar Syrup

1 teaspoon vanilla extract

BURNT SUGAR ICING

½ cup (1 stick) unsalted butter, at room temperature

5 to 6 tablespoons reserved Burnt Sugar Syrup

¼ teaspoon salt

2 to 2½ cups confectioners' sugar, sifted

½ to ¾ cup heavy cream

(photo on page 105)

The crazy love for the taste of burned sugar—caramel—is universal. Caramels are one of the oldest candies, and it is no surprise that the forerunner of the caramel cake we know today was a gentler, more subtle cake made by cooking down white sugar and adding boiling water to create a burnt syrup, which went into both the cake and frosting. It was called a Burnt Leather or Burnt Sugar Cake at the turn of the 20th century and appeared in cookbooks and newspaper columns as early as 1906. (Brownstone Front Cakes were similar but contained a little chocolate to make them darker in color.) To save time baking a Burnt Leather Cake, make the syrup the day before and store it in a glass measuring cup covered with plastic wrap until the next day when you've got time to bake the cake and make the frosting. Use an iron skillet for caramelizing the sugar, and take care when pouring boiling water into the melted sugar. And use caution when pouring the finished caramel syrup into a heatproof glass measuring cup. A trick when pouring very hot liquids into glass is to place a metal spoon in the glass first to absorb the heat from the caramel syrup. This recipe is adapted from Marion Cunningham's cookbook *Lost Recipes*.

1. For the burnt sugar syrup, place the sugar in a 10″ iron skillet over medium heat, and stir with a wooden spoon and cook until the sugar melts and turns a deep brown color, the color of brewed tea, about 8 minutes. Remove the skillet from the heat. Slowly and carefully stir in the boiling water until no lumps remain and the syrup is smooth. If needed, place the skillet back over low heat and stir until smooth. Place a metal spoon in a heatproof measuring cup or jar and pour the syrup into the cup or jar. Set this aside to cool.

2. For the cake, place a rack in the center of the oven, and preheat the oven to 350°F. Butter and flour two 9″ round cake pans, shake out the excess flour, and set the pans aside.

3. Place the butter and sugar in a large mixing bowl, and beat with an electric mixer on medium speed until the mixture is light and fluffy, 1 to 2 minutes. Add the egg yolks and blend to combine. In a separate bowl, stir together the flour, baking powder, and salt. Add a third of the dry ingredients to the creamed batter, blending on low speed until combined. Add half of the milk, and blend. Add another third of the dry

ingredients and blend, then the rest of the milk, and finally the rest of the dry ingredients. Pour in the reserved sugar syrup and blend until smooth, 30 seconds. Set aside.

4. Place the egg whites in a large mixing bowl, and beat with clean beaters on high speed until soft peaks form, about 2 minutes. Fold the egg whites into the batter, along with the vanilla, until just blended. Divide the batter between the 2 pans, and place the pans in the oven.

5. Bake the cakes until they are deeply golden brown and the tops spring back when lightly pressed in the center, 25 to 30 minutes. Place the pans on a wire rack to cool for 10 minutes. Run a knife around the edges of the cakes, and invert the cakes once and then again so they cool right side up on the rack. Let cool for 30 minutes before frosting.

6. For the icing, place the butter, reserved syrup, and salt in a large mixing bowl and blend on medium-low until just combined. Add 2 cups of the confectioners' sugar and $\frac{1}{2}$ cup of the cream and blend until smooth, adding more sugar and more cream if needed to achieve a spreadable consistency.

7. To assemble, place 1 layer on a cake plate or platter, and spread about $\frac{2}{3}$ cup of icing evenly over the top. Place the second layer on top, and pour the remaining icing over the top and let it fall down the sides of the cake. The icing will set as it cools. Let the cake rest for 30 minutes before slicing.

You Say Penuche, I Say Caramel

Making caramel is an old European tradition, and it came to America with the immigrants who knew how to cook down white sugar into an amber syrup. Caramel cakes, syrups, candies, and icings were alive and well before the 20th century. But something called penuche commanded everyone's attention in the early 1900s. It was similar to a caramel icing but thicker, and often contained pecans or walnuts. The frosting was named for the Mexican brown sugar fudge candy called *panocha*, and it would inspire a quick penuche fudge mix of the 1940s. Today much of the Midwest still calls a caramel frosting "penuche."

CHECKERBOARD CAKE

THE BIGGEST NOVELTY CAKE of the early 1900s, the Checkerboard Cake looked like a checkerboard pattern when sliced. With the dark batter of either spice or chocolate and the light batter often flavored with lemon, this cake was first made in the home and then found its way into bakeries.

You have to wonder what cook got it in his or her head to place alternating rings of batter in one cake pan, switch the pattern in the next, repeat the pattern of the first pan, and so on, to create this checkered pattern. And those first cakes were a feat—using round pans. A first mention of the Checkerboard Cake was at the Lehigh County (Pennsylvania) Fair or "The Great Big Fair" in 1897, when 25,000 people packed the Allentown Fairgrounds and witnessed this cake being made. It became the cake to demo as it was quite a showstopper in cooking classes to showcase gas ranges in Philadelphia or to feature Hunt's Perfect baking powder, flour, and extracts in Salt Lake City.

By 1907 someone had gotten the wise idea to bake square cakes, which made the task of alternating batters a little simpler because you poured them in rows instead of concentric circles. Inventive minds couldn't stay away from the notion of capitalizing on our country's fascination with this cake, and in 1928 the three-layer Checkerboard Cake Pan set was born. The set came with two inserts that fit into the pans, and you filled them according to directions with light or dark batter.

Left to right: Wellesley Fudge Cake (page 118), The Lane Cake (page 113), and Burnt Leather Cake (page 102)

LOUISIANA SYRUP CAKE

(GÂTEAU DE SIROP)

MAKES: 12 SERVINGS

PREP: 15 TO 20 MINUTES

BAKE: 35 TO 40 MINUTES

Shortening or oil and flour for prepping the pan

1½ cups granulated sugar

¾ cup vegetable oil

1 cup cane syrup (see Cake Note)

2 teaspoons baking soda

1 cup boiling water

2½ cups all-purpose flour

1 teaspoon ground ginger

½ teaspoon ground cloves

½ teaspoon ground cinnamon

½ teaspoon salt

2 large eggs, lightly beaten

2 teaspoons confectioners' sugar for dusting the top, if desired

CAKE NOTE: Instead of the cane syrup, you can use 1 cup molasses or sorghum.

Steen's Cane Syrup

In 1910 an early winter freeze in Abbeville, Louisiana, forced C. S. Steen to change direction. His sugarcane was frozen, and he had no choice but to mash the harvested cane using mule-driven rollers. He boiled down the juice in open kettles until it turned into an amber-colored syrup, and the Cajun equivalent of molasses was born. Today the mellow-flavored syrup in the distinctive yellow can is used in all sorts of Louisiana recipes, and most often in this syrup cake.

Syrup cake, or *gâteau de sirop* as it is called in French-speaking Acadiana, began as a simple, no-fuss spice cake into which cooks poured a cup of their local cane syrup. According to Poppy Tooker, local historian, it was leavened with baking soda and nearly identical to gingerbreads baked with molasses. Corinne Cook, a longtime Baton Rouge food writer, said people in southwest Louisiana had their own little patches of sugarcane growing out back and thus a steady supply of cane syrup. As soon as the weather turned cool, her mother made syrup cake. "When it got cold, there was gumbo in the air and also syrup cake," she said. "When we came home from school, I could smell that syrup cake before I got to the back door." And with the 6 children her mother had to feed, a syrup cake was simple to throw together, and everyone loved it. Cook was raised in Church Point, Louisiana, a little town outside Lafayette. After college she stayed in Louisiana and raised a family, with 4 children and 10 grandchildren for whom she baked syrup cake. Her recipe is adapted from the back of the Steen's cane syrup can. If you can get your hands on Steen's, buy some for this recipe, for it has a more delicate flavor than molasses. Or add fig preserves instead of cane syrup for an authentic Cajun variation. That's what Corinne's sister does, using the preserves she makes from her home-grown figs.

1. Place a rack in the center of the oven, and preheat the oven to 350°F. Grease a 13″ × 9″ pan with vegetable shortening or oil, and dust with flour. Shake out the excess flour, and set the pan aside.

2. Place the sugar, oil, and cane syrup in a large mixing bowl and stir with a wooden spoon to combine. Dissolve the baking soda in the boiling water and stir into the syrup mixture. Place the flour, ginger, cloves, cinnamon, and salt in a small mixing bowl and stir to combine. Turn these dry ingredients into the batter and blend with the spoon or an electric mixer on low speed until combined. Add the eggs, and stir or blend until well incorporated and smooth, 1 minute more. Pour the batter into the prepared pan, and place the pan in the oven.

3. Bake the cake until it is deeply golden brown and the top springs back when lightly pressed, 35 to 40 minutes. Remove the pan from the oven, let it rest 15 minutes, then slice and serve warm. Dust with the confectioners' sugar, if desired, just before serving.

DATE LOAF CAKE

MAKES: 8 TO 12 SERVINGS

PREP: 20 TO 25 MINUTES

BAKE: 65 TO 75 MINUTES

Butter and flour for prepping the pan

2 cups all-purpose flour, sifted

1 teaspoon baking soda

½ teaspoon ground cloves

¼ teaspoon salt

⅛ teaspoon ground nutmeg

½ cup (1 stick) unsalted butter, at room temperature

¾ cup granulated sugar

1 cup buttermilk, at room temperature

8 ounces dates, chopped

½ teaspoon all-purpose flour

One of America's earliest back-of-the-box cake recipes was for the Date Loaf Cake. Eager to sell dates, the sweet and exotic fruit native to the Arabian peninsula and grown today in California, growers and grocers would share recipes with their customers. Dates were new to the country at the turn of the 20th century and one of the food crops sought for US farmers to grow by "Agriculture Explorers" employed by the US Department of Agriculture. Finding that the growing conditions of California's hot, arid Coachella Valley were much like those in Iraq and Algeria where date palms thrived, the explorers and horticulturalists worked together to plant Algerian date palms in California in 1900 and launched the domestic date industry. The farm-growing towns took on an Arabian theme park–like motif, opened to the public for tours and camel rides, and America got its first taste of the Middle East. In the kitchen, recipes began appearing for both date cakes and date-nut breads. This is an old recipe adapted from the *Yankee Cookbook*, shared by a Mrs. Frank A. Pickering of Methuen, Massachusetts, who received the recipe from her mother-in-law in 1895. Her mother-in-law received it from her local grocer.

1. Place a rack in the center of the oven, and preheat the oven to 325°F. Grease and flour a 9″ loaf pan, and shake out the excess flour. Set the pan aside.

2. Sift together the 2 cups flour, baking soda, cloves, salt, and nutmeg in a large mixing bowl. Resift again, and set the bowl aside.

3. Place the butter and sugar in a large mixing bowl, and beat with an electric mixer on medium speed until the mixture is creamy and light, 1 minute. Alternately add the flour mixture and the buttermilk, beginning and ending with the flour, and beating on low speed until just combined. Toss the dates with the ½ teaspoon flour, and fold them into the batter. Pour the batter into the prepared pan, and place the pan in the oven.

4. Bake the cake until it is lightly browned and a toothpick inserted in the center comes out clean, 65 to 75 minutes. Let rest until cool, then slice and serve.

LADY BALTIMORE CAKE

MAKES: 12 SERVINGS

PREP: 3 TO 4 HOURS TO SOAK
DRIED FRUIT; 1 HOUR TO MAKE
CAKE, FILLING, AND FROSTING

BAKE: 16 TO 18 MINUTES

CAKE

½ cup raisins (see Cake Notes on
page 112), divided use

⅔ cup sherry (see Cake Notes on
page 112)

½ cup chopped dried figs

Butter and flour for prepping the pans

½ cup chopped walnuts (see Cake
Notes on page 112)

2 cups cake flour

2 teaspoons baking powder

¼ teaspoon salt

½ cup (1 stick) unsalted butter, at room
temperature

1¼ cups granulated sugar

¾ cup (6 ounces) whole milk, at room
temperature

½ teaspoon almond extract

3 large egg whites, at room
temperature

SUGAR SYRUP FILLING

½ cup granulated sugar

¼ cup water

½ teaspoon vanilla extract

¼ teaspoon almond extract

1 tablespoon fresh lemon juice

½ teaspoon grated lemon zest

Seven-Minute Frosting (page 317)

Thinly sliced lemon, chopped walnuts,
or lemon verbena or lemon balm sprigs
for garnish

The regal Lady Baltimore Cake—filled with sherry-soaked figs, raisins, and walnuts, scented with just a suggestion of lemon, and crowned with a fluffy boiled-sugar icing makes an impression in real life as well as in fiction. In fact, it's hard to separate what is fictional and what is truth about this storied white layer cake.

Unlike the egg whites–only Lady Baltimore, the Lord Baltimore Cake is made with egg yolks and filled with toasted almonds, crushed macaroons, and candied cherries.

It was baked at the Women's Exchange tearoom in Charleston, South Carolina, before author Owen Wister wrote a 1903 romantic novel by the same name. The following Lady Baltimore recipe is adapted from the cookbook *Two Hundred Years of Charleston Cooking* by Blanche Rhett, a relative of Alicia Rhett Mayberry. According to historian Damon Lee Fowler, Rhett's recipe is the real thing. I have streamlined the filling for the modern cook.

1. Place the raisins in a small glass bowl and pour ⅓ cup of the sherry over them. Toss to coat. Place the figs in a small glass bowl and pour the remaining ⅓ cup of sherry over them. Toss to coat. Let the dried fruit rest lightly covered on the kitchen counter for 3 to 4 hours. The soaked fruit and chopped walnuts will be placed between the layers of the cake.

2. For the cake, place a rack in the center of the oven, and preheat the oven to 375°F. Butter and flour three 8″ cake pans, and shake out the excess flour. Set the pans aside. Place the walnuts in a small baking pan in the preheating oven until lightly browned, 3 to 4 minutes. Set the walnuts aside.

3. Sift the flour, baking powder, and salt into a large bowl. Sift together 2 more times. Set the bowl aside.

4. Place the butter and sugar in a large mixing bowl, and beat with an electric mixer on medium speed until creamy, about 2 minutes. Alternately add the flour mixture and the milk, beginning and ending with the flour mixture, beating on low speed. Blend in the almond extract and set aside.

5. Place the egg whites in a large mixing bowl, and beat with clean beaters on high speed until stiff peaks form, 3 to 4 minutes. Turn a quarter of the beaten whites into the batter, and fold in until just smooth. Add the remaining whites, and fold into the batter until just combined. Divide

continued

the batter between the pans, and place the pans in the oven. Bake until the cake is lightly browned and just pulls away from the sides of the pan, 16 to 18 minutes. Place the pans on a wire rack to cool 10 minutes. Run a knife around the edges of the pans, give the pans a gentle shake, then invert them once and then again onto the racks to cool right side up.

6. For the sugar syrup filling, place the sugar and water in a medium-size saucepan over medium-high heat, stirring, until the sugar dissolves and the mixture bubbles up. Let it cook, stirring, until it thickens slightly, about 1 minute. Remove the pan from the heat and stir in the vanilla, almond extract, lemon juice, and lemon zest. Set aside, and let the mixture cool for 5 minutes. Poke holes in the cake layers with a large toothpick, and drizzle the sugar syrup over the layers so it soaks down into the holes.

7. Prepare the Seven-Minute Frosting.

8. To assemble the cake, place 1 layer on a cake plate or platter. Spread about 1 cup of icing smoothly over the layer. Scatter half of the sherry-soaked raisins and figs, and half of the walnuts, on top of the icing. Place a second layer on top, and spread with 1 cup of icing. Scatter with the remaining raisins, figs, and walnuts. Place the third layer on top. Frost the top and sides of the cake with the remaining frosting.

9. Garnish with thinly sliced lemon, chopped walnuts, a sprig of fresh lemon verbena or lemon balm, or the garnish of your choice.

CAKE NOTES: While figs are an original ingredient in this cake, you can omit them and just use 1 cup raisins. In fact, the raisins soak up more sherry than the figs. For the best walnut flavor, toast the nuts first while the oven is preheating. Choose a medium-sweet to sweet sherry for this recipe. No sherry? Use brandy.

IN OWEN WISTER'S BOOK *LADY BALTIMORE,* a cake impresses the narrator and becomes the centerpiece of a story set in fictional Kings Port (Charleston). A groom, having second thoughts about his upcoming nuptials, goes in a shop to purchase his Lady Baltimore wedding cake; falls in love with Eliza, who is taking his order; and in the end marries her—thanks to the cake.

In real life, Alicia Rhett Mayberry baked Lady Baltimore cakes at the Women's Exchange in Charleston around the turn of the 20th century. Interestingly, her niece and namesake was Alicia Rhett, the actress who would play India Wilkes in the movie *Gone with the Wind.* But it was Nina Ottolengui, who owned the tearoom with her older sister Florrie, who developed the recipe for the Lady Baltimore Cake whom we should credit, according to historians and to Mabel Pollitzer, a neighbor of the family interviewed as part of the University of North Carolina's oral history program in 1974. It is possible Wister tasted Ottolengui's Lady Baltimore Cake before he wrote his novel.

Actually, Lady Baltimore Cake was first mentioned in an August 1889 *Ladies' Home Journal* article. A reader shares her Lady Baltimore recipe, which is a simple white cake—called Silver Cake back then—with English walnuts baked inside.

But when Wister's novel debuted to mixed reviews, newspapers across the country were printing and reprinting recipes for Lady Baltimore Cake. It was clearly the cake of 1906. And it remained popular through the 1930s and in Baltimore up until the 1970s, where in the Hutzler's department store tearoom you could order a slice of this cake. Most likely the cake was named after the real Lady Baltimore—Joan Calvert—who also inspired a Lady Baltimore silver pattern and African violet species, according to author Julia Reed.

THE LANE CAKE

MAKES: 8 TO 12 SERVINGS

PREP: 1½ TO 1¾ HOURS

BAKE: 25 TO 30 MINUTES

FILLING AND FROSTING

2 cups granulated sugar

1 cup (2 sticks) lightly salted butter, at room temperature

10 large egg yolks

2 cups raisins, chopped

1 cup maraschino cherries (save a few for garnish), chopped in half

1 cup chopped pecans, save a few whole for garnish

1 teaspoon vanilla extract

½ cup bourbon

CAKE

Vegetable shortening and waxed paper for prepping the pans

1 cup (2 sticks) lightly salted butter, at room temperature

½ cup (1 stick) margarine, at room temperature (see Cake Notes on page 114)

3 cups granulated sugar

5 large eggs, at room temperature

3 cups all-purpose flour (see Cake Notes on page 114)

½ teaspoon baking powder

¼ teaspoon salt

1 cup whole milk

1 teaspoon vanilla extract

(photo on page 104)

All her life, Mary Jim Merrill Pianowski was known for her Lane Cake, a 3-layer confection filled and frosted with a boozy custard packed with pecans, raisins, and maraschino cherries. When Mary Jim was first married and living in Andalusia, Alabama, in 1937, she was given a copy of a cookbook called *Tried and True*. In the book were recipes for Lane Cake, a Southern superstar put on the culinary map by Emma Rylander Lane of Clayton, Alabama, after Mrs. Lane entered the cake in the state fair and it won first prize. From then on, this cake was often known throughout the South as Prize Cake. Mary Jim tried many Lane and Prize Cakes in the book, and she gathered ideas from the recipes to craft her own rendition. She perfected her recipe over the years and baked at least one Lane Cake during Thanksgiving or Christmas or the first cold months of the year. She used to frost her cake with white seven-minute cooked icing, but her family vetoed that. "They said, 'Mother, don't do that again. That's a lot of trouble. We like the looks of the cherries and raisins and want to see them.'" The secret to making a great Lane Cake, Mary Jim disclosed, is to use only bourbon in the filling—"not brandy, wine, Scotch, or anything else!" Then sprinkle bourbon over leftover cake to keep it moist and flavorful. And cook the filling slowly and thoroughly in a double boiler, stirring constantly, she said, "or it will be grainy." She also saved time by chopping her raisins and nuts ahead of time. This is Mary Jim's recipe. We spoke about 8 months before her death at age 94 in 2014. Her family misses her and her Lane Cake, but her daughter Marianne Weber is carrying on the family tradition and baking this recipe every chance she gets.

1. For the filling and frosting, place the sugar and butter in a large mixing bowl, and beat with an electric mixer on medium speed until the mixture comes together and lightens. In a separate, smaller bowl, beat the egg yolks with a whisk until they turn light yellow in color. Stir the egg yolks into the butter mixture until combined.

2. Fill the bottom saucepan of a double boiler with 2″ of water. Place the pan over medium-high heat and bring to a boil, then reduce the heat so the water simmers. Turn the sugar and egg mixture into the top pan of the double boiler. Cook over simmering water until the custard thickens

continued

and is smooth, stirring constantly, 30 to 40 minutes. Remove the pan from the heat and stir in the raisins, cherries, pecans, and vanilla. Stir to combine the ingredients well, and then stir in up to ¹⁄₂ cup of bourbon, adding the bourbon to taste. Transfer this mixture to a glass bowl and cover with plastic wrap and chill until ready to assemble. It can be made a day in advance.

3. For the cake, place a rack in the center of the oven, and preheat the oven to 350°F. Lightly grease the bottom of three 9″ pans with vegetable shortening and flour. Cut waxed paper rounds to fit the bottom of the pans, and place these in the pans. Set the pans aside.

4. Place the soft butter and margarine in a large mixing bowl with the sugar. Cream the mixture by beating on medium-low speed until the mixture comes together and lightens, 2 to 3 minutes. Add the eggs, one at a time, beating well after each addition.

5. In a separate, smaller bowl, sift together the flour, baking powder, and salt. Add the flour mixture and milk alternately to the butter mixture, beginning and ending with the flour mixture. Blend in the vanilla. Divide the batter between the prepared pans, and place the pans in the oven. Bake until the cakes are lightly browned and spring back when lightly pressed in the center, 25 to 30 minutes. Remove the pans from the oven to a wire rack to cool for 10 minutes. Run a knife around the edges of the cakes, give the layers a gentle shake, and invert the layers once and then again onto the rack to cool completely, right side up, about 30 minutes.

6. To assemble the cake, place the filling between the layers and on top of the cake, leaving the sides bare. Decorate the top of the cake with the reserved cherries and pecans, if desired.

CAKE NOTES: Mary Jim used Fleischmann's original margarine and Gold Medal flour in her cake. For a pretty contrast, use half golden and half dark raisins. Garnish the top with toasted coconut, if desired.

The Lane Cake and To Kill a Mockingbird

When a recipe like the Lane Cake is written about in literature, you take notice. This isn't your average 1-2-3-4 Cake. It is a white layer cake filled with a distinctive boozy bourbon custard and crammed full of raisins, chopped pecans, and cherries. So to write about it, the author must have experienced it in her lifetime. Harper Lee, author of *To Kill a Mockingbird*, lived just 3 hours away from Clayton, Alabama, the home of the Lane Cake, when she wrote the famous novel published in 1960. In the book, the Finches' neighbor Maudie Atkinson gets competitive about baking her Lane Cake and accuses another Maycomb baker of wanting to steal her bourbon-loaded recipe. As Scout said of the generous amount of bourbon in the cake, "Miss Maudie Atkinson baked a Lane Cake so loaded with shinny it made me tight."

LAZY DAISY CAKE

MAKES: 12 TO 16 SERVINGS

PREP: 25 TO 30 MINUTES

BAKE: 28 TO 32 MINUTES

CAKE

Butter or shortening and flour for prepping the pan

½ cup (1 stick) unsalted butter, at room temperature

2 cups granulated sugar

3 large eggs

2 cups all-purpose flour (see Cake Notes)

2 teaspoons baking powder

½ teaspoon salt

1 cup buttermilk

1 teaspoon vanilla extract

TOPPING

½ cup (1 stick) unsalted butter

1 cup light brown sugar, firmly packed

⅓ cup heavy cream

1½ to 2 cups sweetened shredded coconut

1 teaspoon vanilla extract

Pinch of salt (see Cake Notes)

CAKE NOTES: Instead of the all-purpose flour with baking powder and salt added separately, use 2 cups self-rising flour for a quick shortcut. And in the topping, add the pinch of salt if you are using unsalted butter. If using salted butter, omit the salt.

Max Merrell was a high school freshman in Carlsbad, New Mexico, in the early 1950s when he first tasted Lazy Daisy Cake. His mother and grandmother baked the cake for him, and it was a sheet cake, "dripping in brown sugar icing with coconut on top," recalls Max, who now lives in Nashville, Tennessee. "I loved it." Max hadn't given Lazy Daisy much thought until about 10 years ago, when his wife, Mary, and daughter Mindy asked him what cake he'd like for his birthday. "I answered, 'Lazy Daisy,'" he says with a laugh, "and their response was, 'What?' They started digging around, and Mindy came up with this recipe." Mindy's recipe is a little different from some Lazy Daisy recipes in that she creams the soft butter and sugar first to attain a fluffier batter, and she uses buttermilk for flavor instead of milk.

1. For the cake, place a rack in the center of the oven, and preheat the oven to 350°F. Lightly grease and flour a 13″ × 9″ baking pan and set it aside.

2. Place the soft butter and sugar in a large mixing bowl, and blend with an electric mixer on medium speed until the mixture is creamy, 2 minutes. Add the eggs, and blend on medium until the batter is smooth and light, 2 minutes more.

3. In a separate bowl, stir together the flour, baking powder, and salt. Add to the batter along with the buttermilk and vanilla, beginning and ending with the flour mixture. Blend on low until everything is incorporated, then increase the mixer speed to medium and blend to lighten the batter, 30 seconds more. Turn the batter into the prepared pan, and smooth the top. Place the pan in the oven.

4. Bake the cake until it is golden brown and the top springs back when lightly pressed, 28 to 32 minutes. Remove the cake from the oven. Turn the oven broiler on, and carefully position a broiler rack 4″ to 5″ from the broiler.

5. For the topping, place the butter in a medium-size saucepan over medium heat to melt, 1 minute. Stir in the brown sugar and cream and let the mixture come to a boil and boil for 2 minutes, or until it thickens slightly. Take the pan off the heat. Stir in the coconut, vanilla, and salt. Pour the topping over the top of the warm cake, spreading it out to

continued

reach the edges. Place the cake in the oven, leaving the door ajar or the oven light on so you can watch the broiling so it will not overcook. Let the topping broil until it bubbles up and the coconut caramelizes, from 30 seconds to 1 minute, depending on your broiler.

6. Remove the pan from the oven, let it rest for 15 minutes, then cut into squares and serve warm.

A Lazy Daisy Time

One of America's most beloved cakes may be adored because of its catchy name. Popular in the 1930s, this sheet cake with broiled topping of coconut, brown sugar, and cream was written about as early as 1914 in the *Chicago Sunday Tribune* with a recipe submitted by a Margaret Hill of Waterloo, Iowa. And the phrase "lazy daisy" was mentioned in turn-of-the-century poetry—"there's something in the lazy, daisy atmosphere"—to describe the fresh, carefree feel of June. "Lazy daisy" would name a popular stitch in needlework. Once newspaper food columnists got hold of the recipe in the 1920s and Snowdrift shortening ran ads sharing the recipe, well, everyone knew of Lazy Daisy Cake. And its popularity would continue into the wartime 1940s, when America gravitated to quick baking powder-leavened one-bowl cakes: simple, economical, no messing around with creaming butter and sugar and separating eggs. Like the name implies—Lazy Daisy. Variations abound, of course, with this great recipe. You will find cakes with oats that have been soaked until soft in boiling water, and you may find chopped pecans in the topping. It's Lazy Daisy—have fun with it!

WELLESLEY FUDGE CAKE

MAKES: 8 TO 12 SERVINGS

PREP: 40 TO 45 MINUTES

BAKE: 25 TO 30 MINUTES

Butter and flour for prepping the pans

4 ounces unsweetened chocolate, chopped

½ cup water

2 cups granulated sugar, divided use

2 cups all-purpose flour

1 teaspoon baking soda

½ teaspoon salt

¾ cup (1½ sticks) unsalted butter, at room temperature

2 large eggs

1 cup buttermilk, at room temperature

1 teaspoon vanilla extract

Chocolate Pan Frosting (page 310)

(photo on page 104)

S ealed in a centennial time capsule, and placed behind a bronze plaque in the Wellesley College library in 1981, is the recipe for Wellesley Fudge Cake. Why would a chocolate cake recipe be worthy of a time capsule? Well, you have to understand this isn't your average chocolate cake. It has been so admired through the years that when Karyl Bannister was growing up in Needham, Massachusetts, it was the only chocolate cake of her youth. A food writer who now resides in West Southport, Maine, Bannister said Wellesley Fudge Cake isn't just about Wellesley. It is "in the bloodstream of all New Englanders." The deep chocolate layer cake with thick fudge frosting, inspired by the fudge made by Wellesley girls, first made an appearance at a tearoom over Palmer's Shoe Store on Wellesley Square, Bannister said. And it was baked at the old Wellesley Inn. One young woman who made that cake received an immediate marriage proposal from a wealthy widower. The cake got its biggest advertising boost in the 1920s when Baker Chocolate Co. shared recipes for "College Cake" and "Wellesley Fudge Cake" using its unsweetened chocolate. This recipe is adapted from the *Ex Libris* cookbook, a cookbook benefiting the Wellesley Free Libraries. The cake is traditionally baked in square layer pans, and it improves in texture and slices best the next day. The frosting I share is a little lighter and quicker to prepare than the original version.

1. Place a rack in the center of the oven, and preheat the oven to 350°F. Lightly butter and flour the bottoms of two 8″ square baking pans. Shake out the excess flour, and set the pans aside.

2. Place the chocolate and water in a small saucepan over low heat. Stir and heat until the chocolate nearly melts, about 1 minute. Take the pan off the heat, stir in ½ cup of the sugar until smooth, and set the chocolate aside to cool.

3. Meanwhile, place the flour, baking soda, and salt in a medium-size bowl, and stir to combine well. Set aside. Place the butter and the remaining 1½ cups sugar in a large bowl, and beat with an electric mixer on medium speed until the mixture is light and creamy, 1 to 2 minutes. Add the eggs, one at a time, blending on low until combined. Turn the choc-

olate mixture into the batter, and blend on low for 15 to 20 seconds. Add the flour mixture alternately with the buttermilk, beginning and ending with the flour mixture, and blending on low until just combined. Scrape down the sides of the bowl with a rubber spatula, and stir in the vanilla. Divide the batter between the 2 pans, smoothing the top, and place the pans in the oven.

4. Bake the cakes until the tops spring back when lightly pressed with a finger, 25 to 30 minutes. The cakes should just begin to pull away from the sides of the pans. Remove the cakes from the oven, and place on a wire rack to cool for 15 minutes. Run a knife around the edges of the cakes, and give them a gentle shake. Invert the cakes once and then again to cool on the racks, right side up. Let cool completely, 30 to 35 minutes.

5. Meanwhile, prepare the frosting.

6. When the cake layers are cooled, and when the frosting is smooth and still a little warm, place 1 layer on a cake plate or platter and spoon a generous ¾ cup of frosting over the top, smoothing it to let it cover the layer and trickle down the sides. Place the second layer on top, and ladle more frosting over the top, smoothing the top. For a casual look, let the frosting drip down the sides of the cake. Or, for a more finished look, run the frosting around the edges of the cake using a metal spatula, just to seal in the crumbs. Repeat spreading the frosting around the edges of the cake, using long, clean strokes. Let the cake rest for 1 hour before slicing and serving.

Oh, Fudge

College girls have been cooking in their dorm rooms for a long time. Yet in the past, those culinary efforts were frowned on by one university, the prestigious female Wellesley College in Wellesley, Massachusetts, just west of Boston. Girls are said to have cooked fudge in their dorm rooms, melting the butter and chocolate over a Bunsen burner "on loan" from the chemistry lab. They added cream and sugar and cooked the mixture down until thickened, then cut it into squares using a nail file. But making fudge was in violation of the school's rules against snacking, which supposedly diverted too much blood away from the brain. Henry Fowle Durant, the founder of Wellesley, vowed "Pies, lies, and doughnuts should never have a place at Wellesley College." But he didn't mention fudge. Meanwhile, Vassar College girls, according to Mark Zanger in his *The American History Cookbook*, shared the love of fudge. "Oh, Fudge," was an exclamation Vassar girls coined instead of swearing. The inventor of Vassar fudge was Emelyn Hartridge, who was inspired to make fudge in her room after tasting soft chocolate caramels in a Baltimore candy shop. This make-do college fudge became the inspiration for the fudge frosting atop the well-known Wellesley Fudge Cake.

CINNAMON FLOP

MAKES: 8 TO 10 SERVINGS

PREP: 15 MINUTES

BAKE: 30 TO 35 MINUTES

Butter and flour for prepping the pan

4 tablespoons lightly salted butter, at room temperature

1 cup granulated sugar

2 cups all-purpose flour, plus 2 tablespoons

2 teaspoons baking powder

¼ teaspoon salt

1 cup whole milk, at room temperature (see Cake Note)

¼ cup light brown sugar, firmly packed

1 teaspoon ground cinnamon

2 tablespoons cold lightly salted butter, cut into 8 slivers

CAKE NOTE: In this recipe, the milk needs to be at room temperature. Modern cooks pull ingredients from the refrigerator—eggs and milk—and forget their cold temperatures will make the blending of a smooth batter difficult by hand, plus cakes made from cold ingredients do not rise as high.

What's in a Name?

Could this coffee cake be named because the cook forgot the eggs and thought it would be a flop? Or was "flop" a corruption of the word "flap," and could this have been an early breakfast recipe like flapjacks (pancakes) except without eggs? Webster's dictionary says the first use of the word "flop" in America was 1728, a year after the Amish arrived.

As early as 1727, Amish families from Switzerland and Germany settled in farmland in eastern Pennsylvania. Highly disciplined and faithful, the Amish were and are still known for their commitment to church and family. Their vividly patterned quilts and rich fruit and cinnamon-scented baked goods provide a sharp and bold contrast to the restraint the Amish show in appearance. Farm life has its payoffs, and in the Amish world, desserts, especially cakes, are baked and enjoyed daily. This eggless recipe is a simple cake made from staple ingredients on hand in most kitchens. The cake must be mixed by hand so that the ingredients are just combined—the Amish secret to a light cake. Serve as a dessert after a meal or as a coffee cake earlier in the day. Because this cake contains baking powder and milk, it is a quick cake that Pennsylvania Dutch historian William Woys Weaver says was popular in the early 20th century. The 1916 *Club House Cook Book* from Reading, Pennsylvania, contains a flop recipe, and the formula is similar to a 1918 Wisconsin recipe known as "economy cake."

1. Place a rack in the center of the oven, and preheat the oven to 375°F. Lightly grease and flour an 8″ square metal baking pan, and set aside.

2. Place the soft butter and sugar in a large mixing bowl, and cream together with a wooden spoon until well combined. In a separate bowl, stir together the flour, baking powder, and salt. Add a third of the flour mixture to the creamed butter and sugar and stir to combine. Add half of the room-temperature milk, and stir to combine. Add another third of the flour mixture, stir, then the rest of the milk, stir, and then add the remaining flour mixture and stir just until moistened. Do not overbeat.

3. Turn the batter into the prepared pan, and set aside.

4. For the topping, combine the brown sugar and cinnamon in a small bowl, and stir to combine. Sprinkle this sugar mixture evenly over the top of the batter. Stick the butter slivers randomly through the topping and into the batter. Place the pan in the oven.

5. Bake the cake until the center springs back when lightly pressed with a finger, 30 to 35 minutes. Serve warm.

GRANDMA'S MINCEMEAT CAKE WITH CARAMEL ICING

MAKES: 12 TO 16 SERVINGS

PREP: 25 TO 30 MINUTES

BAKE: 53 TO 58 MINUTES

CAKE

Vegetable shortening and flour for prepping the pans

2 cups granulated sugar

½ cup vegetable oil (see Cake Notes)

4 cups all-purpose flour

2 teaspoons baking soda

1 teaspoon salt

2 cups buttermilk

2 cups mincemeat (see Cake Notes)

1 cup finely chopped walnuts

¼ cup bourbon, water, or apple juice

CARAMEL ICING

2 cups light brown sugar, firmly packed

¾ cup (1½ sticks) unsalted butter

7 tablespoons heavy cream

Pinch of salt

¼ teaspoon baking powder

1 teaspoon vanilla extract

1¾ cups confectioners' sugar, sifted

½ cup finely chopped walnuts for garnish, if desired

CAKE NOTES: Beth Campbell's grandmother used melted lard, but the family now uses vegetable oil. If you have homemade mincemeat, use 2 cups of it in this recipe. Or buy mincemeat in the jar at the supermarket and measure out 2 cups.

Mincemeat might mean Thanksgiving pie to many people, but to Beth Campbell and her family of Belleville, Wisconsin, mincemeat signals the end of the garden. With cooler weather approaching, the green tomatoes still on the vine are picked and ground into mincemeat. Campbell was the oldest of 6 children, and she says with big families nothing was ever wasted. In the farmhouse of her youth, down in the basement was a long wooden table with a hand grinder attached to it where the family made mincemeat and she ground the green tomatoes. "I remember the smell of the mincemeat filling cooking down, ready to be put into jars for processing," she said. Her grandmother made cake from the mincemeat, and Campbell entered her recipe in the 2014 Wisconsin State Fair and came home with first place. You can use your own homemade mincemeat in this recipe or use store-bought. As for the nuts folded in, Campbell uses English walnuts, but her grandmother often used black walnuts that grew on the family farm.

1. For the cake, place a rack in the center of the oven, and preheat the oven to 325°F. Grease and flour two 9″ round cake pans with vegetable shortening and flour, and shake out the excess flour. Set the pans aside.

2. Place the sugar and oil in a large mixing bowl, and beat with an electric mixer on medium-low speed until creamy, about 30 seconds.

3. In a separate bowl, sift together the flour, baking soda, and salt. Add a third of the dry ingredients to the oil and sugar mixture, blending on low speed until combined. Add half of the buttermilk and blend until incorporated. Add another third of the dry ingredients and blend, followed by the remaining buttermilk, and finally the last third of the dry ingredients until incorporated. Stir in the mincemeat, walnuts, and bourbon or other liquid. Divide the batter between the 2 prepared pans, and smooth the top with a rubber spatula. Place the pans in the oven and bake until the top springs back when lightly pressed with a finger, 53 to 58 minutes.

4. Remove the pans from the oven, and place them on wire racks to cool for 10 minutes. Run a sharp knife around the edges, give the pans a gentle shake, and invert the layers once and then again onto the racks so they cool right side up.

continued

5. Meanwhile, make the icing. Place the brown sugar, butter, cream, and salt in a large saucepan over medium heat. Stir and bring to a boil, then reduce the heat and let the mixture simmer, stirring occasionally, until thickened, 5 to 7 minutes. Stir in the baking powder and vanilla, and let the mixture cool slightly, then beat vigorously with a wooden spoon until the mixture thickens, about 1 minute. Add the confectioners' sugar, and stir until the frosting is of good spreading consistency. It will harden up from this point on, so you need to work quickly.

6. To assemble, place 1 layer on a cake platter and ladle over about 1 cup of the frosting, smoothing across the top. Place the second layer on top of the first, and ladle the remaining frosting over the top, letting it fall down the sides of the cake. While the frosting is warm, press the chopped walnuts on top or onto the sides of the cake, if desired. Let the cake rest for 20 minutes before slicing.

20TH-CENTURY GAME CHANGER: SHORTENING

WHAT TO DO with the seed of the cotton plant had perplexed scientists and inventors ever since the American cotton boom of the early 1800s. They searched for a way to use the seed, extract the oil, make the oil palatable for human consumption, and possibly find an inexpensive replacement for lard in cooking.

David Wesson, a Chicago chemist, developed a way to process cottonseed oil to remove the offensive odor and brown tint in 1899, and he named his product Wesson. By 1903 his company's chemists had hydrogen-ated Wesson cottonseed oil into a solid and created Snowdrift vegetable shortening.

But according to David Shields, South Carolina historian and author of the book *Southern Provisions*, chemists in the early 20th century were considering "economy and functionality in the invention of their products" and not taste. Procter & Gamble's shelf-stable Crisco was created in 1911, and Crisco shortening would replace lard and change the way Americans cooked and baked a cake. Shortening was less expensive, appealed to vegetarians as a replacement for lard and butter, and nutritionists and physicians thought it was a more digestible and better-tasting substitute.

"We should not lose sight of the fact that housewives, physicians, dietitians, and chefs had nothing to do with the design, taste profile, or manufacture of Crisco," Shields said. Food chemists created it and "were the new aestheticians of food."

NEIGHBORHOOD PRUNE CAKE

MAKES: 8 TO 12 SERVINGS

PREP: 20 TO 25 MINUTES

BAKE: 40 TO 45 MINUTES

CAKE

Vegetable shortening or butter and flour for prepping the pan

1 cup granulated sugar

¾ cup vegetable oil

1 large egg

2 large egg yolks

1½ cups all-purpose flour

1 teaspoon baking soda

1 teaspoon ground cinnamon

1 teaspoon ground allspice

1 teaspoon ground nutmeg

Pinch of salt

4 tablespoons buttermilk

1 cup chopped pitted prunes (see Cake Note on page 127)

BUTTERMILK GLAZE

¼ cup granulated sugar

2 tablespoons buttermilk

1 teaspoon white corn syrup

1 tablespoon unsalted butter

Pinch of salt

½ teaspoon vanilla extract

Plums have been grown in America since Colonial times, planted in what is now California by Spanish Franciscan monks. But it wasn't until Frenchman Louis Pellier came to California during the 1850s gold rush that plums and their dried fruit—prunes—became a viable crop. A horticulturist, Pellier did not strike gold, so he started a nursery in the Santa Clara Valley. Joined by his brother Pierre, who brought cuttings of the sweet French Agen plums with him to plant, the brothers did strike gold, so to speak, with the success of their sun-dried prunes. The California prune farmers shared their wares with the world at the Pan-American Exposition in 1901. They staged a cooking contest and distributed brochures with recipes from stewed prunes to prune whip to prune cake. Oregon, too, produced prunes with plum orchards in the Willamette Valley. The Pheasant Brand of Oregon prunes was considered one of the best, and Oregon became known for its prune cakes. *The Neighborhood Cook Book* of Portland, Oregon, shared this moist and fragrant prune cake recipe in 1914. Beloved of the European immigrants who settled in America and much loved today from the Pacific Northwest into the Midwest, Texas, and throughout the South, prune cake is suitable to serve any time of the year. I substituted oil for the butter, and I added the simple glaze. To feed a crowd, you can double the recipe and bake it in a 13″ × 9″ pan for 45 to 50 minutes.

1. For the cake, place a rack in the center of the oven, and preheat the oven to 350°F. Grease the bottom of an 8″ square baking pan with vegetable shortening or butter and dust with flour. Shake out the excess flour, and set the pan aside.

2. Place the sugar and oil in a large mixing bowl, and blend with an electric mixer on medium speed until combined, 30 seconds. Add the egg and egg yolks, and blend on medium until combined and slightly thickened, about 1 minute. Set aside.

3. Place the flour, soda, cinnamon, allspice, nutmeg, and salt in a medium-size bowl, and whisk to combine. Add half of the flour mixture to the creamed oil and sugar, blend on low to just combine for 15 seconds, then add the buttermilk. Blend on low until combined, then add the

continued

remaining flour mixture until smooth. Fold in the chopped prunes, and turn the batter into the prepared pan. Place the pan in the oven.

4. Bake the cake until the top springs back when slightly pressed in the center, 40 to 45 minutes. About 10 minutes before the cake is done, prepare the glaze.

5. For the glaze, place the sugar, buttermilk, corn syrup, butter, and salt in a small saucepan over medium heat, and bring to a boil, stirring. Reduce the heat to low and let the mixture simmer until smooth and thickened, about 2 minutes. Remove the pan from the heat, and stir in the vanilla.

6. When the cake is done, remove the pan from the oven, and immediately prick the top with a fork to create holes. Drizzle the glaze over the warm cake, and smooth the top of the cake with a small metal spatula so the glaze is absorbed by the cake. Let the cake rest for 30 minutes for the glaze to harden slightly, then slice and serve.

CAKE NOTE: Most prunes are pitted and soft these days. If not, remove the pits with a small paring knife, and place the prunes in ½" of water in a saucepan and let simmer for 3 to 4 minutes, or until they soften. Drain, cool, and chop for this recipe.

SETTLEMENT HOUSES AND CHARITY COOKBOOKS

AROUND 1900 an increasing number of Eastern European immigrants moved to America and settled in cities to find jobs. Working-class neighborhoods emerged, as did the cultural gap between the established middle class and these poor immigrants.

Progressive middle-class women who wanted to help found the best way to raise money to aid the newcomers—they wrote cookbooks. In Milwaukee and in Portland, Oregon, these cookbooks supported the building of settlement houses.

Lizzie Black Kander, a Milwaukee native, with the support of the Federation of Jewish Charities of Milwaukee, led the efforts to create the Settlement. It was a place where immigrant women could learn English, American history, music, and cooking. Kander thought food was a means of social expression, and through cooking classes she helped introduce these women to the American way of life. Kander's recipes, and those of her friends, went into the 1903 cookbook subtitled *The Way to a Man's Heart.* Heavily sprinkled with advertisements from baking-powder companies, range manufacturers, and the utility companies, these early charity

cookbooks also contained housekeeping and cooking advice. Kander's cake recipes are a glimpse back in time—"devil's cake," Sunshine Cake, coffee cakes—plus German and Eastern European influences with tortes, blitz kuchen, and prune cake, as well as a "Cheap Cake" made with just a teaspoon of butter.

In Portland a similar charity was formed by the Council of Jewish Women. They wrote *The Neighborhood Cook Book* in 1912. "The Neighborhood" was the name of their settlement house at the corner of Second and Wood streets, where they helped Portland immigrants adjust to their new home. The cookbook was a big success and led to a 1914 revised and expanded edition containing such classic cakes as the Burnt Leather Cake, caramel cakes, carrot cake, more than a dozen chocolate cake recipes, potato cakes, and a prune cake.

While the settlement house books were raising funds for their communities, so were cookbooks written by women's suffrage supporters. One of the best known was the *Washington Women's Cook Book* of 1909, sharing recipes of the Pacific Northwest and even explaining how to start a campfire and providing sailor recipes to be cooked on a boat, while at the same time educating readers on women's right to vote.

JAPANESE FRUIT CAKE

MAKES: 8 TO 12 SERVINGS

PREP: 1 TO 1½ HOURS, PLUS
3 HOURS TO CHILL FILLING

BAKE: 16 TO 22 MINUTES

FILLING

1 medium coconut (about 1½ pounds)
or 2 bags (6 ounces each) frozen
unsweetened shredded coconut

3 to 4 large oranges, washed and dried

1½ cups granulated sugar

Pinch of salt

CAKE

½ cup chopped raisins

Butter and flour for prepping the pans

1 cup (2 sticks) unsalted butter, at
room temperature

1¾ cups granulated sugar

4 large eggs, separated (save 2 egg
whites for the frosting)

3 cups sifted all-purpose flour

2 teaspoons baking powder

½ teaspoon salt

1 cup whole milk

½ teaspoon ground cinnamon

½ teaspoon ground allspice

½ cup finely chopped pecans

Seven-Minute Frosting (page 317)

Satsuma Oranges

From 1908 to 1911, a million Japanese Owari satsuma tangerine trees were imported from Japan and planted along the Gulf Coast. They were first discovered by the wife of the US minister to Japan. The satsuma is still grown and was an original ingredient in this cake.

The Japanese Fruit Cake isn't a fruitcake in the sense of the heavy English-style cakes of dried fruits, nuts, and whiskey. It is a Southern layer cake of the early 1900s, with an orange and coconut ambrosia-like filling and thick boiled white icing on top. There truly is nothing Japanese about the cake's origin, but it speaks to America's fascination with the Far East at that period in time. Nashville's Kate Brew Vaughn traveled the country between 1912 and 1914 showing cooks how to make a Mikado Cake packed with spices, extracts, dried fruit, wine, and nuts: in essence a fruitcake. But that cake made with Royal baking powder sounded a lot more intriguing to her crowds when she told the story about receiving the recipe from a Japanese chef who had cooked for the Mikado. Soon Japanese-style cakes were the cake to bake, and plates on which to serve them could be ordered from Montgomery Ward & Co. Henrietta Dull was known for her Japanese Fruit Cake, which was one of the most requested recipes at the *Atlanta Journal* during and after her tenure there as food editor. Mrs. Dull has 2 variations in her 1928 cookbook, *Southern Cooking*, and this recipe is adapted from those recipes.

1. For the filling, prepare the fresh coconut for grating (see "Baking with Fresh Coconut" on page 57), or open the bagged coconut, and measure out 3 cups. Set aside.

2. Grate the zest from the oranges and set aside. Cut the oranges in half and juice them to yield 1 cup. Place ³⁄₄ cup of the orange juice in a medium-size saucepan with 1 tablespoon of the reserved orange zest, 3 cups coconut, the sugar, and salt. Bring the mixture to a boil over medium-high heat, stirring to dissolve the sugar. Reduce the heat to medium-low and let simmer until reduced by a third, about 45 minutes. Turn into a bowl, and chill in the refrigerator for at least 3 hours. If you use a fresh coconut, add up to ¹⁄₂ cup of the coconut milk to the orange juice mixture. It will be a little more liquid than without the coconut milk, but the flavor is wonderful.

3. For the cake, place the remaining ¹⁄₄ cup orange juice in a small bowl with the chopped raisins. Set the raisins aside to soften them.

continued

4. Place a rack in the center of the oven, and preheat the oven to 350°F. Butter and flour three 9″ round cake pans, and shake out the excess flour. Set the pans aside.

5. Place the butter and sugar in a large mixing bowl, and blend with an electric mixer on medium speed until light and creamy, 2 to 3 minutes. Add the 4 egg yolks, one at a time, beating just until combined. Place the flour, baking powder, and salt in a large mixing bowl, and stir to combine. Add this and the milk alternately to the butter and sugar mixture, beginning and ending with the flour mixture, and mixing until just combined and smooth, 1 minute. Set aside.

6. Place 2 egg whites (2 egg whites are saved for the frosting) into a large mixing bowl, and beat with clean beaters on high speed until stiff peaks form, about 4 minutes. Fold the whites into the batter until just combined. Divide the batter into thirds.

7. Pour one-third of the batter into a medium-size bowl, and fold in the cinnamon, allspice, soaked raisins, pecans, and ¹/₂ teaspoon of the reserved orange zest. Turn this into one of the prepared pans and smooth the top. Divide the remaining batter between the 2 remaining pans and smooth the tops. Place the pans in the oven.

8. Bake the cake until the white layers are golden brown and spring back when lightly pressed in the center, 16 to 19 minutes, and the spice layer also springs back when pressed, 19 to 22 minutes. Remove the pans from the oven to a wire rack to cool for 10 minutes.

9. Run a knife around the edges of the pans, give the pans a gentle shake, then invert the cakes once and then again onto the rack to cool completely, 30 minutes.

10. Prepare the Seven-Minute Frosting.

11. To assemble the cake, remove the filling from the refrigerator. Measure out ¹/₂ cup of filling and reserve for the top layer. Place 1 white layer on a cake plate or platter. Poke holes in the top of the cake, and spoon half of the filling over the top, almost to the edges. Place the spice layer on top, poke holes in the cake, then spoon the remaining half of the filling over the top. Place the second white layer on top, poke holes in the cake, and spoon over the reserved ¹/₂ cup of filling. Generously pile the frosting over the top of the cake and filling. Frost the sides of the cake, if desired. Slice and serve.

Mrs. Dull, the Queen of Southern Cake Baking

In a time when women were identified by their husbands' initials, Mrs. S. R. Dull crafted a career all her own. She was born Henrietta Celeste Stanley in rural Laurens County, Georgia, in 1863, and she learned to cook by watching the slaves prepare food on her family's plantation. After marriage, six children, and her husband's declining health, Mrs. Dull had to find a way to support her family. Like women in similar situations, she relied on what she knew how to do and baked cakes and made sandwiches to sell to ladies at her church. This grew into a thriving catering business, and eventually her culinary skills got the attention of the Atlanta Gas Light Company. Mrs. Dull was hired to show consumers how to cook with gas. At the time, she compared a gas range to a husband—"you couldn't get the best out of either until you learned how to manage them." Mrs. Dull was offered a job as food editor of the *Sunday Atlanta Journal Magazine*, where she was the South's first celebrity chef, teaching cooking classes throughout the region, and sharing recipes and advice through her columns and her landmark book, *Southern Cooking*, published in 1928.

AMERICAN WEDDING CAKE

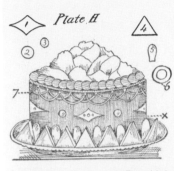

AFTER THE 1840 wedding of Queen Victoria to Prince Albert, the wedding cake went white. Queen Victoria's cake was a massive 300-pound fruitcake with white icing and decorations. The frosting was renamed "Royal Icing" in England.

And in America, white wedding cake, not just the frosting, became the norm. In *Southern Cooking,* author Henrietta Dull shares her mother's wedding cake recipe from 1860—made with 16 egg whites. If you look at the society pages in newspapers from the late 19th century, you will read about grand weddings where the bride's dress and veil, the flowers, and the cake were all white.

Good Housekeeping shared a white wedding cake recipe in 1902, although it was a white fruitcake, often called the Sally White Cake, containing citron, almonds, and coconut. White fruitcakes gave way to white layer cakes and fluffy frosting. As the newspaper recipe columns remarked in 1906, it was a "new departure in wedding cakes . . . eminently delicate."

And a status symbol. As cakes got whiter, they were more expensive to make. A cake baked with white sugar and frosted with an icing of confectioners' sugar indicated you were able to afford it.

Of all the cakes baked today, the wedding cake is the most evolving. A symbol of purity and union, the wedding cake, or "bride cake" as it has been called, is a study in contrasts. It is formal yet feeds a crowd, intimate but useful, traditional and ever changing. And it has an interesting past.

At ancient Roman weddings, the groom would break a cake of barley or wheat over the bride's head, and then the guests would gather and eat the crumbs for good luck. In medieval England, the wedding "cake" was a tower of sugar buns over which the bride and groom would kiss. Success in their attempt to secure a kiss, and the couple would prosper together.

The first recorded recipe for a "bride cake" was included in Elizabeth Raffald's *The Experienced English Housekeeper* in 1769. According to Nicola Humble, author of *Cake: A Global History,* the original recipe was rich fruitcake "banded by layers of candied peel." Cakes at this time might also be covered while hot with a meringue icing called "bliss" and placed back in the oven briefly for the icing to set.

Now wedding cakes come in all shapes, sizes, flavors, and colors—even constructed of cupcakes, macarons, and doughnuts. Pleated frostings, cakes that tell a story of how the couple met, and naked cakes with little or no frosting on the sides are popular. And the tradition of freezing the top layer to eat on your first anniversary? That is a post–World War II trend, possible once homes contained freezers.

CHAPTER 5

1917 *to* 1945

Baking in the Good Times
& the Bad Times

FROM 1917 TO 1945, America rode a roller coaster of economic, political, and cultural events. About 9 of these years—the Roaring Twenties—were good times. The rest were hard, and what you ate and baked had a lot to do with how resourceful you were.

In the 1920s, national wealth doubled, prohibited alcohol flowed in speakeasies, automobiles and railroads crisscrossed the country, and perky Harvey hotel girls served up cake with a smile. Women had won the right to vote. And they had won the right to home refrigeration, too. With the Freon gas invention, the refrigerator was no longer an icebox packed with home-delivered ice. It was a lifesaver, and sales of home refrigerators increased even during the Depression. The crucial ingredient of the icebox cake—a thin chocolate wafer—was created in 1924, just in time for do-ahead refrigerated desserts.

A year later, in Tuskegee, Alabama, George Washington Carver developed 101 ways to use the peanut, including a ground peanut cake flavored with molasses and spices (page 148). It was Carver's plan to persuade farmers to plant peanuts in barren cotton fields and open America's eyes to the infinite possibilities of peanuts. Far from the rural South, New York City's Jewish delicatessens were creating an Ameri-

can cake of a different sort. Made with cream cheese, the New York style of cheesecake was dense and rich on a cookie crumb crust. Even if cheesecake had been baked in America centuries before, it was nothing like this new creation, and the stylish theater crowd loved every bite.

Across the country in Hollywood, where movies were made and stars were born, the fashionable Brown Derby restaurant at the corner of Hollywood and Vine served slices of a new Grapefruit Cake (page 159). It was created for Brown Derby patron and gossip columnist Louella Parsons, who was forever trying to lose weight on a grapefruit diet. Its creator was an insurance salesman turned pastry chef named Harry Baker, who would eventually sell his chiffon cake formula to General Mills. Anything was possible in Hollywood, and it seemed an escape for America during the hard times. As poor as people were in the 1930s and after the Depression, they still went to the movies to see Douglas Fairbanks and W. C. Fields and forget about their troubles. And boy, did America have troubles.

After years of looking inward, isolationist America committed to helping her Allies and sent a generation of boys to the trenches of northern France, where they experienced World War I and a world different from their own. Surviving not just one but two world wars, the stock market collapse and worldwide Depression, as well as the Dust Bowl and a migration to California, our country experienced sacrifice firsthand.

This was the time of making do with what you grew or had on hand, and yet some of our country's best cakes were born in these lean years. The black walnut cake, pineapple upside-down cake, Cold Oven Pound Cake (page 162), and applesauce cake are such classic recipes we still bake today. Spice Meringue Cake and a German-style Blitz Torte called for a simple egg white meringue to make them more interesting, an economical flourish.

Gone were the elaborate multitiered architectural feats popular at the turn of the 20th century. On the table were practical cakes and holiday treats, like Leah Chase's Butter Cake (page 164), saved for Christmas in Louisiana when you opened your home to family and friends. The moist apple butter–filled Appalachian Apple Stack Cake (page 136) originated in the hardscrabble Tennessee and Kentucky mountains, but to the people of this poor region, it was also a wedding cake, a celebration, and a beautiful cake to behold.

Cookbooks such as Marjorie Kinnan Rawlings's *Cross Creek Cookery* and M. F. K. Fisher's *How to Cook a Wolf* contained personal accounts of what it felt like to bake in the tough times. Rawlings shares her mother's World War I eggless cake recipe and the suggestion to top it with "slightly sweetened" whipped cream instead of extravagant frosting. And Fisher recalls her mother's raisin and spice "war cake" and says it means "nothing to me now, but I know that it is an honest cake, and one loved by hungry children."

They say you remember the hard times because they make you stronger. Well, the war cakes and Depression cakes made without eggs, and cakes made with carefully rationed ingredients, are imprinted in the minds of older Americans. These cakes have been baked and rebaked, talked and written about, loved and hated, longed for and never quite forgotten.

World War II followed the struggling 1930s, but the surprise attack on Pearl Harbor on December 7, 1941, created a determination and call to duty not seen before. Times went from bad to worse but brought out the best in everyone. Volunteerism, the ability to bake by a ration list, doing without, thinking of others, uniting as one: These became the themes as America lived with resourcefulness and purpose. Again, dessert and cake became special-occasion fare.

World War II cakes worth noting include the Brooklyn Blackout Cake (page 170), the all-chocolate cake so named by Ebinger's Bakery in 1942 to commemorate the mandatory blackouts enforced to protect Brooklyn's Navy Yard; plus a chocolate loaf cake baked in the most obscure of places, Los Alamos, by a Philadelphia woman who sought the peace and tranquility of the New Mexico desert but ironically baked cakes for scientists developing the atom bomb (page 168). And out of love and duty, many mothers baked and shipped war cakes as a taste of home to their husbands, brothers, and sons serving in the military far away.

After the war, America had changed. The postwar period brought domesticity, growing families, suburbia, Betty Crocker, and Tupperware. But as for the women who, like the icon Rosie the Riveter, had worked outside the home as part of the war effort and who opened businesses in the 1930s as a way to make ends meet didn't want to spend a lot of time in the home kitchen. They became the new market for a myriad of conveniences. The homemade cake was about to meet its rival—the cake mix.

1917 APPLESAUCE CAKE

MAKES: 8 TO 12 SERVINGS

PREP: 15 MINUTES

BAKE: 30 TO 35 MINUTES

Butter for greasing the pan

1 cup granulated sugar

2 tablespoons butter, at room temperature

1 cup unsweetened applesauce (see Cake Notes)

2 cups all-purpose flour (see Cake Notes)

1 teaspoon baking soda

½ teaspoon ground cinnamon

½ teaspoon ground cloves

¼ teaspoon salt

¼ teaspoon ground nutmeg

⅔ cup raisins

The applesauce cake of the early 1900s was ahead of its time. An economical, adaptable, and patriotic way to conserve ingredients—eggs, butter, and sugar—the applesauce cake was also moist, full of spice, needed no frosting, and appealed to all ages. It has never gone out of style. Applesauce has magical properties in baking and can substitute for fat and eggs if needed. In her 1917 book, *Everyday Foods in War Time*, Mary Swartz Rose, who was an assistant professor in the department of nutrition at the Teachers College of Columbia University, New York, said recipes like applesauce cake supported the country's World War I effort. Her slogan was "Food is Fuel for Fighters. Do not waste it. Save WHEAT, MEAT, SUGARS, and FATS. Send more to our Soldiers, Sailors, and Allies." Aimed at what she called the "patriotic housewife," her book emboldened women to upset their normal routine of planning menus and be frugal when cooking. She called for oats and cornmeal in recipes instead of all the flour, and she often omitted eggs. This is Rose's recipe, only slightly adapted for the modern kitchen.

1. Place a rack in the center of the oven, and preheat the oven to 350°F. Lightly grease an 8″ square metal baking pan and set it aside.

2. Place the sugar and butter in a large mixing bowl, and with an electric mixer on medium-low speed or by hand using a wooden spoon, cream the sugar and butter together until well incorporated. Add the applesauce and beat well until smooth. Set aside.

3. In a separate bowl, stir together all but 1 tablespoon of the flour and the baking soda, cinnamon, cloves, salt, and nutmeg. Stir into the creamed mixture just until smooth. Toss the raisins with the reserved tablespoon flour. Fold the raisins into the batter, and turn the batter into the prepared pan. Place the pan in the oven.

4. Bake the cake until it is golden brown and the top springs back when lightly pressed in the center, 30 to 35 minutes. Remove from the oven, let cool for 15 minutes, then slice and serve.

CAKE NOTES: This old recipe did not specify unsweetened or sweetened, but most recipes of that time called for unsweetened applesauce in baking. Applesauce was still made at home, but it was sold in the can as well. The recipe did not advise you to dredge the raisins in a tablespoon of flour before folding them in at the last. Tossing dried fruit with a little flour prevents it from sinking as the cake bakes.

APPALACHIAN APPLE STACK CAKE

MAKES: 12 TO 16 SERVINGS

PREP: 2 HOURS

BAKE: 14 TO 16 MINUTES

APPLE FILLING

15 to 16 ounces dried unsulfured apple rings (4 to 5 packed cups)

1 cup light brown sugar, firmly packed

1 teaspoon ground cinnamon

1 teaspoon ground ginger

½ teaspoon ground nutmeg

4 cups water

CAKE

5 cups all-purpose flour

1 teaspoon baking soda

1 teaspoon baking powder

½ teaspoon salt

⅔ cup vegetable shortening

1 cup granulated sugar

1 cup sorghum or molasses

2 large eggs, at room temperature

1 cup low-fat buttermilk, at room temperature

Confectioners' sugar or sweetened whipped cream for garnish

TIP: The secret to great stack cake is to bake it a day in advance and cover it so that the apple filling slowly seeps into the cake.

I f you were invited to a wedding in the Appalachian mountain areas of Tennessee, North Carolina, or Kentucky, you might have been asked to bring a cake layer. A traditional wedding cake was constructed from these spice cake layers and filled with a thick and fragrant apple butter made from dried apples put up from the fall harvest. The more layers to the cake—12 to 16, perhaps—the more popular the bride, or so the story goes. Stack cakes may contain other fillings, often lemon or coconut, but the original was and still is the apple. Not calling for fancy and expensive ingredients, stack cakes use what people have on hand—modest baking staples like sorghum, flour, and vegetable shortening, and you can bake the cake in a cast-iron skillet. Or you can use 9″ round cake pans, as in the following recipe shared by North Carolina food writer Sheri Castle.

1. For the filling, place the apples in a large nonstick skillet over medium-high heat. Sprinkle the brown sugar, cinnamon, ginger, and nutmeg over the apples. Pour in the water, which should half-cover the apples. Bring the mixture to a boil, and once boiling, reduce the heat to low and allow to simmer, covered, until the apples are soft and the mixture has thickened, about 1 hour. Add a bit more water if needed. Remove the apples from the heat and let them cool. When cool, place them in thirds in a food processor and pulse until smooth but some chunks of apple remain. Or mash the apples by hand with a potato masher. You will have about 5 heaping cups of apples to spread between 6 cake layers. Set aside.

2. Meanwhile, for the cake, place a rack in the center of the oven, and preheat the oven to 350°F. Cut 6 pieces of parchment paper to fit in the bottom of six 9″ round pans. Smear a bit of vegetable shortening on the bottom of the pans to hold the parchment in place, and set the pans aside.

3. Place the flour, baking soda, baking powder, and salt in a large mixing bowl. Whisk to combine, and set the mixture aside. In another large bowl, place the shortening, sugar, and sorghum or molasses. Beat with an electric mixer on medium speed until the mixture is creamy and smooth, about 2 minutes. Add the eggs, one at a time, beating just until blended. Scrape down the sides of the bowl. Add the flour mixture alternately with the buttermilk, beginning and ending with the flour, and beating until smooth, 1 to 2 minutes. The batter will be thick, more like a cookie dough. Use a strong rubber spatula, if needed, to facilitate mixing.

continued

4. Divide the batter into 6 equal parts. Each part will be about 10 ounces. Spread the batter out into the pans, using the rubber spatula or a flexible metal spatula. Place 2 or 3 pans in the oven at a time, depending on the size of your oven. Bake until the cakes are a light golden color and spring back when lightly pressed in the center, 14 to 16 minutes. Remove the pans to a wire rack to cool for 3 minutes, then run a knife around the edges and turn out the warm layers onto the rack. Immediately spread 1 heaping cup of apple filling over the top of the warm layer. Top with a second layer, spread on filling, top with a third, and so on. Repeat the process for the rest of the batter until you end with the sixth layer on top.

5. Place the cake in a cake saver or under a cake dome for 1 to 2 days before serving. Before serving, sprinkle the top of the cake with confectioners' sugar or pile on whipped cream.

WAR CAKES AND HARD-TIMES CAKES

she is doing her part to help win the war

CAKES BY MANY NAMES— Civil War Boiled Raisin Cake, Poor Man's Cake, War Cake, Cowboy Cake, Victory Cake—have made life a little sweeter for cooks during hard times.

One cake based on soft, slowly cooked raisins, sugar (if you had it), and some sort of fat (lard or vegetable shortening) helped Americans bake during the Civil War, on the frontier using a Dutch oven (Cowboy Cake, page 45), and when times were incredibly lean (Poor Man's Cake). Needing no eggs, milk, or butter, this cake was leavened with baking soda and later with baking powder. It was a cake associated with the two World Wars, when it was called War Cake.

M. F. K. Fisher vividly remembered this War Cake in her book *How to Cook a Wolf*, published in 1942. Born in 1908, Fisher recalled that as a child she ate it washed down with milk. The raisin and spice cake was "a remnant of the last war," and "I remember liking it so much that I dreamed about it at night." But she confessed it is a cake you forget about once war is over. "War Cake says nothing to me now, but I know that it is an honest cake, and one loved by hungry children."

Marjorie Kinnan Rawlings, author of *Cross Creek*

Cookery (1942), also has memories of her mother's eggless War Cake. Heavily spiced with cloves, cinnamon, and nutmeg, the cake contained raisins and currants, was made with lard or Crisco, and could be sweetened with honey or brown sugar. Baked in an angel food pan, the cake was, as Rawlings described, "solid . . . moist and flavory and keeps well."

In 1917, once America entered World War I, Americans were encouraged to ration meat, eggs, butter, wheat, and sugar. Bakeries made Victory Bread and Victory Cake, using half wheat and half rye flour. "Conserve the Wheat" was the slogan of the day in an attempt to rally support for the American war effort, conserve wheat, and appeal to the American sense of patriotic sacrifice.

Cooking experts such as Kate Brew Vaughn lectured and showed Americans how to make Victory Cakes—eggless, sugarless, and butterless confections. Someone once called them "joyless," Vaughn told her crowd in Scranton, Pennsylvania, in April 1918, but then he ate three pieces.

"How to Bake by the Ration Book," was Swans Down cake flour's pamphlet and ad campaign in the early 1940s. The company shared an eggless chocolate cake recipe, baked in thin layers. In wartime, less was more. Cake layers were thin, and frosting was spread between the layers and on top, but seldom on the sides.

BLACK WALNUT CAKE

MAKES: 12 SERVINGS

PREP: 20 TO 25 MINUTES

BAKE: 42 TO 47 MINUTES

Butter and flour for prepping the pan

1 cup chopped black walnuts

½ cup (1 stick) unsalted butter, at room temperature

1 cup light brown sugar, firmly packed

2 large eggs, separated

1½ cups sifted all-purpose flour, reserving 1 teaspoon

1 heaping teaspoon baking powder

½ cup water

¼ teaspoon salt

(photo on page 140)

Throughout America, wherever black walnut trees grow—and this is from Pennsylvania south into West Virginia, Kentucky, the Carolinas, Tennessee, and many states in the Midwest—the nutmeats have wound up in family heirloom recipes, namely fudge and pound cake. Known for the pungent, bittersweet flavor and oily texture of its nut, the black walnut tree grows well in fertile limestone soil, and early German settlers in western Pennsylvania looked for the presence of black walnut trees before they stopped and established farms. But the nuts are a mess to harvest and hard to crack. Anyone who has ever lived near black walnut trees has a tale of just how he or she cracked the nuts, from smashing them with a hammer to driving back and forth over them with a car. Baking a cake is a little easier. This recipe is adapted from *The Pennsylvania Dutch Cook Book* by Ruth Hutchison.

1. Place a rack in the center of the oven, and preheat the oven to 350°F. Lightly grease a 9″ loaf pan with butter and dust with flour. Shake out the extra flour, and set the pan aside. Place the chopped black walnuts on a baking pan and place in the oven to toast while the oven preheats. Let them toast for 5 to 7 minutes, and let the nuts cool on the pan.

2. Place the butter and brown sugar in a large mixing bowl, and blend with an electric mixer on medium-high speed until fluffy and pale yellow in color, about 3 minutes. Add the egg yolks, one at a time, beating well after each addition, scraping the bowl as needed. Set this batter aside.

3. Sift the flour and baking powder into a small bowl. Fold a third of the flour mixture into the reserved batter with a rubber spatula, and add half of the water. Add another third of the flour mixture, and then the rest of the water, and the final third of the flour. Toss the toasted nuts with the reserved 1 teaspoon flour, and fold these into the batter.

4. In a medium-size bowl, beat the egg whites and salt with an electric mixer on high speed until stiff peaks form, 3 to 4 minutes. Fold the egg whites into the batter, just until combined, being careful to incorporate the egg whites but not overbeat them. Pour the batter into the prepared pan, smoothing the top with the spatula, and place the pan in the oven.

5. Bake the cake until the top is golden brown and a toothpick inserted in the center comes out clean, 42 to 47 minutes. Place the loaf pan on a wire rack to cool for 10 minutes, then invert the cake once and then again to cool right side up on the rack to room temperature, 1 hour. Slice and serve.

Left to right: Edith Warner's Chocolate Loaf Cake (page 168),
Black Walnut Cake (page 139), and Cold Oven Pound Cake (page 162)

THE BLITZ TORTE

MAKES: 8 TO 12 SERVINGS

PREP: 50 TO 55 MINUTES

BAKE: 28 TO 32 MINUTES

CUSTARD FILLING

1 cup whole milk

½ cup granulated sugar

1 tablespoon cornstarch

2 large egg yolks, lightly beaten

½ teaspoon vanilla extract

CAKE

Butter and flour for prepping the pans

½ cup (1 stick) lightly salted butter, at room temperature

½ cup granulated sugar

4 large egg yolks, lightly beaten, at room temperature

1 teaspoon vanilla extract

3 tablespoons whole milk

1 cup cake flour

1 teaspoon baking powder

TOPPING

6 large egg whites, at room temperature

1 cup plus 1 tablespoon granulated sugar, divided use

½ cup sliced almonds

½ teaspoon ground cinnamon

In Milwaukee, Brooklyn, and other US cities with a large German population, a favorite cake in the 1920s was the Blitz Torte. Meaning "quick" in German, "blitz" described a cake you could pull together easily from ingredients you had on hand. "Blitz" first described turn-of-the-century coffee cakes called blitz kuchen, but the torte was different and more spectacular. Cake layers are spread with a quick meringue before baking and filled with custard. A showstopper anywhere you serve the cake, it has been dear to cooks for generations, appearing in the 1922 *Tested Recipes* cookbook of the Flatlands Dutch Reform Church in Brooklyn. Nancy Stohs, food editor of the *Milwaukee Journal-Sentinel*, says it is Wisconsin's unofficial state cake. When her newspaper asked readers for a Blitz Torte recipe a few years ago, more than 100 readers sent in recipes from their mothers and grandmothers. This recipe, shared by the newspaper, comes from Jeanne Leitl of Oconomowoc, Wisconsin. "My mother, Lorraine Naylor, was well known for her blitz tortes. When we came home from school and saw she was making one, we'd ask who died," says Leitl. "For years she made them for every funeral at St. Joan of Arc Church in Okauchee." Her secret for the high meringue on the cake, Leitl says, was to use 6 egg whites instead of the usual 4. Baked layers are filled with a creamy custard, and you don't need frosting. The meringue, almond, and cinnamon sugar topping is embellishment enough. In hard times, the almonds would have been a costly addition for special occasions.

1. For the filling, place the milk in a medium-size saucepan over medium-high heat, stirring, until steamy and bubbles form at the edges, about 1 minute. Do not boil. Remove the pan from the heat. In a small bowl, stir together the sugar and cornstarch. Slowly whisk the hot milk into the sugar mixture until smooth.

2. Place the egg yolks in the top pan insert of a double boiler. Gradually whisk in the hot milk mixture. Place this pan over an inch of simmering water in the bottom of the double boiler. Cook, stirring, over medium-low heat until the mixture thickens, 10 to 12 minutes. Remove the pan from the heat, and remove the top insert from the double boiler. Whisk until it cools down a bit, about 2 minutes. Whisk in the vanilla, and set the custard aside to cool while you bake the cake.

continued

3. For the cake, place a rack in the center of the oven, and preheat the oven to 350°F. Lightly grease and flour two 8″ round cake pans with removable sides or bottoms. Shake out the excess flour, and set the pans aside.

4. Place the butter in a large mixing bowl, and beat with an electric mixer on medium-high speed until creamy, about 1 minute. Beat in the sugar until the mixture is creamy and light, about 2 minutes. Add the egg yolks, one at a time, and the vanilla and milk, and beat until smooth, 30 seconds more. In a separate bowl, sift together the flour and baking powder. Add gradually to the batter, beating on low in 3 additions, until smooth and just combined. Divide the batter between the 2 prepared pans and set aside.

5. For the meringue topping, place the egg whites in a large mixing bowl, and beat with an electric mixer on high speed until soft peaks form, 2 minutes. Add 1 cup of the sugar to the whites gradually, beating on high until stiff peaks form, 1 minute more. Gently and carefully spread the meringue onto the top of the cake batter. Sprinkle the top of the meringue with almonds, the remaining 1 tablespoon sugar, and cinnamon. Place the pans in the oven, and bake until the meringue has lightly browned and a toothpick inserted in the center comes out clean, 28 to 32 minutes. Remove the pans from the oven, and place on wire racks to cool completely, about 30 minutes. When the cakes have cooled, run a knife around the edges of the pans to loosen the cakes, removing the sides or the bottom. Run a thin knife underneath the layers to remove them from the bottom of the pan. Place 1 layer on a serving plate and spread the custard filling over it. Top with the second layer. Slice and serve.

CAKE NOTE: If you are not using the custard right away, transfer it to a heat-proof bowl, cover with plastic wrap, and refrigerate up to 1 day in advance.

PINEAPPLE UPSIDE-DOWN CAKE

MAKES: 8 SERVINGS

PREP: 20 TO 25 MINUTES

BAKE: 25 TO 30 MINUTES

PINEAPPLE TOPPING

5 tablespoons unsalted butter

⅔ cup light brown sugar, firmly packed

1 can (20 ounces) pineapple slices packed in juice, about 10 slices, reserving 2 tablespoons juice

10 maraschino cherries, if desired

CAKE

1½ cups sifted all-purpose flour

1¾ teaspoons baking powder

¼ teaspoon salt

5 tablespoons butter, at room temperature

¾ cup granulated sugar, divided use

2 large eggs, separated

1 teaspoon grated lemon zest

1 tablespoon fresh lemon juice

1 teaspoon vanilla extract

½ cup sour cream

2 tablespoons reserved pineapple juice

One of the happiest cakes in America, a cake that brings smiles to anyone when it comes out of the oven, the pineapple upside-down cake was created with ingenuity, drama, and a novel ingredient—sliced canned pineapple. Busy cooks in the 1920s gravitated toward the new baking powder cakes that could be easily assembled. What made this cake a little different was its name—first called pineapple skillet cake, then upside-down cake. After all, it was just a vanilla cake batter poured atop butter, sugar, and pineapple rings in an ovenproof skillet. But once baked, it was turned upside down and voilà—the sugar, butter, and pineapple on the bottom of the skillet was now the dramatic topping. Add red maraschino cherries and you had more drama. The cake has seen a lot of variations through the years, whether flavoring the batter with lemon zest or almond extract or swapping in canned pears or sautéed apples for the pineapple. And it once might have been a yeast cake baked by Jewish bakers in Chicago before the 1920s. But what is certain is that this cake was all the rage in the good-times Roaring Twenties. This recipe is adapted slightly from the Dole Food Company and Jean Anderson in her book *The American Century Cookbook.*

1. For the topping, put the butter in a 10″ cast-iron skillet and place over medium-low heat to melt. Remove the pan from the heat, and stir in the brown sugar. Spread out the butter and sugar mixture in the bottom of the pan. Drain the pineapple slices, and place them in an artistic fashion on top. If you have extra slices, you can slice them in half or into chunks and arrange around or inside the whole slices. If desired, place a cherry in the center of each pineapple slice.

2. For the cake, place a rack in the center of the oven, and preheat the oven to 350°F. Sift the flour, baking powder, and salt into a small bowl and set aside. Place the butter and ½ cup of the sugar in a large mixing bowl, and beat with an electric mixer on medium speed until creamy, 1 minute. Add the egg yolks, lemon zest, lemon juice, and vanilla and blend until smooth.

continued

3. In a small bowl, stir together the sour cream and pineapple juice. Beginning and ending with the flour mixture, alternately add the flour and sour cream to the batter, blending only enough to combine. The batter will be thick.

4. Place the egg whites in a large mixing bowl, and beat with clean beaters on high speed until soft peaks form, 2 minutes. Add the remaining ¼ cup sugar, gradually, while beating on high speed until stiff peaks form, 1 to 2 minutes more. Fold the egg whites into the batter. Carefully pour the batter over the pineapple slices, and place the pan in the oven.

5. Bake until the cake is golden brown and firm to the touch, 25 to 30 minutes. Remove the cake from the oven, and let it cool in the pan for 10 minutes. Run a knife around the edges of the pan, invert the pan onto a large platter, and serve warm.

History of Pineapple Upside-Down Cake

In 1925 the Hawaiian Pineapple Company, what is now Dole Food Co., staged a recipe contest asking cooks to submit their best recipe using canned pineapple. Of the 60,000 entries, some 2,500 were for pineapple upside-down cake, variations on early skillet cakes. Pineapple was the ingredient of the moment. And Dole was the largest pineapple packer in the world, founded by Harvard graduate and entrepreneur James Dole. He traveled to Hawaii at the turn of the 20th century and helped create the equipment to peel, cut, and pack canned pineapple.

PINEAPPLES IN EARLY AMERICA

THE FIRST PINEAPPLES to find their way into early American life weren't edible. They were made of wood, stone, silver, brass, and porcelain. Or they were painted on wallpaper. They were the epitome of style and hospitality.

This deep-rooted tradition dates back to when South America and the Caribbean islands were discovered by Europeans. Natives of these New World lands placed fresh pineapples outside their huts as a sign of welcome. Europeans brought pineapples back with them to Spain, but the plant would not grow there. Nevertheless, the pineapple lived on as a symbol of hospitality in Europe and England. And the fact that the tropical pineapples were hard to get and expensive appealed to people of wealth and privilege.

When the American colonists arrived from England, they brought the custom of a pineapple in the home with them. They tried—unsuccessfully—growing pineapple on American soil. But because only wealthy Americans could afford fresh pineapples from the West Indies, the pineapple was carved into wood and stone, styled from silver and brass, and painted onto fine china and thus became the American symbol for hospitality as well.

GEORGE WASHINGTON CARVER'S PEANUT CAKE

MAKES: 12 TO 18 SERVINGS
....
PREP: 20 TO 25 MINUTES
....
BAKE: 25 TO 30 MINUTES
....

Butter, lard, or shortening and flour for prepping the pan

1¾ cups (12 ounces) unsalted roasted peanuts with no skins

1 cup (8 ounces) lard or unsalted butter, at room temperature

1 cup light brown sugar, firmly packed

2 cups molasses or sorghum

4 cups all-purpose flour

2 teaspoons ground cinnamon

1¼ teaspoons baking soda

¾ teaspoon salt

½ teaspoon ground cloves

¼ teaspoon ground nutmeg

2 cups hot water

1 large egg, lightly beaten

2 tablespoons confectioners' sugar

TIP: Take care when using a dripping pan (broiler pan), because if it is dark, the cake will bake more quickly—in about 25 minutes—than if you are using a shiny metal pan—about 30 minutes.

The overplanting of cotton had exhausted Southern soil, and George Washington Carver was on a mission at Tuskegee Normal and Industrial Institute (now Tuskegee University) in Alabama to show farmers how to revive the worn-out dirt and plant something other than cotton—namely peanuts. Carver, a botanist and child of a Missouri slave, wanted to improve the diet and health of the rural black families and show them a way to be self-reliant. So he wrote agricultural bulletins, spoke to church and civic groups, and even addressed the US House Ways and Means Committee in 1921, which allowed him more than an hour to speak on how the peanut could improve the Southern economy. Carver had successfully turned the plant into oil, soap, medicine, and insecticide, and he used the peanut legume to make coffee, oil, cookies, candy, and cake. Carver's peanut cake, adapted here from Carolyn Quick Tillery's cookbook *The African-American Heritage Cookbook,* was originally made with lard. The spices and molasses are reminiscent of gingerbread, but the flavor is decidedly of peanut. This is the perfect cake to take to a large gathering, picnic, or potluck supper.

1. Place a rack in the center of the oven, and preheat the oven to 375°F. Grease and flour an 18″ × 12″ broiler (dripping) pan, and set the pan aside.

2. Grind the peanuts in a food processor fitted with a steel blade until they resemble coarse meal, about 1 minute. Set the peanuts aside.

3. Place the lard and brown sugar in a large mixing bowl, and beat with an electric mixer on medium speed until fluffy, 1 to 2 minutes. Add the molasses and beat until combined, about 30 seconds more. Set the mixture aside.

4. Place the ground peanuts, flour, cinnamon, baking soda, salt, cloves, and nutmeg in a large bowl, and stir to combine well. Add these dry ingredients alternately with the water to the lard mixture, beginning and ending with the flour mixture. Beat just until combined, scraping the bowl often. At the last, beat in the egg until smooth. Turn the batter into the prepared pan, and place the pan in the oven for 10 minutes.

5. After 10 minutes, open the oven door and quickly and carefully sift the confectioners' sugar over the top of the cake. Close the oven door. Continue to bake until the top springs back and a toothpick inserted in the center comes out clean, 15 to 20 minutes more. Remove the pan to a wire rack to cool until ready to serve.

FRANCES VIRGINIA HOT MILK SPONGE CAKE WITH LEMON FILLING

MAKES: 12 TO 16 SERVINGS
....
PREP: 60 TO 65 MINUTES
....
BAKE: 18 TO 22 MINUTES
....

LEMON FILLING

1 cup granulated sugar

4 tablespoons all-purpose flour

⅛ teaspoon salt

2 large egg yolks

1½ cups water

¼ cup fresh lemon juice (from 1 large lemon)

1 teaspoon grated lemon zest

1 tablespoon butter

CAKE

Butter and flour for prepping the pans

4 large eggs, at room temperature

2 cups granulated sugar

2 cups plus 1 tablespoon all-purpose flour, divided use

1 cup whole milk

½ cup (1 stick) unsalted butter

1 tablespoon baking powder

½ teaspoon salt

1 teaspoon vanilla extract

½ teaspoon almond extract

Boiled White Icing (page 318)

I n a bygone time, when ladies lunched on tomato aspic and sponge cake, the Frances Virginia Tea Room was the place to dine in downtown Atlanta. Frances Virginia Wikle Whitaker opened the tearoom in 1928, and in spite of the poor economic times that followed, her restaurant flourished. A larger space was found on the third floor of the Collier Building at the corner of Ellis and Peachtree Streets, word traveled of the good food, and the tearoom with the female silhouette sign became an Atlanta landmark for many years. It closed in 1962, and the Collier Building is now a MARTA rapid rail station. But recipes and memories remain long after restaurants close. Here is one of the favorite cakes served at the Frances Virginia and similar to sponge cakes covered in boiled icing so popular throughout the 1930s and '40s. This recipe is adapted from *The Frances Virginia Tea Room Cookbook* by Millie (Mildred Huff) Coleman, niece of the last tearoom partner and who inherited the tearoom recipes.

1. For the lemon filling, place the sugar, flour, and salt in a medium-size saucepan, and stir to combine. Beat the egg yolks with the water and lemon juice and whisk into the dry ingredients. Stir and cook over medium-high heat until the mixture comes to a boil, then reduce the heat to medium and whisk and cook for 2 minutes more. Remove the pan from the heat, and whisk in the zest and butter. Pour the filling into a bowl, and cover with plastic wrap. Chill in the refrigerator until it is thick and spreadable, about 3 hours.

2. For the cake, place a rack in the center of the oven, and preheat the oven to 350°F. Lightly grease and flour three 9″ cake pans, and shake out the excess flour. Set the pans aside.

3. Crack the eggs into a large mixing bowl, and beat with an electric mixer on medium speed for 30 seconds to combine. Gradually add the sugar while beating until fluffy, 2 to 3 minutes more. Set the mixture aside.

4. Sift the 2 cups of flour twice, and then add to the egg mixture a little at a time, beating on low speed until just combined, 30 to 45 seconds.

5. Place the milk and butter in a medium-size saucepan over medium-high heat. Stir until the butter melts and the mixture comes just to a boil, about 4 minutes. Slowly pour the butter and milk into the batter while

continued

beating on medium speed until smooth, 3 to 4 minutes. The batter will be thin. Sift the remaining 1 tablespoon flour with the baking powder and salt, and beat on low speed into the batter with the vanilla and almond extract until just combined, 1 minute. Divide the batter between the prepared pans, and place the pans in the oven. If your oven is not large enough to place 3 pans on one rack, place 2 on the center rack, and place 1 pan on the rack above, watching to make sure the cake does not overbake.

6. Bake the cake until it is lightly golden brown, 18 to 22 minutes. Remove the layers from the oven, and place them on wire racks to cool for 10 minutes. Run a knife around the edges of the pans, give the pans a gentle shake, and invert the cakes once and then again so they rest right side up on the racks to completely cool, 30 minutes.

7. To assemble the cake, place 1 layer on a cake plate or platter and spread half of the filling to within $1/2''$ of the edges. Top with a second layer, and spread with the other half of the filling. Place the third layer on top. Place these layers and filling back into the refrigerator to chill for 30 minutes.

8. While the cake is chilling, make the icing.

9. To finish the assembly, remove the cake from the refrigerator, and frost the top and sides of the cake. Slice and serve.

SPONGE CAKES

THE DELICATE, light sponge cake soaks up custard sauces and creamy fillings as well as soft summer berries sweetened with sugar. It is lighter than a pound cake, simpler than a fruitcake, and, before baking powder, it was the standard against which all cakes were judged. Unlike the angel food cake, which would appear in American cookbooks and newspapers toward the end of the 1800s, the sponge cake came earlier and called for the whole egg.

Anne Willan, an authority on French and British baking, says those eggs make sponge cakes rise without the traditional creaming of sugar and butter found in pound cake recipes. "A sponge may have some butter added, but not much or it will not rise," Willan says. Cooks later would find that heaviness—the addition of butter or whole milk to the batter—could be counteracted with baking powder.

French-style sponge cakes are of two types, Willan explains. There is the biscuit sponge, common in early America, containing whole eggs and no butter. It has a dry texture and is a little tricky to make. The egg yolks and sugar are whisked together first, and then the beaten egg whites are folded in alternately with flour.

The second French sponge cake is the classic "genoise." Eggs are not separated. The whole eggs and sugar are whisked together, then flour is folded in along with melted butter.

Sponges would become a mainstay of early American cookbooks, and they would be adapted. Some contained a little vinegar. Others included ice water or hot milk. These cakes often contained baking powder, producing a lighter cake, and Willan says these are truly American.

TEAROOMS AND WOMEN'S RIGHTS

 **BELIEVE IT OR NOT,** America's tearooms in the first half of the 20th century served up more than creamed chicken and frozen fruit salad. They helped usher in social change at fashionable places where women could dine without the company of men and run a tearoom as a business.

The decor was as you might expect at home, either cozy with quilts or high-end with chandeliers, Oriental carpets, fresh flowers, and starched white tablecloths, according to Jan Whitaker, consumer historian who wrote *Tea at the Blue Lantern Inn: A Social History of the Tea Room Craze in America.* Their names were often throwbacks to Colonial taverns—the Green Dragon in Philadelphia, the Betsy Ross in Washington, DC, and the Whistling Oyster in Ogunquit, Maine. Or they might be named after the proprietor, such as the Frances Virginia in Atlanta and the Mary Louise in Los Angeles.

Here in these tearooms, whether located on a busy downtown street or tucked in the corner of a crowded department store or grand hotel, you found conversation, fashion, and feminine fare—salads, stuffed tomatoes, and cake. But these were not just places to sip tea,

according to Whitaker, and not everyone wore white gloves. They were where a working woman bought lunch; where a woman brought her family for Sunday dinner. The tearoom preserved a woman's reputation by being a respectable place to dine.

"In the 19th century and before, men dominated public space and women had to be very careful about where they went and who they were with," Whitaker says. "Restaurants were highly associated with drinking, and that was something middle-class white Protestant women, in particular, were supposed to avoid. It was all about reputation, not law."

Because of its delicate texture, degree of difficulty to prepare, and its dramatic presentation, cake went together well with tearooms, says Whitaker. Unlike pie, which was a "crude basic food that was eaten in quantity at all times," cake was associated with a higher level of cuisine. "It was more special, and it was possible to charge more for it."

Sponge cake with lemon filling and a boiled icing was what the ladies ordered at the old Frances Virginia tearoom in Atlanta. Across the country, the angel food and Lady Baltimore were popular cakes, followed by regional favorites like rhubarb.

LA FONDA PUDDING CAKE

MAKES: 8 TO 12 SERVINGS

PREP: 25 TO 30 MINUTES

BAKE: 65 TO 70 MINUTES

Butter and flour for prepping the pan

10 to 11 square graham crackers

3 large eggs, at room temperature, separated

1 cup granulated sugar

½ teaspoon vanilla extract

⅛ teaspoon salt

1 cup finely chopped walnuts, toasted and divided

1 teaspoon baking powder

Graham Cracker Cakes

One of the crust components in Key lime pie and cheesecake, the graham cracker is an old American ingredient, dating back to the mid-1800s when Presbyterian minister and health fanatic Sylvester Graham created crackers from whole grain wheat. The graham crackers we bake with today are a lot sweeter and more processed than the crackers that made Graham famous. When World War I demanded people get resourceful and come up with substitutes for wheat flour, cooks found you could crush graham crackers and use them in baking like flour. A graham cracker cake won the *Chicago Daily Tribune's* 1918 "wartime recipe contest." It was a practical cake that hung around for decades, and this La Fonda Pudding is a variation on that early cake.

When the Fred Harvey Company opened hotels and restaurants along the Santa Fe Railroad in the early 1900s, they offered travelers a fine place to eat and sleep along the way. One of these choice outposts was the La Fonda Hotel in Santa Fe, New Mexico. It was a beautiful 1922-era Mission-style inn, and in 1926 it became one of the prestigious Harvey Houses. Fred Harvey was a British restaurateur who moved to America and saw the railroad boom as a way to improve the food of the American Southwest—and make a fortune, too. His smiling waitresses, the Harvey girls, welcomed tourists. And his hotels and restaurants served great food. But when the automobile replaced the railroad, business started its decline. This recipe was a signature of the La Fonda, which today sits on the historic Santa Fe square where a Spanish inn was operating as early as 1607, making it the oldest hotel corner in America. It is a simple walnut cake, a hybrid of pudding and cake, baked slowly at a low heat until moist and gooey. Based on graham cracker crumbs that lend a warm brown color and distinctive flavor, this recipe is adapted from one shared by author James Porterfield in his book *Dining by Rail*.

1. Place a rack in the center of the oven, and preheat the oven to 275°F. Lightly butter and flour an 8″ square baking pan. Shake out the excess flour, and set the pan aside.

2. Place the graham cracker squares in a plastic bag and crush with a rolling pin, or place in batches in a food processor fitted with a steel blade and pulse until finely crushed. Set aside 1 cup crushed graham cracker crumbs.

3. Place the egg yolks in a medium-size bowl, and beat with an electric mixer on medium speed until thick and lemon colored, 2 to 3 minutes. Gradually beat in the sugar until thickened. Blend in the vanilla and set aside.

4. In a small bowl, stir together the graham cracker crumbs, salt, walnuts, and baking powder. Fold this mixture into the egg yolk mixture and set aside. With clean beaters, beat the egg whites until stiff peaks form, 3 to 4 minutes. Fold the egg whites into the batter until just combined. Turn the batter into the prepared pan. Tent the pan with aluminum foil, and place the pan in the oven.

5. Bake the cake for 20 minutes, then remove the foil and bake until golden brown and cooked through, 45 to 50 minutes more.

NEW YORK CHEESECAKE

MAKES: 12 TO 16 SERVINGS
PREP: 25 TO 30 MINUTES
BAKE: 1 HOUR 32 TO 37 MINUTES

CRUST

¼ cup granulated sugar

½ teaspoon vanilla extract

1 cup sifted all-purpose flour

½ cup (1 stick) cold unsalted butter, cut into tablespoons

FILLING

2½ pounds (five 8-ounce packages) cream cheese, at room temperature

1¾ cups granulated sugar

3 tablespoons all-purpose flour

1½ teaspoons grated lemon zest

1½ teaspoons grated orange zest

½ teaspoon vanilla extract

5 large eggs

2 egg yolks

¼ cup heavy cream

¼ teaspoon salt

DELIS MAY BE KNOWN for their cheesecake, but ask New Yorkers who bakes the best cheesecake, and they will likely say, "My grandmother!"

When you look at the history of the New York cheesecake, you realize that this dessert was destined to be a classic. Cream cheese was being produced by the Breakstone (Breghstein) brothers in New York, and also by James Kraft and his brothers and sold under the Philadelphia brand. Years earlier it had been developed by an upstate New York dairy farmer who had been trying to make the creamy French Neufchâtel cheese. By 1900 half of America's Jewish population lived in New York. "Jews have always baked cheesecake," says Joan Nathan, author and Jewish foodways expert. "It came from early Greece and Rome, and they made it with ricotta or other soft cheeses." Nathan says American cream cheese manufacturers recognized that Jewish people liked it. Their spreading a "schmear" of cream cheese on a bagel was a near religious experience. And many Jewish people baked cheesecake for the religious holiday called Shavuot, which honored the revelation of the Torah and the Ten Commandments at Mount Sinai. So the cream cheese makers advertised, held cooking contests, and Kraft unveiled a Philadelphia Cream Cake. Cooking teachers from Brooklyn to Amarillo, Texas, instructed women how to bake this new cheesecake. The following recipe is adapted from the Lindy's recipe, except that the crust is a tender, shortbread cookie crust adapted from a Maida Heatter recipe. New York–style cheesecake has a creamy texture, both firm and light, and it may have lemon flavor as well. The appearance is a deep nut brown, which comes from baking it briefly in a very hot oven before reducing the oven temperature to finish cooking.

1. For the crust, place a rack in the center of the oven, and preheat the oven to 375°F. Set aside a 9″ ungreased springform pan.

2. Place the sugar and vanilla in a food processor fitted with a steel blade. Pulse until combined, about 6 times. Add the flour and pulse 10 times. Add the cold butter and pulse until the mixture is crumbly, about 15 times. Turn the dough into the springform pan, and press the dough to evenly cover the bottom of the pan. Line the outside of the pan with aluminum foil. Place the pan in the oven, and bake until the crust has lightly browned, 22 to 25 minutes. Remove the pan from the oven, and let it cool to room temperature.

continued

3. Meanwhile, prepare the filling. Increase the oven temperature to 500°F. Place the cream cheese, sugar, flour, lemon and orange zests, and vanilla in a large mixing bowl, and beat with an electric mixer on medium speed until combined and well blended, about 2 minutes. Scrape down the bowl. Add the eggs and egg yolks one at a time, beating on medium until well combined. Add the cream and salt and beat until smooth, 1 minute more. Pour the filling into the prepared crust, and place the pan in the oven.

4. Bake until the top of the cheesecake begins to brown, about 10 minutes. Reduce the oven temperature to 200°F and bake until the filling sets, about 1 hour more. Remove the pan from the oven and let it cool completely on a wire rack. Cover the pan with plastic wrap and chill at least 8 hours or overnight.

5. To serve, remove the collar of the springform pan, slice, and serve.

Lindy's, Reuben's, and the Cheesecake Story

IN THE LATE 1920S, when theater patrons left the showing of *Guys and Dolls*, they went to restaurants like Reuben's or Lindy's for a slice of cheesecake. Arnold Reuben of Reuben's was at a dinner party when he was served "cheese pie," made with cottage cheese. He begged the hostess for the recipe and tweaked it to contain cream cheese. His cheesecake with a cookie crust would win first prize at the 1929 World's Fair in Barcelona. Reuben's cheesecake was the talk of New York, and the world. Then Leo Linderman, the owner of Lindy's Restaurant, hired away the Reuben's baker. Both men competed for the best-loved cheesecake, and Lindy's became more famous. Stories have circulated on how the Lindy's cheesecake recipe was revealed. Some believe it was the *New York Herald Tribune* food writer Clementine Paddleford who asked Linderman for the recipe, and he called his pastry chef Paul Landry to Paddleford's table and instructed him to hand it over. Paddleford shared the recipe in her 1960 book, *How America Eats*. Others think it was *New York Times* food writer Craig Claiborne who got the real recipe from chef Guy Pascal in 1969 after Pascal had hired a Lindy's pastry chef to work at his Las Vegas restaurant and carefully watched him make cheesecake. Either way, Lindy's recipe has been in circulation for a while. And although the original contained a cookie crust, modern versions have gone the way of graham cracker, as baked by icon Junior's Cheesecake in Brooklyn.

BROWN DERBY GRAPEFRUIT CAKE

MAKES: 12 TO 16 SERVINGS
....
PREP: 50 TO 55 MINUTES
....
BAKE: 28 TO 32 MINUTES
....

CAKE

2 large fresh pink grapefruit

1½ cups sifted cake flour

¾ cup granulated sugar

1½ teaspoons baking powder

½ teaspoon salt

⅓ cup vegetable oil

3 large eggs, separated

½ teaspoon grated lemon zest

¼ teaspoon cream of tartar

GRAPEFRUIT FROSTING

8 ounces cream cheese, at room temperature

6 tablespoons unsalted butter

2½ cups confectioners' sugar, sifted

1 tablespoon grated grapefruit zest

½ teaspoon vanilla extract

GARNISH

Reserved grapefruit slices

Grated grapefruit zest

The Brown Derby restaurant was as much a film as it was a restaurant, a place where the Hollywood elite mingled with their colleagues, and where starstruck tourists in the 1920s came to catch a glimpse of someone famous. The most famous cake on the menu was the grapefruit chiffon, first baked by Harry Baker, the legendary creator of the chiffon who would later sell his formula to General Mills. This cake came about because one of the regulars—gossip columnist Louella Parsons—was overweight and on a diet. She insisted that owner Robert (Bob) Cobb come up with a less fattening cake, so Cobb asked Baker to design a grapefruit cake—"put grapefruit on something" is how the story goes. And that grapefruit cake, as well as the Cobb salad, are the 2 recipes that have preserved the Brown Derby legacy long after the restaurant closed. This chiffon cake recipe is adapted from the *Los Angeles Times Cookbook*, written in 1981. It is a beautiful cake, baked in a springform pan, split and layered with fresh grapefruit sections and a cream cheese frosting flavored with grated grapefruit zest.

1. For the cake, first wash and pat the grapefruit dry. Zest the grapefruit to yield 1 tablespoon finely grated grapefruit zest, and set this aside for the frosting. With a sharp knife, cut the skin and pith off the grapefruit. Hold the fruit over a bowl to catch the grapefruit juice. You will use this juice in the cake, and you need a scant ½ cup juice. If you don't collect enough juice, make up the difference in water. Set the juice aside for the cake. Meanwhile, carefully cut the peeled grapefruit into sections, removing the membrane and keeping the slices whole. Set the slices aside in a sieve to drain, and then pat them dry with paper towels. You will use these between layers and on top of the finished cake.

2. Place a rack in the center of the oven, and preheat the oven to 350°F. Set aside an ungreased 9″ springform pan.

3. Sift together the flour, sugar, baking powder, and salt into a large mixing bowl. Add the oil, egg yolks, and lemon zest. Add the reserved scant ½ cup grapefruit juice. Blend with an electric mixer on medium speed until smooth, about 1 minute. In a large bowl, place the egg whites and cream of tartar. Beat with clean beaters on high speed until the whites

continued

come to stiff peaks, but are not dry, 3 to 4 minutes. Fold the egg whites into the batter until just blended. Turn the batter into the springform pan, and place the pan in the oven. Bake until the cake is golden brown and the top springs back when lightly pressed in the center, 28 to 32 minutes. Remove the cake from the oven, and let it cool completely in the pan, about 1 hour.

4. Meanwhile, prepare the frosting. Place the cream cheese and butter in a large mixing bowl, and blend with an electric mixer on medium-low speed until creamy, about 30 seconds. Add the confectioners' sugar, the reserved grapefruit zest, and vanilla, and blend until smooth, 30 to 45 seconds more. Increase the speed to medium and beat until fluffy, about 1 minute. Set aside.

5. When the cake has cooled, run a knife around the edges, and remove the collar of the springform pan. Carefully slice the cake away from the bottom of the pan, and place the cake on a wire rack. With a serrated knife, carefully slice the cake crosswise to make 2 layers. Place the bottom layer on a cake plate, and spread it with about $1/2$ cup of frosting, spreading to the edges. Place about 12 or 13 sections of grapefruit on top of the frosting, placing the sections on in 2 concentric circles. Press down on the sections so they stick to the frosting. Flip the top cake layer over to expose the cut side, and spread this with about $1/3$ cup of frosting. Flip this layer frosting side down onto the grapefruit. With the remaining frosting, frost the top and sides of the cake using clean strokes. Arrange the remaining 7 to 8 slices of grapefruit in a spiral, or arrange as you wish, on top of the cake. If desired, sprinkle grapefruit zest on top. Slice and serve.

COLD OVEN POUND CAKE

MAKES: 12 TO 16 SERVINGS

PREP: 20 TO 25 MINUTES

BAKE: 1 HOUR 15 MINUTES

Vegetable shortening and flour for prepping the pan

3 cups all-purpose flour (see Cake Note)

½ teaspoon salt

5 large eggs

1 cup nonfat milk

1 to 2 teaspoons vanilla extract

1 cup (2 sticks) unsalted butter, at room temperature

½ cup vegetable shortening

2 cups granulated sugar

CAKE NOTE: Gloria Smiley uses Gold Medal all-purpose flour, so use your favorite all-purpose flour.

Gas ovens grew popular at the turn of the 20th century, and you didn't light the oven until you were ready to use it. It was a way to save money. Recipes like this would have made a fine selling point for those early porcelain-clad ovens, says Atlanta cooking teacher and culinary historian Gloria Smiley. Her favorite pound cake is this Cold Oven Pound Cake, a fine-textured cake with a crunchy crust. People baked cold oven pound cakes because they thought no cake should go into a hot oven. It would ruin the texture and rise more unevenly. These pound cakes remained popular up until the 1940s, says Smiley. Not only does this cake rise evenly, "but you get a nice crunchy crust on top of the cake. And the texture is incredible." Smiley, who was raised in Savannah, Georgia, where one of her grandfathers was a baker, says to gradually increase the temperature as the cake bakes. This process adds to the appeal of the pound cake with an interesting past—"in this day and age it is novel to not preheat the oven."

1. Place a rack in the center of the oven. Do not preheat the oven. Grease the bottom and sides of a 10″ tube pan lightly with vegetable shortening. Dust with flour, shake out the excess flour, and set the pan aside.

2. Place the flour in a medium-size bowl and stir in the salt. Set aside.

3. Separate the eggs, placing the yolks in a medium-size mixing bowl and the whites in a large mixing bowl. Set the whites aside. Whisk the milk and vanilla into the yolks until they are well blended, and set the mixture aside.

4. Beat the egg whites with an electric mixer on high speed until soft peaks form, about 2 minutes. Set them aside. Place the butter, shortening, and sugar in another large mixing bowl, and with the same beaters, beat on medium-high speed until the mixture is well creamed and lightened in color, beating for 2 minutes and scraping down the sides of the bowl once or twice. Reduce the mixer speed to low and blend in a third of the flour mixture until combined. Add half of the milk mixture until combined. Add another third of the flour, then the second half of the milk, then the last of the flour. The batter will be thick. Remove the beaters, and pour the beaten egg whites on top of the cake batter. Fold the

(photo on page 141)

whites into the batter with a rubber spatula, using an over-and-under folding method, just incorporating the whites.

5. Turn the batter into the prepared pan, and smooth the top. Place the pan on the center rack of the cold oven. Shut the door. Now heat the oven to 300°F.

6. Bake the cake for 45 minutes. Increase the oven temperature to 325°F. Bake until the cake is golden brown and a toothpick inserted in the center comes out clean, about 30 minutes. Remove the cake from the oven, and let the cake cool in the pan on a wire rack for 20 minutes. It will fall about an inch as it cools.

7. Run a knife around the edges, and invert the cake once and then again so it rests right side up on the rack. Let the cake cool for 1 hour before slicing. The crust will be delicate and crispy. This cake stores well up to a week at room temperature and can be frozen for up to 6 months.

THE MAYONNAISE CAKE

BACK WHEN MAYONNAISE was homemade and not store-bought, and when vegetable oil was known as "mayonnaise oil," clever cooks figured out how to make a cost-cutting cake called Mayonnaise Cake.

In 1927 newspaper columnist Martha Lee comments on the new modern table—its lace doilies are easier and less expensive to care for than heavy table linens of old. And Lee shares a new recipe she calls a Mayonnaise Cake. After you combine dates, nuts, sugar, flour, spices, and a little grated chocolate, you whip together an egg and ½ cup oil and pour this over the date and nut mixture, then bake.

Ten years later, store-bought mayonnaise is added to that cake batter. A reader shares a Mayonnaise Cake recipe in a Greeley, Colorado, newspaper contest, and it calls for ¾ cup mayonnaise. When the World War II rationing years began, cooks who had grown up during the Depression years knew instinctively how to make do and cut back, that cake would surface again.

LEAH CHASE'S BUTTER CAKE

MAKES: 12 TO 16 SERVINGS
PREP: 20 MINUTES
BAKE: 58 TO 62 MINUTES

Vegetable shortening or butter and flour for prepping the pan

1 pound (4 sticks) unsalted butter, chilled but soft to the touch

1 pound confectioners' sugar

6 large eggs, at room temperature (see Cake Note)

2⅔ cups cake flour, sifted once after measuring

½ teaspoon salt, if desired

2 teaspoons vanilla extract

CAKE NOTE: If the eggs are straight from the refrigerator, place them in a large bowl of warm water to come to room temperature.

THE CAKE'S ingredients are what you have on hand. The confectioners' sugar yields a soft and fine crumb, and when done, the crust is crisp and nut brown. And the aroma? Let's just say that as a guest, you would have a difficult time leaving the intoxicating, welcome scent of the home where this cake was baked.

When Leah Chase was a girl growing up in Madisonville, Louisiana, Christmas was a time of celebration and plenty, even if there was little money to spend. Her mother sewed stuffed animals out of scrap fabrics, stewed a chicken for dinner following midnight Mass, and baked cakes to share with neighbors who would visit before church. Leah is the famous chef-owner of Dooky Chase in New Orleans. The way she cooks and bakes is deeply rooted in the 1920s and '30s—years spent in the country. This pound cake recipe is what her family baked for Christmas visitors. It isn't fancy, but there is elegance in its simplicity.

1. Place a rack in the center of the oven, and preheat the oven to 350°F. Grease a 10″ tube pan with vegetable shortening or soft butter, and dust with flour. Shake out the excess flour and set the pan aside.

2. Cut the sticks of butter into 6 to 8 tablespoons each, and place all the butter in the bowl of an electric mixer. Beat on medium-high until the butter is in one mass, 1 minute. Stop the mixer and add the confectioners' sugar. Drape a kitchen towel over the top of the mixer so you don't get showered with sugar. Start on low speed and blend the sugar to incorporate. Then increase the speed to medium and let the mixture beat until creamy, 2 to 3 minutes.

3. Crack 1 egg and add to the butter mixture, beating on medium-low until blended. Add another egg, beating again. Stop the machine after every 2 eggs are added, and scrape down the sides of the bowl with a rubber spatula. Repeat with the remaining eggs.

4. With the machine off, add the flour to the mixture. Add salt, if desired. Mix on low speed to incorporate the flour, 30 seconds. Add the vanilla, and blend on low speed for 15 seconds more.

5. Scrape down the sides of the bowl with the spatula, and turn the batter into the prepared pan, smoothing the top. Place the pan in the oven.

6. Bake until the cake is well browned and the center springs back to the touch, 58 to 62 minutes. A toothpick inserted should come out clean. Remove the cake from the oven, and let it cool in the pan for 20 minutes. Then run a knife around the edges, shake the pan gently to loosen the cake, and turn it out once and then again onto a wire rack to cool right side up. Let cool for 30 minutes to 1 hour before slicing.

MISS SADIE'S SPICE MERINGUE CAKE

MAKES: 12 TO 16 SERVINGS
....
PREP: 25 TO 30 MINUTES
....
BAKE: 55 TO 60 MINUTES
....

Margarine and flour for prepping the pan

2¼ cups all-purpose flour

1 teaspoon baking powder

1 teaspoon baking soda

1 teaspoon ground cinnamon

1 teaspoon ground cloves

1 teaspoon salt

1 cup unsalted margarine, at room temperature (see Cake Note)

4 cups light brown sugar, loosely packed, divided use

4 large eggs, at room temperature (reserving 2 egg whites)

2 teaspoons vanilla extract

1 cup buttermilk, at room temperature

2 large egg whites, at room temperature

½ teaspoon cream of tartar

1 cup coarsely chopped pecans

CAKE NOTE: Margarine was often used instead of butter in the 1930s. You may substitute butter in this recipe.

In the resourceful 1930s, turning egg whites into a meringue was a thrifty stroke of genius. Meringues covered ice cream (Baked Alaska) and every flavor of pie and were turned into cookies, as well as being a handy topping for cake. This simple Spice Meringue Cake, as these cakes were called in the '30s, was what was served to family at home. The meringue went right on top of the batter before the cake went into the oven, and the cake emerged with a beautiful and crunchy topping. Historian Jan Longone says in the 1930s, cooks figured out a way to reserve a few whites for the meringue, thus no need for expensive frosting. Adding the brown sugar to the meringue made the cake a little different and was the creation of Sadie Le Sueur (Miss Sadie), in charge of ladies' luncheons at the Centennial Club in Nashville beginning in 1938. I have adapted her recipe slightly to make it fit a modern 13″ × 9″ pan.

1. Place a rack in the center of the oven, and preheat the oven to 325°F. Lightly grease and flour a 13″ × 9″ metal pan. Shake out the excess flour, and set the pan aside.

2. Sift together the flour, baking powder, baking soda, cinnamon, cloves, and salt into a medium-size bowl. Set aside.

3. Place the margarine in a large mixing bowl, and blend with an electric mixer on medium speed until soft, about 30 seconds. Add 2 cups of the brown sugar; beat to combine until creamy, 1 to 2 minutes. Add 2 whole eggs and 2 yolks, at one time, beating for 15 seconds on medium speed or until combined. Add the vanilla. Alternately add the reserved dry ingredients and the buttermilk, beginning and ending with the dry ingredients. Spread the batter evenly into the pan, and set aside.

4. Place 4 egg whites in a large mixing bowl. Add the cream of tartar, and beat with clean beaters on high speed, slowly adding 2 cups of the brown sugar, until stiff and glossy, 4 to 5 minutes. Spread the meringue evenly over the batter with a rubber spatula. Sprinkle with the pecans. Place the pan in the oven.

5. Bake until the meringue is golden brown (be careful not to let the pecans burn) and a toothpick inserted in the center comes out clean, 55 to 60 minutes. Remove the pan from the oven, and place on a wire rack to cool for 15 minutes. Cut into squares and serve warm.

EDITH WARNER'S CHOCOLATE LOAF CAKE

MAKES: 10 TO 12 SERVINGS

PREP: 30 MINUTES

BAKE: 1 HOUR 15 MINUTES

CAKE

Butter and flour for prepping the pan

1 cup all-purpose flour

1¼ teaspoons baking powder

½ teaspoon salt

1½ ounces unsweetened chocolate, chopped

3 tablespoons unsalted butter

1 cup granulated sugar

½ cup whole milk

3 large eggs

ICING

1¼ cups confectioners' sugar

2 heaping tablespoons unsweetened cocoa powder

Pinch of salt

2 tablespoons unsalted butter, melted

2 tablespoons brewed coffee

HIGH-ALTITUDE TIP: Ironically, in the high elevations of New Mexico, this cake cannot be successfully baked in a loaf pan because it will not rise. You need to decrease the baking powder to 1 teaspoon, increase the milk by 1 tablespoon, and bake the cake in a 9" round pan if baking at high altitude.

(photo on page 140)

Edith Warner was a Philadelphia schoolteacher who yearned for the peace and wide-open space of the West. She was 30 years old when she up and left Philadelphia and settled in Los Alamos, New Mexico. It was 1922, and Edith loved the natural beauty of the Southwest. She befriended the nearby Pueblo Indians and became caretaker of a train depot along the Rio Grande, a place known as Otowi Bridge. Her adobe tearoom was a refuge for friends and visitors, and here Edith shared tea and slices of her blissful chocolate cake with fudge frosting. When the United States entered World War II and the Manhattan Project came to Los Alamos, Edith's idyllic world was forever changed, but her tearoom became a peaceful, family sort of refuge for Robert Oppenheimer, Enrico Fermi, and Niels Bohr, fathers of the atom bomb. They came for dinner, cake, and conversation. This is the chocolate cake with satiny chocolate-coffee icing that fed the souls of the men who built the first atom bomb. It is an incredibly versatile chocolate cake that can be baked in a loaf or square pan. Warner's handwritten recipe for "Chocolate Cake Otowi Bridge" was found in a journal of Joan Neary, who received the journal and recipe as a gift from Warner.

1. Place a rack in the center of the oven, and preheat the oven to 250°F. Lightly grease and flour a 9″ × 5″ loaf pan, and shake out the excess flour. Set the pan aside.

2. For the cake, sift together the flour, baking powder, and salt, and set aside. Place the chocolate and butter in a small saucepan and melt, stirring constantly, over low heat. Pour the sugar into a mixing bowl and pour the melted chocolate and butter over it. Blend with an electric mixer on low speed until the mixture is combined but still grainy, 30 to 45 seconds, or by hand for 1 to 2 minutes. Turn off the mixer, add a third of the flour mixture and half of the milk, blend on low speed to combine, then add another third of the flour, then the remaining milk, and end with the rest of the flour mixture, blending or stirring by hand until just combined. Stop the mixer and scrape down the sides of the bowl with a rubber spatula. Add the eggs, and beat on medium until the batter increases in volume, 1 minute more. Spoon the batter into the prepared pan and place the pan in the oven.

3. Bake for 15 minutes. Then without removing the pan from the oven, increase the temperature to 275°F. Bake for 15 minutes. Increase the oven temperature to 300°F, and bake for 45 minutes more, or until the top is firm when lightly pressed with a finger. Remove the pan from the oven to a wire rack to cool for 20 minutes. Run a knife around the edges of the pan to loosen the cake. Turn it out on the rack to cool completely, right side up, 40 to 45 minutes.

4. For the icing, place the confectioners' sugar, cocoa, and salt in a medium-size mixing bowl, and whisk to combine. Whisk in the melted butter and coffee until the icing is spreadable. Spread the icing over the top and down the sides of the cake. Slice and serve.

BAKING VICTORY CAKES

AFTER AMERICA ENTERED World War II, sugar was the first food to be rationed. US sugar imports from the Philippines were cut off, and cargo ships that might have shipped Hawaiian sugar to the mainland were needed for military uses. So in the spring of 1942, with a third of the nation's supply of sugar reduced, the Office of Price Administration (OPA) issued War Ration Book One, containing stamps used to purchase sugar. The OPA wanted to prevent sugar hoarding and price hiking, so you could only purchase a set amount of sugar with one of your allotted stamps.

Victory Cakes became the cake you baked out of sacrifice, without precious granulated sugar. Bakeries made them, too, advertising that the cakes were made with corn syrup to "keep the lid on the sugar jar." The words "victory cake" were mentioned in World War I,

but the real American Victory Cake was a World War II cake made with corn syrup and often vegetable shortening instead of butter. By today's standards, these cakes might seem subpar, but in the 1940s they were tangible signs that you were doing your part to boost the war effort and celebrate, too.

Victory Cake fairs were staged on lawns, porches, and storefronts across the country. Cooks baked their best "sugar-shy" cakes. Visitors to the patriotic fairs bought war stamps at the door and pasted them into the stamp book next to the cake they deemed best. The winner often received war bonds as a prize.

An interesting note is that at the end of World War II, Admiral William Halsey cut a special Victory Cake with a bayonet on board the USS *Missouri*, a battleship that helped win the war. It is not certain whether that cake was baked with corn syrup or granulated sugar. But it was obviously quite a grand Victory Cake celebration. Sugar rationing continued for 2 more years, or until American sugar supplies returned to normal.

BROOKLYN BLACKOUT CAKE

MAKES: 12 TO 16 SERVINGS
PREP: 1½ TO 2 HOURS
BAKE: 30 TO 35 MINUTES

FILLING

⅔ cup granulated sugar

2 tablespoons cornstarch

¼ teaspoon salt

1½ cups whole milk

3 ounces unsweetened chocolate, chopped

1 teaspoon vanilla extract

CAKE

Butter and flour for prepping the pans

¾ cup unsweetened cocoa powder

1 cup whole milk

½ cup (1 stick) unsalted butter, at room temperature

¼ cup vegetable shortening

2 cups granulated sugar

3 large eggs, at room temperature

2 teaspoons vanilla extract

2¼ cups cake flour

2 teaspoons baking powder

½ teaspoon salt

FROSTING

12 ounces (about 2 cups) semisweet chocolate

¾ cup (1½ sticks) unsalted butter, cut into tablespoons

½ cup hot tap water

1 tablespoon light corn syrup

1 tablespoon vanilla extract

The Brooklyn Blackout Cake is more than a cake. It is a legendary bakery cake that lives on in memory. And it is a chocolate cake named for the mandatory blackouts in Brooklyn during World War II that protected the battleship and aircraft carrier assembly, and the 71,000 workers, at the Brooklyn Navy Yard. Near the Yard was a bakery named Ebinger's, where a 3-layer dark chocolate cake filled with chocolate custardy pudding, frosted with chocolate icing, and packed with chocolate cake crumbs was baked. It was a visual blackout, and Ebinger's named its cake the Blackout Cake, a name that stuck for a chocolate cake made in the war years when chocolate was hard to find and sugar rationed. Ebinger's closed in 1972. But the cake lives on in memory and is baked in new variations today at bakeries like Brooklyn's Ovenly, where it contains Black Chocolate Stout, and at other bakeries selling smaller bites of history—blackout cupcakes. But there were other blackout cakes in America—in Iowa and the Midwest—as "blackout" seemed to describe any chocolate cake, whether the layers were dark or light. Chocolate cakes continued to be called "blackout" after World War II, referring to power outages and other modern uses of the term. But no cake has been as long-lasting and beloved as Ebinger's, sold in the signature pale green boxes with brown cross-hatch pattern, and now re-created in recipe form for baking at home. The following recipe is adapted from 2 cookbooks—the *Brooklyn Cookbook* and Molly O'Neill's *New York Cookbook*.

1. For the filling, place the sugar, cornstarch, and salt in a small heavy saucepan, and stir to combine. Gradually whisk in the milk. Fold in the chocolate, and place the pan over medium-high heat, stirring constantly until the mixture bubbles up and thickens, 8 to 10 minutes. Remove the pan from the heat, and stir in the vanilla. Let the filling cool to room temperature, then place in a glass bowl, cover with plastic wrap, and chill until ready to assemble the cake.

2. For the cake, place a rack in the center of the oven, and preheat the oven to 350°F. Grease and flour two 9″ cake pans, shake out the excess flour, and set the pans aside.

3. Place the cocoa in a medium-size bowl. Pour some of the milk—about ½ cup—into the cocoa, and stir to make a paste. Whisk in the remaining

continued

milk until the mixture is smooth. Set aside. In a large mixing bowl, combine the butter, shortening, and sugar, and blend with an electric mixer on medium speed until light and creamed, 1 minute. Add the eggs and vanilla and blend on medium-high until smooth and fluffy, 1 minute more.

4. Sift together the flour, baking powder, and salt in a small bowl. Add these dry ingredients to the batter alternately with the cocoa, beginning and ending with the dry ingredients. Beat until just combined. Scrape down the sides of the bowl with a rubber spatula and stir the batter until smooth. Divide the batter between the 2 pans, and place the pans in the oven.

5. Bake until the cake just pulls away from the sides of the pans, 30 to 35 minutes. Remove the pans to a wire rack to cool 10 minutes. Run a knife around the edges of the pan, give the pans a gentle shake, and invert them once and then again to cool completely right side up, about 45 minutes.

6. Meanwhile, make the frosting. Place the chocolate in the top pan insert of a double boiler. Place this pan over an inch of boiling water in the bottom of the double boiler over medium heat. Whisk until the chocolate melts. Remove the pan insert, and whisk in the butter, a little at a time. Place back over the simmering water if needed to melt the butter. Whisk in the hot water, corn syrup, and vanilla. Place the pan insert in a large mixing bowl filled with ice. Beat with an electric mixer on medium-high speed until the frosting is thickened and spreadable, 5 to 8 minutes. Set the frosting aside.

7. To assemble the cake, slice the cake layers in half crosswise using a long serrated knife. You will have 4 layers. Crumble 1 layer with your fingers into crumbs that will cover the cake. Place these in a small bowl and set aside. Remove the filling from the refrigerator. Place 1 cake layer on a cake platter and spread half of the filling over the top of it, spreading to ½″ from the edge. Place a second layer on top, and repeat with the remaining filling. Place on the top layer. If needed, insert 5 or 6 long toothpicks down into the cake from the top to stabilize it. Place the cake in the refrigerator to chill for 15 minutes.

8. Remove the cake from the refrigerator, and frost the top and sides of the cake with smooth strokes. Press the cake crumbs onto the sides of the cake first, then pile the remaining crumbs on top of the cake. Slice and serve.

ICEBOX CAKE

THE WORDS "icebox cake" conjure a bygone era of 1950s bridge club luncheons where a novel do-ahead dessert was assembled ahead of time, refrigerated, and ready when you were. It wasn't a cake in the sense that it was baked, but it was very much cakelike in appearance.

But the cake dates back to the 1920s and earlier, named after the "icebox," an insulated compartment filled with ice and the forerunner to our modern home refrigerators. Even as iceboxes phased out and refrigerators phased in, the term "icebox" was still used to describe a refrigerator, and "icebox cakes" stayed in vogue, too. They were a symbol of 1930s preparedness, the idea that you are ready for anything, even if it means unannounced relatives staying over for dinner and dessert.

Icebox cakes are made by layering sponge cake, ladyfingers, or thin chocolate wafers with whipped cream, custard, or pudding in a pan or bowl until it is full. Cover and chill until firm.

The first American icebox cakes were mentioned in newspaper articles before they were shared in cookbooks. A 1919 *Houston Post* chocolate mousse icebox cake recipe took 12 hours to "harden" before it was stiff enough to slice. By the 1920s, they were the go-to cake and featured in *McCall's* magazine in 1926.

MRS. HARVEY'S
WHITE FRUITCAKE

MAKES: 5 POUNDS OF FRUITCAKE

PREP: 45 TO 50 MINUTES

**BAKE: 1¾ TO 2 HOURS FOR
LOAVES; 2 HOURS 20 MINUTES
FOR TUBE PAN**

Butter or shortening and parchment
paper for prepping the pans

4 cups pecan halves

1 pound candied cherries (see Cake
Notes)

1 pound candied pineapple

1¾ cups all-purpose flour, divided use

1 cup (2 sticks) lightly salted butter, at
room temperature

1 cup granulated sugar

5 large eggs

½ teaspoon baking powder

2 tablespoons vanilla extract

1 tablespoon pure lemon extract

Bourbon for brushing the baked loaves

CAKE NOTES: Candied cherries
and pineapple are found more easily in
late November and early December.
You can substitute dried, sugared
pineapple for the candied pineapple.
And while Mrs. Harvey seasoned her
fruitcake with vanilla and lemon
extracts, you can use up to ¼ cup
bourbon or rum instead.

When World War II called American men to fight, the women at home stayed in touch by writing letters and shipping food. Lucile Plowden Harvey of Tampa baked fruitcake, and it is said she shipped her famous fruitcakes to servicemen in 13 foreign countries. Even after the war, she baked fruitcake, winning a *Tampa Tribune* recipe contest for the recipe known as the "fruitcake people like to eat" in 1956. And each year, right after Thanksgiving, the newspaper repeats that recipe. According to her daughter-in-law Betty Harvey of Bradenton, people bake fruitcake at Thanksgiving to get ready for the upcoming holidays. Even people who think they don't like fruitcake like Mrs. Harvey's fruitcake recipe, she said. "People love that cake so much." While the cake doesn't contain a smidgen of alcohol, Mrs. Harvey brushed her baked cakes with bourbon, using a special brush. And she wrapped her loaves in aluminum foil, not too tightly, and placed them in a chest of drawers to wait until Christmas. When Mrs. Harvey died, she left Betty all her dried fruit and nuts for baking fruitcake. Now Betty bakes 4 cakes each year, 1 to send to her sister in Atlanta, 1 for her daughter, and 2 to serve at Thanksgiving and Christmas.

1. Place a rack in the center of the oven. Select either a 10″ tube pan or two 9″ loaf pans for baking. Grease the bottom of the pans, and line the bottom with parchment paper or waxed paper. Grease again, and set aside.

2. Chop the pecans, cherries, and pineapple into medium-size pieces. Toss with ¼ cup of the flour in a large bowl. Set aside.

3. Place the butter and sugar in a large bowl, and beat with an electric mixer on medium speed until light and creamy, about 1 minute. Add the eggs, one at a time, beating after each addition until smooth. Sift together the remaining 1½ cups flour and the baking powder, and stir these dry ingredients into the batter along with the extracts. Fold in the reserved fruit and nut mixture. Pour the batter into the prepared pans. Place the pans in a cold oven.

4. Set the oven temperature to 250°F. Bake for about 2 hours 20 minutes for the tube pan and 1¾ to 2 hours for the loaf pans. To test for doneness, stick a long toothpick in the center of the cake. It should come out clean.

continued

5. Let the fruitcake cool in the pan, about 30 minutes for the loaves and about 1 hour for the tube pan. Run a knife around the edges of the pan, give the pan a gentle shake, and turn the cake out onto a wire rack. Brush the top of the cake liberally with bourbon. Wrap the cake in clean cheesecloth and then aluminum foil for storage. These cakes keep for several weeks at room temperature. Brush with more bourbon every week during storage.

BAKING WITH ALCOHOL

UP UNTIL THE 1900s, America was awash in alcohol. Spirits were inexpensive, and immigrants turned corn and rye into the first American whiskeys. By 1830, according to *Time* magazine, the average American was drinking the equivalent of 1.7 bottles of hard liquor a week.

Alcohol was used as a preservative in cooking, especially in mincemeat, and it was also used as a flavoring in pound cakes, Queen Cakes, Washington Cakes, fruitcakes, plum cakes, and great cakes of all types. But in 1826, the temperance movements began, and one advocate was Catherine Beecher, author of *A Treatise on Domestic Economy* in 1841 and *Miss Beecher's Domestic Receipt Book* in 1846. She wove temperance talk into her prose focused on homemaking. Maine banned the sale of alcohol in 1851, and in 1869 the Prohibition Party was founded.

Beecher broke temperance cooks into three camps—those who consider alcohol a sin, those who do not advocate alcohol, and those who shun alcohol for drinking but find nothing wrong with cooking with it or using it medicinally, like herself. She used alcohol in her recipes.

Prohibition, from 1920 to 1933, was America's long-fought answer to public drunkenness, and cooks who needed to find alcohol for a cake recipe often received a prescription for it from their pharmacist, or they had an underground source. Some recipes themselves went underground during Prohibition because without alcohol as an ingredient, they were not used and forgotten.

1946 *to* 1962

Tupperware, Bake-Offs,®
& a New Domesticity

～～

CAKES FLOURISHED in the peaceful, affluent post–World War II America, growing sweeter, lighter, and more decorative than ever before. In contrast to the previous decades, when cakes were baked with less sugar, no frosting, and without eggs and butter, these new cakes were baked to celebrate the good times.

Experiencing the largest baby boom in history, America's Greatest Generation lived in the suburbs, drove station wagons, took vacations on new interstate highways, hosted Tupperware parties, and fell in love with television.

Women who saw cake baking as an extension of their femininity and took on the challenge of difficult recipes to please family and friends created the decorated white birthday cake, the German chocolate cake, the red velvet cake, and the caramel cake. In classic Donna Reed style, donning heels and a ruffled apron, they baked cakes for picnics, garden parties, the Junior League, and bridge luncheons. And their children baked small cakes in Easy-Bake Ovens.

"Cake was love, femininity, happiness, and a man around the house," according to historian Laura Shapiro in her book *Something from the Oven*. In 1950

McCall's became the first women's magazine to place a cake on its cover.

But working women baked cakes, too. Inspired by Rosie the Riveter, 6 million American women had worked in the war effort, and afterward many chose to be employed outside the home. As company clerks and salesladies behind a counter, they experienced a new freedom, independence, and paycheck that were the quiet beginnings of the women's movement, which would culminate in the 1960s.

Food companies sensed a market directed at the busy working woman who needed the convenience of a cake mix, microwave, and TV dinner. And Shapiro says, cakes fit right in. "You could come home as a working girl and make a cake and decorate it with peppermint and feel just as feminine as women who didn't work."

And no American had more influence on the way

working women and homemakers baked after World War II than Betty Crocker. Betty spoke to everyone because she was the best of everyone—smart, attractive, and in charge. She suggested we bake cakes for all occasions. In 1945 *Fortune* magazine named Betty Crocker the second most popular woman in America, following Eleanor Roosevelt, in spite of the fact that Betty was a fictional character created by General Mills to boost slipping flour sales. Her first cake mix was sold in 1947, and the legendary *Betty Crocker's Picture Cook Book,* published in 1950, sold 1 million copies the first year.

While cake mixes had been developed during the war, they wouldn't become a fixture in the home pantry until the end of the 1950s. Cake mixes would evolve, dropping the powdered eggs in favor of the addition of fresh eggs to create a from-scratch experience the earlier mixes lacked. And it wasn't long before cooks lent their creative hand to the mixes, adding Jell-O to create colorful "poke" cakes and plenty of alcohol to concoct the famed Bacardí Rum Cake and other boozy confections.

This was the heyday of the 13" × 9" rectangular pan, a pan used in the late 1930s but made popular by the Rice Krispies squares recipe of 1948. Cakes baked in it didn't need assembly and served a crowd, and you could take The Wacky Cake (page 187), the Fruit Cocktail Cake (page 190), or a Cherry Upside-Down Cake (page 215) with you. Americans on the go gravitated toward simple-to-prepare recipes like an apple cake called Ozark Pudding, which would later be called the Huguenot Torte (page 181) in the 1950 *Charleston Receipts,* the oldest Junior League cookbook still in circulation. Junior League cookbooks were hugely popular and became a way for regional recipes to be shared with the rest of America.

Postwar also brought the debut of the chiffon cake, the brainchild of insurance salesman turned pastry cook Harry Baker, who baked for the Hollywood stars and sold his chiffon formula to General Mills in 1948. The new cake of the century, it was America's "greatest

cake," says Rose Levy Beranbaum, author of *The Cake Bible,* not only because "it was truly invented in America, but also because it has such a fantastic texture."

In the 1950s and early '60s, great cakes flowed out of Texas like crude oil and aspiring politicians. The German chocolate, red velvet, and Hershey bar cakes are thought to have beginnings in Texas and neighboring Oklahoma. Helen Corbitt of the Neiman Marcus Zodiac Room transformed rough-and-tumble Texas cowboy fare into something more civilized. Her popovers as well as her coffee-flavored angel food cake were a new type of Texas baking. And Texas fare would benefit from the exposure of Lyndon Johnson's time in the White House, when First Lady Lady Bird's beautification luncheons featured Helen Corbitt's signature flowerpot cakes.

But no presidency affected American food like the short-lived Kennedy administration, when a French chef entered the White House kitchen in 1961. It helped usher in a shift to a French style of baking cakes, and Dione Lucas's near flourless Chocolate Roulade (page 211) was the catalyst behind the popular roulades of the 1970s and the chocolate molten cakes that would come later.

America enjoyed a peaceful time to bake cakes, whether from scratch or from a mix. The end of the 1960s brought new thoughts and experimentation, and that included those in the kitchen.

ORANGE CHIFFON CAKE

MAKES: 12 TO 16 SERVINGS

PREP: 35 TO 40 MINUTES

BAKE: 63 TO 65 MINUTES

2 medium-size lemons

2 large oranges

2 cups sifted all-purpose flour

1½ cups granulated sugar

1 tablespoon baking powder

½ teaspoon salt

½ cup vegetable oil

7 large eggs, separated, at room temperature

½ teaspoon cream of tartar

> **ORANGE GLAZE:** *Place 1 cup confectioners' sugar in a small bowl and whisk in 2 tablespoons orange juice. When smooth, spoon the glaze over the top of the cooled cake. If desired, sprinkle a little confectioners' sugar on top.*

Beauty of the Chiffon

The real beauty of a chiffon cake is that it is light like an angel cake, moist from the vegetable oil and egg yolks, and quick to prepare. It was Harry Baker's idea to create a cake that is the best of these worlds—light, moist, and fast. He carefully whisked the oil into the batter to make sure the batter was thickened properly before baking. This recipe is a little simpler. You place the oil, orange juice, egg yolks, and zest in the bowl with the dry ingredients and then mix.

One of the most authentically American cakes, a cake that didn't originate in Europe and doesn't date back to Colonial times, is the chiffon. It was created by Harry Baker, an insurance salesman and hobby baker who moved to Los Angeles in the 1920s and baked cakes for restaurants such as the Brown Derby in Hollywood. Baker's chiffon cake had a secret ingredient—vegetable oil. Baker closely guarded that secret, removing his garbage and disposing of it himself so no curious food sleuths might discover what made his cakes so moist. Baker eventually sold his recipe to General Mills in 1948, and the cake was introduced as "the cake discovery of the century." It was not only a discovery but it opened the door to oil substituting for butter in all sorts of cakes. Rose Levy Beranbaum, author of *The Cake Bible,* calls the chiffon America's "greatest cake." Here is the orange chiffon, adapted slightly from Maida Heatter.

1. Wash and dry the lemons and oranges. Grate the lemons to yield 1 tablespoon zest. Reserve lemons for another use. Grate the oranges to yield 3 tablespoons zest. Cut the oranges in half and juice to yield ¾ cup. Set zests and juice aside.

2. Place a rack in the center of the oven, and preheat the oven to 325°F. Set aside an ungreased 10″ tube pan.

3. Place the flour, sugar, baking powder, and salt in a large mixing bowl, and stir to combine. Make a well in the middle of the dry ingredients. Add in the following order, without mixing, the oil, egg yolks (reserve the whites), the lemon and orange zest, and the orange juice. With a strong wire whisk, beat until smooth, about 1 minute. Set aside.

4. In a large mixing bowl, beat the egg whites and cream of tartar with an electric mixer on high speed until a stiff peak holds when the beater is raised, 3 to 4 minutes. In 3 additions, fold about three-quarters of the yolk mixture into the whites. Next fold the whites into the remaining yolk mixture. Gently pour the batter into the prepared pan.

5. Bake for 55 minutes at 325°F. Then increase the temperature to 350°F and bake for an additional 8 to 10 minutes. Remove the cake from the oven, and immediately hang the pan upside down over the neck of a bottle or a funnel, so that it is cooling upside down for 1 hour. With a sharp knife, trim the cake away from the edges of the pan. Give the pan a gentle shake, and invert the cake once and then again onto a serving plate. If desired, drizzle with Orange Glaze.

HUGUENOT TORTE

MAKES: 6 TO 8 SERVINGS

PREP: 15 MINUTES

BAKE: 30 TO 35 MINUTES

Butter and flour for prepping the pan

1 cup pecans

2 tablespoons plus ¾ cup granulated sugar, divided use

2 large eggs

¼ cup all-purpose flour

2 teaspoons baking powder

¼ teaspoon salt

1 medium tart apple, peeled and finely chopped, about 1 cup

1 cup unsweetened whipped cream for topping

Ozark Pudding

Bess Truman's favorite Ozark Pudding recipe, appearing in the *Congressional Club Cook Book,* contained black walnuts, which grew wild in northwest Arkansas and Missouri. The Ozarks were populated with German settlers. The Ozark Pudding was more of a torte than a pudding, and it is similar to the fruit and ground nut tortes of Germany.

A cross between a pecan pie and a macaroon, with the addition of apples, this might seem to be the quintessential Southern coastal dessert. And for generations, the families of Charleston, South Carolina, proudly thought this torte was their own, brought on the boat with the first French Huguenots who fled to Charleston in the 17th century for religious freedom, right? Wrong. . . . It was centuries later that a South Carolina food writer and historian, John Martin Taylor, sought out the woman who placed the first Huguenot Torte recipe in the venerable *Charleston Receipts* cookbook. And who first shared the recipe with the other ladies at the St. Philips Episcopal Tearoom and who baked this cake for the Huguenot Tavern in Charleston. The recipe, divulged its creator Evelyn Anderson Florance, didn't date back to the Huguenots. It was a dessert she'd enjoyed on vacation and couldn't wait to get home and try out in her own kitchen. It was most likely an Ozark Pudding, what Mrs. S. R. Dull shared as Apple Torte in her 1928 book, *Southern Cooking.* And what Bess Truman shared in the 1948 *Congressional Club Cook Book.* Whether made in Charleston, the Ozarks, or any city on the map, enjoy.

1. Place a rack in the center of the oven, and preheat the oven to 350°F. Lightly grease and flour a 9″ springform pan. Shake out the excess flour, and set the pan aside.

2. Place the pecans and 2 tablespoons of sugar in a food processor fitted with a steel blade (or finely chop the pecans by hand, then combine with the sugar). Pulse 3 or 4 times so that the pecans are finely minced and nearly ground. Set aside.

3. Place the eggs in a large mixing bowl, and whisk by hand or beat with an electric mixer on high speed until they double in volume. Reduce the mixer speed to medium, and gradually beat in ³⁄₄ cup sugar until the eggs are thick and pale yellow in color. Scatter the pecans over the top of the eggs. Combine the flour with the baking powder and salt, and sprinkle this over the pecans. Add the chopped apple. Fold the ingredients together lightly with a rubber spatula, and turn the batter into the prepared pan.

4. Place the pan in the oven, and bake until the torte is golden and just pulls away from the sides of the pan, 30 to 35 minutes. Remove the pan from the oven and cool for 20 minutes. Unfasten the collar of the pan, and remove. Slice the torte and serve with the whipped cream.

BETTY CROCKER

TO AMERICANS it did not matter that Betty Crocker was a fictional character who advised them how to bake cake and get dinner on the table. They revered her as much as a First Lady and gathered around the radio to listen to her. To many, she *was* America's First Lady of food. In 1945 *Fortune* magazine named Betty Crocker the second most popular woman in America, following Eleanor Roosevelt.

Betty was born out of a promotional campaign. The Washburn Crosby Company, the maker of Gold Medal flour and the forerunner of General Mills, placed a puzzle in the *Saturday Evening Post* in 1921 and promised readers who solved the puzzle a pincushion shaped like a flour sack. Not only did thousands of people solve the puzzle successfully, but they included baking questions with their entries. The advertising department convinced executives to create a female person to reply to those questions. That woman would be Betty Crocker.

"Betty" was a popular name of the time. "Crocker" was the surname of the recently retired company director, William G. Crocker. And the signature was a result of an informal contest between female employees. But behind the scenes, Marjorie Child Husted, a University of Minnesota home economics grad, quietly built the Betty Crocker brand and wrote her scripts when radio brought Betty into the home in the 1930s and '40s.

Proving to be more than a signature and a voice, Betty "reached a huge swath of people, especially married women cooking for families who needed advice," says historian Laura Shapiro. She was the new baking authority, appealing to homemakers across the land who put their trust in her. And she was also a working woman, in charge of the test kitchens and a "fount of knowledge." The first portrait of Betty in 1936 showed a motherly but buttoned-up woman. By contrast, her fifth portrait in 1972 showed Betty resembling the popular actress of the time, Mary Tyler Moore, appearing attractive and confident. Many more portraits would follow, but always Betty wore her signature white blouse and red jacket.

Betty Crocker's Picture Cook Book was published in 1950 and sold 1 million copies the first year. The more popular Betty Crocker cake recipes through the years have been her devil's food, angel food, chiffon, and the Daffodil Cake, an angel food cake batter divided into two parts. One part stays white, and to the other you add beaten egg yolks, making it yellow. You spoon the batters alternately into a tube pan, and when it bakes and you slice it, this popular Easter cake looks just like the springtime flower. Which is how Betty Crocker would like it.

JUNIOR LEAGUE COOKBOOKS

THE HUGUENOT TORTE (page 181) was first baked by many Americans in 1950 after it was published in one of the best-known Junior League cookbooks, *Charleston Receipts*. That cookbook wasn't the first Junior League book—the first was from Augusta, Georgia, in 1940 and called *Recipes from a Southern Kitchen*. But the *Charleston Receipts* would be the most successful of the League cookbooks, and it is still in print.

Junior League cookbooks have helped share regional cakes and other recipes with Americans in other parts of the country. And they have been key fund-raising tools to raise money to benefit local communities.

The Junior League itself was founded on service in 1901 by Mary Harriman, a young New York socialite who gathered 80 like-minded women to help the new immigrants living on Manhattan's Lower East Side. Her friend Eleanor Roosevelt would be inspired to join the League and volunteer at New York's Rivington Street Settlement House.

CAKE CARRIERS, SAVING A CAKE, AND TUPPERWARE

AUTOMOBILE TRAVEL gave Americans incentive to take a cake with them. Outings, picnics, and rides to the country for family reunions were all good reasons to bake and go.

In the 1920s, cooks were advised to be frugal and economical in planning their movable feasts. Save egg boxes, said Wanda Barton in her column "Home-Making Helps" of 1923. "They are fine for carrying boiled or deviled eggs. By removing the compartments they are good for sandwich and cut-cake carriers."

And even into the early 1940s, practical cooks were inventing ways to make their own carriers. In March 1941, an East Liverpool, Ohio, cook creates the simple carrier with a deep box and lid. Place the cake on the lid, and top it with the box over the cake. "You will have no difficulty removing the cake from the box."

But in the early 1930s, shiny aluminum and painted enamel-over-metal carriers were all the rage. They came with locking covers, with handles, and with elaborate floral decorations. And soon, they were recognized for their ability to take a cake with you and also store the cake at home.

By 1936 there were square cake carriers, and a year later a combination carrier with room for one cake and one pie. In hardware as well as department stores, cake carriers were the must-have for busy cooks. Every household seemed to own one.

The metal carrier and saver would be replaced by plastic in the 1940s, and not just any plastic, but Tupperware, billed as "the miracle plastic."

Inspired by the tight seal of a paint can lid, Earl Tupper, a home inventor and chemist, purified and molded polyethylene into a plastic bowl with a "burp." Tupper was raised on a New England farm and lived outside Boston. He established Tupper Plastics in 1939 and introduced the Tupperware brand 10 years later. But the products didn't sell well in stores.

Then Tupper met Brownie Wise, a young mother and self-taught saleswoman who had sold Stanley Home Products through home parties and said she could do the same with Tupperware. She became vice president of sales, and the rest really is history.

Wise trained and organized women for "patio parties," where sellers invited friends and neighbors over for food and a good time. Wise motivated sellers with incentives of minks, home appliances, and fancy vacations and held annual fun-filled glitzy meetings called Jubilees.

The timing was perfect. Postwar America was mobile, casual, and moving to the suburbs. They were barbecuing in the backyard. And they baked and carried cakes to parties, using Tupperware's Cake Taker.

It was also a time when women had just left their World War II jobs to head back to the home kitchen. Selling Tupperware allowed them to embrace domesticity and also make money.

Tupper sold his company in 1954 to Rexall Drugs for $16 million. He thought the company had peaked. Today Tupperware is a billion-dollar multinational company with products offered online and in retail stores, and still through Tupperware parties. In fact there is a Tupperware party being held somewhere in the world every 2.5 seconds.

GOOEY BUTTER CAKE

MAKES: 16 SERVINGS
....
PREP: 2½ HOURS
....
BAKE: 25 TO 30 MINUTES
....

CAKE

¼ cup whole milk

2¼ teaspoons (1 package) active dry yeast

6 tablespoons unsalted butter, at room temperature

3 tablespoons granulated sugar

¾ teaspoon salt

1 large egg

1¾ cups all-purpose flour

Soft butter for prepping the pans

FILLING

¾ cup (1½ sticks) unsalted butter, at room temperature

1½ cups granulated sugar

½ teaspoon salt

¼ cup light corn syrup

1½ teaspoons vanilla extract

2 large eggs, at room temperature

¼ cup whole milk, at room temperature

1 cup cake flour

Confectioners' sugar for dusting the cake

T he signature dessert of St. Louis, this cake is what the name suggests—a wonderfully gooey cake that doesn't quite set when baked. Cake mix versions exist with cream cheese, but locals know that the original was made from scratch using yeast. But is the original from St. Louis? Or was this cake a typical German

> *Marjorie Child Evans, a cooking teacher with a school in Joplin, Missouri, located in the southwestern corner of the state, was demonstrating how to make butter cakes—or butter kuchen—in the 1920s. Kuchen, affectionately called kucha, are a part of the German baking heritage, both in Germany and with German Americans. They were well advertised in Missouri and Illinois newspapers throughout the 1950s. Not far away, in Louisville, Kentucky, butter kuchen dates to the 1920s with both Heitzman and Plehn's bakeries offering not a gooey but a "runny" butter kuchen. It is possible that the runny butter cake and gooey butter cake evolved about the same time, as both Louisville and St. Louis were cities with a strong German population and a wealth of bakeries.*

kuchen (cake) of the early 20th century, baked and sold in German bakeries that dotted the Midwest and other big cities? Locals in St. Louis like to say the cake originated there in the 1930s, and the stories go that a baker was in a hurry and left out a key ingredient or that the baker intentionally was experimenting to create something new. Judy Evans, who was the longtime food editor for the *St. Louis Post-Dispatch*, often searched for the origin of this cake, but "surprisingly no one takes credit for it." Here is the recipe that Evans shared each time a reader wanted the most authentic St. Louis recipe.

1. For the cake, place the milk in a small saucepan over medium heat for about 1 minute, or in the microwave on low power for 45 seconds, and heat until the milk is 100°F. Sprinkle the yeast over the milk, and stir to dissolve. Set aside.

2. Place the butter, sugar, and salt in a large bowl, and beat with an electric mixer on medium speed until light and fluffy, 2 to 3 minutes. Add the egg, and beat until incorporated. Stop the mixer, and scrape down the sides of the bowl. Add the flour alternately with the yeast and milk mixture, beginning and ending with the flour. When all the flour has been

continued

added, blend on low speed until the dough is smooth and elastic, about 5 minutes.

3. Lightly rub butter into the bottom of two 8″ square pans. Divide the dough in half, and press one half into the bottom of each pan. Cover each pan loosely with plastic wrap, and place in a warm place to rise until nearly doubled, about 2 hours.

4. When the dough has nearly finished rising, make the filling. Place the butter, sugar, salt, and corn syrup in a large mixing bowl, and beat on medium speed until light and fluffy, about 3 minutes. Scrape down the bowl and add the vanilla and 1 egg. Beat on medium speed until combined, then add the second egg. Add the milk and half the flour, beating until combined. Add the rest of the flour, and beat until smooth. Set aside.

5. Place a rack in the center of the oven, and preheat the oven to 350°F. Pour the filling over the rising dough, dividing it evenly between the 2 pans, and spread it to the edges. Place the pans in the oven.

6. Bake the cakes until the tops are golden brown, 25 to 30 minutes. Remove from the oven, and let the cakes cool for 20 minutes. Dust with confectioners' sugar, slice, and serve warm.

THE WACKY CAKE

MAKES: 12 TO 16 SERVINGS
PREP: 10 TO 15 MINUTES
BAKE: 25 TO 30 MINUTES

CAKE

3 cups all-purpose flour

2 cups granulated sugar

6 tablespoons unsweetened cocoa powder

2 teaspoons baking soda

¼ teaspoon salt

¾ cup (6 ounces) vegetable oil

2 tablespoons white vinegar

1 tablespoon vanilla extract

2 cups warm water

CARAMEL ICING

1½ cups light brown sugar, lightly packed

6 tablespoons unsalted butter or vegetable shortening, cut into tablespoons

6 tablespoons milk

½ teaspoon salt

½ teaspoon vanilla

½ cup finely chopped pecans, if desired

Whether spelled "wacky" or "whacky," this crazy cake of simple ingredients dates back to the late 1940s and has been a fixture in small-town American cookbooks and newspapers ever since. Its popularity grew after being shown to cooks at home demonstration meetings. At the time, "emergency" desserts were all the rage. As this cake's ingredients were on the pantry shelf, it was a cake you could prepare at the last minute for unexpected guests. Plus the cake's unconventional preparation had all the drama of a magician pulling a rabbit out of a hat. The flour, cocoa, baking soda, salt, and sugar are mixed right in the pan, then you burrow 3 holes into the dry ingredients with your fingers for the vinegar, vanilla, and oil. And finally you pour warm water over all, creating a giant mess that doesn't resemble cake batter. But behold, the cake slides into the oven and emerges tall and gorgeous, moist and chocolatey. It was advice columnist Amy Vanderbilt's dessert suggestion for first-time cooks in the 1960s because of its economy and ease. This recipe is from the *Recipes from Old Virginia* cookbook, a compilation of recipes used by home demonstration agents in the 1940s and '50s in Virginia. The caramel icing is simple and excellent. Garnish with finely chopped toasted pecans while the icing is still warm, if desired. By the way, this recipe helped Mrs. Russell Inskeep of Culpepper County, Virginia, win the 1957 Mrs. America contest.

1. For the cake, place a rack in the center of the oven, and preheat the oven to 350°F. Set aside an ungreased 13″ × 9″ metal baking pan.

2. Sift flour, sugar, cocoa, baking soda, and salt several times to combine well. Place in the baking pan, and sift several times to combine well. With your fingers, make 3 wells in the dry ingredients. Into one well, pour the oil. Into another, pour the vinegar. Into the third, pour the vanilla. Stir with a wooden spoon to combine the ingredients loosely. Pour 1 cup of the warm water over the ingredients in the pan, and stir to combine. Pour the second cup into the pan, and stir to combine well. Place the pan in the oven.

3. Bake the cake until the top springs back when lightly pressed with a finger, 25 to 30 minutes. Remove the pan from the oven to cool.

continued

4. For the icing, place the brown sugar, butter, milk, salt, and vanilla in a medium-size saucepan over medium heat. Bring to a boil, stirring. Let the mixture boil for 1 minute. Remove the pan from the heat. Place the pan in a large bowl filled with 2 cups of ice. Whisk the icing until it begins to thicken and is of spreading consistency.

5. Pour the caramel icing over the warm cake, spreading the icing to the edges and corners using a small spatula. If desired, sprinkle on chopped pecans while the icing is warm. Let the cake rest for 30 minutes so the icing hardens and makes slicing easy.

THE POWER OF COOKING SCHOOLS AND HOME DEMONSTRATION AGENTS

BEFORE THE AGE of televised cooking shows and YouTube, before someone on camera showed you how to frost a cake or make a meal, you bought a ticket to the cooking school coming to town. Or you awaited the next visit of the home demonstration agent.

Cooking schools date from the turn of the 20th century, when oven companies, utilities, and manufacturers for baking powder, oil, and shortening showcased their new products. The cooking school was held in a local auditorium, often at the newspaper, and was sponsored by the newspaper, food companies, and utilities.

The stars of the show were attractive, professional women who made a living traveling the country teaching others to cook. They weren't the big-name Fannie Farmers of the turn of the century, and they weren't the TV beauty stars of today. But they were well-respected good cooks of the region whom people wanted to meet, such as Henrietta Dull in Georgia and Leona Rusk Ihrig, Julia Jones, or Jessie Hogue in Texas. Jones worked for Chambers Range Company in Harlingen, Texas, in 1947, and developed recipes with "the new range that cooks with the gas turned off." Their razzmatazz recipes and well-choreographed shows packed the house.

Another way new recipes entered the home was via homemaker clubs and home demonstration agents. The Wacky Cake was loved by demonstration agents, repeated over and over again because it was easy, showy, and delicious. Ditto the Fruit Cocktail Cake (page 190), a favorite to demo because the ingredients were in everyone's pantry. Both recipes were cost cutting, an important feature in postwar America. Justina Crosby, a Carroll County, Maryland, home demonstration agent, visited rural families and showed them how to make the Wacky Cake and manage their money in 1944. She offered more than a new recipe and was a role model to rural women and girls.

Often the recipes these agents showed to cooks were so new they had only been shared between friends or printed in the local newspaper. In this pre-Internet era, these ladies were the disseminators of new food fads and flavors. By the time the German chocolate cake recipe made it to the pages of the *Dallas Morning News* in 1958, it had already been baked across Texas and Oklahoma, a recipe shared by the home demonstration agents.

FRUIT COCKTAIL CAKE

MAKES: 12 TO 16 SERVINGS

PREP: 15 TO 20 MINUTES

BAKE: 22 TO 27 MINUTES

CAKE

Butter and flour for prepping the pan

2 cups all-purpose flour

1½ cups granulated sugar

2 teaspoons baking soda

¾ teaspoon salt

2 large eggs

1 teaspoon vanilla extract

3 tablespoons fresh lemon juice

1 can (15.25 ounces) fruit cocktail, packed in juice

½ cup light brown sugar, firmly packed

½ cup grated unsweetened coconut

SAUCE

¼ cup evaporated milk, cream, or buttermilk

¾ cup granulated sugar

1 teaspoon vanilla extract

½ cup (1 stick) unsalted butter

½ cup grated unsweetened coconut

½ cup chopped pecans or walnuts

I f you are a baby boomer and you were served fruit cocktail during your childhood or at camp, you can picture its combination even if a can isn't in your pantry. The soft, sweet, only slightly colorful bits of peaches, pineapple, pears, grapes, and often red cherries—that's fruit cocktail. It was first created by Del Monte to use up small pieces of fruit left over from processing. And while fruit salads have been around for ages, the term "fruit cocktail" might have come from *Mrs. Rorer's New Cookbook* of 1902. It was a combination of fruit, sugar, and alcohol, appropriate for serving at luncheon or a "12 o'clock breakfast." But there never was alcohol in the canned product—only the name sounded exotic. In the mid-1950s, clever cooks started adding it to cake batter. In a 1955 *Chicago Daily Herald* article, Fruit Cocktail Cake was touted as being a perfect hot-weather dessert—quick to prepare and light because it contains no shortening.

1. For the cake, place a rack in the center of the oven, and preheat the oven to 350°F. Lightly grease and flour a 13″ × 9″ baking pan, and shake out the excess flour. Set the pan aside.

2. Place the flour, sugar, baking soda, and salt in a large mixing bowl, and stir to combine well. Add the eggs, vanilla, lemon juice, and fruit cocktail, and blend with an electric mixer on medium speed until smooth but chunks of fruit cocktail remain, 1 to 2 minutes. Pour the batter into the prepared pan.

3. Stir together the brown sugar and coconut in a small bowl, and sprinkle this mixture over the top of the batter. Place the pan in the oven, and bake until the cake is golden brown, 22 to 27 minutes.

4. While the cake is baking, prepare the sauce. Place the milk, sugar, vanilla, butter, coconut, and nuts in a medium-size saucepan and bring to a boil, stirring, over medium-high heat. Reduce the heat to low, and let the sauce simmer until it begins to thicken, 3 to 5 minutes. Remove the pan from the heat, and keep the sauce warm.

5. When the cake has baked, remove it from the oven, and immediately pour the sauce over the cake. Let it cool to room temperature, about 30 minutes, then slice and serve.

HELEN CORBITT'S COFFEE ANGEL FOOD CAKE

MAKES: 12 TO 16 SERVINGS

PREP: 40 TO 45 MINUTES

BAKE: 35 TO 40 MINUTES

CAKE

1½ cups sifted granulated sugar, divided use

1 cup sifted cake flour

½ teaspoon salt

1¼ cups egg whites (from 8 to 9 large eggs)

1¼ teaspoons cream of tartar

½ teaspoon vanilla extract

1 tablespoon espresso powder (see Cake Note)

Coffee Butter Icing (page 320)

GARNISH

Toasted sliced almonds, if desired

Semisweet chocolate shavings, if desired

CAKE NOTE: Helen Corbitt called for powdered instant coffee. You can find the espresso powder, which has more flavor and intensity than instant coffee, in most supermarkets today.

Texas food doyenne Helen Corbitt baked cakes in clay flowerpots for Lady Bird Johnson and made black-eyed peas elegant for the tearoom crowd during her reign as tastemaker at Neiman Marcus's fashionable Zodiac Room in the 1950s and '60s. A New York native and home economics graduate from Skidmore College, Corbitt moved to Texas to work for a large hospital but was hired away by Neiman Marcus, where she would introduce popovers, poppyseed dressing, and soufflés to the white-glove set and have an everlasting imprint on Texas cuisine. Corbitt also wrote 5 cookbooks that would remain popular for decades. In her first book, *Helen Corbitt's Cookbook*, was this recipe, described in Corbitt's own words as "the most talked about cake at Neiman Marcus." After baking it, I completely see why. It is beautifully flavored with coffee, and the soft fine texture of the angel food cake pairs perfectly with the creamy coffee-infused buttercream frosting. You have 1 slice, and then you want another. And then you feel you are back in time at the Zodiac Room, saving room for cake.

1. For the cake, place a rack in the center of the oven, and preheat the oven to 350°F. Set aside an ungreased 10″ tube pan.

2. Stir ½ cup of the sugar into the flour in a large bowl. Sift together 4 times and set aside.

3. Add the salt to the egg whites in a large mixing bowl, and beat with an electric mixer on high speed until foamy, 2 to 3 minutes. Sprinkle the cream of tartar over the eggs and beat until soft peaks form, another 2 to 3 minutes. Add the remaining 1 cup sugar to the egg whites, about ¼ cup at a time, beating on high about 1 minute, until the whites are nearly stiff. Sift the flour and sugar mixture again over the beaten egg whites, folding into the whites with a rubber spatula until no flour can be seen. Fold in the vanilla and espresso powder until just combined. Pour the batter into the ungreased pan, smoothing the top. Place the pan in the oven.

4. Bake the cake until it is firm when pressed gently on top, 35 to 40 minutes. Remove the pan from the oven, and invert it onto a wire rack to let the cake cool upside down in the pan for at least an hour, or until completely cool.

5. To assemble, run a knife around the edge of the pan, give the pan a gentle shake, and invert the cake once and then again to let it rest right side up on a serving plate. Frost the top and sides with the Coffee Butter Icing. Top with toasted almonds and grated chocolate. Slice and serve.

TEXAS SHEATH CAKE

MAKES: 16 SERVINGS
....
PREP: 30 TO 35 MINUTES
....
BAKE: 20 TO 25 MINUTES
....

CAKE

Butter and flour for prepping the pan

2 cups all-purpose flour

2 cups granulated sugar

1 cup (2 sticks) lightly salted butter

4 tablespoons unsweetened cocoa powder (see Cake Notes on page 196)

1 cup water

1 teaspoon baking soda

½ cup buttermilk

2 large eggs, slightly beaten

1 teaspoon ground cinnamon

1 teaspoon vanilla extract

ICING

½ cup (1 stick) lightly salted butter (see Cake Notes on page 196)

4 tablespoons unsweetened cocoa powder

⅓ cup whole milk

3¾ cups confectioners' sugar, sifted

1 teaspoon vanilla extract

¾ to 1 cup chopped pecans, toasted (see Cake Notes on page 196)

When Sarah Hooton was growing up in Fort Worth, Texas, there was one cake that was sure to be on the kitchen counter during the Thanksgiving and Christmas holidays—Texas sheet cake, or in Sarah's family, her grandmother Mary Hooton's recipe for Texas Sheath Cake, as they call it. A simple cake based on cocoa and seasoned with the distinctive pinch of cinnamon, this cake is so named because you pour it into a sheet (or, in this case, a 13″ × 9″) pan, and while the cake is still hot, pour over a warm chocolate-pecan icing. This cake is a Texas favorite, distinctive because of the cinnamon in the cake and pecans in the icing. "To be honest, if you asked me to name my favorite birthday cake, it would be this cake," says Sarah, who is Culinary Institute of America–trained in pastry and baking and worked in London's Savoy Hotel, as well as at restaurants in Portland and cooking schools in Austin and Dallas, before joining the Fort Worth Central Market as cooking school manager. "It may be the most unattractive cake you've ever seen, but it is delicious and nostalgic and everyone in Texas loves it," she adds. And Texas is divided, too, as to the name of the cake—some saying, "sheet," and others "sheath," which Hooton guesses might be a Scottish pronunciation. When the Central Markets were updating their bakery cakes, Sarah suggested this cake and offered her grandmother's recipe. Now it is one of the store's most popular desserts. A perfect grab-and-go dessert, this sheet, or sheath, cake is suitable year-round for tailgates, picnics, and casual entertaining. Always toast the pecans first in a 350°F oven for a few minutes before adding to the icing, says Sarah. "That is a must."

1. For the cake, place a rack in the center of the oven, and preheat the oven to 400°F. Lightly grease and flour a 13″ × 9″ metal baking pan. Shake out the excess flour, and set the pan aside.

2. Place the flour and sugar in a large mixing bowl, and stir to combine. Set aside.

3. Place the butter, cocoa, and water in a medium-size saucepan over medium heat, and stir until the butter melts and the mixture just comes

continued

to a boil, 3 to 4 minutes. Remove from the heat and pour into the bowl with the flour and sugar. Stir to combine. Stir the baking soda into the buttermilk, and stir into the batter along with the eggs, cinnamon, and vanilla. Stir until smooth. Pour the batter into the prepared pan, and place the pan in the oven.

4. Bake the cake until the top springs back when lightly pressed, 20 to 25 minutes. Remove the cake from the oven to cool on a wire rack.

5. About 5 minutes before the cake is done, start preparing the icing. Place the butter, cocoa, and milk into a medium-size saucepan over medium heat, stir to combine, and bring to a boil, 2 to 3 minutes. Place the confectioners' sugar in a large mixing bowl, and pour the hot cocoa mixture into the sugar. Stir until smooth. Fold in the vanilla and pecans until well combined. Pour the icing over the warm cake. Let the cake cool for at least 1 hour before slicing.

CAKE NOTES: Sarah's family uses Hershey's regular baking cocoa. But the Central Markets use a dark unsweetened Valrhona cocoa. This cake needs a bit of salt, so that is why lightly salted butter is called for in the recipe. If you are baking with unsalted butter, add ½ teaspoon salt to the cake, and ¼ teaspoon salt to the icing. Toast the pecans before folding into the icing. Place the pecans in a small baking pan in the oven for 4 to 5 minutes while the oven preheats, watching to make sure they turn golden brown and do not burn.

MARY HOOTON loved to cook. She had three sons, and before each son left for college, she typed recipes onto index cards and sent the cards with the boys. On each index card, she wrote personal notes to the son, such as that the chocolate cake recipe was the one he liked and it is "easy and good." Judging from the stains and smudges on the cards today, it is obvious those sons and their families have enjoyed baking by Mary's recipes.

THE 13" X 9" PAN

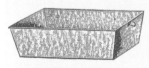

AS LONG AS THERE HAVE BEEN roasting pans and ovens large enough to hold them, there have been cakes baked in a roasting pan. By the end of the 1800s, you could buy an oblong pan with handles just for roasting. It was called the dripping pan.

Along came baking powder and jelly rolls, and that dripping pan was just the right size in which to pour a cake batter, bake a thin cake, spread it with jelly, and roll it up.

By the 1930s, cooks were concerned with the specific size of a pan so that it fit the measurements in their recipe. You started to see pans measuring 12" × 9", and then, in 1938, a 13" × 9" jelly roll pan to bake cakes and also to chill gelatin salads. But the real turn-

ing point was in 1948, when Kellogg's introduced a Rice Krispies squares recipe and instructions to press it into a 13" × 9" pan. If you didn't own that pan, you bought one. Later manufacturers developed plastic tops that snapped onto the pans so that Rice Krispies squares, brownies, and coffee cakes could be taken with you.

Today the 13" × 9" pan, also known as the sheet pan, is the most-used baking pan in America. That's because it is convenient. Historian Darra Goldstein says with a sheet pan you don't have to prepare two pans to bake a cake. And sheet cake is immediate—quick to cool, easy to frost, even simpler to slice and serve. But the big layer cakes will always be preferred in communities that pride themselves on cake baking, Goldstein adds. And they keep well, too.

HERSHEY BAR CAKE

MAKES: 12 TO 16 SERVINGS
PREP: 20 TO 25 MINUTES
BAKE: 65 TO 70 MINUTES

Butter and flour for prepping the pan

1 cup (2 sticks) unsalted butter, at room temperature

1¼ cups granulated sugar

4 large eggs, at room temperature

6 bars (1.55 ounces each) Hershey's milk chocolate

2½ cups all-purpose flour

¼ teaspoon baking soda

⅛ teaspoon salt

1 cup buttermilk, at room temperature

½ cup Hershey's chocolate syrup

2 teaspoons vanilla extract

GARNISH

½ cup chopped toasted pecans (see Cake Note)

2 teaspoons confectioners' sugar

CAKE NOTE: To toast the pecans, place them in a small baking pan in the turned-off oven for 3 to 5 minutes, or until medium brown and fragrant.

Milton Hershey was born into a Pennsylvania Mennonite farm family, but his interests were clearly off the farm. He apprenticed with a Philadelphia confectioner at 14 and went west to Denver to learn the art of caramel making. Hershey turned that into a successful venture, sold it, and set his sights on chocolate, and more importantly, on making chocolate bars affordable to everyone. An entrepreneur at heart, Hershey remembered the dairy farms of his youth and located his new milk chocolate plant in his birthplace of Derry Church, Pennsylvania (which would be renamed Hershey, Pennsylvania), smack-dab in the middle of dairy country, with fresh milk and an ample labor source available. The first Hershey milk chocolate bars came off the line in 1900, and they were cleverly embossed with the name "Hershey" right in the bar so they could self-advertise once unwrapped. Kisses were produced in 1907, and the almond chocolate bars a year later. This cake is an homage to the Hershey bar, an all-American ingredient. It was first seen in the 1950s, and a 1958 recipe printed in the Kerrville, Texas, newspaper, contributed by Ruth Harrison, is a simple pound cake made with 6 melted Hershey bars and the instruction that "8 makes it better." Later versions of this cake reduce the sugar but include a half cup of Hershey's chocolate syrup, invented in 1926. And while some recipes instruct you to drizzle more chocolate syrup on top of the cake before slicing, this cake is best unadorned, or if you must, dressed up with just a sprinkling of confectioners' sugar and/or toasted pecans.

1. Place a rack in the center of the oven, and preheat the oven to 350°F. Lightly grease and flour a 10″ tube pan. Shake out the excess flour, and set the pan aside.

2. Place the butter in a large mixing bowl, and beat with an electric mixer on medium speed until creamy, 1 to 2 minutes. Gradually add the sugar, and beat until light and fluffy, 2 to 3 minutes. Add the eggs, one at a time, beating after each addition. Set aside.

3. Unwrap the chocolate bars, break them in half, and place them on a glass pie plate in the microwave on medium power for 1 to 1½ minutes, stirring every 30 seconds. Fold the melted chocolate into the batter.

continued

4. Sift together the flour, baking soda, and salt in a large bowl, and add this to the chocolate batter alternately with the buttermilk, beginning and ending with the dry ingredients. Add the chocolate syrup and vanilla, and stir until well incorporated. Pour the batter into the prepared pan, and place the pan in the oven.

5. Bake the cake until a toothpick inserted in the center comes out clean, 65 to 70 minutes. Remove the cake from the oven, and place on a wire rack to cool for 15 minutes. Run a knife around the edges of the cake, and then give the pan a gentle shake to loosen the cake. Invert it once and then again onto the rack so that it cools completely right side up, about 1 hour.

6. Before serving, garnish the top with chopped pecans and/or sifted confectioners' sugar. Slice and serve.

ICE CREAM SUNDAE CAKE: *For a fun presentation, just before serving, fill the center of the cake with vanilla ice cream. Drizzle the top with chocolate syrup, toasted pecans, and maraschino cherries.*

Hershey Bars and World War II

If you eat a chocolate bar to give you extra energy to survive the day, consider this: American troops serving in World War II were provided the same sustenance in 4-ounce chocolate Field Ration D bars and later Tropical bars made by Hershey. Before America entered World War II, Hershey was approached by the military about creating a chocolate bar for troops. It had to be high in energy and withstand high temperatures. The resulting D bar was a blend of chocolate, sugar, cocoa butter, nonfat milk powder, and oat flour. Too thick for Hershey's machinery, it had to be packed into molds by hand. It came with instructions to "eat slowly," and it supposedly tasted like a potato. But when those Allied troops stormed the beaches of Normandy on D-Day and when they liberated Paris, Hershey D ration bars were with them. The Tropical bar was made later, designed to be a bit better tasting and withstand the hot and humid conditions of the Pacific. These weren't the milk chocolate bars we know today, but Hershey manufactured 40 million of them for the war effort. They were much appreciated at the end of the war when American soldiers handed them to locals as a gesture of peace. The French children especially loved the bars, as they were hungry and had not tasted chocolate for years due to rationing.

SISTER SADIE'S HONEY CAKE

MAKES: 8 SERVINGS
PREP: 15 TO 20 MINUTES
BAKE: 55 TO 60 MINUTES

CAKE

Vegetable oil or shortening and flour for prepping the pan

1 cup honey

½ cup granulated sugar

2 large eggs

¼ cup Coca-Cola (or strong coffee)

¼ cup vegetable oil

1¾ cups all-purpose flour

1¾ teaspoons baking powder

¾ teaspoon ground cinnamon

½ teaspoon ground allspice

¼ teaspoon salt

TOPPING

2 tablespoons honey

2 tablespoons sliced toasted almonds (see Cake Note)

CAKE NOTE: To toast sliced almonds, you want to be very careful and leave them in the oven only for a few minutes. Place them in a small baking pan in the oven while it preheats. Turn the light on, and watch the almonds so they don't get too brown—2 to 3 minutes is about right.

Honey cake is one of the oldest cakes in the world. Also called *Lebkuchen* in German, this cake of flour and honey was made as far back as ancient Rome. It is to the Jewish new year—Rosh Hashanah—what fruitcake is to Christmas—a must. And it has a religious significance, too, because honey represents sweetness and good living. Every Jewish cook has her own version of honey cake, says Marcie Cohen Ferris, Southern Jewish foodways historian and author. Most recipes call for spices and a liquid such as coffee or tea. But an American honey cake, and in this case, a Southern honey cake, calls for flat Coca-Cola. Jews who grew up living in hot and humid Savannah, Charleston, Atlanta, Mobile, and New Orleans have a personal connection with ice-cold Coca-Cola, Ferris says. This honey cake recipe comes from Ferris and is adapted from a recipe shared by Sadie Gottlieb of the old Gottlieb's Bakery in Savannah and printed in Ferris's cookbook, *Matzoh Ball Gumbo*. Whereas most honey cake recipes call for coffee, a flat Coke might have been easier to find in the South than coffee on warm afternoons. Sister Sadie's recipe originally made 2 loaves of honey cake, but I have halved the recipe.

1. For the cake, place a rack in the center of the oven, and preheat the oven to 325°F. Lightly grease and flour a 9″ × 5″ loaf pan, and shake out the excess flour. Set the pan aside.

2. Place the honey, sugar, eggs, Coca-Cola, and oil in a large mixing bowl, and stir with a wooden spoon for 50 strokes or blend with an electric mixer on medium-low speed until smooth, 1 minute. Set aside.

3. Place the flour in a separate mixing bowl, and stir in the baking powder, cinnamon, allspice, and salt. Fold the dry ingredients into the honey mixture, stirring just to combine. Pour the batter into the prepared pan, and place the pan in the oven.

4. Bake until the cake springs back in the center when lightly pressed, 55 to 60 minutes. Remove the cake from the oven. While it is warm, spread the honey lightly over the top of the cake to glaze it. Let the cake cool in the pan for 15 minutes.

5. Run a sharp knife around the edges of the pan, give the pan a gentle shake, then invert the cake once and then again onto a wire rack. Scatter the toasted almonds over the top. Let the cake cool for 30 minutes before slicing.

GERMAN CHOCOLATE CAKE

MAKES: 12 TO 16 SERVINGS
PREP: 1½ HOURS
BAKE: 28 TO 32 MINUTES

CAKE

Butter and flour for prepping the pans

2 cups all-purpose flour

1 teaspoon baking soda

½ teaspoon salt

1 package (4 ounces) German's Sweet Chocolate

½ cup boiling water

1 cup (2 sticks) unsalted butter (see Cake Notes on opposite page), at room temperature

2 cups granulated sugar

4 large eggs, separated

1 teaspoon vanilla extract

1 cup buttermilk

COCONUT AND PECAN FILLING

1½ cups (12-ounce can) evaporated milk

1½ cups granulated sugar

4 egg yolks, slightly beaten

¾ cup (1½ sticks) unsalted butter, cut into 12 tablespoons

1½ teaspoons vanilla extract

¼ teaspoon salt

2⅓ cups (about 7 ounces) unsweetened flaked coconut (see Cake Notes on opposite page)

1½ cups chopped toasted pecans (see Cake Notes on opposite page)

(photo on page 204)

While America was starstruck by Elvis Presley in 1956, an American classic cake was in its infancy. Irving, Texas, newspaper columnist Daisy Pearce shared a Summer German Chocolate Cake recipe that year, given to her by her daughter in Oklahoma. In one year, that recipe was baked for the Texas State Fair, printed in newspapers across the state, and shared by home demonstration agents. A homemaker sent the recipe to the *Dallas Morning News* that year, and the food editor ran it once, then again, reducing the amount of chocolate. The cake wasn't German, but it did contain German's Sweet Chocolate, named for Sam German, the Englishman who invented it in 1852. German chocolate sales shot up 73 percent following the recipe's appearance in the Dallas paper, and Baker's chocolate realized it had a publicity dream come true and sent the recipe to food editors across the country. By the next year, the recipe was printed on the back of the chocolate box. German chocolate cakes weren't new—they were sold frozen in Wisconsin supermarkets in the 1940s and, in Texas, had been written about in Corsicana and Denton. But those cakes didn't have the distinctive cooked frosting of evaporated milk, sugar, butter, pecans, and coconut that made the new German chocolate cake unique. Handy to cooks in Texas, Oklahoma, and all of the West, evaporated milk would keep in the cupboard for puddings and fillings. It was a holdover from frontier times and needed no refrigeration, and cooks liked the richness it added to their recipes. Coconut, like canned milk, was available nationwide and a pantry staple. But pecans were a nut of our country's southern tier, which makes it believable that this recipe originated in Oklahoma or Texas, where pecans grow. The frosting was originally intended as a filling, and the earliest German chocolate cakes were frosted with a coffee buttercream or a seven-minute frosting. But through the years, it has been the filling that everyone's been crazy about, and the filling became the frosting, making this cake, like Elvis, an American classic.

1. For the cake, place a rack in the center of the oven, and preheat the oven to 350°F. Lightly grease and flour three 9″ cake pans, and shake out the excess flour. Set the pans aside.

2. Place the flour, baking soda, and salt into a large mixing bowl, and sift to combine. Set aside.

3. Chop the chocolate into ½″ pieces, and place in a small bowl. Pour the boiling water over it, and stir to melt the chocolate. Set aside.

4. Place the butter and sugar in a large bowl, and beat with an electric mixer on medium speed until light and fluffy, 2 minutes. Add the egg yolks, one at a time, beating after each addition. Add the vanilla. Alternately add the flour mixture and buttermilk to the batter, blending on low speed, beginning and ending with the dry ingredients. Set aside.

5. Place the egg whites in a large mixing bowl, and beat with clean beaters on high speed until almost-stiff peaks form, about 4 minutes. Fold the egg whites into the batter. Divide the batter between the 3 prepared pans. Place the pans in the oven.

6. Bake the cakes until they spring back when lightly pressed in the center, 28 to 32 minutes. Remove the cakes from the oven, and place on a wire rack to cool for 15 minutes. Run a knife around the edges of each pan, and gently shake them to loosen the cakes. Invert the cakes once and then again onto the racks to cool completely, right side up, 45 minutes.

7. Meanwhile, prepare the filling. Place the milk, sugar, egg yolks, butter, vanilla, and salt in a large saucepan over medium heat. Cook and stir constantly, until the mixture thickens and is caramel in color, about 15 minutes. Remove the pan from the heat and stir in the coconut and pecans. Let the mixture cool until it is thick enough to spread. You can refrigerate the filling while the cake layers cool. (Or to speed the process along, you can make the filling before you bake the cake.)

8. To assemble, place 1 cake layer on a serving plate and cover with 1 cup of filling, spreading it to the edges. Top with the second layer and repeat. Top with the third layer, and pile the remaining filling on top, leaving the sides bare. Chill for 1 hour for easier slicing.

CAKE NOTES: If you use lightly salted butter, reduce the salt in the cake to ¼ teaspoon, and you can omit salt from the filling. Use unsweetened coconut, but if you cannot find it, sweetened will do. Pecans are much more delicious if toasted first. Place them on a baking pan in the turned-off oven while you are preparing the filling. When they are medium brown and fragrant, 3 to 5 minutes, remove from the oven.

German Chocolate Cake (page 202) and Red Velvet Cake (opposite) are two American classics.

RED VELVET CAKE

MAKES: 12 SERVINGS

PREP: 1 TO 1½ HOURS

BAKE: 16 TO 18 MINUTES

CAKE

Butter or vegetable shortening and unsweetened cocoa powder or flour for prepping the pans

½ cup unsalted butter or shortening, at room temperature

1½ cups granulated sugar

2 large eggs, at room temperature

2 teaspoons vanilla extract

2 tablespoons red food coloring

2½ cups all-purpose flour, sifted

3 tablespoons unsweetened cocoa powder

½ teaspoon salt

1 cup buttermilk, at room temperature

1 tablespoon white vinegar

1 teaspoon baking soda

ERMINE FROSTING

5 tablespoons all-purpose flour

1 cup cold whole milk

1 teaspoon vanilla extract

Pinch of salt

1 cup (2 sticks) unsalted butter, at room temperature

1 cup granulated sugar

Never has an American cake caused such a stir as the red velvet. From the name to the ingredients to the place and time in which the first red velvet cake landed in America, historians and cooks have disagreed about its origin. It is from Texas. No, it's from Indiana. It should have cream cheese frosting. No, only the cooked Ermine Frosting. What is known can be found in the pages of old cookbooks, newspapers, and magazines, and they reveal the cake dates back to the 1920s. Cora Scott shared a recipe for a "Velvet Cake" in the Fort Scott, Kansas, newspaper in June 1921, and it called for a tablespoon of red food coloring, but no cocoa. "Velvet" was a common adjective for cakes from the 1870s on, implying they contained cornstarch or rice flour to soften the hard wheat flour and thus had a fine texture. But the "red" color was originally that chemical reaction between an acid (cocoa, buttermilk) and a base (baking soda) that created a naturally reddish batter. Hershey's shared a Demon Cake with such a color in 1934. Interestingly, a popular lipstick hue was "red velvet" in 1936. And chocolate cakes with a reddish tint had come to

A plausible story goes that the red velvet started in the 1930s at the Waldorf Astoria Hotel in New York, a place awash in red velvet decor.

be known as red velvet cake by 1951. Throughout the 1950s, cakes baked with or without the red food coloring were called "Red Velvet" or "Waldorf Red Velvet." One such cake won first prize at the Maryland State Fair in 1960. That year in Terre Haute, Indiana, columnist Beatrice Biggs writes that she is indebted to a local cook for sharing a Waldorf Red Velvet Cake, containing both cocoa and red food coloring. Down in Texas, red velvet cakes are everywhere, and Texas has always had a strong connection with the cake. From the Austin-based Adams Extract company that claims it provided homemakers with the first recipe to use with its red coloring, to the 1989 movie *Steel Magnolias* in which the groom's cake is an armadillo-shaped red velvet, this cake has been as big as Texas. Patricia Adam of Navasota, Texas, remembers teaching in 1960 in Port Arthur, and sampling one of the first red velvet cakes. "It was baked by a lady who supposedly created the recipe," Adam says, and "the cake was absolutely delicious." But the heavy use

continued

of the red food coloring? Makes you wonder, what were they thinking? The late John Egerton summed it up best when he said, "To me there seems no culinary reason why someone would dump that much food coloring into a cake." Unless they were trying to sell you food coloring, and extract companies like Adams have contributed much to the staying power of this recipe. Or you might rationalize that the red velvet is a Depression-cra cake, and the red food coloring made up for the lack of cocoa. But reason is not an ingredient of the red velvet. It was popular in postwar times and has remained an American favorite, baked for Christmas, birthdays, the Fourth of July, and potlucks across the country.

Here is a recipe adapted from the Adams Extract company and the *New York Times*. It is frosted with the classic Ermine (cooked) Frosting. If you prefer, use Cream Cheese Frosting on your red velvet; see page 320. The Adams method calls for vegetable shortening, but you can use butter, if desired.

1. For the cake, place a rack in the center of the oven, and preheat the oven to 350°F. Grease three 9″ round cake pans, and dust them with cocoa or flour. Shake out the excess cocoa or flour, and set the pans aside.

2. Place the butter and sugar in a large mixing bowl, and beat with an electric mixer on medium speed until light and creamy, 3 minutes. Add the eggs, one at a time, beating well after each addition. Blend in the vanilla and red food coloring. Set aside.

3. In a separate bowl, stir together the flour, cocoa, and salt. In a small bowl, stir together the buttermilk, vinegar, and baking soda. Add the dry ingredients and the buttermilk mixture to the batter alternately on low speed, beginning and ending with the dry ingredients. Scrape down the bowl, and stir to blend the batter one last time. Divide the batter between the pans, and place the pans in the oven.

4. Bake the cakes until they just begin to pull away from the sides of the pan, 16 to 18 minutes. Remove the pans from the oven, and place them on a wire rack to cool for 10 minutes. Run a knife around the edges of the pans, give them a shake to loosen the cakes, then turn the layers out once and then again onto the rack so they cool right side up.

5. While the cakes cool, make the Ermine Frosting. Whisk together the flour and milk in a small saucepan over medium heat until it is very

Why Red?

Throughout American cake history, cooks have figured out ways to dye their cakes a different color, from the simplest use of extra egg yolks for the yellow Daffodil Cake to the vivid red velvet cake. Why red and not green or blue? That may be a question for psychologists. The color red has always attracted attention. Look to nature and see the male cardinal as an example. And red has long been a color that signifies royalty and wealth as it was more costly to dye fabrics and garments red than other colors.

thick and puddinglike, 4 to 5 minutes. Remove the pan from the heat, and whisk in the vanilla and salt. Pour the mixture into a small heatproof bowl. Cover the surface of the mixture with plastic wrap and place in the refrigerator to cool for 1 hour.

6. Place the butter and sugar in a large mixing bowl, and beat with an electric mixer on medium speed until light and fluffy, 4 minutes. Remove the milk and flour mixture from the refrigerator, and slowly add it to the butter and sugar while beating on medium. Continue to beat until the mixture is light and fluffy and resembles whipped cream, about 2 minutes.

7. To assemble the cake, place 1 layer on a cake plate. Spread about ¾ cup of the frosting evenly to the edges. Place a second layer on top and repeat. Place the third layer on top, and spread a thin layer of frosting on the sides and on top, making what is called a skim coat. Chill the cake for 15 minutes. (This seals in the crumbs and prevents them from being dragged into the frosting and turning the frosting pink.)

8. Remove the cake from the refrigerator and, with the remaining frosting, frost the top and sides of the cake. Slice and serve.

WATERMELON CAKE AND RED CAKES

BEFORE RED VELVET CAKE, America's obsession with red cake started in the late 1800s, at the end of the Victorian era. It was a time when objects were designed to look like other objects, and the Watermelon Cake was created to look like a real watermelon.

A crucial ingredient was an early red food coloring called cochineal. A tropical beetle used by the Aztecs and Mayans to dye clothing scarlet red, cochineal was ground to a much-valued powder and traded around the world.

It wasn't long until pastry chefs and home cooks found they could dye food red and pink—depending on how much you added—with cochineal. And then the Victorians created something masterful—a pinkish-red Watermelon Cake around 1877.

Cross Creek author Marjorie Kinnan Rawlings recalls the Watermelon Cake her mother baked for her 5th birthday: "The cake was a deep loaf cake. Its base was white, it was thickly streaked with watermelon pink, and choco-late blobs were scattered through it to represent seeds. It was iced with pistachio frosting in a delicate green."

Caroline King writes of her Watermelon Cake memories in her 1941 book *Victorian Cakes* and reveals her natural dye for tinting the cake. She and her sister Emily would prepare a white batter and dye half of it with beet juice. They added 1 cup of currants dusted with flour to look like seeds and folded these into the pink batter.

Even before Caroline took the natural route for tinting the cake red, food colorings made from fresh fruit were concocted in home kitchens. In 1839 the *Kentucky Housewife* shares a simple red food coloring recipe made from the juice of ripe cherries and strawberries. But the Victorians used cochineal, and there was no fear in ingesting it. The *New York Tribune* wrote in October 1890 that cochineal "is perfectly harmless." And perhaps less harmful than the artificial food colorings that would come our way in 1907. Although Red 40 and Red 3 are banned from coloring cosmetics today, they are allowed to tint maraschino cherries, candies, and red velvet cake.

DELTA CARAMEL CAKE

MAKES: 12 SERVINGS

PREP: 1½ HOURS

BAKE: 25 TO 30 MINUTES

Vegetable shortening and flour for prepping the pans

1 cup (2 sticks) unsalted butter, at room temperature

1¾ cups granulated sugar

3 large eggs

1 teaspoon vanilla extract

2 cups all-purpose flour

1½ teaspoons baking powder

¼ teaspoon salt

⅔ cup whole milk, warmed

Old-Fashioned Caramel Icing (page 314)

Tips on Caramel Icing

How to make the real caramel icing? You need two pans. One simmers the sugar and milk, and the second, a cast-iron skillet, caramelizes a small portion of the sugar that is added to the first pan. Variations exist, as some icings use evaporated milk, others cream; many vary on the amount of sugar to be caramelized and how long to beat the icing before spreading it onto the cake. But they do agree that you must frost this cake while the icing is still warm. And you must let the cake air-dry and set as it cools.

Caramel cakes have been a part of American baking for as long as cooks have put granulated sugar over heat and allowed those white crystals to melt into an amber-brown liquid. That slightly burnt flavor, the interplay of sweet and bitter, the color, the creamy consistency: These are reasons we have been forever drawn to caramel. But the caramel cake has a special place in the Mississippi Delta region. With a ready source of sugar in the cane grown in Louisiana and the New Orleans influence on the way people cooked, caramel cake became a fixture there, says Susan Puckett, Mississippi native and author of *Eat Drink Delta: A Hungry Traveler's Journey through the Soul of the South*. "So many food traditions in the Delta

> *A fixture at funerals, the caramel cake is listed as one of the 10 must-haves at Delta funerals in* Being Dead Is No Excuse, *by Delta writers Gayden Metcalfe and Charlotte Hays.*

came right up the river." Plus, she says, caramel cakes are part of the strong entertaining culture of this region devoid of fruit trees, where people grew accustomed to making custards and layer cakes. For Delta women who loved to bake, a caramel cake took time and patience and was a badge of honor, says Puckett, "an ordeal to make, and in the Delta we celebrate those ordeals." And while a lot of wealthy women in Mississippi have had the help of African American women in making their caramel cakes—think Minnie in *The Help*—the cake is still baked today by those without help, and it remains something to brag about. In recent years, Puckett says, a lot of busy Delta cooks have substituted cake mix for the scratch cake, but they still make their family's recipe for caramel icing. Because really, this cake is all about the icing, another reason why caramel cakes have stood the test of time in the Delta. The icing is a little temperamental to prepare, and good cooks say you should never attempt it during a rainstorm or on a humid day, but once frosted, this cake can sit unaffected on a summer picnic table in the sweltering heat and humidity and not weep, not run, just sit there majestically, like some great god

continued

of Delta cooking, a shrine to the hard work that went into the cake. And a visible reminder that who needs fruit trees in the Delta when you have caramel cake?

1. Place a rack in the center of the oven, and preheat the oven to 350°F. Lightly grease the bottom of two 9″ round or square pans with vegetable shortening and dust with flour. Shake out the excess flour, and set the pans aside.

2. Place the butter and sugar in a large bowl, and beat with an electric mixer on medium speed until the mixture comes together and lightens, about 2 minutes. Add the eggs, one at a time, beating well after each addition. Blend in the vanilla. Set aside.

3. In a smaller bowl, sift together the flour, baking powder, and salt. Alternately add the dry ingredients and the milk to the batter, beginning and ending with the dry ingredients. Blend on low speed until just incorporated, 1 minute more. Divide the batter between the 2 prepared pans, and place the pans in the oven.

4. Bake the cake until it is golden brown and the top springs back when lightly pressed with a finger, 25 to 30 minutes. Remove the pans from the oven, and place on a wire rack to cool for 10 minutes. Run a knife around the edges of the pans, give them a shake to loosen, then turn the layers out once and then again onto the rack so they cool right side up.

5. While the cakes are cooling, prepare the icing.

6. To assemble while the icing is still warm, place 1 cake layer on a serving plate. Spoon over a generous ladle of the warm icing, and spread it to the edges of the cake with a metal spatula. Place the second layer on top, and spoon several generous ladles of frosting over the top of the cake, smoothing it out with a metal spatula, and letting the icing run down the sides. When the top of the cake is frosted and pretty, use the remainder of the icing to frost the sides. If the icing has gotten hard and is not spreadable, place the pan over very low heat, stirring just a minute to warm it. Or place the saucepan into a large bowl filled with 2″ of hot water. Dip the spatula into the saucepan and run this icing around the cake in clean strokes, being careful not to tear the cake. Let the cake rest for 30 minutes so the icing will harden, then slice and serve.

DIONE'S CHOCOLATE ROULADE

MAKES: 10 TO 12 SERVINGS
PREP: 45 TO 50 MINUTES
BAKE: 16 TO 18 MINUTES
CHILL: UP TO 3 HOURS

CAKE

Vegetable oil and waxed paper for prepping the pan

8 ounces bittersweet chocolate

⅓ cup water

8 large eggs, separated

1 cup superfine sugar

⅛ teaspoon salt

½ cup unsweetened cocoa powder

FILLING

1¾ cups heavy cream

2 to 4 tablespoons confectioners' sugar

⅓ whole vanilla bean or 1 teaspoon vanilla extract

How to Make Your Own Superfine Sugar

Place granulated sugar in a food processor fitted with a metal blade. Pulse for 20 to 30 seconds, or until fine.

While many Americans were trying their hands at easy Betty Crocker recipes, Dione Lucas was showing her 1946 US television audience how to make a flourless chocolate roulade, an omelet, and a crown roast of lamb. The daughter of a London architect and the first woman to graduate from the prestigious Le Cordon Bleu cooking school in Paris, Lucas was instrumental in starting the London Cordon Bleu, and she moved to New York in 1940. She opened restaurants, taught cooking classes in her apartment kitchen, wrote cookbooks, and appeared on TV. Her first show, called *To the Queen's Taste*, aired more than 15 years before Julia Child would dazzle viewers in *The French Chef*. Although Lucas isn't as well-known as Child, her signature chocolate cake/roulade Leontine—a flourless chocolate roll filled with whipped cream—is beloved. The recipe, writes Lucas, came from a French chef named Leontine who was cooking in the Adirondacks. "When I arrived in New York the temperature was 101, and a cousin took me by train to the cool air of the Adirondacks," she writes in *The Dione Lucas Book of French Cooking*. The dinner Leontine prepared was fresh sea bass and corn, and this chocolate roll. The recipe, which I have adapted only slightly, was way ahead of its time, and when Lucas shared it in her 1947 cookbook, it sparked the American interest in flourless chocolate cakes that would continue for decades.

1. For the cake, brush a jelly roll pan (18″ × 12″) with a thin coat of vegetable oil. Line the pan with waxed paper, leaving about 3″ hanging over each end. Set the pan aside.

2. Place a rack in the center of the oven, and preheat the oven to 350°F.

3. Place the chocolate and water in a small saucepan over low heat. Stir to combine until the chocolate is slowly melted, 2 to 3 minutes. Remove the pan from the heat, and set it aside.

4. Place the egg yolks, sugar, and salt in a medium-size bowl, and beat with an electric mixer on medium speed until very light and fluffy, 1 minute. Beat in the melted chocolate just until combined. Set the mixture aside, and wash the beaters.

5. In a medium-size bowl, beat the egg whites on high speed until stiff peaks form, 4 to 5 minutes. Pour the chocolate mixture gently into the

continued

whites and fold in with a rubber spatula until well combined. Pour this batter into the prepared pan, smoothing the batter evenly to the edges. Place the pan in the oven.

6. Bake the cake until a toothpick inserted in the center comes out clean, 16 to 18 minutes. Don't overbake. Remove the pan to a wire rack and gently place on it a strip of 4 damp paper towels. Cover the wet towels with a layer of dry paper towels. Let the roulade stand at room temperature until it is lukewarm, then remove all the paper towels. Run a knife around the edges of the cake to loosen it. Sprinkle the top of the cake with cocoa. Cover the top with 2 sheets of waxed paper, and carefully but quickly flip the cake onto the counter, so that the waxed paper sheets are on the bottom. Remove the jelly roll pan and peel the waxed paper lining off the cake.

7. For the filling, place the heavy cream in a large metal bowl over another bowl full of ice. Beat with a large whisk or an electric mixer until the cream starts to hold its shape. Add the confectioners' sugar and vanilla. Continue beating the cream until it holds its shape. Divide the whipped cream into 3 rows of 3 heaping tablespoons each so as to distribute the cream and make spreading over the delicate cake easier. Spread it evenly across the top of the cake. Carefully roll up the cake like a jelly roll and serve seam side down on a platter or pretty board.

CAKE NOTE: This assembled roulade is best made the day of serving, and you can keep it covered and refrigerated for 2 to 3 hours.

FLOURLESS CHOCOLATE CAKE AND CHOCOLATE DECADENCE

DIONE LUCAS introduced the flourless chocolate roulade to America in the 1950s. James Beard would later describe her cake as a chocolate soufflé in a roll. Whatever the description, Lucas changed the way we looked at chocolate cake. *McCall's* magazine published a chocolate cake recipe in 1959 that had only a small amount of flour, making the chocolate flavor intense and the texture moist and like cheesecake.

Then two more cakes followed, one in the *New York Times* in 1969, and the other from restaurateur Narsai David of Berkeley, California, in the early 1970s. Both recipes were dense, pâté-like, and briefly baked, and they became vehicles to show off good chocolate. David would name his recipe Chocolate Decadence, and he obtained a trademark for it.

The *Times* recipe from Evelyn Sharpe contained 1 pound semisweet chocolate, 10 tablespoons soft butter, 1 tablespoon flour, 1 tablespoon sugar, and 4 eggs,

separated. The cake is baked in a small springform pan, the chocolate melted and mixed with the butter, flour, sugar, and egg yolks. The whites are beaten until they form peaks and folded in carefully. The cake is baked at a high heat—425°F—for only 15 minutes, and then it rests in the oven with the door ajar, similar to cooking a rare filet of beef.

Narsai David created his chocolate cake for a friend who was having a dinner party and needed a good dessert. The friend was an aficionado of port, so the dessert had to pair well with port. David's recipe is the same as Evelyn Sharpe's, but his preparation is a little different. He also bakes the cake for 15 minutes at 425°F, but then he removes it from the oven. He says the cake will still be liquid in the center, and he freezes the cake overnight in the pan. The next day, he unmolds the cake by dipping the pan into hot water first.

David's classic accompaniment was a raspberry puree, just a simple puree in the blender of thawed frozen raspberries, run through a sieve to remove the seeds and sweetened. It was the ketchup of the late '70s, accompanying all things chocolate.

MARY'S CHERRY UPSIDE-DOWN CAKE

MAKES: 10 TO 12 SERVINGS
PREP: 20 TO 25 MINUTES
BAKE: 45 TO 50 MINUTES

CAKE

6 tablespoons unsalted butter

1¼ cups light brown sugar, firmly packed

1¼ pounds (2½ to 3 cups) fresh pitted or frozen pitted tart cherries, thawed and drained

¾ cup (1½ sticks) unsalted butter, at room temperature

1½ cups granulated sugar

3 large eggs, separated

2 teaspoons vanilla extract

½ teaspoon almond extract

2¼ cups all-purpose flour (see Cake Note on page 217)

1 tablespoon baking powder

½ teaspoon salt

¾ cup whole milk, at room temperature

TOPPING

1 cup heavy cream, chilled

⅓ cup granulated sugar

1 teaspoon vanilla extract

Sour Cherries

Make sure you use sour or tart cherries in this recipe. Unlike sweet cherries, they have a tartness and acidity that pack a lot of flavor. If they don't grow near you, you can use frozen cherries. Thaw them and pat dry before using in this recipe.

When Mary Drabik was growing up in a large family on the south side of Chicago in the 1950s, summer meant sour cherries to be pitted for pie, lemonade, and this upside-down cake. Her mother was a good cook who stretched every penny and stayed up nights after the 10 children were in bed to make her own bread. She couldn't turn down free sour cherries from her sister's cherry trees. So Mary, her mother, and her older sisters would walk to her aunt's yard and fill shopping bags with cherries. "Then the cherry craziness would begin," as Mary describes the endless baking. "We didn't have a lot of freezer space, so when those cherries came in, we had cherry everything. That was how it used to be. When food came into season, that was what you ate." One year Mary's sister used her babysitting money to buy their mother her own cherry tree. The children watered it and kept the birds away. "I remember peering out of the back window of our upstairs bedroom checking on the condition of the cherry tree, especially if we had a lot of snow during the winter." Today Mary, who lives in Shoreview, Minnesota, picks cherries from a farm in Wisconsin and relives those good old days by baking this cake. While her mother used vegetable shortening to save money, Mary prefers butter. And Mary has been successful baking her mom's recipe, entering it in the Minnesota State Fair in 2014 and winning first prize.

1. For the cake, place a rack in the center of the oven, and preheat the oven to 350°F. Line the bottom of a 13″ × 9″ baking pan with parchment paper (this makes the turning-out process less messy).

2. Place the 6 tablespoons butter and brown sugar in a small saucepan over medium heat and let the butter melt, stirring, 1 to 2 minutes. Turn the mixture into the prepared pan, spreading it evenly over the parchment paper. Place the drained, pitted cherries in an even layer on top of the butter and sugar mixture. Set the pan aside.

3. For the cake batter, place the ¾ cup butter and granulated sugar in a large mixing bowl, and beat with an electric mixer on medium speed until light and creamy, 3 minutes. Add the egg yolks, one at a time, beating well after each addition. Beat in the vanilla and almond extract, and scrape down the sides of the bowl.

continued

4. Whisk together the flour, baking powder, and salt. Add this to the batter alternately with the milk, beginning and ending with the dry ingredients. Set aside.

5. Place the egg whites in a large mixing bowl, and beat with an electric mixer on high speed until stiff peaks form, about 4 minutes. Fold a small amount of beaten egg whites into the batter to lighten it. Then fold in the rest of the egg whites, lifting and folding as you incorporate the egg whites. Gently spread the batter over the cherries so as not to disturb them. Place the cake in the oven, and bake until the top is golden and a toothpick inserted in the center comes out clean, 45 to 50 minutes. Remove the cake from the oven and let cool for 15 minutes.

6. After 15 minutes, run a knife around the edges of the pan. Turn the cake onto a serving platter and cut into servings. Serve warm with the whipped cream topping or with vanilla ice cream.

7. For the topping, place the cold cream into a large mixing bowl. Whip with an electric mixer with cold beaters on high speed until soft peaks form, about 2 minutes. Then, while the mixer is on, gradually add the sugar, and beat until the cream holds stiff peaks. Fold in the vanilla, and serve.

CAKE NOTE: Mary's mother used Gold Medal flour in this cake. Mary does, as well.

Family Heirloom State Fair Recipes

This recipe is just one of many family heirloom recipes that have been entered in state fairs throughout the Midwest. The contests are coordinated by the Greater Midwest Foodways Alliance. According to contest director Catherine Lambrecht, who attends all the fairs and comes up with a contest theme each year, this upside-down cake won the "Picnics and Family Reunions" theme. I can't think of a better cake to tote to a summer gathering than this dessert.

THE ORIGINAL CUPCAKES

 WITHOUT THE HEAVY FROSTING and sprinkles that bedeck cupcakes today, the original "cup cake" was simply a cake based on cup measurements versus weights. It was the forerunner of the 1-2-3-4 Cake and the "yellow" cake of modern times. These simple cakes contained 1 cup butter, 2 cups sugar, 3 cups flour, and 4 eggs, beaten. Sometimes a little rosewater, lemon juice, or brandy was added for flavoring, as Lettice Bryan suggested in *The Kentucky Housewife*, published in 1839. Once baking powder was invented, the recipe spun off in all directions.

By the 1940s, "cupcake" was one word. It described the cakes baked in muffin pans lined with paper baking cups. During the World War II years, they were a way for working women to bake quickly and take the cakes to share with coworkers. A Mrs. J. D. Harper writes in the *Hutchinson News* (Kansas) in 1943 about her chocolate cupcakes: "My war workers like them very much, and I like them because they are so easy to make and easy to pack."

Throughout the 1950s and '60s, cupcakes fit into the easy entertaining lifestyle enjoyed by America, as well as the trend of fund-raising bake sales. Then they took a little hiatus until 2000, when TV character Carrie Bradshaw of *Sex and the City* walked into Magnolia Bakery in New York City's West Village and ate a vanilla cupcake with thick buttercream frosting. And cupcakes were back.

PINK CHAMPAGNE CAKE

MAKES: 12 SERVINGS
PREP: 50 TO 55 MINUTES
BAKE: 23 TO 27 MINUTES

CAKE

Butter and flour for prepping the pans

3 cups cake flour

1 tablespoon baking powder

½ teaspoon salt

6 large egg whites, at room temperature

1 cup pink champagne, at room temperature

2 teaspoons vanilla extract

2 tablespoons vegetable oil

2 cups granulated sugar

1 cup (2 sticks) unsalted butter, at room temperature

Tiny amount of pink food coloring (see Cake Note on page 220)

PINK CHAMPAGNE BUTTERCREAM FROSTING

1¾ cups (3½ sticks) unsalted butter, at room temperature

8 cups confectioners' sugar, sifted

4 to 5 tablespoons pink champagne

1 teaspoon vanilla extract

Tiny amount of pink food coloring (see Cake Note on page 220)

White chocolate shavings, sliced strawberries, coconut, or edible rose petals for garnish

In 1960, women who frequented the nightclub scene sipped pink champagne, or at least that's what the gossip columnists said. In England, Princess Margaret was out sipping pink champagne in the wee hours, and pink champagne was the drink of choice of Hollywood starlets, too. Women's clubs hosted pink champagne luncheons on festive occasions. And when not poured into glasses, pink champagne was a fashionable color of jewelry, even a shade of shag carpeting. Johnson's Model Bakery in Medford, Oregon, that same year baked a Christmas Pink Champagne Cake, and later variations popped up in Oregon and California. From the Yosemite Bakery in Modesto, California, to the Modern Cake Shop in Eureka, Kansas, where the cake was "filled with Bavarian champagne-flavored butter cream," this cake was fun, fresh, and hip. It is still baked at McGavin's Bakery in Bremerton, Washington, containing no champagne, and at the Madonna Inn in San Luis Obispo, California. The *Los Angeles Times* has said this cake is one of its most requested cake recipes of all time. It is just right for showers, bachelorette parties, weddings, and graduations. This recipe is adapted from the one shared in the *Los Angeles Times*.

1. For the cake, place a rack in the center of the oven, and preheat the oven to 350°F. Grease and flour three 8″ layer pans. Shake out the excess flour, and set the pans aside.

2. Place the flour, baking powder, and salt in a medium-size bowl, and sift to combine well. Set aside.

3. Place the egg whites, champagne, vanilla, and oil in a large mixing bowl, and whisk by hand until well blended. Set aside.

4. Place the sugar and butter in a large bowl, and beat with an electric mixer on medium speed until creamy and light, 3 to 4 minutes. Add the flour mixture and the egg white mixture alternately, beginning and ending with the dry ingredients. Stir in the pink coloring. Divide the batter between the prepared pans, and place the pans in the oven.

5. Bake until the cakes just pull back from the sides of the pans, 23 to 27 minutes. Remove the pans from the oven, and place them on a wire rack to cool for 10 minutes. Run a knife around the edges of each pan,

continued

give each cake a gentle shake, then invert it once and then again onto the rack to cool completely, right side up, 30 minutes.

6. While the cakes are cooling, prepare the frosting. Place the butter in a large mixing bowl, and beat on medium speed until creamy and smooth, 1 minute. Add 6 cups of the confectioners' sugar and the champagne and vanilla. Blend on medium speed until smooth. Add the remaining confectioners' sugar, adding what you need to make the frosting thick but spreadable. Increase the mixer speed to medium-high, add the pink coloring, and beat until the frosting is fluffy, 30 seconds.

7. To assemble the cake, place 1 layer on a cake plate. Spread about $3/4$ cup of the frosting to the edges. Place a second layer on top and repeat. Place the third layer on top, and frost the top and sides of the cake with the remaining frosting. Garnish as desired, depending on the occasion. Slice and serve.

CAKE NOTE: We used Wilton pink coloring paste. Use a toothpick to dab into the paste and use only a small amount to create a pale pink cake.

TRAINING WORLD WAR II VETERANS IN THE CULINARY ARTS

AFTER WORLD WAR II, many American vets came home to no jobs and with few marketable skills. Two important initiatives opened their doors to vets, and these businesses are now fixtures in the American culinary scene.

In 1946 the New Haven Restaurant Institute in New Haven, Connecticut, offered culinary classes to veterans. Five years later, that school became the Culinary Institute of America, which would grow into one of the best culinary schools in the world—the CIA. In the 1970s, the CIA expanded its enrollment and moved to its Hudson Valley, New York, location, and it added on-campus restaurants and a culinary library.

One of those restaurants—American Bounty—was ahead of its time in 1982 in focusing on the foods of regional America. It was through this training that Amer-

ican chefs became comfortable with cooking and baking in an American style with local ingredients.

Another endeavor to put postwar vets to work was the Wilton method of decorating; like the CIA, it is still in full force today. Dewey McKinley Wilton, a Chicago pulled-sugar artist, opened a cake decorating school in 1929, offering to teach hotel pastry chefs the art of pulled sugar. They, in turn, taught Wilton how to decorate cakes with French buttercream frosting.

Wilton combined these techniques in 1946 when he, his wife, and their five grown children taught classes in their home dining room. Word spread about the Wilton Method of Cake Decorating, a style that emphasized buttercream frosting, shell borders, swags, and piped icing flowers. The classes filled quickly, and veterans on the GI Bill used the training to work in bakeries or open their own bakeries. By 1948 there were more than 250,000 male bakery workers in America, three and a half times as many as before the war.

RUM CAKE THROUGH THE YEARS

COOKS HAVE DOCTORED cake mixes ever since the mixes hit the shelves. One of the more popular recipes beginning with a cake mix has been the Bacardí Rum Cake baked in a Bundt or tube pan lined with chopped pecans. Dark rum goes into the batter, and once baked, the cake is saturated with rum sauce, a hallmark of the recipe.

But rum cake in America dates back well before cake mix came along. Colonists added rum to their fruitcakes, and Americans continued to drink and cook with rum throughout the 1800s. At the turn of the 20th century, home cooks placed newspaper ads in Wisconsin offering rum cakes for sale. The cakes were known in the early 1900s as being the "confectionery with a kick." One Pittsburgh, Pennsylvania, dance hall couldn't get a liquor license, so the owner baked a potent rum cake and served it to the patrons. "Never before anywhere did cake make such a hit," wrote the *Pittsburgh Post-Dispatch* the following day, April 14, 1919. "Men and women fought to get to the cake counter . . . rum cake is in a class by itself. A few pieces of it produce a marvelous effect . . . after the third, the feet simply refuse to behave."

With the titillating publicity, rum cakes took off in the 1920s and '30s. And there were clear regional variations—the "Ba Ba Rum" cakes of Brooklyn, the pecan rum cakes in Chicago, and the Cuban rum cakes of South Carolina. Missouri and Oklahoma rum cakes had cashews on top, and Pennsylvania cooks added molasses. But at the end of the day, rum cake was just a lot of fun to eat and stayed in the news.

A Massachusetts attorney tried to get his client off the hook for drunk driving in 1944 by pleading it was the man's overconsumption of rum cake that did it. Burglars in Santa Cruz, California, broke into a home in 1947 and stole the family's ham, cottage cheese, and rum cake.

But liquored-up cakes yielded to teetotaling versions such as the one prepared at a 1956 Illinois cooking school sponsored by the local newspaper and electric utility. Cooking teacher Mae Ellen Bruce used rum flavoring in the batter, which she poured atop chopped pecans in the bottom of the tube pan. Two years later, the Piggly Wiggly supermarkets in California were selling "Bacardi" Rum Cakes, with the assurance of "no hangovers guaranteed!"

By the time America baked the rum cake with a cake mix, Bacardí dark rum, not rum flavoring, was the addition of choice. It made a cake that was festive, moist, a good keeper, and easy to assemble.

In 1976 Bacardí president William Walker was having a party at his home in Miami, and his neighbor brought a rum cake for dessert. Walker loved the cake so much he asked his corporate chef to create the cake for a Bacardí board meeting. The directors loved it, too, and the cake became part of Bacardí's advertising campaign and a great sales tool, calling for 6 ounces dark rum. Even housewives who didn't drink rum needed to buy it for their cake. And liquor stores were happy to hand out the recipe with a purchase.

CAKE MIX EVOLUTION

THE CAKE MIX was developed long before it became popular in postwar America. Here are some highlights of its timeline.

• Between 1930 and 1936, the Duff Company of Pittsburgh introduces white, spice, and devil's food mix.

• In 1943 General Mills begins its Betty Crocker cake mix research.

• Duncan Hines begins cake mix testing in 1946.

• The first Pillsbury Bake-Off,® called the Grand National Recipe and Baking Contest, takes place in 1949.

• Duncan Hines creates its first cake mix—the Three Star Special—in 1951.

• In 1954 Betty Crocker introduces an Answer Cake, offering a foil pan, cake mix, and frosting aimed at busy people. It had been discontinued by 1968.

• Jiffy Cake Mixes are made by Michigan's Chelsea Milling in yellow, white, and devil's food in 1955.

• In 1977 Pillsbury places pudding in the cake mixes to make them more moist. General Mills follows this lead.

1963 *to* 1979

American Cake Times
Are a-Changin'

~~~

EVENTS UNFOLDING on television news in the 1960s were a stark contrast to the sweet and simple cakes coming out of the oven. As America neared a nuclear missile crisis, grieved at the death of President John Kennedy, fought in Vietnam, and staged protests against the war and for civil rights, our cakes were edible escapes from the tumultuous real world.

They were often simple butter cakes with fruit like the Huckleberry Cake of James Beard (page 224), the dean of American cooking. Beard's recipes revolved around his culinary raising in the bountiful Pacific Northwest and learning to cook from his mother, who ran a Portland, Oregon, boardinghouse. He wanted Americans to turn to local chefs and native soil for inspiration.

Or the cakes were elegantly French in style, dense and chocolatey, like the Reine de Saba, or Queen of Sheba Cake, a creation of Julia Child (page 238). With the French joie de vivre and the American can-do spirit of her California upbringing, Child arrived back in America on a book tour in 1961. Her new book, *Mastering the Art of French Cooking*, which she coauthored with Simone Beck and Louisette Bertholle, explained in detail how to cook French food, a popular fascination of the time. Child was a former member of the Office of Strategic Services who took French cooking

classes in Paris as a newlywed. The two volumes of her best-selling book and a television series called *The French Chef*, which followed on PBS, won over America.

Had it not been for television, the public would never have witnessed Julia Child's on-air gaffes, not to mention the Saturday-morning cartoons, comedies like *Rowan & Martin's Laugh-In*, and the endless run of game shows that gave a troubled America something to laugh about. In the food world, the Pillsbury Bake-Off® which launched in 1949, capitalized on America's craving for celebrity and love of a good contest. Bakers vied to represent their state in the grand Bake-Off,® a mix of patriotic vibe and beauty contest appeal, and the winners took home stardom, cash, and legal agreements allowing their recipes to appear in Pillsbury cookbooks. One of those recipes was the 1966 second-place winner—the Tunnel of Fudge Cake (page 226)—a gooey chocolate cake baked in a

Bundt pan that made its Texas creator, Ella Rita Helfrich, famous in her home state and propelled the Bundt pan to stardom.

Down South, Coca-Cola, the popular cold drink in the little bottles, found its way into a cake of its own. Essentially a chocolate sheet cake with Coke as the liquid and more Coke in the frosting, the Coca-Cola Cake (page 232) blurred racial lines in a still-segregated South. It was baked by both blacks and whites for church suppers and neighborhood picnics, and that cake is still baked today, as are other 1960s greatest-hits cakes like the Hummingbird (page 235), the multilayer Doberge Torte (page 241), and the Italian Cream Cake (page 246).

The Hummingbird, or Dr. Bird Cake as it was originally called in marketing materials from Jamaica Airlines, combined banana and pineapple. The tropical theme was all over the '60s in Hawaiian shirts, muu-muu dresses, and piña coladas, and this new cake was moist and different, topped with cream cheese frosting, and embraced by Southern cooks. And yet away from backyard suburban luaus and little umbrellas floating in tropical drinks, much of America was donning black armbands in protest of the Vietnam War. In 1969 we witnessed the Peace Moratorium—the largest antiwar demonstration in US history—as well as the Woodstock music festival and men walking on the moon.

Berkeley, California, the epicenter of the new hippie movement, was a revolutionary university town where Alice Waters would put down roots and open Chez Panisse in 1971. Waters, a visionary who educated America on fresh, local, seasonal, and sustainable ingredients, brought a radical chic style to fine cooking. She was joined by Lindsey Shere as pastry chef, and Shere's Chez Panisse Almond Torte (page 231) is an American classic: unfrosted, uncluttered, sleek, and timeless. It set the tone for other sophisticated cakes to come out of California restaurant kitchens. The look of American cake would no longer be just comforting layers with frosting or filling and candles on top.

Once the 1970s arrived, America was having a huge '60s social hangover, and the news settled back into economic woes—inflation and recession—and new cultural mores—such as feminism, *The Joy of Sex*, and working women. In 1975, 44 percent of married women were in the job market. Which means there wasn't a whole lot of cooking at home. One of the more popular quick cakes of the time was the Watergate Cake, based on white cake mix and pistachio pudding mix, topped with—what else?—Cover-Up Icing.

But the best cakes coming out of the 1970s were products of the activist '60s—carrot cakes and cakes with decidedly vegetarian, California, and Mediterranean tones. Mollie Katzen and the cooks of the Moosewood Collective in Ithaca, New York, taught a generation of young people how to cook vegetarian meals. Their cakes, such as a cinnamon and cardamom coffee cake (page 251), were rich and moist, heavy and unapologetic.

At the end of the decade, it was neither French culinary techniques nor convenient canned soups that intrigued America's cooks. Working women didn't have time to cook anymore and were drawn to takeout fare with bold, sophisticated flavors. Sheila Lukins had been catering such food out of her New York apartment kitchen and joined Julee Rosso in 1977 to open a gourmet shop on New York's Upper West Side. Called the Silver Palate, it was a one-stop resource for bright and clever dinner party fare, and a new style of American cooking dawned. Lukins's carrot cake, packed with pineapple, coconut, walnuts, and cinnamon (page 252), was like no other.

The war was over, the marches were done, and heroes were buried. The first e-mail message had been sent between two California computers. Apple and Microsoft were born. And baby boomers who had new jobs on Wall Street were hungry for carrot cake, chicken Marbella, and a big slice of Chocolate Decadence.

JAMES BEARD'S HUCKLEBERRY CAKE

MAKES: 8 TO 9 SERVINGS

PREP: 20 MINUTES

BAKE: 38 TO 42 MINUTES

Butter and flour for prepping the pan

1 cup (2 sticks) unsalted butter, at room temperature

1 cup granulated sugar

3 large eggs

2 cups all-purpose flour, sifted

2 teaspoons baking powder

Pinch of salt

1 to 1½ cups fresh huckleberries or blueberries (see Cake Notes)

1 teaspoon vanilla extract

Sweetened whipped cream for serving, if desired

No Huckleberries? Use Blueberries

Wild huckleberries are smaller and more tart than blueberries, and if you have access to fresh berries, use them. You can also order several pounds of frozen huckleberries online from a number of companies, such as Northwest Wild Foods in Burlington, Washington. They are pricey, but they arrive at your kitchen frozen and ready to thaw and use in this cake. And you can share leftover berries with friends. Blueberries make a good stand-in, and although Beard was a stickler about this being better as a huckleberry cake, we found it worked just fine with blueberries. The cake is so delicious, it would be wonderful with fresh raspberries, too.

When James Beard was a boy growing up in Portland, Oregon, his family spent summers at the beach on the Oregon coast. Beard writes about those good times in his 1964 cookbook, *Delights and Prejudices*. A pleasant memory was going berrying for blue-black–hued huckleberries in the hills on the other side of the railroad tracks. Huckleberries are one of America's great indigenous berries, at home in the wet, acidic soil of the Pacific Coast, Idaho, and Montana, ready for picking in summertime, and beloved by humans and bears. Beard writes that the tart taste and fragrance of fresh huckleberries were "absolutely ravishing." This cake was a favorite recipe of Beard's mother's best friend, Polly Hamblet, who baked it for Beard when he was a boy. It's dead simple, and that is its appeal. There are no distractions—no almond or lemon, and the amount of sugar is kept to a refreshing minimum—so what you taste are the berries.

1. Place a rack in the center of the oven, and preheat the oven to 375°F. Lightly grease and flour an 8″ square metal baking pan with butter, and shake out the excess flour. Set the pan aside.

2. Place the butter and sugar in a large mixing bowl, and blend with an electric mixer on medium speed until light and fluffy, 1 to 2 minutes. Add the eggs, one at a time, blending on low until just combined.

3. Remove 2 tablespoons of the flour and set aside. Sift together the remaining flour, baking powder, and salt in a small bowl, and fold this into the creamed mixture. Toss the reserved flour with the berries, and fold them into the batter along with the vanilla. Turn the batter into the prepared pan, and smooth the top. Place the pan in the oven.

4. Bake the cake until the top is deeply browned and a toothpick inserted in the center comes out clean, 38 to 42 minutes. Remove the cake from the oven, and place it on a wire rack to cool for 20 minutes. Slice and serve with the whipped cream, if desired.

CAKE NOTES: While James Beard's recipe calls for 1 cup of berries, I like a few more. And if you like the flavor of lemon, add this simple glaze to brush on the cake as it cools: Whisk together ½ cup confectioners' sugar and the juice and grated zest of half a lemon. Brush onto the cake with a pastry brush.

TUNNEL OF FUDGE CAKE

MAKES: 12 TO 16 SERVINGS
PREP: 30 TO 35 MINUTES
BAKE: 45 MINUTES

2 cups chopped pecans or walnuts (see Cake Notes)

2 tablespoons unsalted butter, melted

Pinch of salt

Butter or vegetable shortening and flour for prepping the pan

1¼ cups (2½ sticks) unsalted butter, slightly cool, cut into tablespoon-size pieces (see Cake Notes)

1 cup granulated sugar

¾ cup light or dark brown sugar, lightly packed

1 teaspoon vanilla extract

⅓ cup vegetable oil

½ teaspoon salt

2 large egg yolks, at room temperature

4 large eggs, at room temperature

2 cups confectioners' sugar

¾ cup unsweetened cocoa powder

2¼ cups all-purpose flour

CAKE NOTES: Pecans were used in the Bake-Off® recipe. The butter should not be cold and also not be at room temperature, thus "slightly cool."

The story of the Tunnel of Fudge Cake is a good lesson that coming in second place has its rewards. In the 1966 Pillsbury Bake-Off® staged in the San Francisco Hilton Hotel ballroom, Mari Petrelli of Las Vegas took home the $25,000 grand prize for her Golden Gate Snack Bread. But the second-place winner, Ella Rita Helfrich's Tunnel of Fudge Cake, would forever be the real winner. For weeks, months, even 50 years after that '66 Bake-Off,® you still hear about the Tunnel of Fudge Cake and Helfrich of Houston, Texas, while the snack bread is but a distant memory. What made the Tunnel of Fudge such an interesting cake was its secret ingredient—a box of Pillsbury Double Dutch Fudge Buttercream dry frosting mix—that when baked into the cake oozed a soft and fudgy chocolate filling, thus the tunnel of fudge. And the pan in which the cake was baked was the fluted Bundt, relatively new to the baking landscape. After the Bake-Off,® it became a fixture in American kitchens. Although Pillsbury no longer makes the Double Dutch Fudge Buttercream dry frosting mix used in Helfrich's recipe, many people have tried to re-create the recipe that calls for it. Here is one devised by Atlanta food chemist and author Shirley Corriher in which the cake is intentionally underbaked—45 minutes—to yield a fudgy core.

1. Place a heavy baking sheet on a shelf in the lower third of the oven. Preheat the oven to 350°F.

2. Place the pecans on a large baking sheet, and place in the oven while it preheats. Toast the nuts until nicely browned, 5 to 7 minutes. Keep watch that they do not burn. Turn the pecans into a small bowl, and add the 2 tablespoons melted butter and salt. Toss to coat and set aside.

3. Grease and flour a 10″ Bundt pan. Shake out the excess flour, and set the pan aside.

4. Place the 1¼ cups butter in a large mixing bowl, and beat with an electric mixer on medium speed until soft and fluffy, about 2 minutes. Add the granulated and brown sugars, and beat until creamy. While beating, if the bowl does not feel cool, place it in the refrigerator for 5 minutes, then resume beating. Add the vanilla, oil, and salt, and blend until incorporated.

continued

5. Add the 2 egg yolks. Crack the 4 whole eggs into a medium-size mixing bowl, and blend with a fork lightly. Add to the batter in 3 batches, blending on low speed. Add the confectioners' sugar and cocoa, just until combined.

6. In a large mixing bowl, stir the flour and toasted nuts. Fold them into the batter, and turn the batter into the prepared pan.

7. Place the pan in the oven, and bake exactly 45 minutes. You cannot use the toothpick test to check doneness because the center will not be set. Remove the cake from the oven. It will still have a runny, fudgy core and an air pocket above the tunnel of fudge. Let it cool for 15 minutes. Press down on the cake with a clean kitchen towel to deflate the air pocket. Run a knife around the edges of the cake, and invert it onto a platter to cool for 45 minutes. Slice and serve.

The Cake Lady

A Houston mother of five entered the 1966 Pillsbury Bake-Off® using two of her favorite flavors—pecans from her backyard pecan tree and a package of chocolate frosting mix. Ella Rita Helfrich became known as "the Cake Lady," and according to longtime *Houston Chronicle* food editor Ann Criswell, "Ella Rita made Houston famous." She used the $5,000 prize money to buy a new Impala. But her family says Helfrich didn't like all the national attention she received for creating the chocolate cake baked in a Bundt pan, and she once considered disconnecting the home telephone to avoid the calls. In 1999 Pillsbury named her one of its inaugural inductees in the Bake-Off® Hall of Fame. In 2012 she and the Bundt pan were featured in the Smithsonian's exhibit called "Food: Transforming the American Table 1950–2000." A longtime lover of sugar, butter, chocolate, and pecans, Helfrich died in 2015 at 98 years. Had it not been for the Cake Lady, the Bundt pan would never have been so popular in America.

BUNDT-MANIA

 THE CLASSIC PAN of the American kitchen—the pan that has launched Bake-Off®-winning cakes, pleased millions of brides-to-be, and had everyone laughing in the movie *My Big Fat Greek Wedding*—the Bundt originated in Europe. According to Mimi Sheraton in *The German Cookbook*, the American Bundt pan was a take-off on the turban-shaped pans used to bake the traditional German coffee cake called *Bundkuchen* or *Kugelhopfs*. The story goes that after the Turks were defeated at the gates of Vienna in 1683, the Viennese bakers created a victory cake shaped like the sultan's turban. The turban-shaped cakes were beloved in Germany and baked in fragile ceramic pans or heavy cast-iron pans. As early as 1903, *The Settlement Cook Book* of Milwaukee, Wisconsin, shared two recipes for "Bundt Kuchen," both rich yeast cakes, one with lemon and the other with raisins. It is quite possible those ladies baking the Bundt Kuchen had brought their pans with them to America. Nearly a half century later, in the 1950s, a group of ladies from the Minneapolis chapter of the Hadassah

Society met with H. David Dalquist, whose company Nordic Ware was making bakeware for the Scandinavian community. The ladies pleaded with Dalquist to create a lightweight turban-shaped pan so they could make *Bundkuchen* like they did in Germany. Dalquist agreed, cast the pan in aluminum, and called it a Bundt. After enduring sluggish sales for 10 years, Dalquist got his big break in 1966 when seemingly out of nowhere, Ella Rita Helfrich of Texas baked her Bake-Off® second-place-winning Tunnel of Fudge Cake in his Bundt pan. Sales skyrocketed, and Bundt-mania swept the nation. Pillsbury received more than 200,000 phone and mail requests to locate the mysterious fluted pan. Now there are countless variations of the original Bundt, and Nordic Ware has sold some 60 million pans. The pan is so popular that it is no longer an adjective used to describe a cooking pan but is a noun on its own, as witnessed in *My Big Fat Greek Wedding*. The best way to prepare a Bundt for baking is to brush it with vegetable oil or shortening, then dust with flour. The 12-cup Bundt holds 12 cups of cake batter, and the cake yields 16 slices.

SOCK-IT-TO-ME CAKE

THE PHRASE "sock it to me" was repeated throughout *Rowan & Martin's Laugh-In*, a television comedy show debuting in 1968 and running until 1973. When someone said "Sock it to me," and it was usually actress Goldie Hawn, he or she got doused with water. Richard Nixon was campaigning for president in 1968 and agreed to come on the popular show that dabbled in comedy, political commentary, and sexual innuendo. Nixon deadpanned, "Sock it to me," and his ratings

soared. (He didn't get doused with water, by the way.) It was only a matter of time before a cake was named after the catchy phrase. The Sock-It-to-Me Cake was a sour cream coffee cake, based on a cake mix. It was swirled with cinnamon, brown sugar, and finely chopped pecans. Recipes for these cakes circulated in Texas and Oklahoma in the late 1960s. And Duncan Hines ran a Sock-It-to-Me Cake recipe on the back of the box for a long time.

CHEZ PANISSE
ALMOND TORTE

MAKES: 12 SERVINGS
PREP: 20 TO 25 MINUTES
BAKE: 48 TO 52 MINUTES

Butter for prepping the pan

7 to 8 ounces almond paste (see Cake Note)

1¼ cups granulated sugar

1 cup (2 sticks) unsalted butter, at room temperature

1 teaspoon vanilla extract

6 large eggs, at room temperature

1 cup unbleached flour

1½ teaspoons baking powder

½ teaspoon salt

2 teaspoons confectioners' sugar for dusting

Cake Bites for a Crowd

On Shere's 80th birthday, the current pastry chef at Chez Panisse, Mary Jo Thoresen, who trained with Shere as an intern, stamped out rounds of Shere's almond torte and served them with peaches soaked in red wine. It was a fitting tribute to a talented chef and the sign of a simple and versatile recipe. To do likewise, bake your favorite cake recipe in a half sheet pan, or a large jelly roll pan. Cut the cake into squares, or stamp out small circles of the cake with a cookie cutter. Transfer the squares or circles to a long platter. Dust the top with confectioners' sugar. Garnish the platter with fresh berries or with peaches that have been soaked in red wine and a little sugar and garnish as desired.

Lindsey Shere was 12 when her family left Chicago and moved to a ranch outside Healdsburg, California. Her mother didn't anticipate how much work that ranch would require, and so Shere, the oldest of five daughters, did a lot of the family cooking. Shere became an accomplished self-taught cook with a flair for desserts when her friend and neighbor Alice Waters opened Chez Panisse restaurant in Berkeley in 1971. Their dinner parties had demonstrated Shere's ability with pastry, so Waters felt no interview was required. And in the early years, when Chez Panisse was just a remodeled house with a cottage out back, Shere's baking was done in that cottage. She carried her tarts and tortes across the yard to the restaurant until the health department prohibited that, she says, and a pastry kitchen was attached to the restaurant. One of Shere's signature cakes was this almond torte, which was an old Italian recipe that she tweaked a little. As her father's family was from northern Italy, she adds, "I was drawn to Italian food."

1. Place a rack in the center of the oven, and preheat the oven to 325°F. Lightly grease a 9″ springform or deep layer cake pan with soft butter, and set the pan aside.

2. Crumble the almond paste into pieces in a food processor fitted with a steel blade. Add the sugar. Pulse until the almond paste is finely chopped. Stop the machine and add the butter and vanilla. Pulse until the mixture is creamy and light. Add the eggs, one at a time, and pulse until the eggs are well combined. Stop the machine.

3. Place the flour, baking powder, and salt in a large mixing bowl, and whisk to combine. Add the flour mixture to the food processor, and pulse until just blended. Turn the batter into the prepared pan, smoothing the top. Place the pan in the oven.

4. Bake the cake until it is deeply golden brown and the center is slightly firm when pressed, 48 to 52 minutes. Remove the pan from the oven. Let the cake cool for 20 minutes. If using a springform pan, run a knife around the edges and unfasten the collar. Slice and serve. Or, if using a layer pan, run a knife around the edges, give the pan a gentle shake, and invert the cake once and then again onto a serving plate.

CAKE NOTE: Almond paste is found in the baking aisle. Most brands are 7 to 8 ounces. Some versions of this recipe call for a little almond extract, but Shere says there was no almond extract in her original recipe.

COCA-COLA CAKE

MAKES: 16 SERVINGS

PREP: 35 TO 40 MINUTES

BAKE: 30 TO 35 MINUTES

CAKE

Butter and flour for prepping the pan

2 cups all-purpose flour

1¾ cups granulated sugar

½ cup (1 stick) lightly salted butter

½ cup vegetable oil

3 heaping tablespoons unsweetened cocoa powder

1 cup Coca-Cola

½ cup buttermilk

1 teaspoon baking soda

2 large eggs

2 teaspoons vanilla extract

1½ cups miniature marshmallows

FROSTING

½ cup (1 stick) lightly salted butter

3 heaping tablespoons unsweetened cocoa powder

6 tablespoons Coca-Cola

3 to 4 cups confectioners' sugar, sifted

1 teaspoon vanilla extract

1 cup chopped pecans (see Cake Note)

CAKE NOTE: If you want the best flavor from the pecans, toast them first while the oven preheats, 4 to 5 minutes. It is your choice to fold the pecans into the icing, to omit them, or to scatter them on top of the cake once the cake has been frosted.

In 1886 Atlanta pharmacist John Pemberton was looking for new sources of income and created a pharmaceutical tonic. This was not only a time when pharmacists were the ones to invent new drugs and tonics, but it was also when the Temperance movement shunned alcohol consumption. Hanging out at a soda fountain sipping a soft drink was preferable to spending time at the saloon. Pemberton created the formula for Coke but would die long before Coke became "the Real Thing," and even before it was bottled. Asa Candler stepped in, bought the company, and marketed Coca-Cola with modern-day savvy, handing out coupons and placing the well-known logo on merchandise. Coke developed a strong Southern identity and was called the "Champagne of the South." And as Coke's popularity spread throughout the country, it wasn't long before cooks added it to recipes. A Coca-Cola chocolate spice cake was first mentioned in 1959 in Galveston, Texas. By 1967 Coca-Cola cake recipes appeared in local Arkansas and Oklahoma newspapers. Nell Amburn writes in the *Emporia Gazette* in Emporia, Kansas, on July 20, 1967, "We have made cakes with soup and with Jell-O—why not make one with Coca-Cola?" This cake, based on a classic Texas sheet (sheath) cake recipe of cocoa, buttermilk, and the poured fudge frosting, is adapted from an Atlanta Junior League recipe.

1. For the cake, place a rack in the center of the oven, and preheat the oven to 350°F. Grease and flour a 13″ × 9″ metal baking pan, and shake out the excess flour. Set the pan aside.

2. Place the flour and sugar in a large mixing bowl, and stir to combine. Set aside.

3. Place the butter, oil, cocoa, and Coca-Cola in a medium-size saucepan, and bring to a boil over medium heat. Stir until the butter melts and the mixture just comes to a boil. Pour the cocoa mixture over the sugar and flour. Blend with an electric mixer on low speed, or with a wooden spoon, until just combined. Measure the buttermilk, and stir the baking soda into it to dissolve. Add to the batter along with the eggs and vanilla. Blend on medium speed until well combined, 1 minute. Fold in the marshmallows. Turn the batter into the pan, and place the pan in the oven.

continued

4. Bake the cake until the top springs back when lightly pressed with a finger, 30 to 35 minutes. Remove the pan from the oven.

5. While the cake cools, make the frosting. Place the butter, cocoa, and Coca-Cola in a small saucepan over medium heat, and when the butter has melted and the mixture just comes to a boil, remove it from the heat. Measure 3 cups of the confectioners' sugar into a large mixing bowl, and pour the hot cocoa mixture over it. Blend with an electric mixer on low speed until smooth, adding the vanilla and more confectioners' sugar to make the frosting spreadable but also easy to pour from the pan. If desired, fold the pecans into the frosting before spreading it onto the cake. Or frost the cake, and top with the pecans. Let cool for 20 minutes, then slice and serve.

Other Cakes Made with Soda Pop

Coca-Cola may be the oldest soft drink, but it is not the only one added to cake batter. Through the years, cooks have poured their regional soft drink favorites into cakes. Avoiding the sugar but capitalizing on their flavor, Weight Watchers cake recipes have called for diet soft drinks. Here are a few of the soft drink favorites.

DR PEPPER: According to Vance Ely, Austin chef and Texas native, the best Dr Pepper for adding to a cake recipe was one made in Dublin, Texas, and called Dublin Dr Pepper. It included Imperial Sugar's pure cane sugar from Plano, Texas, instead of corn syrup. And it was one of the original small-batch soda manufacturers that dotted the American landscape. Legal battles with the parent company Dr Pepper Snapple shut the doors on Dublin Dr Pepper production, but the company makes other sodas now. Ely says if you are going to bake a cake with a soft drink, it will taste better if the soda is made with cane sugar.

7UP: A staple pound cake in Savannah, Georgia, and along the coastal South, says food historian Damon Lee Fowler, this cake even gets a mention in Sue Monk Kidd's book *The Secret Life of Bees.* It is most often flavored with lemon, either lemon zest or lemon extract.

CHEERWINE: A North Carolina soft drink invented in 1917, bright red, cherry-flavored Cheerwine folds well into cake batter. Raleigh, North Carolina, food writer Sheri Castle makes a Cheerwine pound cake, flavoring it with almond and lemon extracts.

ALE-8-ONE: Entrepreneur G. L. Wainscott of Winchester, Kentucky, was eager to enter the soda market, but in order to compete with big manufacturers like Coca-Cola he needed something new. Traveling in Europe, Wainscott tasted ginger beer and came home to create his own. Needing a name for his new beverage, Wainscott held a contest in 1926 at a county fair. The winning name Ale-8-One was a play on words, rhyming with "a late one," because this soft drink was "the latest thing." Still made in Winchester, Ale-8-One is beloved in the Bluegrass State and is poured into a pound cake batter flavored with ginger.

THE HUMMINGBIRD CAKE

MAKES: 12 SERVINGS

PREP: 1 HOUR

BAKE: 18 TO 22 MINUTES

Vegetable shortening or butter and flour for prepping the pans

3 cups all-purpose flour

2 cups granulated sugar

1 teaspoon ground cinnamon

1 teaspoon baking soda

½ teaspoon salt

3 large eggs, slightly beaten

1 cup vegetable oil

1½ teaspoons vanilla extract

1 can (8 ounces) crushed pineapple packed in juice, drained

1 cup finely chopped pecans, if desired

2 cups mashed ripe bananas (about 4 medium)

Cream Cheese Frosting for a 3-layer cake (page 320)

½ cup chopped toasted pecans for garnish

Who would have thought that a marketing promotion by Jamaica Airlines would evolve into one of America's best-loved cakes? The Hummingbird—a sweet cake of mashed bananas, cinnamon, and crushed pineapple—not only resonated with the tropical-themed late 1960s, but it still speaks today. Moist, flavorful, a good keeper, the Hummingbird Cake has stood the test of time. But it began as the Dr. Bird Cake, created to bring exposure to Jamaica Airlines and Jamaica as a travel destination in 1969. The airline's symbol, emblazoned on the jets, was the hummingbird, or as it was known in Jamaica, Dr. Bird. Press parties were held in New York and Miami to unveil a new promotional cake containing mashed bananas and crushed pineapple and baked in a tube pan. Its tropical flavors were supposed to conjure up some idyllic beach holiday in the islands. Helen Moore, the food editor of the *Charlotte Observer* at the time, remembers receiving the press release and sharing the cake recipe with her readers in North Carolina. Some time passed, and a Mrs. L. H. Wiggins, of Greensboro, North Carolina, sent the recipe to *Southern Living*, where in February 1978 it appeared in the magazine transformed into a layer cake containing pecans and topped with cream cheese frosting. The recipe shot to instant stardom. It is still considered one of *Southern Living*'s most popular cake recipes. And according to Brandi Stafford of the *Tulsa World*, the Hummingbird has another name in Oklahoma—"The Cake That Doesn't Last."

1. Place a rack in the center of the oven, and preheat the oven to 350°F. Grease and flour three 9″ round cake pans. Shake out the excess flour, and set the pans aside.

2. Place the flour, sugar, cinnamon, baking soda, and salt in a large bowl, and whisk to combine well. Add the eggs, oil, and vanilla, and blend with a wooden spoon or an electric mixer on low speed. Increase the speed to medium and blend until well combined, 1 minute. Or stir more briskly until well combined. Fold in the pineapple, pecans, if desired, and the bananas. Divide the batter between the prepared pans, and place the pans in the oven.

3. Bake until the cake just pulls away from the edges of the pans, 18 to 22 minutes. Remove to wire racks to cool for 10 minutes. Run a knife

continued

around the edges of the pans, and give them a gentle shake to loosen the cakes. Invert the cakes once and then again onto the racks. Let the layers cool to room temperature, at least 30 minutes.

4. Meanwhile, prepare the frosting. If using the pecans as a garnish, toast them in a 350°F oven for 4 to 5 minutes.

5. To assemble the cake, place 1 layer on a serving plate. Spread with about $^2/_3$ cup of frosting. Top with a second layer and repeat with the frosting. Top with the third layer and frost the top and sides of the cake with smooth strokes. Garnish the top of the cake with pecans. Slice and serve. Or chill for 1 hour uncovered for easier slicing.

TAKE ME TO THE ISLANDS

FOOD FADS, like fashion trends, have been influenced by cultural choices, world events, and economic times. They have also been affected by Madison Avenue. In the early 1960s, before tie-dye swept the nation, the advertising world convinced Americans to go tropical. Hawaii had just become a state in 1959, and bright floral shirts, long and colorful muumuu dresses, and appetizer pupu platters of fried pork and dipping sauces enlivened leisure life.

The hit musical *South Pacific* was touring the nation, and everyone dreamed of the idyllic islands and sipping Trader Vic's rum drinks of bananas, pineapple, and coconut. These ingredients had been around for decades, but not until the '60s were they used in combination to create something tropical.

The Hummingbird Cake, the cherry-pineapple dump cake, ham and pineapple casseroles, and curried chicken salad with pineapple and coconut were fun and different. Sara Lee unveiled a frozen banana cake. Coconut made its way into cream pies with mile-high meringues, into piña coladas, and into a super-successful suntan lotion called Hawaiian Tropic.

JULIA CHILD'S QUEEN OF SHEBA CAKE (REINE DE SABA)

MAKES: 12 SERVINGS
PREP: 40 TO 45 MINUTES
BAKE: 24 TO 28 MINUTES

CAKE

Butter and flour for prepping the pan

¼ cup whole almonds

½ cup (1 stick) unsalted butter, at room temperature

⅔ cup granulated sugar plus 1 tablespoon (to add to the egg whites)

3 large eggs, at room temperature, separated

4 ounces (⅔ cup) chopped good semisweet chocolate

2 tablespoons rum

Pinch of salt

¼ teaspoon almond extract

¾ cup sifted cake flour

CHOCOLATE BUTTER ICING (*GLAÇAGE AU CHOCOLAT*)

1 ounce chopped semisweet chocolate

3 tablespoons unsalted butter

1 tablespoon rum

8 to 12 toasted whole or sliced almonds for decoration

Julia Child had Betty Crocker's "zeal for teaching," M. F. K. Fisher's "love for food," and a command of the kitchen at 6′ 2″ tall, according to food historian Laura Shapiro. Julia also advocated moderation even if her cream-laden recipes were developed in the guilt-free 1960s, as she said. Child would have said to enjoy a small slice of this intensely chocolate, rum, and almond cake, one of her signatures. It was included in the first volume of *Mastering the Art of French Cooking*, which she coauthored with Louisette Bertholle and Simone Beck in 1961. This cake is intentionally soft and creamy, containing no baking powder. It rises with beaten egg whites, and Julia Child advised us to beat them until they form peaks and fold them "swiftly and delicately" so they retain their volume. Each recipe she shared over her lifetime involved well-explained classic technique so that you might find joy in cooking well.

1. For the cake, place a rack in the center of the oven, and preheat the oven to 350°F. Butter and flour the bottom of an 8″ round cake pan that is at least 1½″ deep. Shake out the excess flour. If you have an 8″ springform, or a pan with a removable bottom, use it. Set the pan aside.

2. Place the almonds in a food processor fitted with a steel blade, and pulverize until you get a meal-like texture, 60 to 90 seconds. Set the ground almonds aside.

3. Place the butter and ⅔ cup of the sugar in a large bowl and beat with an electric mixer on medium-high speed until light and fluffy, 4 to 5 minutes. Add the egg yolks and beat until just blended, scraping down the bowl with a rubber spatula. Set the mixture aside.

4. Place the chocolate in a small glass bowl, and heat in the microwave on high power, 30 to 45 seconds, stirring 2 or 3 times, so that the chocolate melts. Once it cools down a bit, stir it into the butter mixture, and blend with the mixer until just combined. Add the rum, salt, almond extract, and ground almonds and stir with the rubber spatula to combine. Set aside.

5. Beat the egg whites in a medium-size bowl with the electric mixer on high speed until soft peaks form, 3 to 4 minutes. Add the remaining 1 tablespoon sugar slowly, and continue beating until stiff peaks form, another 1 to 2 minutes. Stir about a quarter of the whites into the chocolate batter

continued

with the spatula until just combined and the batter is lightened. Fold in about a third of the remaining whites until just combined. Sift in a third of the flour and gently fold to just combine. Continue to add the rest of the whites and flour until all is incorporated. Pour the batter into the prepared pan. With the spatula, spread the batter up the sides of the pan so a well forms in the center. Place the pan in the oven.

6. Bake the cake until a toothpick comes out clean when inserted about 2″ from the edges and the middle is still underdone, 24 to 28 minutes. Cool the cake in the pan on a wire rack for 10 minutes. Run a knife around the edges of the cake, and unmold it onto a serving plate and let cool to room temperature before frosting.

7. For the icing, place the chocolate and butter in a microwaveable bowl and place in the microwave on the defrost setting for 1 minute. Remove and stir. If needed, place back on defrost for another 60 to 90 seconds. Remove and stir to melt the chocolate. Stir in the rum. Place the bowl in the refrigerator until the icing firms up and is spreadable, 5 to 10 minutes.

8. To finish, spread the icing smoothly over the top of the cake. Press the toasted almonds into the icing in a decorative pattern on top.

The French Chef

The first TV episode of *The French Chef* starring Julia Child aired in black and white from Boston on February 11, 1963. The subsequent episodes spanning several years would be groundbreaking and refreshing to watch, a primer on classic French cooking produced live but taped. Mistakes would not be corrected, and millions tuned in over the course of the show. America was smitten with Julia Child because she was knowledgeable and refreshingly honest, dropping an egg or forgetting an ingredient, which was her appeal. This Queen of Sheba Cake was from episode 100. Years later Child would write *The French Chef Cookbook*, a companion to the TV shows. She explains the behind-the-scenes events, how tough it was in the beginning years to get the shows off the ground. But she would never take credit for the show's lasting success. She credited the Kennedy factor—that the Kennedys brought their French chef René Verdon to the White House kitchen and that Americans could easily fly to France, which would "awaken American palates to the pleasures of the table." But we all know the success was due to Julia and her ability to inspire us to think outside the box and enjoy the process.

THE DOBERGE TORTE

MAKES: 12 TO 16 SERVINGS

PREP: 1 DAY, ON AND OFF

BAKE: 10 TO 12 MINUTES PER LAYER (8 LAYERS BAKED 2 AT A TIME)

CUSTARD

2 cups granulated sugar

½ teaspoon salt

4 tablespoons all-purpose flour

4 tablespoons cornstarch

2 heaping tablespoons unsweetened cocoa powder

4 large eggs

1 tablespoon unsalted butter

2 ounces unsweetened chocolate, chopped

4 cups whole milk

1 tablespoon vanilla extract

CAKE

Butter and flour for prepping the pans

¾ cup (1½ sticks) unsalted butter, at room temperature

2 cups granulated sugar

¼ teaspoon salt

4 large eggs, at room temperature, separated

3½ cups sifted cake flour

1 tablespoon baking powder

1 cup whole milk, at room temperature

1 teaspoon vanilla extract

1 scant teaspoon fresh lemon juice

I f bakery owners needed new ideas, they headed to the big city and visited other bakeries for inspiration. That's how a French/Austrian torte became one of the legacy cakes of New Orleans. Baker Beulah Ledner saw the cake while on vacation and modified the classic Dobos Torte to have a Big Easy vibe. Ledner knew her Southern patrons would approve of the thin buttery layers scented with vanilla, and she knew they would approve of a filling of lemon or chocolate. But what type of filling could stand up to the New Orleans heat and humidity? That's where Ledner had to get creative. She cooked up a homemade pudding, thickened it with cornstarch, and enriched it with chocolate and eggs. And on top, she spread a rich buttercream frosting. Since the 1950s, the Doberge—pronounced "doe bash"—Torte has been the cake New Orleans parents ship their children on their birthdays. It was the cake food writer Dale Curry remembers most about her childhood—on trips to New Orleans to visit her grandmother. Beulah Ledner's Doberge Torte, according to Curry, has "so many layers I could hardly count them." This spectacular 8-layer cake takes a good part of a day to make. To save time, make the custard filling the day before you bake the cake.

1. For the custard, place the sugar, salt, flour, cornstarch, and cocoa in a medium-size bowl, and whisk to combine. Set aside. Place the eggs in another medium-size bowl, and lightly beat until lemon colored. Set aside. Place the butter and chocolate in a large saucepan over low heat. Stir to melt the butter and chocolate. Add the milk and beaten eggs, and whisk until combined. Add the dry ingredients, and whisk to combine. Increase the heat to medium and cook until the mixture is very thick, whisking constantly, 12 to 15 minutes. Remove from the heat, then whisk in the vanilla. Pour the hot custard into a large heatproof bowl. Cover the surface of the custard with plastic wrap, sealing to the edges. This prevents the custard from developing a tough surface as it cools. Cool on the counter for 30 minutes, then place in the refrigerator until cold. This takes as little as 4 hours, or overnight.

2. For the cake, place a rack in the center of the oven, and preheat the oven to 375°F. Grease and flour the bottom of as many 9″ layer pans as you have. You will be baking 8 layers. Shake out the excess flour, and set the pans aside.

continued

3. Place the butter, sugar, and salt in a large mixing bowl, and beat with an electric mixer on medium speed until light and creamy, 1 to 2 minutes. Add the egg yolks, one at a time, beating well after each addition. Set aside. Place the egg whites in the large bowl of an electric mixer, and beat on high speed until stiff peaks form, about 5 minutes. Set aside.

4. Sift together the flour and baking powder in a medium-size bowl. Add the flour mixture to the butter mixture alternately with the milk, beginning and ending with the flour. Fold in the vanilla and lemon juice. Fold in the egg whites until just combined.

5. Divide the batter into eighths—about 6 ounces batter or a full $^3/_4$ cup per pan. Spread this into each cake pan, using a metal spatula to spread the batter to the edges. Bake 2 to 3 layers at a time, depending on the size of your oven. Bake until the layers are lightly golden brown and the edges pull away from the sides, 10 to 12 minutes. Remove to wire racks, cool for 5 minutes, then run a knife around the edges and invert onto the racks to cool. The layers will cool quickly because they are thin. Wipe out the pans, grease and flour again, and repeat with the remaining batter.

6. To begin assembly, place 1 layer on a serving plate. Dollop about $8^1/_2$ ounces of custard (about $^7/_8$ cup) on top, and spread it out evenly, to within $^1/_2$″ of the edges. Continue stacking layers and custard. There will be 7 layers of custard, with a top cake layer bare. Lightly cover the cake, and place it in the refrigerator to firm up the custard, about 1 hour.

7. Meanwhile, prepare the frosting. Place the confectioners' sugar and butter in a large mixing bowl, and beat with an electric mixer on low speed for 30 seconds. Increase the speed to medium and beat until creamy, 2 to 3 minutes. Add the cocoa, melted chocolate, and vanilla, and beat until smooth, 1 minute. If the frosting is too thick, add a little hot water, 1 teaspoon at a time, very slowly until the consistency is right.

8. Remove the cake from the refrigerator. Frost the sides of the cake first, spreading on a thin layer. Frost the top, spreading a thin layer to the edges. Store the cake in a cake saver in the refrigerator for up to 3 days. Slice and serve.

CHOCOLATE BUTTERCREAM FROSTING

2 cups confectioners' sugar, sifted

1 cup (2 sticks) unsalted butter, at room temperature

1 cup unsweetened cocoa powder

1 (1-ounce) square unsweetened chocolate, melted

1 teaspoon vanilla extract

4 to 5 teaspoons hot water

FRENCH KING CAKE

(GALETTE DES ROIS)

MAKES: 12 SERVINGS

PREP: 15 TO 20 MINUTES PLUS
2 HOURS TO LET PASTRY REST

BAKE: 40 TO 45 MINUTES

1 package (17.3 ounces) frozen puff
pastry (2 sheets), thawed

FILLING

½ cup (1 stick) unsalted butter, at room
temperature

½ cup granulated sugar

1 large egg

½ cup sliced almonds

1 tablespoon confectioners' sugar

¼ cup all-purpose flour

1 tablespoon rum

1 teaspoon vanilla extract

EGG WASH

1 large egg, lightly beaten

The tradition of serving King Cake in New Orleans on Epiphany and during the time leading up to Mardi Gras is old and dear. While brioche-style King Cake was the first King Cake in New Orleans, and most bakeries today make cakes with a Danish dough and decorate it with bright yellow, green, and purple sprinkles, home cooks are more likely to bake this version. It is a French King Cake or Frangipane King Cake that originated in the northern part of France to serve on Epiphany. Ever since Pepperidge Farm brought frozen puff pastry sheets to US supermarkets and the food processor came into American kitchens, this cake has been the easy King Cake of choice. And it's just the kind of recipe passed from one good cook to another. Caroline Bauerschmidt of Nashville, Tennessee, used to live in Covington, Louisiana, where she picked up this recipe from Anne Butts, who was originally from New Orleans. It has become a tradition in the Bauerschmidt home to have this cake on Mardi Gras morning.

1. Unfold the sheets of puff pastry. Place each one onto a baking sheet. Press down on any cracks to repair them, and gently roll the pastry to smooth it out. Place the baking sheets in the refrigerator for 1 hour.

2. Meanwhile, for the filling, place the butter and sugar in a large mixing bowl, and beat with an electric mixer on medium speed until light and creamy, 30 seconds. Add the egg, and beat until creamy, 30 to 45 seconds more. Set aside.

3. Place the almonds and confectioners' sugar in the bowl of a food processor fitted with a steel blade. Pulse until the mixture resembles meal. Turn the almond meal into the bowl with the butter and sugar. Add the flour, rum, and vanilla, and stir with a wooden spoon or a rubber spatula until just incorporated. Set aside. (If your kitchen is warm, cover and place in the refrigerator until ready to assemble.)

4. Remove the baking sheets from the refrigerator. Paint a 1″ border of the egg wash around the edges of 1 pastry sheet. Spoon the almond mixture into the center of the pastry, pressing it with the spoon just until it meets the egg wash. Do not let the filling get onto the egg wash border. Place the second pastry sheet over the filling, and press down on the edges firmly so they seal. Brush the top with egg wash, and let the cake rest for 1 hour before baking.

5. Place a rack in the center of the oven, and preheat the oven to 400°F. Bake until the cake is puffed and brown, 40 to 45 minutes. Slice and serve.

ITALIAN CREAM CAKE

MAKES: 12 SERVINGS
....
PREP: 1 HOUR
....
BAKE: 22 TO 25 MINUTES
....

CAKE

Vegetable shortening and flour for greasing the pans

8 tablespoons (1 stick) unsalted butter, at room temperature

½ cup vegetable shortening

2 cups granulated sugar

5 large eggs, at room temperature, separated

2 teaspoons vanilla extract

2 cups all-purpose flour

1 teaspoon baking soda

1 cup buttermilk, at room temperature

1 cup sweetened flaked coconut

¾ cup finely chopped pecans

FROSTING

¼ cup finely chopped pecans

8 tablespoons (1 stick) unsalted butter, at room temperature

8 ounces cream cheese

2 teaspoons vanilla extract

4 to 4¾ cups confectioners' sugar

Dash of salt

Extra sweetened flaked coconut as garnish, if desired

You might wonder what is American about an Italian Cream Cake. Well, it depends on the type of Italian Cream Cake. The first version is truly Italian, and an early mention of it is in 1913 in Salem, Ohio, as made by Long's Bakery at the corner of Howard and Main streets. By 1925 Italian Cream Cake was all over California, on restaurant menus and in newspaper grocery ads. Italian grandmothers added a dash of liqueur to the filling, and if you go into an Italian American bakery today, chances are there will be an Italian Cream Cake—filled with sweetened ricotta cheese, candied fruit, and often chocolate. But there is another version, which we will call the pseudo–Italian Cream Cake, or Southern Italian Cream Cake. It contains coconut and pecans and in the 1970s was frosted with cream cheese frosting. It has nothing to do with Italy, but it has everything to do with community cookbooks throughout the South, Texas, and Midwest. The alter ego of the German chocolate cake? Maybe. Truly American? No doubt. Where else but in America would we call a cake with coconut and pecans "Italian"? This recipe is from Eugenia Moore of Nashville and was her signature ending to elaborate Italian dinner parties.

1. For the cake, place a rack in the center of the oven, and preheat the oven to 325°F. Grease and flour three 9″ round cake pans. Shake out the excess flour, and set the pans aside.

2. Place the butter and shortening in a large mixing bowl, and blend with an electric mixer on high speed until creamy, 1 minute. Gradually add the sugar, blending on medium speed. Add the egg yolks, one at a time, beating just until combined. Add the vanilla and combine.

3. Sift the flour and baking soda in a small bowl, and sift to combine well. Spoon a third of the flour mixture into the butter mixture and blend on low, then add ½ cup of the buttermilk and blend. Add another third of the flour mixture, then the rest of the buttermilk, blending, then the rest of the flour mixture. Fold in the coconut and pecans just until combined. Set aside.

4. Place the 5 egg whites in a large mixing bowl, and beat with clean beaters on high speed until stiff peaks form, 4 minutes. Fold the beaten whites into the batter until the whites are well combined. Divide the batter between the 3 pans, and smooth the tops. Place the pans in the oven.

continued

5. Bake until the cakes are golden brown and just pull away from the sides of the pans, 22 to 25 minutes. Remove the pans to a wire rack to cool for 10 minutes, then run a knife around the edges. Shake the layers gently, then invert onto the rack right side up to cool completely, 30 minutes. Leave the oven on.

6. Meanwhile, make the frosting. Place the ¼ cup nuts in a small pan in the oven to toast for 3 to 4 minutes. Remove and set aside to cool. Place the butter and cream cheese in a large mixing bowl, and beat with an electric mixer on medium speed until creamy, 1 minute. Add the vanilla and half of the confectioners' sugar, beating on medium until combined. Add another cup of sugar and the salt and blend on medium-high until combined and light. Add the remaining sugar as needed, and beat on medium-high to lighten the frosting. Fold in the cooled toasted nuts.

7. To assemble the cake, place 1 cooled layer on a cake stand and cover with ¾ cup of frosting, spread to the edges. Place a second layer on top, and spread it with ¾ cup of frosting. Place the third layer on top, and add 1 to 1½ cups frosting to the top of the cake, spreading it decoratively across the top. Use the remaining frosting to frost the sides of the cake, using smooth, clean strokes. Pat extra coconut on top of the cake for garnish, if desired.

THE AMERICAN COFFEE CAKE STORY

 **A MUCH-LOVED BREAK-FAST CAKE** that knows no regional boundaries, the coffee cake is just that—cake to accompany a cup of coffee. It's part of the American story, for as Europeans settled here, they brought with them family recipes and a need to stay connected with people who spoke their language, knew their customs, and shared their tastes in food.

Women who did not work outside the home established a sense of community by sharing morning coffee, conversation, and cake with others. For Germans this cake might have been "blitz kuchen" or "quick cake." The Polish would share poppyseed cake, the Hungarians a sour cream and cinnamon coffee cake, and Scandinavians a cake with fruit such as cherries. Ranging from fragrant yeast breads to quick baking-powder cakes like Cinnamon Flop, coffee cakes were a new development in the first decade of the 20th century.

The 1903 *Settlement Cook Book* of Milwaukee, subtitled *The Way to a Man's Heart,* contains not only a German blitz kuchen recipe flavored with lemon rind but also a coffee cake made with grated chocolate and a cup of strong coffee, proof that coffee cakes often contained coffee. And in Portland, Oregon's *The Neighborhood Cook Book*, published in 1914, coffee cakes looked as they might today, baked in a tube pan with a thick ribbon of brown sugar, cinnamon, and walnut streusel inside.

Coffee cakes popularized ingredients such as sour cream, which came with the Eastern and Central European immigrants who as easily spooned it into their coffee cake as they did their borscht. Isaac Breakstone (born Breghstein) of Lithuania brought the dairy business to New York City in 1882 and supplied cooks with the sour cream to make their traditional streusel-topped sour cream coffee cakes.

Coffee cake with sour cream would become the standard, appearing in grocery advertisements in newspapers in the late 1930s. Syndicated food writers Gaynor and Dorothy Maddox shared a recipe for such a coffee cake in 1939. Jewish delis in Brooklyn; Hartford, Connecticut; and San Francisco became known for their crumb cakes.

By the 1960s, this European tradition of entertaining friends over a cup of coffee and cake had taken hold in postwar America. Junior League cookbooks were filled with cinnamon-infused sour cream coffee cake recipes, and if there was one cake you needed to know how to bake, it was a coffee cake.

MOOSEWOOD CARDAMOM COFFEE CAKE

MAKES: 12 TO 16 SERVINGS
PREP: 25 TO 30 MINUTES
BAKE: 60 TO 65 MINUTES

CAKE

Butter and flour for prepping the pan

2 cups (4 sticks) unsalted butter, at room temperature

2 cups light brown sugar, firmly packed

4 large eggs, at room temperature

2 teaspoons vanilla extract

4 cups all-purpose flour

2 teaspoons baking powder

2½ teaspoons baking soda

1½ teaspoons ground cardamom

½ teaspoon salt

2 cups sour cream

FILLING

¼ cup light brown sugar, firmly packed

1 tablespoon ground cinnamon

½ cup finely chopped walnuts

Cardamom and Scandinavian Cakes

Cardamom-scented coffee cake is a gift from the Scandinavian countries of Sweden and Finland to America. With the immigrants came the love of cardamom, the aromatic spice from the ginger family. It is used whole in Indian cooking, but in Scandinavian cakes and breads the seeds are ground to a powder.

In 1973 in Ithaca, New York, a group of Cornell students opened a mostly vegetarian restaurant called the Moosewood Collective. Here they cooked simple, seasonal meals with ingredients from local farms. Mollie Katzen was one of the cooks, and Katzen went on to publish her recipes in *The Moosewood Cookbook*. Katzen introduced America to vegetarian cooking and her signature sweet was this big, rich coffee cake. Similar to other coffee cakes of the 1970s with sour cream and cinnamon, this cake also contained ground cardamom, new to much of the country. Putting bold flavors together and making cooking and eating fun was what Katzen did so well. Which explains why so many people have learned to cook vegetarian food with her recipes. So many that, in 2007, the James Beard Foundation named *The Moosewood Cookbook* to its Cookbook Hall of Fame.

1. For the cake, place a rack in the center of the oven, and preheat the oven to 350°F. Butter and flour a 10″ tube pan, and shake out the excess flour. Set the pan aside.

2. Place the butter and brown sugar in a large mixing bowl, and beat with an electric mixer on medium speed until light and fluffy, 3 to 4 minutes. Add the eggs, one at a time, beating after each addition. Blend in the vanilla, and set the batter aside.

3. Sift together the flour, baking powder, baking soda, cardamom, and salt in a large mixing bowl. Add this to the batter alternately with the sour cream, beginning and ending with the dry ingredients. Don't overmix. Set aside.

4. For the filling, stir together the sugar, cinnamon, and walnuts in a small bowl. Spoon a third of the batter into the bottom of the prepared pan and spread the batter to the edges. Scatter half of the filling over the top. Spread another third of the batter on top, and scatter the remaining filling over it. Spread the last third of the batter over the filling, and place the pan in the oven.

5. Bake the cake until it has browned well on top and a long toothpick inserted in the center comes out clean, 60 to 65 minutes. Remove the cake from the oven, and place it on a wire rack to cool in the pan for 20 minutes.

6. Run a knife around the edges of the pan, give the pan a gentle shake, and invert the cake once and then again so it cools completely on the rack, right side up, about 1 hour. Slice and serve.

SILVER PALATE CARROT CAKE

MAKES: 12 TO 16 SERVINGS

PREP: 45 TO 50 MINUTES

BAKE: 32 TO 37 MINUTES

6 medium carrots (about 14 to 15 ounces)

Vegetable shortening and flour for prepping the pans (see Cake Note)

¾ cup (8-ounce can) crushed pineapple, drained

1½ cups finely chopped walnuts

3 cups unbleached flour

3 cups granulated sugar

1 teaspoon salt

1 tablespoon baking soda

1 tablespoon ground cinnamon

1½ cups corn oil

4 large eggs, at room temperature, lightly beaten

1 tablespoon vanilla extract

1½ cups loosely packed sweetened shredded coconut

Cream Cheese Frosting for a 3-layer cake (page 320)

CAKE NOTE: To make these layers containing pineapple and coconut easy to remove from the pan, grease and flour generously. Or line the pan bottoms with a round of parchment paper.

C arrots have been used for centuries in cake baking in Europe because once they were cooked down, they could naturally sweeten a cake. One of the earliest carrot cake recipes printed in America was in *The Neighborhood Cook Book* by the Council of Jewish Women in Portland, Oregon, in 1912. And while carrot cake recipes have been shared in newspapers as early as the 1930s, the carrot cake we know really came into its own in the 1970s. Carrot cake in the '70s was everywhere, the carrots were most often raw and shredded into the batter, and the frosting was and still is cream cheese frosting. This recipe from the *Silver Palate Cookbook*, by Sheila Lukins and Julee Rosso, is made in the old-style way using cooked carrots. It was the landmark cake of the Silver Palate gourmet shop, which opened its doors in 1977 in Manhattan. Lukins's mother baked the cake in her Connecticut kitchen and then drove it to the shop each morning. Moist, jam-packed with goodies like walnuts and coconut, and scented with cinnamon, this cake makes any kitchen smell otherworldly. It must have been very difficult to bake this fragrant cake, drive it to the shop, and never get to eat a slice. Here is the Silver Palate recipe, adapted a bit so that it bakes in three 9″ pans.

1. Wash and peel the carrots. Trim off the tops, and slice the carrots into ¼″ pieces. Place them in a medium-size saucepan, and add water just to barely cover them. Place the pan over high heat and bring to a boil, then reduce the heat to medium-low and let the carrots simmer, uncovered, until fork-tender, about 15 minutes. Drain the carrots, and place them in a food processor fitted with a steel blade. Pulse for 45 to 60 seconds or until they are coarsely pureed and yield 1⅓ cups. Set aside.

2. Place a rack in the center of the oven, and preheat the oven to 350°F. Grease and flour three 9″ round cake pans, and shake out the excess flour. Set the pans aside. Drain the pineapple well in a sieve. Put the walnuts on a baking sheet and place in the oven to toast until lightly browned, 5 to 7 minutes. Remove the walnuts, and set aside to cool.

3. Sift together the flour, sugar, salt, baking soda, and cinnamon in a large mixing bowl. Add the oil, eggs, and vanilla. With a large spoon, stir the wet ingredients together and then sift into the dry ingredients until just

continued

combined. The batter will be thick. Fold in the coconut, carrots, pineapple, and walnuts until well blended. Divide the batter between the prepared pans, and place the pans in the oven.

4. Bake the cakes until they turn dark brown and a toothpick inserted in the center comes out clean, 32 to 37 minutes. Remove the cakes to a wire rack to cool for 10 minutes. Run a knife around the edges of the pans, and give the pans a gentle shake. Invert them once and then again onto the rack to cool right side up, 30 minutes.

5. While the layers cool, prepare the frosting.

6. To assemble the cake, place 1 layer on a cake plate and spread with a generous ¾ cup of frosting. Top with the second layer and repeat. Top with the third layer, and spread the frosting on the top and sides of the cake. Chill for at least 30 minutes to make slicing easier.

The Muffin Method

With the rise in popularity of cakes with vegetable oil, an easier method of cake preparation resulted, called the muffin method. So named because this was the easy way to assemble them with the dry ingredients combined and the wet ingredients—the eggs, oil, flavorings—folded in. The batter is thick, and the add-ins like nuts, raisins, or pineapple are added last. The cake has a moist, dense texture, and it should not be overmixed, which would make it tough.

SUNDAY CAKES AND FUNERAL CAKES

IN COMMU-
NITIES across
America, the Sun-
day cake tradition
placed a freshly
baked cake on
the table each week. After church on Sunday, the
preacher visited homes, and you invited him to stay for
dinner. You wanted to have something nice to serve, and
you also didn't know how many people to plan to feed.

The late cookbook author and chef Edna Lewis
called yellow layer cake with chocolate frosting "Sunday cake"—what you baked and served to company vis-
iting after church. Corinne Cook, of Baton Rouge,
Louisiana, remembers her mother baking layer cakes
for the church to raffle off after Mass on Sunday.

A cake that could be baked ahead of time, and one
that stayed moist, was a good Sunday cake candidate.
Pound cakes were popular. In Elberton, Georgia, one
pound cake is called the Bishop Asbury Pound Cake, so
named for Francis Asbury, who brought American Meth-
odism to the South.

In Kentucky, a similar story circulates about a cinnamon coffee cake called "Bishop Cake." Methodist bish-
ops traveled the countryside on horseback and would
stop at rural farmhouses for breakfast. If the bishop
paid an unexpected visit, this easy coffee cake could be
assembled quickly from buttermilk, flour, sugar, and
eggs—ingredients at hand.

Similar to the tea and sympathy tradition well known
in the South, cakes also were served as funeral food.
The late John Egerton explained the custom well in his
book *Side Orders* in 1990. Back when funeral wakes
were held in the home, when parlor doors had to be
wide enough for the pallbearers to pass through with
the coffin, relatives often traveled great distances to
come home to the funeral. And as there were no motels,
they stayed in the family home or in the home of friends.
To support the bereaved, the community brought food,
and the cakes were the same favorites as Sunday
cakes—chocolate layer cake, pineapple upside-down
cake, and pound cake.

Egerton said that in the South, the greetings "come
on in" and "help yourself" are throwbacks to a time
when people opened their doors to the preacher and
the community to join in the meal.

CHAPTER

{ 8 }

1980 to 1999

Cakes Born *in the* USA

~~~

IN THE 1980S, fine chocolate, imported butter, Madagascar vanilla, and boutique coffee could be bought at your corner market. A new and creative American style of cooking was born, and it bid farewell to simple homespun postwar cakes. The cakes of the '80s were surprising and bold—flourless almond cakes, plum tortes, and chocolate cakes so dense and creamy you ate them with a spoon.

Embraced by food writers, superstar chefs, California winemakers, small food producers, and farmers, this new American food scene was the beginning of the local food movement we now know. Highbrow pastry chefs loaded their squirt bottles with crème Anglaise, raspberry coulis, caramel sauce, and balsamic vinegar reductions and painted edible squiggles and swirls on dessert plates. They stacked cakes and brownies high on the plate, creating a three-dimensional architectural presentation that was larger than life.

The luxurious offerings of the 1980s emanated from restaurant kitchens staffed by talented young cooks trained in France or from high-profile California restaurants like Chez Panisse and Spago. What emerged was an army of superstar chefs who led a gourmet movement of regional flavors. American Spoon Foods of Michigan started with chef Larry Forgione's salute to the sour cherries of his home state. According to Chez Panisse alum and pastry chef

Lindsey Shere, the fine food of the period came out of the creative 1960s.

The Chantilly Cake from Hawaii (page 273) and Chocolate Earthquake Cake from San Francisco (page 258) were great American regional cakes with their origins in the '80s and '90s. They were intense, rich, thick, chewy, and fruity: everything that mattered, according to restaurant consultant Clark Wolf when interviewed in the '80s on what people eat. They also wanted chocolate. Magazines such as *Chocolatier* were devoted just to chocolate, and a flourless chocolate cake was on every dessert menu. Flourless chocolate cakes had been baked for Passover for years, and now they came out of Jewish bakeries and cookbooks and into the spotlight, embraced by those who cook gluten-free.

And while "gourmet" was everywhere, "foodie" was only coined by food writer Gael Greene in 1980. But not everyone could afford to eat at these bastions of new American cuisine. In 1984 Bruce Springsteen's best-selling songs on the *Born in the USA* album spoke of the struggles of average working-class families. The elitist style of American cooking that emanated from California had little in common with regional small-town America. And small-town America continued to bake at home. Regional recipes continued to be published in church and community cookbooks. On Ocracoke Island, on the Outer Banks of North Carolina, a spice cake made with locally produced fig preserves (page 267) was popular. As was a peach layer cake called Mother Ann's Birthday Cake in New England (page 264). In New York, readers of the *New York Times* could not get enough of a Plum Torte recipe (page 261) every September.

One of the biggest advocates of regional cooking turned out to be Martha Stewart, who urged women not to give up on cooking at home. She challenged women to be creative, making magnolia wreaths for the front door, growing their own herbs, and putting up jams and jellies. And to bake just like Martha, you could go to your local Williams-Sonoma or Sur La Table store and get all the supplies and equipment. Or you could take cooking classes. Peter Kump ran one of the most prestigious cooking schools in New York, and after James Beard died in 1985, Kump led the effort to buy Beard's Greenwich Village brownstone from Reed College, the benefactor. The James Beard Foundation began.

But just as Black Monday in October 1987 jolted the stock market, the 1990s were the correction for the decadent '80s. America woke up from the chocolate and butter dream and felt terribly hung over. We replaced the fat with a puree of prunes. In pound cakes, we used applesauce instead of butter. Weight Watchers cake recipes with a cake mix and diet soda spread via the Internet. Fat was the enemy, and we sought ways to bake cakes without it. But those cakes didn't taste very good, and thus, they didn't last long. Had it not been for cupcakes, the '90s would have been a terribly depressing period in American cake baking.

Cupcakes had fit into the easy entertaining lifestyle enjoyed by America in the '50s and '60s. But they took a little hiatus until 2000 when Carrie Bradshaw of TV's *Sex and the City* walked into Magnolia Bakery in New York City's West Village and ate a vanilla cupcake with thick buttercream frosting. Women across America and the world craved those cupcakes as much as they coveted Carrie's Jimmy Choo shoes. Copycat cupcake shops sprang up in New York, Washington, DC, and Los Angeles. In 1999, when Ina Garten wrote her first *Barefoot Contessa* cookbook, she shared her recipe for coconut cupcakes, which became a national obsession.

These new cupcakes were retro but stylish. They were large and generous, down-home and gourmet, often boozy, with icing piled 3 inches high. They had all the decadence of the 1980s, with a dose of moderation from the '90s and ushered in a bite-size approach to baking that would continue well into the new millennium.

CHOCOLATE EARTHQUAKE CAKE

MAKES: 10 TO 12 SERVINGS

PREP: 60 TO 65 MINUTES

BAKE: 50 TO 55 MINUTES

2 teaspoons unsalted butter, at room temperature

1 teaspoon unsweetened cocoa powder

10 ounces bittersweet chocolate, broken into 1" pieces

½ cup (1 stick) unsalted butter, cut into 1" pieces

6 large eggs

1 cup granulated sugar, divided use

2 teaspoons rum or brandy

1 teaspoon vanilla extract

GARNISH

1 teaspoon confectioners' sugar for dusting

Vanilla ice cream and/or fresh raspberries for serving

Without flour to give them stability, and with beaten egg whites folded in to give them height, flourless chocolate cakes often soar in the oven but fall and crack when removed to cool. Some recipes advise you to level off the cracked top of the cake and flip the cake so the smooth and flat bottom is on top. But other chefs embraced the cracked, sunken appearance of a cooled flourless cake. In San Francisco in the 1980s, this cake was known as the Earthquake Cake. Dense and fudgelike, this cake is allowed to cool and is dusted with confectioners' sugar before serving. One of the first Earthquake Cakes was baked by Carlo Middione at the Italian restaurant Vivande in San Francisco.

1. Place a rack in the center of the oven, and preheat the oven to 375°F.

2. Rub the soft butter on the bottom and sides of an 8″ springform pan or tall metal baking pan with removable bottom. Dust with the cocoa, and set the pan aside.

3. Place the chocolate and butter in a heavy saucepan over low heat, and stir until the chocolate melts, 2 minutes. Turn off the heat and set the chocolate-butter mixture aside.

4. Separate the eggs, placing the yolks in a large mixing bowl and the whites in a separate large mixing bowl. Set the whites aside. Beat the egg yolks with an electric mixer on medium-high speed, gradually adding ¾ cup of the sugar as you beat. Beat until they are pale yellow and the consistency of mayonnaise, 1 to 2 minutes. Turn off the mixer and pour the chocolate mixture into the yolks. Beat on low until just combined, 30 seconds. Add the rum and vanilla, and beat again on low until just combined, 10 seconds. Set aside.

5. With clean beaters, beat the egg whites on high speed until soft peaks form, 1 to 2 minutes. Gradually beat in the remaining ¼ cup sugar, and beat until stiff peaks form, about 1 minute longer. Turn off the mixer, and fold the whites into the chocolate mixture with a rubber spatula until the whites are well combined. Pour the batter into the prepared pan, and place the pan in the oven.

continued

6. Bake the cake for 15 minutes, then reduce the temperature to 350°F, leaving the cake in the oven. Bake the cake for another 15 minutes, then reduce the temperature to 250°F. Bake the cake until the cake smells very chocolatey, the top has a nice firm crust, and the cake jiggles a bit when the top is touched, 20 to 25 minutes. Turn off the oven, but leave the cake in the oven. Prop the oven door open 2″ with kitchen towels, and let the cake sit in the turned-off oven for 25 minutes.

7. Remove the cake from the oven, and let it cool for 20 to 30 minutes in the pan on the kitchen counter. The cake will fall as it cools. Run a knife around the edge of the pan, and remove the sides or bottom of the pan. Place the cake on a serving plate, sift confectioners' sugar over the top, and slice while warm. Serve with the ice cream and/or berries.

8. Or, for easier slicing, leave the cake in the pan and chill, covered, at least 2 hours, then slice and serve.

Molten Cake Craze

Little did Ella Rita Helfrich know when she came in second place in the 1966 Pillsbury Bake-Off® that her Tunnel of Fudge Cake (page 226) would inspire the molten chocolate cake craze of the 1990s. There was something pretty wonderful about forking into a cake and having the center ooze warm chocolate onto the plate. Especially if a scoop of vanilla bean ice cream was to the side. In 1987 Jean-Georges Vongerichten, star chef of Jean-Georges and JoJo in New York, placed a Molten Chocolate Cake on his menu. He said the cake was created by accident after he underbaked small chocolate cakes. But these cakes have been around for years in France as well as California. By 1991, when Florence Fabricant wrote in the *New York Times* that molten cakes had taken over the city's best restaurants, these molten cakes, or lava cakes as they were called, were everywhere. Unintentional or intentional, the underbaked chocolate cake never tasted so good.

LOIS'S ORIGINAL PLUM TORTE

MAKES: 8 TO 12 SERVINGS

PREP: 15 TO 20 MINUTES

BAKE: 40 TO 45 MINUTES FOR 10" PAN; 45 TO 50 MINUTES FOR 9" PAN

1 teaspoon butter for greasing the pan

8 to 12 whole purple or red plums

¾ cup granulated sugar

½ cup (1 stick) unsalted butter, at room temperature

1 cup unbleached flour, sifted

1 teaspoon baking powder

Pinch of salt

2 large eggs, lightly beaten

1 tablespoon granulated sugar

1 teaspoon ground cinnamon or 1 teaspoon grated lemon zest

When Lois Levine and her friend Marian Burros shared Lois's recipe for a fruit torte in their 1960 *Elegant but Easy Cookbook*, they had no idea that recipe would become one of the *New York Times'* most requested cakes. Burros wrote about food for the *Times* for many years, and in the early 1980s she shared that recipe with newspaper readers. A blueprint sort of recipe to use with most any seasonal fruit—plums, peaches, apples, etc.—it was an instant hit with plums, which come into season in late summer. And so readers became accustomed to seeing that recipe each September, and when they didn't, they let the food department know they wanted the recipe republished. According to the *Times*, one reader put it like this: "Summer is leaving, fall is coming. That's what your annual recipe is all about." Plum tortes are an old recipe, with roots in Germany, and in America they were popular in the 1930s when made with crushed zwieback, a sweetened toast used in baking. By 1969 newspaper recipes for plum tortes included the buttery cake batter found in this recipe. The California fruit industry was busy sending food editors recipes using their purple plums, and it didn't take long for the plum torte fad to really take off in the 1980s. Food writer Amanda Hesser says the appeal of this recipe is that it contains only a few ingredients that you already have in your kitchen. And you don't need an electric mixer to make it, although you can use one if you like. Any size pan will do as well, either a 9" or a 10" springform pan. The larger is preferable, as there is more surface area so more crispy cake on top. And you can customize the amount of fruit versus cake by adding the number of plum halves you like. Fit them closely together, and you will have a cobblerlike cake. Use fewer and space them apart, and you will have cake with some fruit, which makes it easier to slice.

1. Place a rack in the center of the oven, and preheat the oven to 350°F. Lightly grease the bottom of a 9" to 10" springform pan with butter, and set the pan aside.

2. Wash and pat dry the plums. Cut them in half, and remove the pits and discard. Set the plum halves aside.

continued

3. Place the sugar and butter in a large mixing bowl, and beat with an electric mixer on medium speed until light and creamy, 1 minute. In a separate bowl, stir together the flour, baking powder, and salt. Set aside.

4. Add the eggs to the butter and sugar mixture, and blend on low to incorporate. Fold in the flour mixture just to combine. Spoon the batter into the bottom of the prepared pan. Place the plum halves cut side down on top of the batter. (If you want more plums, use 12 whole or 24 halves. If you want fewer, use 8 whole or 16 halves, or as many as you like.) Sprinkle the plums with the 1 tablespoon sugar and either cinnamon or lemon zest. Place the pan in the oven.

5. Bake the cake until the top is golden brown and the center springs back when lightly pressed with a finger, 40 to 45 minutes for a 10″ pan, and 45 to 50 minutes for a 9″ pan. Remove the pan from the oven, and set it on a wire rack to cool for 20 minutes. Run a knife around the edges of the pan, and unfasten the collar of the pan. Carefully slice the cake away from the bottom of the pan, and place it on a cake plate to serve.

CAKE NOTE: To reheat the cake, place uncovered in a 300°F oven until warmed through, about 20 minutes.

MOTHER ANN'S BIRTHDAY CAKE

MAKES: 12 TO 16 SERVINGS
PREP: 25 TO 30 MINUTES
BAKE: 23 TO 27 MINUTES

CAKE

Butter and flour for greasing the pans

3 cups all-purpose flour

½ cup cornstarch

1 tablespoon baking powder

1 teaspoon salt

1 cup (2 sticks) unsalted butter, at room temperature

2 cups granulated sugar

1 cup whole milk

2 teaspoons vanilla extract

12 large egg whites

BUTTERCREAM FROSTING

½ cup (1 stick) unsalted butter, at room temperature

2 cups confectioners' sugar

2 tablespoons whole milk

½ teaspoon vanilla extract

FILLING

1 generous cup peach jam or preserves for spreading between the layers (see Cake Note on page 266)

Martha Chapman received a copy of the 1978 *Colorado Cache* Junior League cookbook as a shower gift when she married. One of her favorite recipes from the book is Mother Ann's Birthday Cake, a popular New England recipe that Martha made for her children's birthdays through the years. The inspiration for the recipe was Ann Lee, or Mother Ann, the founder of the American Shaker religious movement who emigrated from England in 1774. The first community of Shakers settled in the Hudson River Valley, where peaches once grew. The story goes that this cake was first made by whisking the egg whites with freshly cut peach twigs. It was common to whisk egg whites with twigs or sticks, whatever you had on hand, before the metal whisk was invented. Nowadays you can breathe a sigh of relief and use an electric mixer to beat 12 egg whites to stiff peaks. Mother Ann's birthday was on February 29, but you can bake this cake on any birthday and fill it with your favorite jam, preferably peach.

1. For the cake, place a rack in the center of the oven, and preheat the oven to 350°F. Grease and flour three 9″ round cake pans, and shake out the excess flour. Set the pans aside.

2. Measure the flour, cornstarch, baking powder, and salt into a large mixing bowl, and sift the mixture together into another large bowl. Set aside.

3. Place the butter into a very large bowl, and beat with an electric mixer on medium speed until soft, 15 seconds. Add the sugar a little at a time, beating until creamy, 1 minute. Spoon a third of the flour mixture into the sugar and butter mixture and beat on low to incorporate. Add a third of the milk. Continue to add the flour mixture and milk alternately until the batter is smooth. Stir in the vanilla, and set the batter aside.

4. Place the 12 egg whites in a large clean bowl and beat with clean beaters on high speed until stiff peaks form, about 4 minutes. Turn the beaten whites on top of the batter, and using a rubber spatula, fold the whites into the batter until they are well incorporated. Use a turning motion and rotate the bowl as you fold in the whites. Divide the batter between the 3 prepared pans, and smooth the tops with a rubber spatula. Place the pans in the oven.

continued

5. Bake the cakes until they are lightly golden around the edges and the center springs back when lightly pressed, 23 to 27 minutes. Remove the pans from the oven, and place them on a wire rack to cool for 10 minutes. Run a knife around the edges of the pans, give the pans a gentle shake, and turn the cakes out onto racks to cool right side up for 30 minutes.

6. While the cake layers are cooling, make the frosting. Place the soft butter, sugar, milk, and vanilla in a large bowl, and beat with an electric mixer on low speed to combine, 30 seconds. Increase the mixer speed to medium and beat until smooth, 1 to 2 minutes more.

7. To assemble the cake, place 1 cake layer on a serving plate. Spread with half of the peach jam. Place a second layer on top. Spread the remaining jam on top of the second layer, and top with the third layer. Spread the top and sides of the cake with frosting. Store up to 3 days at room temperature, if needed.

CAKE NOTE: Some stores have peach jam and others peach preserves. The jam is a little easier to spread than preserves. If you want a more pronounced peach flavor, slice the cake layers in half horizontally and spread jam between all the half layers. You will need 2 cups jam for this method.

TIP FOR BEATING EGG WHITES: *Even a smidgen of egg yolk mixed in with the egg whites will reduce the volume of the beaten egg whites. So to be careful, separate each egg over a small bowl. Then pour the egg whites into a larger bowl.*

BIRTHDAY CAKES

EARLY AMERICANS brought birthday cake rituals with them from their home countries. Most often fruitcakes were baked for birthdays. After the Revolutionary War, people not only celebrated their birthdays but they celebrated the birthdays of the country's founding fathers.

And with fewer bakeries than in Europe, Americans developed a habit of baking cake in the home. According to the *Oxford Encyclopedia of Food and Drink*, American women were bakers because of an "abundance of oven fuel and New World sparsity of professional bakers."

The American layer cake—layers, filling, fluffy frosting—became the image of the American birthday cake. It was leavened with baking powder, the invention that produced faster, taller cakes.

OCRACOKE FIG CAKE

MAKES: 10 TO 12 SERVINGS

PREP: 25 TO 30 MINUTES

BAKE: 50 TO 55 MINUTES

Vegetable shortening and flour for prepping the pan

1 cup walnut or pecan halves

2 cups all-purpose flour

2 teaspoons baking powder

1 teaspoon ground nutmeg

1 teaspoon ground allspice

1 teaspoon ground cinnamon

1 teaspoon salt

1½ cups granulated sugar

1 cup vegetable oil

3 large eggs

1 teaspoon vanilla extract

½ cup buttermilk

1 cup good fig preserves (see Cake Note)

CAKE NOTE: The best fig preserves are made by a friend or found at a roadside stand or farmers' markets. They are dark and syrupy and wonderful. If you must substitute store bought, look for dark Italian fig preserves or jam.

It's nothing new to fold jam or preserves into a spice cake batter. Americans have been doing that for generations. But a cake that incorporates fig preserves is special on the Outer Banks of North Carolina. As popular as American regional ingredients were in the late 1980s, on Ocracoke Island, it was never about the local food movement, as it was a way of life. This is where figs grow prolifically, where they are a part of the island's history, and where each summer a Fig Cake Bake-Off occurs at the annual August Fig Festival. North Carolina food writer Sheri Castle says Ocracoke Island figs thrive because of the salt and the wind, the sand, and the heat of summer. "Figs can be happy in punishing conditions," Castle says. A fragile fruit, figs don't ship well, and their appeal is their seasonality and the localness of the harvest, best eaten in your backyard. Because they don't keep well you've got to preserve them. Which is the same scenario in Louisiana, where fig preserves cakes are coated with caramel frosting and served at Christmas. Figs have been grown in America for centuries. The Spanish and Italian explorers brought them to coastal locations, where they flourished and became a staple addition in cooking. This recipe is adapted from one shared for many years by the Ocracoke United Methodist Church Women. The first fig cake published in their cookbook placed fig preserves between yellow layers. This buttermilk and spice fig cake was an adaptation of an old date spice cake recipe, and it is the fig cake Sheri Castle says is the real thing.

1. Place a rack in the center of the oven, and preheat the oven to 325°F. Lightly grease and flour a 10" tube pan, shake out the excess flour, and set the pan aside. Place the walnuts in a small baking pan in the oven to toast while the oven preheats until they are golden brown, 4 to 5 minutes. Remove the walnuts from the oven, and let them cool. When cool, finely chop and set aside.

2. Sift together the flour, baking powder, nutmeg, allspice, cinnamon, and salt in a large bowl, and set aside.

3. Place the sugar and oil in a large bowl, and beat with an electric mixer on low speed until well combined, about 1 minute. Add the eggs, one at a time, and beat until well incorporated, 1 minute. Add the vanilla.

continued

Alternately add the reserved flour mixture and the buttermilk to the batter, beginning and ending with the flour. Beat on low speed until just incorporated, 30 seconds. Fold in the fig preserves and reserved nuts, and stir until smooth. Turn the batter into the prepared pan, and place the pan in the oven.

4. Bake the cake until a long toothpick inserted in the cake comes out clean and the top springs back when lightly pressed, 50 to 55 minutes. Remove the pan from the oven, and let the cake cool in the pan for 20 minutes.

5. Run a knife around the edges of the pan, give the pan a gentle shake, and invert the cake once and then again onto a wire rack to completely cool, about 1 hour. Slice and serve.

How to Make Fig Preserves Any Time of the Year

When figs aren't in season, you can create fig preserves using dried figs. Chop about 8 ounces dried figs (1½ cups) into small pieces and place in a saucepan with water to cover, about 1 cup. Bring to a boil, cover the pan, reduce the heat, and simmer for about 10 minutes. Stir in ¼ cup sugar and 1 teaspoon fresh lemon juice. Uncover the pan, and let the mixture simmer until thick, 8 to 10 minutes. Spoon into a heat-proof bowl and let cool to room temperature. Store in the refrigerator, and bring to room temperature before using in the cake recipe. Makes about 1⅓ cups.

ROBERT REDFORD CAKE

MAKES: 12 SERVINGS

PREP: 1½ HOURS

BAKE: 52 TO 57 MINUTES

CAKE

Butter, parchment paper, and flour for prepping the pan

1 cup blanched hazelnuts or almonds (see page 272)

¾ cup (1½ sticks) unsalted butter, at room temperature

½ cup honey

10 large eggs, separated

12 ounces semisweet chocolate, chopped, or chips

¼ teaspoon salt

GANACHE FROSTING

¾ cup heavy cream

12 ounces semisweet chocolate, chopped, or chips

GARNISH

Semisweet chocolate shavings

Oregon Hazelnuts

Hazelnuts are native to the Pacific Northwest, but the hazelnuts grown today in Oregon's Willamette Valley is a cultivated variety introduced from Europe. Also known as filberts, hazelnuts are an old nut, dating back to prehistoric times. The first Oregon hazelnut trees were planted by an English sailor in 1858. The hazelnut grows naturally as a bush, but in Oregon it is grown as a single-trunk tree.

In the late 1970s, when actor Robert Redford was in New York and dining at Hisae's restaurant in Greenwich Village, he supposedly was served a slice of this dense and flavorful chocolate honey cake. *Chocolate News* magazine ran the recipe with Redford's photo, which is where cake maven Maida Heatter first saw it. With her usual wit, Heatter says she broke the 4-minute mile getting into her kitchen to try out the recipe. And she later traveled to New York and dined at Hisae's to sample the cake. Heatter deemed her recipe better than the restaurant cake and included this cake in her *Maida Heatter's New Book of Great Desserts* in 1982. She named the cake after Robert Redford, and while other cakes have been named for the heartthrob actor, this one is the original. As was done in the 1980s, the uneven top of the cake was sliced off after baking to level it, the cake was flipped over to have the flat bottom side on top, and it was frosted with a sleek ganache. But this cake, just like Robert Redford, is timeless and always in vogue. You can bake it as is, without leveling and flipping, and serve it with a dusting of confectioners' sugar. Or you can do the '80s thing and spread it with ganache. The hazelnuts are a little tricky to prepare because they have to be blanched first—their skins removed—and then ground. Do the nuts ahead of time, and in fact make the whole cake ahead of time and keep it chilled. Slice small servings, think about Robert Redford, and smile.

1. For the cake, place a rack in the center of the oven, and preheat the oven to 375°F. Lightly grease the bottom and sides of a 10″ springform pan with butter. Line the bottom of the pan with a circle of parchment paper. Grease the parchment paper, and dust with flour. Shake out the excess flour, and set the pan aside.

2. Place the reserved, cooled, blanched hazelnuts in a food processor fitted with a steel blade. Pulse until the nuts resemble coarse meal, about 1 minute. They will be a little sticky. Set aside.

3. Place the butter and honey in a large mixing bowl, and beat with an electric mixer on medium speed until smooth and creamy, 1 minute. Add the egg yolks, 2 at a time, and blend until each round of egg yolks is incorporated. Scrape down the bowl with a rubber spatula, and fold in the ground hazelnuts. Set aside.

continued

4. Put the chocolate in a medium-size glass bowl, and place in the microwave on the defrost setting for 3 minutes, stirring until the chocolate has melted. Cool a few minutes, stirring, and then fold into the batter. Beat on medium speed until blended. Set aside.

5. Place the egg whites and salt in a large bowl, and beat with clean beaters on high speed until nearly stiff peaks form, 4 minutes. Fold the whites into the batter in 3 portions, folding just until combined. Turn the batter into the prepared pan, and place the pan in the oven.

6. Bake the cake for 20 minutes. Then reduce the oven temperature to 350°F and bake until the cake has welled in the center and a toothpick inserted in the center comes out clean, 32 to 37 minutes. Remove the pan from the oven, and place on a rack to cool for 20 minutes.

7. While the cake bakes, prepare the frosting. Place the cream in a small saucepan over medium heat until it nearly boils, about 2 minutes. Place the chopped chocolate in a large bowl. Pour the hot cream over the chocolate and stir with a wooden spoon until the chocolate melts and the frosting is smooth. Let the frosting cool to room temperature. It will thicken as it cools.

8. Run a knife around the edges of the cake. Unfasten the collar of the springform pan, and remove the bottom and the parchment paper from the bottom of the cake. Place the cake on a serving platter. Level the top of the cake with a long serrated knife. Flip the cake so it is bottom up. Spread the top and sides of the cake with the frosting. Garnish with chocolate shavings. Let the cake rest for 30 minutes, then slice and serve.

How to Blanch Hazelnuts or Almonds

Place 3 cups water and 4 tablespoons baking soda in a medium-size saucepan. Stir to dissolve the soda, and bring the water to a boil over high heat. Add 1 cup hazelnuts or almonds (about 4½ ounces raw nuts). Reduce the heat to low and let the nuts boil in the water for 5 minutes. Spoon off the foam that results on the top of the water and discard. Remove the pan from the heat, and pour the nuts into a colander. Rinse the nuts under cold water and rub them between the palms of your hands to remove the skins. When all the skins have been removed, turn the nuts onto a kitchen towel to drain for 15 minutes. Preheat the oven to 350°F. Spread the nuts onto a baking sheet, and when the oven has preheated, place the pan in the oven. Bake the nuts for 20 minutes. Remove the pan from the oven, and let the nuts cool before using in recipes such as this.

HAWAIIAN CHANTILLY CAKE

MAKES: 12 TO 16 SERVINGS

PREP: 4 HOURS IN ADVANCE TO
CHILL FROSTING, 3 HOURS TO
CHILL FILLING

BAKE: 22 TO 26 MINUTES

FROSTING

1 can (12 ounces) evaporated milk

1½ cups granulated sugar

¾ cup (1½ sticks) lightly salted butter,
melted

4 large egg yolks

1½ teaspoons vanilla extract

FILLING

¼ cup granulated sugar

4 teaspoons cornstarch

¼ teaspoon salt

1 large egg, lightly beaten

1 cup whole milk

1 tablespoon unsalted butter

½ teaspoon vanilla extract

GARNISH

¼ to ½ cup chopped macadamia nuts

CAKE

Butter and flour for prepping the pans

3 large eggs

1½ cups granulated sugar, divided use

1⅔ cups sifted cake flour

¾ teaspoon baking soda

¾ teaspoon salt

1 ounce unsweetened chocolate,
melted

⅓ cup vegetable oil

1 cup whole milk, at room temperature,
divided use

Jann Fujimoto left her native Hawaii to attend college at the University of Indiana, and what she missed most about the islands was Chantilly Cake—the chocolate cake with a creamy and rich German chocolate cake–like frosting, except without the coconut. The Oconomowoc, Wisconsin, resident remembers trying to find a Chantilly Cake outside of Hawaii and discovering that Chantilly Cake must be uniquely Hawaiian. It originated in the 1950s, when the Liliha Bakery on Oahu began offering this cake. Now it is still baked at Liliha and in homes, too. Some versions are just cake plus the cooked frosting, and others have the cake, frosting, and a creamy puddinglike filling between the layers. But one thing is constant—toasted macadamias are sprinkled on top of the cake. That's what makes it Hawaiian. Set off from the US mainland and not a state until 1959, Hawaii developed its own cuisine, a blend of Polynesian flavors and influences from around the world. Sailors and explorers who spent time in Hawaii left their culinary marks—the Scottish scones and shortbread, the Portuguese sweetbread and red bean soup, and the American fish chowders. But this cake was a bakery creation using evaporated milk, a staple on the islands before fresh milk was readily available. Evaporated milk has a higher fat content than whole milk, and for that reason it has been a rich and favorite addition to fillings and frostings. Based on the Liliha Chantilly Cake, this cake has a filling and frosting, so it takes a while to assemble. Plan ahead and make what you can the night before you plan on baking the cake.

1. For the frosting, place the milk, sugar, melted butter, and egg yolks in a large mixing bowl, and whisk to combine. Pour the mixture into a medium-size heavy saucepan, and place over medium heat. Cook, whisking vigorously, until the mixture comes to a boil. Boil for 1 minute. Remove the frosting from the heat, and whisk for 1 minute to cool it down. Whisk in the vanilla. Pour into a heatproof bowl, cover the top of the frosting with plastic wrap, and place the bowl in the refrigerator to chill for 4 hours.

2. For the filling, place the sugar, cornstarch, and salt in a medium-size heavy saucepan and stir to combine. Add the egg and milk, and stir to combine. Place the pan over medium heat and cook, stirring until the mixture comes to a boil, and then thickens, 3 to 4 minutes. Take the pan

continued

off the heat, and stir in the butter and vanilla. Pour into a heatproof bowl, cover the top of the filling with plastic wrap, and place the bowl in the refrigerator to chill for 3 hours.

3. For the macadamia nut garnish, place a rack in the center of the oven, and preheat the oven to 350°F. Place the macadamia nuts in a small baking pan, and place in the preheating oven. Toast until golden brown, 4 to 5 minutes, watching carefully so the nuts do not burn. Remove the pan from the oven, and set aside.

4. For the cake, lightly grease and flour two 9″ round cake pans, shake out the excess flour, and set the pans aside.

5. Separate the eggs, placing the whites in a large mixing bowl and the egg yolks in a smaller one. Beat the egg whites with an electric mixer on high speed until foamy, 1 to 2 minutes. Gradually add ½ cup of the sugar, continuing to beat on high until stiff peaks form, 1 to 2 minutes more. Set the egg whites aside.

6. Sift the remaining 1 cup sugar and the flour, baking soda, and salt into a large mixing bowl. Add the melted chocolate, oil, and ½ cup of the milk. Blend on low speed until just combined. Add the egg yolks and remaining milk, and beat on medium speed until smooth, 1 minute. Fold in the egg whites until no traces of white remain. Divide the batter between the prepared pans, and place the pans in the oven.

7. Bake the cakes until they spring back when lightly pressed in the center, 22 to 26 minutes. Remove the pans from the oven and let cool 10 minutes. Run a knife around the edges of the pans, give the cakes a gentle shake, and then invert once and then again onto a wire rack to cool completely, 1 hour. Slice each layer in half horizontally.

8. To assemble the cake, remove the filling and frosting from the refrigerator. Place the bottom half of 1 layer on a cake plate with the cut side up. Divide the filling into thirds, and spread 1 part onto the top of the cake. Place the top of the layer over the filling, and spread with another third of the filling. Place the bottom of the second layer on top of the filling, and spread with the remaining filling. Place the top of the second layer over the filling. Place the cake in the refrigerator for 15 minutes to make the cake easier to frost.

9. Remove the cake from the refrigerator, and spread a thin layer of frosting around the edges of the cake to seal the crumbs. Place the cake back in the refrigerator to set the frosting, about 30 minutes. Remove the cake from the refrigerator, and spread the remaining frosting on the top and sides of the cake. Garnish with the toasted macadamia nuts.

JOHN EGERTON'S POUND CAKE

MAKES: 12 TO 16 SERVINGS

PREP: 20 TO 25 MINUTES

BAKE: 75 TO 80 MINUTES

Vegetable shortening and flour for prepping the pan

1 cup (2 sticks) unsalted butter, at room temperature

Pinch of salt (see Cake Notes)

3 cups granulated sugar

6 large eggs, at room temperature

3 cups sifted all-purpose flour (see Cake Notes)

1 cup heavy cream

2 teaspoons vanilla extract (see Cake Notes)

CAKE NOTES: You can make this cake with any all-purpose bleached or unbleached flour. You can substitute almond extract for ½ teaspoon of the vanilla. If using salted butter, omit the salt.

John Egerton was a widely known Southern scholar of history, civil rights, race, and food. He grew up in the country ham district of Cadiz, Kentucky, but he traveled extensively throughout the South and wrote about the people and places behind the recipes in his 1987 cookbook, *Southern Food.* Nashville was Egerton's home, where he mentored food writers at meat-and-threes like Arnold's. This pound cake recipe comes from his book, and it is a recipe that pound cake aficionados consider one of the best. The secret is the addition of heavy cream, which lends the cake a tender crumb and keeps it moist for up to a week. But it won't last that long. It will be eaten the day you bake it. John Egerton died in 2013. Reflecting about this cake in his book, Egerton said, "A warm slice is special." So was he.

1. Place a rack in the center of the oven, and preheat the oven to 325°F. Generously grease and flour a 10″ tube pan. Shake out the excess flour, and set the pan aside.

2. Place the butter and salt in a large mixing bowl, and beat with an electric mixer on medium-low speed until creamy, 1 minute. Add the sugar, gradually, while beating on medium-low. Increase the mixer speed to medium once all the sugar has been incorporated, and beat until pale in color, 1 minute more. While the mixer is running on low speed, add the eggs, one at a time, making sure each one is incorporated. Scrape down the sides of the bowl with a rubber spatula.

3. With the mixer on low speed, add the flour and cream alternately, until combined, beginning and ending with the flour. Blend in the vanilla, and scrape down the sides of the bowl. Turn the batter into the prepared pan, smoothing the top with the rubber spatula. Place the pan in the oven.

4. Bake until the cake is golden brown and crackly on top and a toothpick inserted near the center comes out clean, 75 to 80 minutes. Remove the pan to a wire rack to cool for 20 minutes.

5. Run a knife around the edges of the pan, give the pan a gentle shake, then turn the cake out onto the rack then turn again to cool right side up. Let it cool for 1 hour before slicing. To store, wrap in aluminum foil or place in a cake saver at room temperature. Or freeze leftovers wrapped in foil for up to 6 months.

CHAPTER 9

2000 *to the* Present

The Cakes
of the New Millennium

〜〜

THE CAKES OF THE NEW MILLENNIUM—from 2000 to the present—like their predecessors use American ingredients, European techniques, and a creativity bubbling from our giant culinary melting pot.

But unlike the cakes of America's first settlers, these new cakes aren't necessarily made with a handwritten recipe given from mother to daughter. They might come from a recipe Web site or be shared via social media. These new cakes might not use wheat flour at all, or they may call for a cup of ground almonds, a generous amount of cocoa powder, or a cup of cornmeal in addition to flour to create a rustic, hearty cake reminiscent of baked goods from Italy.

These new American cakes are often smaller than the cakes of the last 50 years, harkening back to a time when ovens, pans, and portions were smaller. Only now can we appreciate a Half Pound Cake (page 284). Only now do we applaud less icing on the cake and the popularity of so called "naked" cakes, those cakes with the sides left unfrosted.

The restaurant world's transformation from old into artisanal continues to influence the way we bake at home. Chefs often bake cakes in cast-iron pans, a throwback to frontier times, because the heavy pan gives cakes such a nice smooth crumb. And pastry chefs have turned their noses up at artificial red food coloring in red velvet cake and instead look for natural ways to color it red, such as roasting fresh beets, recalling the early Idaho and Midwestern chocolate beet cakes. Dessert portions of cake have shrunk compared with the '80s, and now bites of cake are served in single-serving jars, even shot glasses. With the popularity of cupcakes and cake balls and a new interest in small, beautiful bites of cakes, could the reinvention of petits fours be next?

Fresher and local have replaced gourmet and grandiose. Cakes from Kentucky contain bourbon and sorghum. Chocolate cakes in Brooklyn or in Massachusetts might include the local stout. Cakes in California give a nod to Native American heritage flavors like maple, cranberries, and cornmeal as well as

Mediterranean olive oil and citrus. And in Alaska in the springtime, fresh rhubarb is folded into a simply delicious coffee cake (page 283).

Our growing Hispanic population introduced us to Chocoflan (page 297) and Tres Leches Cake (page 300). Creamy, comforting, and perfect for entertaining, these Hispanic recipes work well in restaurants as well as the home, and they can be easily improvised to include coconut, chocolate, and rum.

Today ordinary cake isn't good enough. Pound cake can't be just pound cake—it needs to be flavored with the juice of Meyer lemons or tiny Key limes. It needs to be baked with real butter and local eggs. Someday soon, locally milled flour from an old heritage grain such as Purple Straw might go into your cake. In fact all the ingredients of cake might one day be mindfully selected. In a stark contrast to the 1980s, when American foodies went in search of the best and most expensive ingredients, sustainable cake bakers of the future will, like their ancestors, use what they have and use every ounce of it.

Throughout its history, America has loved cake. It has been with us as we've celebrated the good times and mourned the losses. Along the way, only the best cakes have survived. Still prepared from family cookbooks the way they used to be, these cakes have stories to tell. Only time will tell what great American cakes of the present live on into the future.

CRANBERRY AND CORNMEAL RICOTTA CAKE

MAKES: 12 TO 16 SERVINGS

PREP: 30 TO 35 MINUTES

BAKE: 1 HOUR 15 TO 20 MINUTES

Butter for prepping the pan

2 cups all-purpose flour

1 cup yellow cornmeal

1 tablespoon baking powder

1 teaspoon salt

¾ cup plus 2 tablespoons (1¾ sticks) unsalted butter, at room temperature

1½ cups plus 2 tablespoons granulated sugar, divided use

3 large eggs

¼ cup maple syrup

¼ cup plus 2 tablespoons light olive oil

1 tablespoon vanilla extract

Grated zest of 1 orange or 1 lemon

1 container (15 ounces) whole milk ricotta cheese, about 2 cups

2½ cups fresh cranberries, divided use

An homage to early New England baking, this sturdy cake of cornmeal, maple syrup, and fresh cranberries is as suitable today as those flavors have been throughout American history. And the inclusion of ricotta cheese, grated citrus, and light olive oil show how European and Mediterranean ingredients have influenced how we bake today. The cake is baked in a deep 9" pan and needs only a dusting of confectioners' sugar for garnish. Old world meets new world in this cake inspired by Zoe Nathan of the Rustic Canyon restaurants in Santa Monica, California.

1. Place a rack in the center of the oven, and preheat the oven to 375°F. Lightly grease a 9" springform pan with butter, and place the pan on a baking sheet and set aside.

2. Place the flour, cornmeal, baking powder, and salt in a large mixing bowl, and stir to combine. Set aside.

3. Place the butter in a large mixing bowl and beat with an electric mixer on medium speed until creamy, 30 seconds. Add the 1½ cups sugar, and beat on medium until the mixture is light and fluffy, 1 to 1½ minutes. Scrape down the sides of the bowl. Add the eggs, one at a time, beating until each egg is incorporated, about 20 seconds each. Add the maple syrup, oil, vanilla, and grated citrus zest, and blend on medium speed until well combined, 45 seconds.

4. Turn about a third of the dry ingredients into the batter and blend on low until just incorporated. Add half of the ricotta cheese and blend. Add another third dry ingredients and blend, then add the rest of the ricotta, and finally the rest of the dry ingredients, blending just to incorporate. Fold 1½ cups of the cranberries into the batter, and blend on low speed to break up the cranberries a bit, about 30 seconds. Turn the batter into the prepared pan. Scatter the remaining cup of cranberries on top of the batter, and sprinkle with the remaining 2 tablespoons sugar. Place the baking sheet with the springform pan in the oven.

5. Bake until the cake is well browned and a toothpick inserted in the center comes out clean, 1 hour 15 to 20 minutes. After 1 hour, gently cover the top of the cake with aluminum foil to protect it from overbrowning. Remove the cake from the oven, and let the cake cool in the pan for 20 to 25 minutes. Run a knife around the edges of the pan, and unfasten the sides of the pan. Let the cake cool completely before serving, about 1 hour. Slice and serve with vanilla ice cream.

ALASKA RHUBARB CAKE

MAKES: 12 TO 16 SERVINGS

PREP: 25 TO 30 MINUTES

BAKE: 38 TO 42 MINUTES

Butter or vegetable shortening and flour for prepping the pan

2 cups (about 7.25 ounces) chopped fresh rhubarb stalks, cut into ¼" pieces

2 cups granulated sugar, divided use

½ cup (1 stick) unsalted butter, at room temperature

2 large eggs

2 cups all-purpose flour

1 teaspoon baking soda

1 teaspoon ground cinnamon

¼ teaspoon salt

1 cup buttermilk, at room temperature

1 teaspoon vanilla extract

2 teaspoons confectioners' sugar for dusting the cake, if desired

A large, leafy green plant with fat, reddish, celery-like stalks, rhubarb grows well in cool climates like New England, Minnesota, and the upper Midwest, as well as in Alaska. It is the first edible item to appear in many spring gardens. Whereas the leaves are poisonous and contain oxalic acid, the stalk or stem of the plant is edible. It is chopped and added to pies and cakes and often blended with other sweeter fruits like strawberries in baking. In America rhubarb has been nicknamed "pie plant." But rhubarb is much older than America. Its origins can be traced to 206 BC in bitterly cold Mongolia, where the roots could survive the frozen ground. In Asia and Europe, rhubarb root was valued as a medicine, and the first rhubarb root was introduced to America by Benjamin Franklin as a medicine. But the French and British began cooking with the brightly colored stalks and turned them into jams, preserves, sauces, pies, and cakes. That inventiveness caught on in America. This coffee cake is adapted from a University of Alaska Cooperative Extension Service recipe. It is a delicious reminder that wherever you live, when rhubarb is in season in the spring, you should seize the moment and bake with it.

1. Place a rack in the center of the oven, and preheat the oven to 350°F. Grease and flour a 13" × 9" baking pan, and shake out the excess flour. Set aside.

2. Place the chopped rhubarb and ½ cup of the sugar in a small glass bowl. Stir and let the mixture rest while you prepare the rest of the cake.

3. Place the butter and the remaining 1½ cups sugar in a large mixing bowl, and beat with an electric mixer on medium speed until well combined and creamy, about 1 minute. Add the eggs, one at a time, beating on medium speed until light and fluffy. Set aside.

4. Sift the flour, baking soda, cinnamon, and salt into a medium-size bowl. Add this flour mixture to the creamed butter and sugar alternately with the buttermilk, beginning and ending with the flour. Beat on low speed until combined. Fold in the rhubarb and sugar mixture and the vanilla. Pour the batter into the prepared pan, and place the pan in the oven.

5. Bake the cake until it is golden brown and a toothpick inserted in the center comes out clean, 38 to 42 minutes. Remove the cake to a rack and let cool in the pan for 30 minutes. Dust the top with the confectioners' sugar, if desired, slice, and serve from the pan.

HALF POUND CAKE

MAKES: 8 TO 12 SERVINGS
....
PREP: 20 TO 25 MINUTES
....
BAKE: 1 HOUR 18 TO 22 MINUTES
....

Butter and flour for prepping the pan

4 large eggs (weighing 8 ounces; use
5 eggs if needed), at room temperature

1 cup (2 sticks; 8 ounces) unsalted
butter, at room temperature (see Cake
Notes)

Pinch of salt

1¼ cups (8 ounces) granulated sugar

2 cups (8 ounces) unbleached flour

3 tablespoons bourbon, rum, sherry, or
Herbsaint

½ teaspoon vanilla extract or almond
extract

CAKE NOTES: If using salted butter, omit the salt. John Martin Taylor
lets his baked pound cake loaf rest in
a turned-off oven for 30 minutes
before removing. But the cake was
done after the baking time, and I felt
you do not need this step.

The original pound cake called for a pound each of butter, sugar, flour, and eggs. But more realistically, however many eggs the hen had laid were put on the scale, and the cook used enough of the other ingredients to weigh the same. If there were just 4 eggs, the batter might yield a medium loaf of cake. Cookbook author John Martin Taylor goes so far as to share a recipe for a Half Pound Cake in his book *The New Southern Cook*. In today's weights, about 4 large eggs equal 8 ounces. Two sticks of butter, 1 generous cup of sugar, and about 2 cups of unbleached flour also weigh 8 ounces. Taylor, who bakes by old recipes, likes to flavor his batter with a little vanilla extract and 3 tablespoons bourbon, rum, sherry, or Herbsaint, a New Orleans anisette. It makes exactly one delicious loaf that is both historically correct and the right size for today's families.

1. Place a rack in the center of the oven, and preheat the oven to 325°F. Lightly butter and flour a 9″ loaf pan. Shake out the excess flour, and set the pan aside.

2. Separate the eggs, placing the whites in a large mixing bowl and the yolks in a medium-size bowl. Beat the yolks lightly to combine and set aside. With an electric mixer or whisk, beat the egg whites on high speed until they are foamy, about 2 minutes. Set the whites aside.

3. Place the butter and salt in a large mixing bowl, and beat with the same beaters (no need to wash them) on medium speed until creamy, 1 min-ute. Add the sugar, and beat until smooth and light, 2 minutes. Lower the mixer speed and add a third of the yolks just to combine. Add half of the flour, and blend to combine, then another third of the yolks, the rest of the flour, and the final third of the yolks, and blend until smooth. Pour in the bourbon and vanilla, and blend. The batter will be thick.

4. Put a wire whisk down in the egg whites and finish beating them by hand until they hold firm peaks but are not dry, 2 minutes. Fold them gently into the batter with a rubber spatula just until combined. Turn the batter into the prepared pan, and smooth the top. Place the pan in the oven.

5. Bake the cake until it is deeply golden brown and a straw inserted deep into the center comes out clean and dry, 1 hour 18 to 22 minutes. Remove the cake from the oven to a wire rack to cool for 20 minutes. Run a knife around the edges of the pan, and give the pan a gentle shake. Turn the cake onto the rack right side up to cool completely, 1 hour.

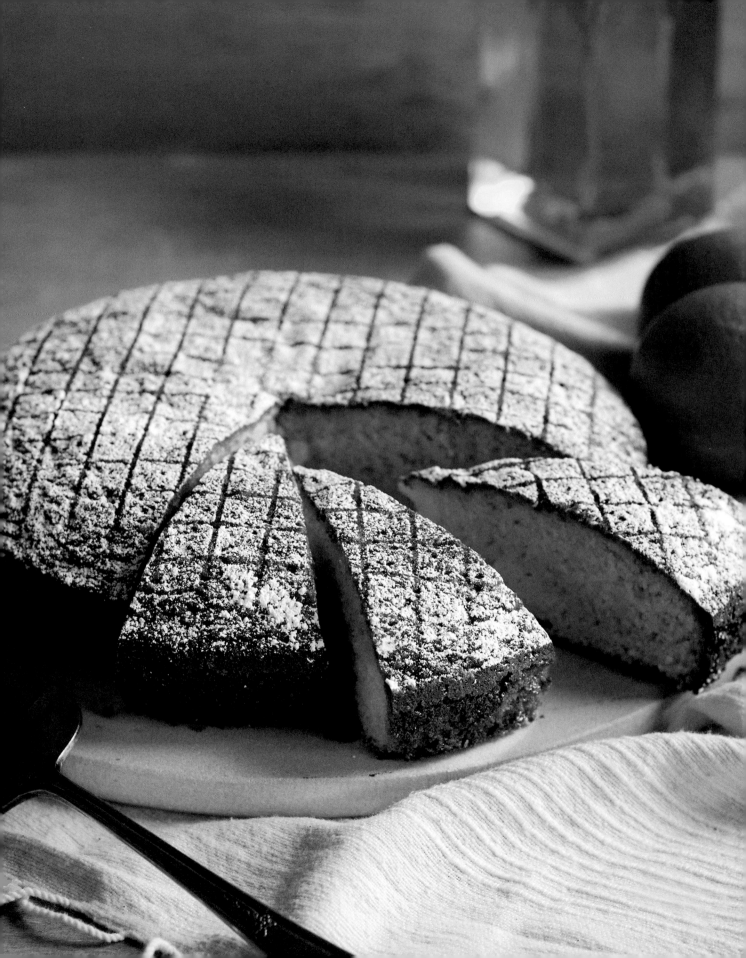

CALIFORNIA ORANGE AND OLIVE OIL CAKE

MAKES: 12 SERVINGS

PREP: 20 TO 25 MINUTES

BAKE: 38 TO 42 MINUTES

Light olive oil and flour for prepping the pan

1½ cups all-purpose flour

1½ cups granulated sugar

1 teaspoon baking powder

¼ teaspoon baking soda

¼ teaspoon salt

2 large eggs

⅔ cup orange juice (see Cake Notes)

2 teaspoons grated orange zest

⅔ cup light olive oil

Confectioners' sugar, for dusting

CAKE NOTES: If you have 2 or 3 fresh oranges, you should be able to juice them and obtain enough juice to measure ⅔ cup. Grate enough of the zest from 1 or 2 oranges to make 2 teaspoons.

Olive Oil Tip

How to substitute olive oil for butter in your favorite cake recipe? The rule of thumb for swapping a liquid fat for a solid fat like butter is to use 75 percent of the amount of butter. So if the recipe calls for 8 ounces butter, you would use 6 ounces (¾ cup) oil. But unlike butter, which may be creamed with sugar to aerate and produce little gas bubbles that will expand in baking and help the cake rise, oil won't help the cake rise through beating. There must be a chemical leavening present— baking powder or soda.

Baking with olive oil has been a way of life for Mediterranean cooks, and it is gaining steam in America now. In California, where olive oil is produced and citrus grown, this cake is as common as a yellow birthday cake with chocolate frosting. Natalie Haughton, the retired food writer from Los Angeles, says this cake speaks California, and we can thank pastry chef Emily Luchetti of San Francisco and chocolate maven Alice Medrich of Berkeley, as well as authors of Italian cookbooks such as Lynne Rosetto Kasper for sharing olive oil cakes and introducing Americans to the benefit of baking with olive oil. For one, it is healthier to bake with olive oil, which contains monounsaturated fat, compared with butter's saturated fat. And because olive oil is a natural emulsifier, it improves the moisture and texture of a cake. A cake baked with olive oil will bake higher than one baked with butter. Franciscan monks from Spain brought the first olive trees to the San Diego area in 1769, and while olive oil production didn't take off at first, today the California olive oil industry has experienced huge growth. Use a light olive oil in this recipe, and save your more flavorful extra virgin oil for dressing a salad.

1. Place a rack in the center of the oven, and preheat the oven to 375°F. Lightly grease and flour a 9″ springform pan with the olive oil and flour. Shake out the excess flour, and set the pan aside.

2. Place the flour, sugar, baking powder, baking soda, and salt in a large mixing bowl and whisk to combine. Crack the eggs into the bowl and stir to break the yolks, then add the orange juice, zest, and olive oil. Mix with a wooden spoon until well combined, 60 to 70 strokes, or mix with an electric mixer on medium speed until smooth and combined, 1 to 2 minutes.

3. Turn the batter into the prepared pan, and place the pan on a sheet pan or baking sheet to protect your oven from batter leaking from the bottom of the pan. Place the pan in the oven, and bake until the cake is well browned and the top springs back when lightly pressed with a finger, 38 to 42 minutes.

4. Remove the pan from the oven. Let it rest on a wire rack for 20 minutes. Run a knife around the edges, unsnap the collar rim, and let it rest on the rack until cool, 30 minutes more. To serve, run a sharp knife underneath the cake to remove the bottom of the pan. Place the cake on a plate, dust with confectioners' sugar, if desired, and slice and serve.

CHOCOLATE STOUT CAKE

MAKES: 12 TO 16 SERVINGS
PREP: 40 TO 45 MINUTES
BAKE: 30 TO 35 MINUTES

GANACHE FROSTING

1⅓ cups heavy cream

16 ounces (1 pound) bittersweet or semisweet chocolate, chopped

CAKE

Butter and flour for prepping the pans

2 cups stout (see Cake Note)

2 cups (4 sticks) unsalted butter

1½ cups unsweetened cocoa powder

4 cups all-purpose flour

4 cups granulated sugar

1 tablespoon baking soda

1½ teaspoons salt

4 large eggs

1⅓ cups sour cream

CAKE NOTE: Use Barrington Brewery's Black Bear Stout in this recipe, or use a local freshly made stout from a brewery near you. Or use Guinness.

Cakes have been baked with ale, porter, and cider for centuries. It was a ready ingredient freshly made at home by many early Americans and added moisture and flavor to cakes. In fact these were the earliest of the true American fruitcakes, baked on a wood hearth, filled with dried fruit and spices, and flavored with what alcoholic beverages you had on hand. But this cake is unlike its predecessors, for it is a chocolate cake made moist and flavorful with stout. A dark and earthy beer most often associated with Ireland's Guinness, stout is made today across America. This recipe was created by Barrington Brewery in Great Barrington, Massachusetts, one of the country's first microbreweries, and it showcases Barrington's Black Bear Stout. Owner Gary Happ said the stout was so named for the growing population of black bears in the area. This is a slightly adapted version of a recipe featured in a 2002 issue of *Bon Appétit* magazine. The cake is made daily at the brewery by chef Odille Carpenter, and it is a whopper of a cake—a pint of stout, a pound of butter, a pound of flour, and nearly 2 pounds sugar. It is not for the faint of heart or calorie counter. But it is indulgent and wonderful, an autumn cake that stays moist on the kitchen counter for days. If it lasts that long!

1. For the frosting, place the cream in a medium-size heavy saucepan over medium heat. Bring to a simmer, and then remove from the heat. Stir in the chopped chocolate, and stir until all the chocolate has melted and the mixture is smooth. Pour the icing into a stainless steel bowl, and set aside on the counter until ready to frost the cake. You can make this up to 3 hours in advance.

2. For the cake, place a rack in the center of the oven, and preheat the oven to 350°F. Grease and flour three 8″ round cake pans that are at least 2″ deep, and shake out the excess flour. Set the pans aside.

3. Place the stout and butter in a large saucepan, and stir over medium heat until the butter melts, 3 to 4 minutes. Whisk in the cocoa until smooth. Remove the pan from the heat and let it cool.

4. Place the flour, sugar, baking soda, and salt in a large bowl, and whisk to combine. Set aside. Place the eggs and sour cream in a large bowl, and blend with an electric mixer on medium speed until just combined, 1 minute. Add the chocolate and butter mixture and blend just to combine.

continued

Fold in the flour mixture, and scrape down the sides of the bowl with a rubber spatula. Divide the batter between the prepared pans, and place the pans in the oven.

5. Bake the cake until the top springs back when lightly pressed with a finger, 30 to 35 minutes. Remove the cake from the oven, and place the pans on a wire rack to cool for 10 minutes. Run a knife around the edges of the pans, give the pans a gentle shake, and invert the layers once and then again so the layers cool completely right side up, about 1 hour.

6. To assemble the cake, stir the frosting until smooth enough to spread. Place 1 layer on a cake plate, and spread with about ²/₃ cup of frosting. Top with the second layer, and spread with another ²/₃ cup of frosting. Top with the third layer and spread the top and sides of the cake with the remaining frosting. Slice and serve.

ODE TO CHOCOLATE CAKE

AMERICA HAS BEEN IN LOVE with a lot of cakes through the years, but we completely, madly fell for chocolate cake. From 1847 when grated chocolate first crept into spice cakes and marbled cakes, to when cooking school teachers Sarah Rorer and Maria Parloa added a modest amount of baking chocolate to cake batters at the end of the 19th century, to the deep, dark devil's food cakes popular today, chocolate cake has won state fairs, Pillsbury Bake-Off® contests, and hearts from shore to shore. Even offshore—in our 50th state, Hawaii—the chocolate Chantilly Cake (page 273) with its creamy cooked caramel frosting and macadamia garnish is a local favorite.

Every part of the country, every place in time, has a favorite chocolate cake, from the German chocolate, Texas sheet cakes, Minnesota fudge cake, and faintly chocolate-flavored red velvets of contemporary Texas and Oklahoma, to the World War II chocolate loaf cake baked by Edith Warner near Los Alamos (page 168), to the deeply chocolate Earthquake Cakes of California, coffee-infused chocolate cakes of Washington State and Wisconsin, to the heartland's chocolate upside-down cakes and Hoosier cakes, and the most loved chocolate dessert of all time—the American brownie.

From the chocolate glaze that first trickled down the sides of a Boston cream pie, to New York's French-inspired flourless chocolate cakes, to the rich Brooklyn Blackout now laced with stout at Brooklyn's Ovenly bakery, to the peanut butter and chocolate Smith Island Cake of the Chesapeake (page 294), and into the South with more chocolate cakes than you can imagine—chocolate pound cakes, Hershey bar cakes, Mississippi Mud Cake, and sweet Coca-Cola Cake—we love chocolate cake.

RUM SIZZLE CAKE

MAKES: 12 TO 16 SERVINGS

PREP: DRIED FRUIT SOAKS IN RUM FOR 24 HOURS; CANDIED FRUIT NEEDS TO DRY OVERNIGHT; 50 TO 55 MINUTES TO PREPARE CAKE

BAKE: 1 HOUR 40 TO 50 MINUTES

1¼ cups dark raisins

1¼ cups golden raisins

1 cup chopped pitted prunes

1½ cups dark rum, divided use

2 tablespoons finely chopped candied ginger (see "Candied Fruit" on page 293)

⅓ cup chopped candied orange and lemon peel (see "Candied Fruit" on page 293)

1 cup (2 sticks) unsalted butter, at room temperature, plus a little for greasing the pan

Parchment paper

1⅔ cups dark brown sugar, firmly packed

2 cups all-purpose flour

2 teaspoons baking powder

1 teaspoon ground cinnamon

½ teaspoon ground cloves

⅛ teaspoon ground mace

6 large eggs, at room temperature

4 tablespoons molasses

Not your run-of-the-mill fruitcake, that doorstop of a cake you give your worst enemy. No, this is a fruitcake you'll want to bake and eat yourself. Poet, author, actor, screenwriter, and accomplished cook Eugene Walter left a legacy of boozy and wonderful cakes such as this when he died in 1998. He was Mobile, Alabama's bon vivant Renaissance man who lived around the world but dearly loved Southern food and culture. His rum fruitcake recipe, so named because of the sizzling sound the rum makes when poured into the holes of a warm baked cake, is adapted from the book *The Happy Table of Eugene Walter: Southern Spirits in Food and Drink*, edited by Donald Goodman and Thomas Head. It doesn't have the fruitcake ingredients Walter remembered seeing in Mobile groceries in November— "insanely red cherries for color" and candied fruit that "resembled a wild, baroque display of costume jewelry." Instead this cake is packed with the dried fruit you probably have in your pantry right now— raisins and prunes. The candied ginger and candied orange and lemon peel are a little time consuming to prepare, but together with the rum, brown sugar, butter, and spices, they give you new hope that American fruitcake is here to stay.

1. The day before baking, soak the dried fruit. Place the dark and golden raisins and the prunes in a medium-size bowl. Pour about ¾ cup of the rum over the fruit, toss to coat, and cover the bowl. Let soak for 24 hours. Stir occasionally.

2. For the candied fruit, see the box on page 293.

3. Place a rack in the center of the oven, and preheat the oven to 300°F. Grease a 10″ tube pan with soft butter, and line it with parchment paper. First cut a piece of parchment to fit the bottom of the pan (turn the pan over and use the bottom as an outline for cutting), then cut a strip that is deep enough to go around the sides of the pan. To allow for the widening of the pan, cut the strip at intervals so it fans out. Lightly grease the parchment with a little butter, and set the pan aside.

4. Place the butter and brown sugar in a large mixing bowl, and beat with an electric mixer on medium speed until light and fluffy, 3 to 4 minutes. Set aside.

continued

5. Sift the flour, baking powder, cinnamon, cloves, and mace into a large bowl. Alternately add the flour mixture to the creamed butter and sugar with the eggs, beginning and ending with the flour mixture, until just blended. Scrape down the sides of the bowl with a rubber spatula, and stir in the molasses. Fold in the chopped ginger and orange and lemon peel. Fold in the soaked dried fruit and rum (do not drain). When the batter is well combined, turn it into the prepared pan, smoothing the top with the spatula. Place the pan in the oven.

6. Bake the cake until a wooden skewer comes out clean, about 1 hour 40 to 50 minutes. Remove the pan from the oven, and place it on a wire rack. Immediately poke holes in the cake with the skewer. Pour the remaining $^3/_4$ cup rum slowly and evenly over the top of the cake. The cake will sizzle as the rum goes into the hot cake—thus the name. When the sizzling stops, cover the pan loosely with a clean kitchen towel and let it cool to room temperature, about 3 hours. Turn the cake out onto a plate, slice, and serve.

CAKE NOTE: Place it in a cake saver or under a cake dome. It will keep for up to 2 weeks.

CANDIED FRUIT
Candied Ginger

| 1 cup granulated sugar | ⅝ cup water | 3 ounces fresh ginger, peeled and sliced about ⅛" thick |

Place the sugar and water in a medium-size saucepan over medium heat. Stir until the sugar dissolves and the syrup comes to a simmer. Drop the gingerroot slices into the pan, and stir so that all the ginger is covered in syrup. Let this simmer for 1½ hours, or until the ginger is translucent. With metal tongs, transfer the ginger to a wire rack and let it dry several hours or overnight. Store in a tightly covered plastic container. Finely chop before adding to the recipe.

Candied Orange and Lemon Peel

| 1 cup granulated sugar
⅝ cup water | 1 medium orange, washed and dried | 2 medium lemons, washed and dried |

Place the sugar and water in a medium-size saucepan over medium heat. Stir until the sugar dissolves and the syrup comes to a simmer. With a sharp zester, remove the peel from the orange and lemons in long strips. Drop the strips into the pan, and stir so that all the strips are covered in syrup. Let this simmer for 1½ hours, or until the peel is translucent. With metal tongs, transfer the peel to a wire rack and let it dry several hours or overnight. Store in a tightly covered plastic container. Finely chop before adding to the recipe.

SMITH ISLAND CAKE

MAKES: 16 SERVINGS
....
PREP: 1 TO 1½ HOURS
....
BAKE: 14 TO 17 MINUTES
....

CAKE

Butter or vegetable oil spray for prepping the pans

1 cup (2 sticks) unsalted butter, at room temperature

2 cups granulated sugar

5 large eggs

3 cups all-purpose flour

1 tablespoon baking powder

½ teaspoon salt

1½ cups (12-ounce can) evaporated milk

2 teaspoons vanilla extract

FROSTING

¾ cup (1½ sticks) unsalted butter

½ cup unsweetened cocoa powder

¼ teaspoon salt

½ cup plus 3 tablespoons evaporated milk

1 teaspoon vanilla extract

6 cups confectioners' sugar, sifted

8 Reese's peanut butter cups (about 12 ounces total), frozen, for garnish, if desired (see option at end of recipe)

I n 2008 the Maryland legislature named not the crab cake but the 10-layer, chocolate-fudge–frosted Smith Island Cake as its state cake. It brought a good deal of attention to this old barrier island located 10 miles offshore in Chesapeake Bay. Settled in the 1600s by the English in the company of Captain John Smith, the island with its bounty of blue crab and oysters has been a fishing hub for generations. Pretty much everyone on Smith Island has something to do with fishing. In fact, Frances Kitching, the boardinghouse owner and author of the 1981 cookbook called *Mrs. Kitching's Smith Island Cookbook,* is said to have invented the Smith Island Cake. The cake resembles the stack cakes of Appalachia in construction and appeal—thin layers, a good keeper, and feeds a crowd. But most people will tell you this cake is all about the frosting, and in a newspaper interview years ago, Mrs. Kitching said she made her layers thin because her children liked the frosting so much. I have slightly modified Mrs. Kitching's frosting to make it a little easier to pull together. A modern variation on this cake is to add finely chopped Reese's peanut butter cups between the layers. Yet the crucial ingredient in the cake and the frosting is canned evaporated milk—a godsend to remote locations like Smith Island. While this cake is a little time consuming to prepare, you can always visit Smith Island yourself and buy a cake from the Smith Island Baking Co., founded in 2009 to bring the baking of this legendary cake back to the island.

1. For the cake, place a rack in the center of the oven, and preheat the oven to 350°F. Lightly grease as many 9″ round layer pans as you have (you need 10 layers) with soft butter or oil. Set the pans aside. (Or buy ten 9″ round aluminum foil pans to save time.)

2. Place the butter and sugar in a large mixing bowl, and beat with an electric mixer on medium speed until light and creamy, 1 minute. Add the eggs, one at a time, beating on medium until just combined. Set aside.

3. Sift the flour, baking powder, and salt into a medium-size bowl. Add the flour mixture to the butter and sugar mixture alternately with the evaporated milk. Begin and end with the flour mixture. Beat on low speed until smooth, about 1 minute. Scrape down the sides of the bowl, and fold in the vanilla.

continued

4. Spoon about a generous $^1/_2$ cup batter into each prepared pan, using the back of a large spoon to spread the batter across the bottom of the pan. Place up to 3 pans in the oven at a time, or place in as many layers as your oven will accommodate. Bake until the top of the cake springs back when lightly touched with a finger, 14 to 17 minutes. Remove the cakes from the oven, let them rest in the pans for 5 minutes, then carefully remove to a wire rack to cool. Repeat the process with the remaining batter and layers.

5. Once all the layers have baked and are cooled, prepare the frosting. Melt the butter in a large saucepan over low heat, 2 to 3 minutes. Stir in the cocoa, salt, and evaporated milk. Cook and stir until the mixture thickens and just begins to come to a boil, 1 minute longer. Remove the pan from the heat. Stir in the vanilla and the confectioners' sugar, continuing to stir until the frosting is thickened and smooth and the consistency of hot fudge sauce. To keep the frosting from hardening, place the saucepan over low heat while frosting the layers.

6. To assemble the cake, place 1 layer on a cake plate and spoon about $^1/_4$ cup of the frosting on top, spreading it thinly to the edge. Place another layer on top, and continue adding $^1/_4$ cup of frosting and stacking the layers. When all the layers have been stacked, frost the top and sides of the cake thinly with the remaining frosting. Store this cake at room temperature under a cake dome or in a cake saver for up to 3 days. It will keep 1 week in the refrigerator.

CHOCOLATE PEANUT BUTTER OPTION: *Chop 3 frozen peanut butter cups into chunks and set aside as the garnish for the top of the cake. Pulse the remaining 5 peanut butter cups into a fine powder in the food processor. As you are stacking the cake layers, scatter 2 teaspoons peanut butter cup powder on top of each frosted layer. Once finished, garnish the top of the cake with the reserved peanut butter cup chunks.*

Canned Milk

What would America's remote locations—barrier islands, the islands of Hawaii, small towns, and pioneer farms—have done without the convenience of canned evaporated milk? It was a ready source of milk for drinking and cooking when fresh milk wasn't available. In the early 1900s, fresh milk posed a health risk because it was either contaminated with bacteria from the cow or people were unable to store it at home without refrigeration. The process of evaporating milk is an old one. Gail Borden received a patent for his sweetened condensed milk in 1856. And by the end of the 19th century, the patents, technology, and inventions were in place to produce an unsweetened evaporated milk by Borden and competitor Pet Milk. Sugar was originally added to condensed milk not for flavor but to slow bacterial growth. Even as the quality of fresh American milk improved in the 1900s and the refrigerator came into the home, family recipes continued to call for "Pet milk." There was just something rich and creamy about a frosting made with canned evaporated milk. Still is. The Smith Island Cake, Tres Leches Cake (page 300), and Chocoflan (next page) are recipes that were created with and still rely on canned milk.

CHOCOFLAN (CHOCOLATE IMPOSSIBLE CAKE)

MAKES: 12 SERVINGS

PREP: 50 TO 55 MINUTES

BAKE: 48 TO 52 MINUTES

CAKE

Butter and flour for prepping the pan

10 tablespoons lightly salted butter, at room temperature

1 cup granulated sugar

1 large egg, at room temperature

3 tablespoons brewed espresso

¾ cup all-purpose flour

1 cup cake flour

¾ teaspoon baking powder

¾ teaspoon baking soda

⅓ cup plus 1 tablespoon unsweetened cocoa powder

½ teaspoon ground cinnamon, if desired

9 ounces buttermilk, at room temperature

FLAN

1 can (12 ounces) evaporated milk

1 can (14 ounces) sweetened condensed milk

4 large eggs, at room temperature

1 teaspoon vanilla extract

1 cup store-bought cajeta (goat milk caramel)

For as long as Mexican flavors have been influencing the baking of California and Texas, there have been flan cakes in the oven. As early as 1954, bake shops in Texas sold flan cakes, and through the 1970s flan cakes starring flavors like pumpkin and cherry appeared in newspaper columns. But flan cake really made its presence known when Chicago's Rick Bayless opened his restaurants, wrote his cookbooks, and went on public television explaining the foods of Mexico. And it was in season 6 of *Mexico—One Plate at a Time* that Bayless shared the beauty and mystery of Chocoflan with us all. Here is how the cake with the split personality works: A chocolate cake batter is poured over *cajeta*, which is sweetened, caramelized goat milk that has been spread on the bottom of the deep cake pan. (You can buy cajeta at many supermarkets or at markets specializing in Hispanic foods.) Then you pour a flan batter over the top of the chocolate batter, and during baking the mystery takes place. The layers of cake and flan magically reverse themselves. The cake rises to the top, the flan sinks to the bottom. And when unmolded (turned upside down), you have the amber-brown flan sitting beautifully atop the dark chocolate cake. A throwback to the Bisquick "impossible pie" that made its own crust, this cake is just as miraculous although more dazzling. It is perfect for a large gathering, following a meal with Mexican flavors.

1. Place a rack in the center of the oven, and preheat the oven to 350°F. Generously butter and flour a 10″ springform pan or a 10″ round layer pan that is at least 3″ deep. Set the pan aside. Set aside a large roasting pan. Place 8 to 10 cups of water in a large saucepan over medium-low heat, and keep the water hot and steamy, but not boiling, while you prepare the cake.

2. For the cake, place the butter and sugar in a large mixing bowl, and beat with an electric mixer on medium speed until light in color and texture, 3 minutes. Scrape down the sides of the bowl with a rubber spatula. Add the egg and espresso, and beat just until blended. Set aside.

3. Sift together the flours, baking powder, baking soda, cocoa, and cinnamon, if desired. Add half of the flour mixture to the batter, blending at medium-low speed. Scrape down the bowl. Add half of the buttermilk

continued

and blend. Add the remaining flour and blend, then the remaining buttermilk, and blend until smooth. Scrape down the sides of the bowl and then increase the speed to medium-high and beat for 1 minute. Set aside.

4. For the flan, place the milks, eggs, and vanilla in a blender or food processor and blend until smooth, about 15 seconds. Set aside.

5. To assemble the cake for baking, pour the cajeta into a glass measuring cup. Place the cup in the microwave on high power for 15 to 20 seconds. Pour the cajeta evenly into the prepared pan, spreading it to the edges using a small metal spatula. Dollop the cake batter over the cajeta, spreading to the edges of the pan. Using a ladle, gently pour the flan mixture over the batter. The pan will be very full. Place the cake pan into the roasting pan and place on the middle rack in the oven. Using a heatproof glass measuring cup, gently pour hot, steamy water into the roasting pan around the cake pan until the water is 1″ deep. Close the oven door.

6. Bake the cake until it is firm to the touch and cracked on top, 48 to 52 minutes. Remove the roasting pan from the oven. Carefully remove the cake pan from the roasting pan. Place it on a wire rack and let it cool for 1 hour.

7. To serve, carefully run a thin-bladed knife around the edge of the cake and flan to free the edges. Invert a rimmed serving platter over the pan, grasp the two tightly together, and then flip the two over. Gently jiggle the pan back and forth several times to make sure the cake and flan have dropped, and then remove the pan. Scrape any remaining cajeta from the mold onto the cake. Slice and serve.

TRES LECHES CAKE

MAKES: 12 TO 16 SERVINGS

PREP: 45 TO 50 MINUTES

BAKE: 20 TO 25 MINUTES

CAKE

Vegetable oil spray or soft butter for greasing the pan

½ cup (1 stick) unsalted butter, at room temperature

1 cup granulated sugar

4 large eggs

½ teaspoon vanilla extract

1½ cups all-purpose flour

1 teaspoon baking powder

¼ teaspoon salt

MILK SYRUP

1 cup whole milk

1 cup evaporated milk

1 cup sweetened condensed milk

3 tablespoons rum, if desired

1 teaspoon vanilla extract

WHIPPED CREAM

1 cup heavy cream

1 tablespoon granulated sugar

Sliced fresh strawberries for garnish, if desired

L ong before the Tres Leches Cake made its way to Pittsburgh, Charlotte, or Portland, it was entrenched in Texas. As Austin food writer MM Pack said in a 2004 *Austin Chronicle* column, it is "the new tiramisu of the millennium." Named for the syrup of 3 milks—whole milk, evaporated milk, and sweetened condensed milk—that is spooned onto a baked butter or sponge cake, *pastel de tres leches* has been a fixture in Mexican, Nicaraguan, and Cuban kitchens for 2 generations. *Texas Monthly* writer Patricia Sharpe surmised in 1999 that the cake was so well-known it might have originated as a promotional recipe by a canned milk manufacturer. Sure enough, in the 1940s Nestlé opened an evaporated milk manufacturing plant in Mexico, and a recipe for this cake was on the label of those cans. But MM Pack, who discovered the Nestlé and Mexico connection, says the cake is even older and originated in Europe, where old Portuguese and Spanish desserts were often sponge cake soaked in egg cream. No doubt that the popularity of Tres Leches in America has much to do with our country's increasing Hispanic population. Now Tres Leches Cake and its myriad variations are found in homes, bakeries, and restaurants across the country. Baked large enough to feed a party or made smaller and individual like cupcakes, the Tres Leches is a blank canvas. Top it with whipped cream or meringue, sliced fresh fruit, or flavor it with caramel, rum, chocolate, or coconut.

1. Place a rack in the center of the oven, and preheat the oven to 350°F. Lightly grease a 13″ × 9″ baking pan with the vegetable oil spray or soft butter. Set the pan aside.

2. For the cake, place the butter and sugar in a large mixing bowl, and beat with an electric mixer on medium speed until the mixture is light and fluffy, 1 to 2 minutes. Add the eggs, one at a time, beating about 15 seconds after each egg. Blend in the vanilla, and set the batter aside.

3. Sift the flour, baking powder, and salt into a small bowl. Add the flour mixture to the batter about 2 tablespoons at a time, blending on low speed after each addition. Pour the batter into the prepared pan, and place the pan in the oven.

continued

4. Bake the cake until the top springs back when lightly pressed with a finger and a toothpick inserted comes out clean, 20 to 25 minutes. Remove the cake to a wire rack, and poke holes on the top of the cake with a wooden skewer. Let the cake cool for 15 minutes.

5. Meanwhile, make the milk syrup. Pour the milks, rum, if desired, and vanilla into a medium-size bowl and stir. Spoon the syrup over the top of the cake, letting it soak into the holes. Cover the cake with plastic wrap, and place it in the refrigerator to chill for 2 hours.

6. For the whipped cream, chill the heavy cream and the beaters of the electric mixer. When cold, pour the cream and sugar into a large mixing bowl, and beat on high speed until stiff peaks form. Remove the cake from the refrigerator and spread the whipped cream evenly over the top. Return the cake, covered, to the refrigerator until time to serve.

7. To serve, cut into squares and top with the fresh strawberries, if desired.

BEET RED VELVET CAKE

MAKES: 12 TO 16 SERVINGS

PREP: ABOUT 2 HOURS TO ROAST AND PREPARE BEETS (CAN BE DONE A DAY AHEAD); 40 TO 45 MINUTES TO PREPARE CAKE AND FROSTING

BAKE: 22 TO 25 MINUTES

2 medium beets

Butter and flour for prepping the pans

¾ cup buttermilk, at room temperature

3 tablespoons fresh lemon juice, from 1 large lemon

2 teaspoons white vinegar

1½ teaspoons vanilla extract

2 cups sifted cake flour

3 tablespoons unsweetened cocoa powder

1⅛ teaspoons baking powder

½ teaspoon salt

½ teaspoon baking soda

¾ cup (1½ sticks) unsalted butter, at room temperature

1¾ cups granulated sugar

3 large eggs, at room temperature

Cream Cheese Frosting (page 320)

As much as red velvet cake has been a national favorite, many cooks find it unacceptable to add artificial red food coloring to the recipe. Beets have become today's go-to fresh and natural alternative to red food dye. They will never create a cake as crimson red as one made with artificial coloring, but they do make a wonderfully flavored cake nevertheless. This recipe comes from pastry chef Pamela Moxley of Miller Union restaurant in Atlanta. Best known for her whimsical homemade ice cream sandwiches, Moxley plays with classic American cake recipes in creative but respectful ways. She grew up on a New Hampshire farm with an eye on the land, creating cakes that are simple and fresh, not fancy and with elaborate fondant. For this reinvented red velvet, Moxley roasts the beets, which caramelizes them and brings out their natural sugars. This recipe is slightly adapted from one shared in Miller Union chef Steven Satterfield's *Root to Leaf* cookbook and shared in the *New York Times*. I use regular cocoa to bring out the reddish color of the cake. I also share a basic cream cheese frosting, or you may prefer a frosting made with fresh goat cheese that follows, on page 305.

1. Place a rack in the center of the oven, and preheat the oven to 350°F. Wash the beets and wrap in aluminum foil. Place on a rack in the oven or on a baking sheet in the oven and bake until the tip of a small sharp knife can slide easily into the larger beet, about 1 hour and 20 to 30 minutes. Remove the beets from the oven, and when cool enough to handle, open the foil, peel the beets, and cut them into quarters. Place the cooled, quartered beets in a food processor fitted with a steel blade. Pulse until they are chopped finely, 10 to 12 pulses. Measure out 1 cup and set it aside. If there are extra beets, use them for another purpose.

2. Grease and flour two 9″ cake pans. Shake out the excess flour, and set the pans aside. Place the 1 cup beets back in the food processor or a blender with the buttermilk, lemon juice, vinegar, and vanilla, and pulse until smooth, 15 to 20 seconds. Set aside.

3. Sift the flour, cocoa, baking powder, salt, and baking soda into a medium-size bowl, and set the bowl aside.

continued

4. Place the butter in a large mixing bowl, and beat with an electric mixer on medium speed until soft, about 30 seconds. While the mixer is running, slowly add the sugar, beating until the mixture is creamy, 1 to 2 minutes. Beat in the eggs, one at a time, beating just until combined. Alternately add the flour mixture and the beet mixture to the butter mixture, beginning and ending with the flour, and beat on medium speed just until each is incorporated. Scrape down the sides of the bowl. Divide the batter between the prepared pans, and place the pans in the oven.

5. Bake the cakes until the top springs back when lightly pressed with a finger and a toothpick inserted in the center comes out clean, 22 to 25 minutes. Remove the pans to a wire rack to cool for 10 minutes. Run a knife around the edges of the pans, give the pans a gentle shake, and invert the cakes once and then again so the layers are right side up. Cool completely, 30 to 35 minutes.

6. Prepare the Cream Cheese Frosting.

7. To assemble the cake, place 1 cake layer on a serving plate. Spread about ³/₄ cup of frosting over the top of the cake. Place the second layer on top. Spread a thin coating of frosting over the top and sides of the cake to seal in the crumbs. Place the cake in the refrigerator to chill for 15 minutes.

8. To complete the assembly, spread the remaining frosting generously over the top and sides of the cake. This 2-step frosting process seals in the dark red crumbs and makes for a neater frosting of the cake.

GOAT CHEESE FROSTING

THE FLAVOR COMBINATION of roasted beets and goat cheese, or chevre, is a favorite in salads, and it works in the pastry kitchen, too. Here is how to make this frosting.

Place 6 tablespoons soft unsalted butter in an electric mixer and beat until creamy. Add 1³/₄ cups sifted confectioners' sugar, a teaspoon of vanilla, and a pinch of salt and beat until just combined. While the motor of the mixer is running, add 4 ounces soft cream cheese and 4 ounces soft goat cheese and blend until smooth. Adjust with more sugar, salt, or vanilla as needed.

Frostings & Icings

JUST AS AMERICAN CAKES have evolved through the years, so have our frostings. They have been dead simple, fluffy and elaborate, sleek and elegant, and nonexistent.

Much depends on the key ingredient in frostings—sugar—and its availability to us. Back when the colonists were buying white sugar by the loaf and cutting it with special scissors, that hard sugar could not be whipped into a buttercream frosting like we prepare today. It had to be ground and sprinkled onto the cake, turned into a white glaze, or cooked down with water, milk, or other ingredients to make a cooked icing. When the simplest topping of an egg white and sugar beaten together was brushed onto cakes and returned to the oven, the topping created a shiny appearance, looking like ice. Thus the name "icing" was coined.

Later, Americans were more inventive, turning beaten egg whites into Victorian seven-minute, White Mountain, and other fluffy frostings. Sweetened with granulated sugar, and stabilized with a pinch of cream of tartar or a little lemon juice, these whipped frostings were elegant, of the moment, and versatile.

Then we made Ermine Frosting (page 205), the

sturdy cooked frosting based on flour and fat, to which butter and sugar were added. It became the first frosting for red velvet cake. Chocolate fudge candy became a fudge icing all its own, and industrious cooks cooked down white sugar into a caramelized syrup to make caramel icing and penuche icing, often adding chopped walnuts or pecans.

But the invention of a commercially powdered sugar—confectioners' sugar—changed the way we frosted an American layer cake. With no cooking, the simple buttercream frosting could be blended with soft butter, a little milk, and a box of sugar. Frosting quantities increased, we frosted bigger cakes, and our frostings got sweeter, too. Interestingly this was at a time when sugar prices were at an all-time low. Compared with a century earlier, when sugar was kept locked away, confectioners' sugar was cheap and available to most everyone.

These buttercream frostings inspired the cream cheese frostings that followed. But they were compromised when bakeries made a fluffy white frosting based on vegetable shortening. Crisco made frosting lighter and whiter, but it didn't necessarily make it taste better. Thankfully when the French culinary influence of the 1960s took hold, we tried the French ganache with its two ingredients—sweetened chocolate and cream. It was a sleek, bold change of pace from buttercream, and it appealed to those seeking a less sweet icing.

Frostings and icings took the front seat when the cupcake craze captivated America at the end of the 1990s and the beginning of the 21st century. Frostings of all types added height, interest, sex appeal, and flavor to the lowly cupcake. At this writing, cakes of all types are getting smaller. So we're using less frosting.

Will we return to the bare-sided cakes of old? Will we minimally ice cakes by ladling over warm caramel icing? Will a pungent lemon glaze drizzled down the sides of the molasses and lemon cake suffice? Or will we stop making homemade frostings and buy premade frosting instead? Hopefully not.

Homemade frosting makes all the difference on a home-baked cake. It is the first and last bite, the soft and creamy, sweet and tangy counterpoint to moist and flavorful cake.

Here are some favorite American frostings that go with most any cake in this book. And there are even more frostings throughout the book, placed with individual recipes. Feel free to mix and match cake and frosting and find the combination that works for you.

BUTTERCREAM FROSTING

MAKES: ABOUT 1½ CUPS; ENOUGH FOR THE TOP AND CENTER OF A 2-LAYER CAKE, OR THE TOP OF A 13" x 9" CAKE, OR TO THINLY FROST 12 CUPCAKES

4 tablespoons unsalted butter, at room temperature

Pinch of salt

2 cups confectioners' sugar, sifted

1 teaspoon vanilla extract

½ teaspoon almond extract, if desired

3 tablespoons heavy cream

Chocolate Buttercream Frosting

For a delicious chocolate frosting to adorn most any cake, see the recipe on page 243.

Before "buttercream" was 1 word, it was 2 words and described the 2 ingredients that went into an easy butter frosting— butter and cream. To prepare this frosting, there is a delicate dance back and forth of adding the soft butter, a bit of the sugar, your flavorings, then more sugar, then some cream, then more sugar, a tad more cream, and so on until you have a beautifully blended and smooth frosting that is worthy of any cake. Here is a recipe adapted from the 1948 *Rumford Complete Cook Book*. If you are making it with unsalted butter, you need to add a pinch of salt. And the almond extract is quite pronounced, so if you are not an almond lover in frostings, go easy on it or omit it altogether. Like the frostings of a bygone era, this recipe makes a modest amount, about 1½ cups. It is sufficient for filling and frosting the top of a 2-layer cake or spreading thinly atop a 13" × 9" cake, and it will glaze the top of 12 cupcakes.

1. Place the butter in a medium-size mixing bowl, and blend with an electric mixer on low speed until smooth, about 1 minute. Add the salt and about 1 cup of the sugar, and blend on low until coarse crumbs form. Add the vanilla and almond extract, if using, along with 1 tablespoon of the cream, blending on low. Add ½ cup of the sugar and another tablespoon of cream, and blend on low until smooth. Add the final ½ cup sugar and the last tablespoon cream. When smooth, increase the mixer speed to medium-high and blend for 30 seconds to lighten the frosting.

2. Frost your favorite cake, or store, covered, in the refrigerator for up to 2 days.

MODERN BUTTERCREAM FROSTING

MAKES: 3½ CUPS; ENOUGH TO FROST A 2- OR 3-LAYER CAKE OR 24 CUPCAKES

....

½ cup (1 stick) lightly salted butter, at room temperature

3¾ cups confectioners' sugar, sifted

3 tablespoons whole milk, or more as needed

1 to 2 teaspoons vanilla extract

Easy Chocolate Ganache

You cannot beat the ease or elegance of ganache to frost a cake. The recipe on page 270 generously frosts a 2-layer cake, and the recipe on page 288 frosts a larger cake.

Through the years, the amount of confectioners' sugar called for in buttercream frostings has greatly increased over those first buttercream frostings. And that is not necessarily a good thing for flavor. So be careful when making this modern buttercream to add only as much sugar as needed to pull the frosting together and make it spreadable. This frosting does not contain egg yolks as the classic French buttercream does. Instead the American style of butter frosting is egg-free and simple—just butter, confectioners' sugar, a little liquid—milk or cream—and flavoring. I use salted butter in making frostings, as the bit of salt in the butter balances the sugar. If you don't have salted butter, use unsalted butter and add a pinch of salt. And always sift the confectioners' sugar before adding it to the bowl to prevent lumps from getting in your frosting.

1. Place the butter in a medium-size mixing bowl, and beat with an electric mixer on low speed until smooth, 30 seconds. Add 3 cups of the confectioners' sugar, 2 tablespoons of the milk, and the vanilla, and beat on low until the sugar is incorporated. Add the remaining ¾ cup sugar and the remaining 1 tablespoon milk, and beat until smooth. Increase the mixer speed to medium and beat until the frosting is light and fluffy, 1 minute more. If the frosting is too thick to spread, beat in 1 more tablespoon milk.

2. Frost your cake as desired, or store, covered, in the refrigerator for up to 2 days.

   FOR A PEPPERMINT BUTTERCREAM, *add ¹/₂ cup crushed peppermint candy and ¹/₄ teaspoon peppermint extract. For chocolate buttercream, add up to ²/₃ cup unsweetened cocoa powder and increase the milk to ¹/₃ cup.*

   FOR ORANGE AND LEMON BUTTERCREAMS, *omit the vanilla and add 1 teaspoon grated fresh lemon or orange zest.*

(photo on pages 311 & 313)

CHOCOLATE SOUR CREAM FROSTING

MAKES: 2 TO 3 CUPS; ENOUGH TO
FROST A 2- OR 3-LAYER CAKE
....

6 ounces semisweet chocolate, chopped (or 1 cup chocolate chips)

4 tablespoons unsalted butter

½ cup (4 ounces) sour cream

1 teaspoon vanilla extract

Pinch of salt

2¼ cups confectioners' sugar, sifted

S our cream is a natural partner to chocolate, and in frostings it not only adds rich flavor but gives the frosting body. This frosting is delicious on the Chocolate Sauerkraut Cake (page 84) or the 1-2-3-4 Cake (page 96).

1. Place the chocolate and butter in a medium-size saucepan over low heat. Stir and melt the chocolate and butter, about 2 minutes. Remove the pan from the heat and whisk in the sour cream, vanilla, and salt until well blended and smooth. Whisk in the confectioners' sugar, a little at a time, until the frosting is smooth and all the sugar has been incorporated.

2. Frost the cake of your choice, and keep the cake refrigerated.

CHOCOLATE PAN FROSTING

MAKES: 3 CUPS; ENOUGH TO
FROST A 2-LAYER CAKE (SEE
NOTE)
....

½ cup (1 stick) lightly salted butter

4 heaping tablespoons unsweetened cocoa powder

⅓ cup whole milk

3½ cups confectioners' sugar, sifted

1 teaspoon vanilla extract

A simple alternative to the more time-consuming way of making fudge icing with a candy thermometer, this frosting requires just a saucepan, some basic ingredients from your kitchen, and a wooden spoon or spatula to stir the frosting together.

1. Place the butter in a medium-size saucepan over low heat. When the butter melts, stir in the cocoa and milk. Let the mixture come just to a boil, stirring, and then remove the pan from the heat. Stir in the confectioners' sugar and vanilla until the frosting is thickened and smooth.

2. Spread the frosting over the cake of your choice. Work quickly, because this frosting goes on best while still warm.

NOTE: For a larger amount of frosting to frost the Wellesley Fudge Cake (page 118) and other 3-layer cakes, increase the butter to 1½ sticks (12 tablespoons), use ½ cup unsweetened cocoa powder, ½ cup milk, 2 teaspoons vanilla, and 5½ cups confectioners' sugar, sifted.

(photo at right)

Clockwise from top: Chocolate Pan Frosting (left), Cream Cheese Frosting (page 320), Chocolate Pan Frosting (left), Old-Fashioned Caramel Icing (page 314), and Modern Buttercream Frosting (page 309)

American frostings come in all shades, including (clockwise from top left) the Quick Caramel Icing (page 315), Buttercream Frosting (page 305), Coffee Butter Icing (page 320), Chocolate Fudge Icing (page 319), and Boiled White Icing (page 318).

OLD-FASHIONED CARAMEL ICING

MAKES: 4 CUPS; ENOUGH TO FROST A 3-LAYER CAKE

3 cups granulated sugar, divided use

1 cup evaporated milk

¼ teaspoon salt

½ cup (1 stick) unsalted butter

1 teaspoon vanilla extract

ICING VS. FROSTING

IF YOU WANT TO KNOW if early Americans first iced or frosted their cakes, the answer would be neither. Most of the early cakes were unadorned. Sugar was a dear and expensive ingredient, plus powdered or confectioners' sugar as we know it did not exist. For sugar to be powdered, it had to be hand-ground into a powder using a mortar and pestle. The earliest hint of a frosting was simply a sprinkling of sugar on the cake before it was baked, or the cake was "iced" with beaten eggs before baking. So icing did predate frosting.

This is the classic icing that is spread onto yellow layers to make the Delta Caramel Cake (page 208). It's a labor of love to make, and it is delicious. For the faint of heart, opt for Quick Caramel Icing, on the opposite page.

1. Place 2½ cups of the sugar, the evaporated milk, and salt in a large heavy saucepan over medium heat. Stir constantly until the mixture boils and the sugar has dissolved, and continue to stir and let the mixture boil for 3 minutes. Remove the pan from the heat.

2. Place the remaining ½ cup sugar in a small cast-iron skillet over medium heat. Let the sugar caramelize—turn from granulated into a deep golden brown—without stirring, 4 to 5 minutes. When the mixture is just deep golden, remove it from the heat. Do not let it become dark brown. The heat in the skillet continues to cook the sugar, so if you let it get dark, it will burn. (If this happens, remove the skillet from the heat, let it cool completely, and clean the skillet. Repeat the process with a clean skillet and ½ cup granulated sugar.)

3. Stir about ½ cup of the sugar and evaporated milk mixture into the hot caramelized sugar to bring the heat down. Then pour the contents of the iron skillet back into the saucepan with the remaining sugar and evaporated milk mixture. Stir until incorporated. Add the butter and vanilla, and stir until the butter melts and the mixture is smooth.

4. Place the saucepan into a large bowl filled with 2″ of ice water. Stir the icing with a wooden spoon until it cools and thickens, 4 to 5 minutes. You don't want the icing to thicken too much or it will be difficult to spread. When it is of a spreadable consistency, nearly as thick as peanut butter, remove the pan from the ice water bath. Frost the cake quickly. The icing will harden as it cools.

(photo on pages 311 & 312)

QUICK CARAMEL ICING

12 tablespoons (1½ sticks) unsalted
butter, cut into tablespoons

¾ cup light brown sugar, lightly packed

¾ cup dark brown sugar, lightly packed

⅓ cup whole milk

2½ to 3 cups confectioners' sugar,
sifted

2 teaspoons vanilla extract

¼ teaspoon salt, or to taste

(photo on page 312)

Here is the icing recipe my mother handed down to me many years ago. It is a lot easier to prepare than the old-fashioned method of caramelizing the sugar. Caramel cake snobs may turn up their nose because it contains brown sugar and confectioners' sugar, but this frosting has great flavor, dirties few pans in the kitchen, and is ready in a snap.

1. Place the butter and brown sugars in a medium-size saucepan over medium heat, and stir until the butter melts and the mixture begins to boil, 2 to 3 minutes. Add the milk, stir, and let the mixture come back to a boil.

2. Remove the pan from the heat, and whisk in 2½ cups of the confectioners' sugar, the vanilla, and salt. Whisk until smooth, and if the icing is too runny, add another ½ cup confectioners' sugar. Do not add so much sugar that the frosting thickens and hardens. It needs to be smooth enough to spread. It will set as it cools. Frost between the layers and on the top and sides of the cake.

WAYS TO MIX AND MATCH FROSTINGS

The beauty of cake and frosting is that they mix and match. It's a lot like pairing tops and bottoms in your wardrobe. So take a look at these other great frostings in the book, and get creative.

ORANGE AND LEMON ICING (page 58): Slather this icing onto the Coconut Layer Cake (page 55) layers, and you have a festive cake ready for any celebration.

TEXAS SHEATH CAKE ICING (page 194): Try on the 1-2-3-4 Cake (page 96) or German Chocolate Cake (page 202).

PINK CHAMPAGNE BUTTERCREAM FROSTING (page 218): Spread onto cupcakes made from the 1-2-3-4 Cake (page 96) or Mahogany Cake (page 86) batter.

BUTTERCREAM FROSTING (page 308): This is delicious spread onto a sheet pan of Ocracoke Fig Preserves Cake (page 267), Neighborhood Prune Cake (page 125), Grandma's Mincemeat Cake (page 122), or your favorite spice cake.

HAWAIIAN CHANTILLY CAKE FROSTING (page 273): For a showstopper cake, spread this frosting onto the Wellesley Fudge Cake (page 118) layers.

GANACHE FROSTING (page 288): Gild the lily and spread ganache over the Wellesley Fudge Cake (page 118), or opt for an orange-chocolate combination and spread it on the top and sides of the Orange Chiffon Cake (page 178).

SEVEN-MINUTE FROSTING

MAKES: 2 TO 3 CUPS; ENOUGH TO
FROST THE TOP AND SIDES OF A
2- OR 3-LAYER CAKE

2 large egg whites, at room
temperature

⅛ teaspoon cream of tartar

1½ cups granulated sugar

5 tablespoons water

1½ teaspoons corn syrup

1 teaspoon vanilla extract

The classic frosting of the early 1900s, this recipe is so named because you beat the egg whites with sugar and other ingredients for 7 minutes over simmering water. This length of time cooks the egg whites and makes a fluffy frosting. But you need to count in another 3 minutes of beating those egg whites after the pan is removed from the heat. Those are the extra 3 minutes no one ever tells you about, but they ensure your frosting will be thickened, smooth, and spreadable. Use this frosting on just about any cake in this book, especially the Coconut Layer Cake (page 55), Mahogany Cake (page 86), Lady Baltimore Cake (page 110), and Japanese Fruit Cake (page 128).

1. For the frosting, bring 2″ of water in the bottom of a double boiler to a boil.

2. Meanwhile, place the egg whites, cream of tartar, sugar, water, and corn syrup in a medium-size metal bowl, and beat with an electric mixer on high speed until well combined, about 4 minutes. Place the bowl on top of the double boiler. While over simmering water, beat on high speed for about 7 minutes.

3. Remove the pan from atop the water, and beat another 3 minutes on high until the frosting is stiff and spreadable. Add the vanilla and beat until combined.

4. Frost your favorite cake. This frosting is best made just before using.

EVERY WOMAN NEEDS A GOOD ICING RECIPE

THOSE WERE THE WORDS of Texas cook and author Helen Corbitt, who transformed the way Texas ate with her sophisticated fare at Neiman Marcus. But she thought you needed only a handful of great frosting recipes such as Seven-Minute or Boiled White Icing. Here are her suggestions for dressing up a simple frosting.

• Add fresh coconut or toasted coconut flakes on a frosted chocolate or yellow cake.
• Melt bitter chocolate and dribble it over a frosted chocolate or angel food cake.
• Split layers of yellow cake, fill with lemon custard, and frost lightly with Seven-Minute Frosting.
• Fold grated lemon or lime zest into the frosting over angel food cake.

• Scatter toasted nuts of all types over a frosted chiffon cake.
• Fold sliced fresh strawberries into the frosting before topping an angel food cake.
• Pour a little peppermint schnapps or crème de cacao into frosting to go on a chocolate cake.

BOILED WHITE ICING

MAKES: 2 TO 3 CUPS; ENOUGH TO
FROST THE TOP AND SIDES OF A
2- OR 3-LAYER CAKE

1 cup plus 1 tablespoon granulated
sugar, divided use

¼ cup water

Dash of cream of tartar

Dash of salt

2 large egg whites, at room
temperature

2 tablespoons confectioners' sugar

½ teaspoon vanilla extract

Not all egg white icing is the same. And while the Seven-Minute Frosting can be temperamental and weep on rainy days, this Boiled White Icing is more durable. It is preferred by caterers and tearooms, places that need to bake and frost cakes ahead. And it was a favorite of our ancestors—they often called it White Mountain Frosting or Colonnade Icing. The trick is to keep beating the egg whites as the temperature on the candy thermometer climbs.

1. Place the 1 cup granulated sugar, water, cream of tartar, and salt in a small saucepan over medium-high heat. Stir to combine, then cover and bring to a boil. Once the mixture is boiling, remove the cover and reduce the heat to keep the mixture at a low boil over medium-low heat. Attach a candy thermometer to the side of the pan.

2. Meanwhile, place the egg whites in a large bowl, and beat them with an electric mixer on high speed until they almost form stiff peaks, about 4 minutes. Add the 1 tablespoon granulated sugar gradually while beating, until the whites come to stiff peaks. Set them aside.

3. Check the mixture on the stove, and let the candy thermometer reach 238°F or soft-ball stage. The syrup will slowly drop from a metal spoon. While beating the egg whites again on medium-high speed, slowly drizzle about a third of the syrup into the whites. Place the pan back on the burner and let the syrup come back to a low boil. Let the syrup reach 244°F on the thermometer, when a thin hair of syrup drops from the metal spoon. Slowly drizzle half of this syrup into the whites while beating on medium-high speed. Place the pan back on the burner and let the syrup come to a low boil, and let the temperature reach 250°F. This happens quickly. About 2 thin hairs will drop from the spoon. Slowly drizzle the remaining syrup into the whites, beating at medium-high speed. Immediately beat in the confectioners' sugar and vanilla until just incorporated. The icing should be thick, smooth, and spreadable. Spread at once onto cooled cake layers.

(photo on page 312)

CHOCOLATE FUDGE ICING

MAKES: 2 TO 2½ CUPS; ENOUGH TO FROST THE CENTER AND TOP OF A 2-LAYER CAKE AND LET FROSTING RUN PARTIALLY DOWN THE SIDES, OR SPOON OVER 20 TO 24 CUPCAKES, OR A 13" X 9" CAKE

2 cups granulated sugar

½ cup unsweetened cocoa powder

½ cup whole milk

½ cup (1 stick) lightly salted butter

¼ teaspoon salt

1 teaspoon vanilla extract

Just as the candy known as fudge was cooked slowly on the stove, a cake icing based on fudge was cooked much the same way before it was spread warm onto cake. This old-fashioned recipe was a simple way of using pantry staples in the days before tubs of premade frosting. This was my mother's recipe. She got it from a good friend named Dot Wallman. As children my sisters and I were drawn to the delicious scent of this chocolate icing cooking on the stove.

1. Place the sugar, cocoa, milk, butter, and salt in a medium-size heavy saucepan over medium heat. Stir until the butter melts and the mixture is smooth, 2 to 3 minutes. When the mixture comes to a full and rapid boil, start timing it. This needs to boil for 2 minutes, while you are gently stirring but not scraping the sides of the pan. Remove the pan from the heat and stir in the vanilla. Let the pan cool for 15 minutes.

2. Place the saucepan in a large bowl with ice and beat with a wooden spoon for several minutes or until thickened enough to spread. Or pour the icing into a heatproof bowl and place the bowl in the refrigerator for 10 to 15 minutes so it cools and thickens. Remove the bowl from the refrigerator, and stir with the wooden spoon until smooth.

3. Frost the center and top of a layer cake. If the frosting cools too quickly, reheat it gently in the microwave or on the top of the stove until it has reached spreading consistency.

(photo on page 313)

CREAM CHEESE FROSTING

FOR A 3-LAYER CAKE

12 ounces cream cheese, at room temperature

½ cup (1 stick) unsalted butter, at room temperature

Pinch of salt

5 cups confectioners' sugar, sifted

1½ teaspoons vanilla extract or ½ teaspoon grated lemon zest

FOR A 2-LAYER CAKE

8 ounces cream cheese, at room temperature

½ cup (1 stick) unsalted butter, at room temperature

Pinch of salt

3½ cups confectioners' sugar, sifted

1 teaspoon vanilla extract or ½ teaspoon grated lemon zest

(photo on page 311)

A perennial classic recipe, cream cheese frosting has been spread on some of America's favorite cakes—the carrot cake, red velvet, and Hummingbird. And as long as cream cheese has been used in baking, it has been folded into frostings. An early chocolate cream cheese frosting recipe can be found in the 1948 *Rumford Complete Cook Book*. Here are 2 variations for preparing this frosting, depending on the number of layers in your cake. Make sure your cream cheese and butter are at room temperature before beginning. If needed, place them in a glass bowl in the microwave on high power for 20 seconds to soften.

1. Place the cream cheese and butter in a large mixing bowl, and beat with an electric mixer on low speed until combined, 30 seconds. Add the pinch of salt and half of the confectioners' sugar. Blend until smooth. Add the vanilla and the rest of the confectioners' sugar, and blend until smooth. Increase the mixer speed to medium and beat the frosting until fluffy, about 1 minute more.

2. Frost the cake of your choice. Store the frosting, covered, in the refrigerator for up to 2 days. Let it come to room temperature before spreading on the cake.

COFFEE BUTTER ICING

MAKES: ABOUT 2½ CUPS; ENOUGH TO FROST A 2-LAYER CAKE OR ANGEL FOOD CAKE
....

½ cup (1 stick) unsalted butter, at room temperature

Pinch of salt

2 to 3 teaspoons espresso powder

2½ cups sifted confectioners' sugar

2 to 3 tablespoons milk, or as needed

1 teaspoon vanilla extract

(photo on page 313)

This easy coffee buttercream frosting is adapted from the recipe created by the late Helen Corbitt. It goes well on her Coffee Angel Food Cake (page 193) and any chocolate cake.

1. Place the butter and salt in a large mixing bowl, and beat with an electric mixer on low speed until soft, 30 seconds. Add the espresso powder and blend. Add the sugar and milk alternately until smooth and fluffy. Beat in the vanilla.

2. Spread on the cake of your choice. Or store, covered, in the refrigerator for up to 2 days.

Acknowledgments

WHEN AUTHOR Alice Randall walked up to me at a book launch party several years ago with the suggestion that I should research and write about the history of American cake, it was an idea I could not shake. I thought about it morning, noon, and night. My husband and I were trying to make the difficult decision about whether to buy and restore an old home that my grandfather built and where my father was raised. Did we have the energy and resources to rebuild fireplaces, deal with a 100-year-old roof, and so on? Somehow researching a book on American cake history and rediscovering my family's history at the same time seemed right. So we bought the house, and I dove into this book. Along the way, with each new recipe discovery or nugget of history, I was amazed that this book had not been written. The stories and recipes were out there—in family lore, on pages of community cookbooks, on restaurant menus, and in libraries and museums.

What I gained from the time spent poring over old recipes and cookbooks, interviewing experts in their fields, listening to someone tell a story of their family's favorite cake, and searching newspaper archives was an understanding that our ancestors went through much to bake something simple for the people they loved. And even though the cake of yesterday looked different from the cake of today, and we can bake a cake in a fraction of the time today versus years ago, cakes are timeless confections. They have been baked for the same reasons through the years—to celebrate, honor, and welcome others. I thank my family for their thoughtfulness and humor during these past

2 years of research and redoing our old house. Thanks to my agent David Black and his team for believing in this book and finding it a good home. Thanks to my editor Dervla Kelly, creative wizard Amy King, Rodale's art director; and Marilyn Hauptly, Sara Cox, and Chris Krogermeier in Rodale's managing editorial department, who gave organization and editing to my manuscript. Many thanks to photographer Mitch Mandel and assistant Troy Schnyder for the gorgeous photos in this book. And I am forever thankful to food stylist Paul Grimes and his team for making even the simplest cake look dazzling. Carla Gonzalez-Hart, prop stylist, gave careful thought to the plates, linens, and garnishes in each photograph so that the photos would be not only beautiful but historically correct. A big hug and thanks to Amy Fritch and the Rodale Test Kitchen, who prebaked a multitude of cakes for the photo shoot, which allowed us to stay on schedule. Thanks also to Rodale publisher Gail Gonzales, as well as the publicity and marketing duo of Susan Turner and Melissa Miceli, who now grab the baton and tell the world about this book. Thanks also to Aaron Pattap for his creativity and diligence in shooting video while the photography session was in full swing.

One disclaimer: The recipes I have selected to appear in this book are my choice. So do not be offended if I did not include your favorite cake. Each one of us with a curiosity about the past and a passion for food and the future could take this assignment and run differently with it.

I would like to thank the following people for taking my phone calls, answering my e-mails, and offering advice, a lead, a recipe, an old cookbook, a suggestion, a nugget of information, or just a new way of looking at something. I am grateful for your help.

JANICE BLUESTEIN LONGONE

LAURA SHAPIRO

JOAN NATHAN

LINDSEY SHERE

DAMON LEE FOWLER

DARRA GOLDSTEIN

ALICE RANDALL

DAVID SHIELDS

NATHALIE DUPREE

LEAH CHASE

LENI SORENSEN

NIC BUTLER

GREG PATENT

ROSE LEVY BERANBAUM

ANNE WILLAN

JACK BASS

DORIE GREENSPAN

WILLIAM WOYS WEAVER

SUSAN PUCKETT

MINDY MERRELL

MARTHA BOWDEN

FRONDA ALLEY

KATHLEEN PURVIS

JUDITH EVANS

CLAY BAILEY

SARAH HOOTON

MARCIE COHEN FERRIS

SHERI CASTLE

RIEN FERTEL

JOHN T. EDGE

JUDY WALKER

TONI TIPTON-MARTIN

LUANN SEWELL WATERS

LIZ WILIAMS

BRUCE KRAIG

CORINNE COOK

CATHY BARBER

SANDY BAKER

POPPY TOOKER

NANCY STOHS

NATALIE HAUGHTON

DALE CURRY

JANET KEELER

JILL SILVA

VANCE ELY

CAROL MEEKS

PETER G. ROSE

STEPHEN SCHMIDT

MARY HORNER

BETH CAMPBELL

JAN WHITAKER

BARBARA WEST

JOHN MARTIN TAYLOR

DANA R. CHANDLER

I would like to thank the staff of the following libraries for making their collections accessible and for answering my inquiries.

JANICE BLUESTEIN LONGONE CULINARY ARCHIVE, CLEMENTS LIBRARY, UNIVERSITY OF MICHIGAN

FEEDING AMERICA: THE HISTORIC AMERICAN COOKBOOK PROJECT, MICHIGAN STATE UNIVERSITY

KENTUCKY DIGITAL LIBRARY

KANSAS STATE UNIVERSITY

DUKE UNIVERSITY'S CATALOG OF ADVERTISING COOKBOOKS

BEATRICE McINTOSH COOKERY COLLECTION AT THE UNIVERSITY OF MASSACHUSETTS

MARGARET COOK COOKBOOK COLLECTION, TEXAS WOMAN'S UNIVERSITY

PEACOCK-HARPER CULINARY COLLECTION, VIRGINIA TECH

HERMILDA LISTEMAN CULINARY COLLECTION OF COMMUNITY COOKBOOKS AT THE UNIVERSITY OF ILLINOIS AT URBANA-CHAMPAIGN

UNIVERSITY OF ALABAMA'S AFRICAN-AMERICAN COOKBOOK COLLECTION

UNIVERSITY OF MINNESOTA LIBRARIES

UNIVERSITY OF VERMONT LIBRARIES

HARVARD UNIVERSITY'S SCHLESINGER LIBRARY

FORD MOTOR COMPANY LIBRARY, TUSKEGEE UNIVERSITY

Thank you to the following online research sources.

Gutenberg.org

Npr.org

Nytimes.com

Newspapers.com

Epicurious.com

Chicagotribune.com

Accessible.com (Accessible Archives)

Saveur.com

Foodtimeline.org (and the late Lynne Olver)

Connecticuthistory.org

Britannica.com (Encyclopedia Britannica)

Nps.org

Theoldfoodie.com

Wikipedia

Thank you to the following organizations that opened a window into the past and present.

Julia Child Foundation

New-York Historical Society

Greater Midwest Foodways Alliance

Old Sturbridge Village

Southern Foodways Alliance

Plimoth Plantation

The National Society of the Colonial Dames of America

Colonial Williamsburg

Monticello

Keystone Center for the Study of Regional Foods and Food Tourism

History Colorado Center

Lincoln Home: National Historic Site

Massachusetts Historical Society

American Museum of Natural History

Historical Society of Pennsylvania

University of Alaska–Fairbanks Cooperative Extension Service

Brooklyn Historical Society

Bibliography

Anderson, Jean. *The American Century Cookbook*. New York: Clarkson Potter, 1997. Print.

Andrews, Glenn. *Food from the Heartland: The Cooking of America's Midwest*. New York: Prentice-Hall, 1991. Print.

Anyone Can Bake. New York: Royal Baking Powder Co., 1929. Print.

Baird, Sarah C. *Kentucky Sweets: Bourbon Balls, Spoonbread & Mile High Pie*. Charleston, SC: The History Press, 2014. Print.

Balsley, Betsy. *The Los Angeles Times California Cookbook*. New York: H.N. Abrams, 1981. Print.

Beard, James. *Delights and Prejudices*. New York: Atheneum, 1964. Print.

Beck, Simone, Louisette Bertholle, and Julia Child. *Mastering the Art of French Cooking*. New York: Alfred A. Knopf, 1971. Print.

Bienvenu, Marcelle, and Judy Walker, editors. *Cooking Up a Storm*. San Francisco: Chronicle Books, 2008. Print.

Bomberger, Maude A. *Colonial Recipes: From Old Virginia and Maryland Manors, with Numerous Legends and Traditions Interwoven*. New York: The Neale Publishing Co., 1907. Print.

Boorstin, Daniel J. *The Americans: The Colonial Experience*. New York: Random House, 1958. Print.

Booth, Letha. *The Williamsburg Cookbook: Traditional and Contemporary Recipes*. Williamsburg, VA: Colonial Williamsburg Foundation, 1975. Print.

Brown, Marion Lea. *Marion Brown's Southern Cook Book*. Chapel Hill, NC: University of North Carolina, 1968. Print.

Bryan, Lettice. *The Kentucky Housewife*. Columbia, SC: University of South Carolina, 1991. Print.

Byrn, Anne. *The Cake Mix Doctor*. New York: Workman Publishing Co., 1999. Print.

Cannon, Poppy, and Patricia Brooks. *The Presidents' Cookbook: Practical Recipes from George Washington to the Present*. New York: Funk & Wagnalls, 1968. Print.

Carter, Jimmy. *Christmas in Plains: Memories*. New York: Simon & Schuster, 2001. Print.

Castle, Sheri. *The Southern Living Community Cookbook: Celebrating Food & Fellowship in the American South*. Birmingham, AL: Oxmoor House, 2014. Print.

Chandonnet, Ann. *Gold Rush Grub: From Turpentine Stew to Hoochinoo*. Fairbanks, AK: University of Alaska, 2005. Print.

Chase, Leah. *The Dooky Chase Cookbook*. Gretna, LA: Pelican Publishing, 1990. Print.

Clark, Marian. *The Route 66 Cookbook*. Tulsa, OK: Council Oak, 1993. Print.

Coleman, Mildred Huff. *The Frances Virginia Tea Room Cookbook*. Atlanta, GA: Peachtree Publishers, 1981. Print.

Cooking with Soup. Camden, NJ: Home Economics Department, Campbell Soup, 1977. Print.

Corbitt, Helen. *Helen Corbitt's Cookbook*. Boston: Houghton Mifflin, 1957. Print.

Corriher, Shirley. *BakeWise*. New York: Scribner, 2008. Print.

Cunningham, Marion. *Lost Recipes: Meals to Share with Friends and Family*. New York: Alfred A. Knopf, 2003. Print.

Donovan, Mary, Amy Hatrak, Frances Mills, and Elizabeth Shull. *The Thirteen Colonies Cookbook*. New York: Praeger Publishing, 1975. Print.

Dull, Mrs. S. R. *Southern Cooking*. New York, NY: Grosset & Dunlap, 1941. Print.

Dupree, Nathalie, and Cynthia Graubart. *Mastering the Art of Southern Cooking*. Salt Lake City, UT: Gibbs Smith, 2012. Print.

Egerton, John. *Side Orders: Small Helpings of Southern Cookery & Culture*. Atlanta, GA: Peachtree Publishers, 1990. Print.

———. *Southern Food: At Home, on the Road, in History*. New York: Alfred A. Knopf, 1987. Print.

Ex Libris: A Treasury of Recipes. Wellesley, MA: Friends of the Wellesley Free Libraries, 1987. Print.

Ferris, Marcie Cohen. *Matzoh Ball Gumbo: Culinary Tales of the Jewish South*. Chapel Hill, NC: University of North Carolina, 2005. Print.

Fisher, M. F. K. *How to Cook a Wolf*. San Francisco: North Point Press, 1988. Print.

Flexner, Marion W. *Out of Kentucky Kitchens*. Lexington, KY: University of Kentucky, 1989. Print.

Fowler, Damon Lee. *Dining at Monticello: In Good Taste and Abundance*. Charlottesville, VA: Thomas Jefferson Foundation, 2005. Print.

Fussell, Betty Harper. *I Hear America Cooking*. New York: Viking, 1986. Print.

General Foods Cook Book. New York: Consumer Service Department, General Foods Corporation, 1932. Print.

Goodman, Donald, and Thomas Head, editors. *The Happy Table of Eugene Walter: Southern Spirits in Food and Drink*. Chapel Hill, NC: University of North Carolina, 2011. Print.

Grierson, Alice Kirk, and Mary L. Williams. *An Army Wife's Cookbook with Household Hints and Home Remedies*. Globe, AZ: Southwest Parks and Monuments Association, 1972. Print.

Hachten, Harva, and Terese Allen. *The Flavor of Wisconsin: An Informal History of Food and Eating in the Badger State*. Madison: Wisconsin Historical Society, 2009. Print.

Haller, Henry, and Virginia Aronson. *The White House Family Cookbook*. New York: Random House, 1987. Print.

Harbury, Katharine E. *Colonial Virginia's Cooking Dynasty*. Columbia, SC: University of South Carolina, 2004. Print.

Heatter, Maida. *Maida Heatter's Cakes*. Kansas City, MO: Andrews McMeel Publishing, 1997. Print.

Heller, Edna Eby. *The Art of Pennsylvania Dutch Cooking*. Garden City, NY: Doubleday, 1968. Print.

Hess, John L., and Karen Hess. *The Taste of America*. New York: Grossman Publishers, 1977. Print.

Horry, Harriott Pinckney, and Richard J. Hooker. *A Colonial Plantation Cookbook: The Receipt Book of Harriott Pinckney Horry, 1770*. Columbia, SC: University of South Carolina, 1984. Print.

Humble, Nicola. *Cake: A Global History*. London: Reaktion, 2010. Print.

Hutchison, Ruth. *The Pennsylvania Dutch Cook Book*. New York: Harper & Row, 1977. Print.

Jamison, Cheryl Alters, and Bill Jamison. *Tasting New Mexico: Recipes Celebrating One Hundred Years of Distinctive Home Cooking*. Albuquerque, NM: Museum of New Mexico Press, 2012. Print.

Jones, Evan. *American Food: The Gastronomic Story*, 2nd edition, New York: Random House, 1981. Print.

Kander, Mrs. Simon, and Mrs. Henry Schoenfeld. *The "Settlement" Cookbook: 1903 (The Way to a Man's Heart)*. Carlisle, MA: Applewood Books, 1996. Print.

Katzen, Mollie. *The Moosewood Cookbook*. Ithaca, NY: Glad Day Press, 1974. Print.

Kimball, Marie Goebel. *The Martha Washington Cook Book*. New York: Coward-McCann, 1940. Print.

———. *Thomas Jefferson's Cook Book*. Charlottesville, VA: University of Virginia Press, 1976. Print.

King, Caroline B., and Thelma Wise. *Victorian Cakes: A Reminiscence with Recipes*. Berkeley, CA: Aris Books, 1986. Print.

Klapthor, Margaret Brown, and Helen Claire Duprey Bullock. *The First Ladies Cook Book: Favorite Recipes of All the Presidents of the United States*. New York, NY: Parents' Magazine Press, 1982. Print.

Koock, Mary Faulk. *The Texas Cookbook: From Barbecue to Banquet—An Informal View of Dining and Entertaining the Texas Way*. Denton, TX: University of North Texas Press, 1965. Print.

LeClercq, Anne Sinkler Whaley. *An Antebellum Plantation Household: Including the South Carolina Low Country Receipts and Remedies of Emily Wharton Sinkler*. Columbia, SC: University of South Carolina Press, 2006. Print.

LeSueur, Sadie. *Recipes and Party Plans: A Cookbook for the Hostess*. New York: Hearthside Press, 1958. Print.

Lewis, Edna, with Mary Goodbody. *In Pursuit of Flavor*. New York: Alfred A. Knopf, 1988. Print.

Lucas, Dione, and Marion Gorman. *The Dione Lucas Book of French Cooking*. Boston: Little, Brown, 1973. Print.

Mariani, John F. *The Dictionary of American Food and Drink*. New York: Ticknor & Fields, 1983. Print.

Metcalfe, Gayden, and Charlotte Hays. *Being Dead Is No Excuse: The Official Southern Ladies Guide to Hosting the Perfect Funeral*. New York: Miramax Books, 2005. Print.

Mintz, Sidney W. *Sweetness and Power: The Place of Sugar in Modern History*. New York: Penguin Books, 1985. Print.

Nathan, Zoe. *Huckleberry: Stories, Secrets, and Recipes from Our Kitchen*. San Francisco: Chronicle Books, 2014. Print.

Neal, Bill. *Bill Neal's Southern Cooking*. Chapel Hill, NC: University of North Carolina Press, 1985. Print.

Ojakangas, Beatrice A. *Great Old-Fashioned American Recipes*. Minneapolis: University of Minnesota Press, 2005. Print.

O'Neill, Molly. *New York Cookbook: From Pelham Bay to Park Avenue, Firehouses to Four-Star Restaurants*. New York: Workman Publishing Co., 1992. Print.

Page, Linda Garland, and Eliot Wigginton, editors. *The Foxfire Book of Appalachian Cookery*. New York: E. P. Dutton, 1984. Print.

Patent, Greg. *Baking in America: Traditional and Contemporary Favorites from the Past 200 Years*. Boston: Houghton Mifflin Co., 2002. Print.

Perkins, Mrs. N. R., and Virginia Federation of Home Demonstration Clubs. *Recipes from Old Virginia*. Richmond, VA: Dietz Press Inc., 1958. Print.

Piercy, Caroline B. *The Shaker Cook Book: Not by Bread Alone*. New York: Crown Publishers, 1953. Print.

Puckett, Susan. *Eat Drink Delta: A Hungry Traveler's Journey through the Soul of the South*. Athens, GA: University of Georgia Press, 2013. Print.

Randolph, Mary. *The Virginia House-wife*. Birmingham, AL.: Oxmoor House, 1988. Print.

Rawlings, Marjorie Kinnan. *Cross Creek Cookery*. New York: Charles Scribner's Sons, 1942. Print.

Reed, Julia. *Ham Biscuits, Hostess Gowns, and Other Southern Specialties: An Entertaining Life (with Recipes)*. New York: St. Martin's Press, 2008. Print.

Rhett, Blanche S. *200 Years of Charleston Cooking*. New York: Random House, 1934. Print.

River Road Recipes. Baton Rouge, LA: Junior League of Baton Rouge, 1959. Print.

Roberts, Cokie. *Founding Mothers: The Women Who Raised Our Nation*. New York: William Morrow, 2004. Print.

Rombauer, Irma S. *The Joy of Cooking*. New York: Charles Scribner's Sons, 1959. Print.

Rosso, Julee, and Sheila Lukins. *The Silver Palate Cookbook*. New York: Workman Publishing Co., 1979. Print.

Russell, Malinda, and Janice Bluestein Longone. *A Domestic Cook Book: Containing a Careful Selection of Useful Receipts for the Kitchen*. Ann Arbor, MI: Longone Center for American Culinary Research, William L. Clements Library, University of Michigan, 2007. Print.

Satterfield, Steven. *Root to Leaf: A Southern Chef Cooks through the Seasons*. New York: Harper Wave, 2015. Print.

Sax, Richard. *Classic Home Desserts: A Treasury of Heirloom and Contemporary Recipes from around the World*. New York: Houghton Mifflin, 1994. Print.

Scaggs, Deirdre A., and Andrew W. McGraw. *The Historic Kentucky Kitchen: Traditional Recipes for Today's Cook*. Lexington: University Press of Kentucky, 2013. Print.

Sewell, Ernestine P., and Joyce Gibson Roach. *Eats: A Folk History of Texas Foods*. Fort Worth: Texas Christian University Press, 1989. Print.

Shapiro, Laura. *Perfection Salad: Women and Cooking at the Turn of the Century*. New York: Farrar, Straus, and Giroux, 1986. Print.

————. *Something from the Oven: Reinventing Dinner in 1950's America*. New York: Viking Press, 2004. Print.

Shere, Lindsey Remolif. *Chez Panisse Desserts*. New York: Random House, 1985. Print.

Shields, David S. *Southern Provisions: The Creation & Revival of a Cuisine*. Chicago: University of Chicago Press, 2015. Print.

Simmons, Amelia, and Mary Tolford Wilson. *The First American Cookbook: A Facsimile of "American Cookery," 1796*. New York: Dover Publications, 1984. Print.

Smith, Andrew F. *The Oxford Companion to American Food and Drink*. New York: Oxford University Press, 2007. Print.

Sohn, Mark F. *Appalachian Home Cooking: History, Culture, and Recipes*. Lexington, KY: University of Kentucky Press, 2005. Print.

Sokolov, Raymond A. *Why We Eat What We Eat*. New York: Simon & Schuster, 1991. Print.

Spaulding, Lily May, and John Spaulding. *Civil War Recipes: Receipts from the Pages of Godey's Lady's Book*. Lexington, KY: University of Kentucky Press, 1999. Print.

Staib, Walter, and Paul Bauer. *The City Tavern Cookbook: Recipes from the Birthplace of American Cuisine*. Philadelphia, PA: Running Press, 2009. Print.

Taylor, John Martin. *The New Southern Cook: 200 Recipes from the South's Best Chefs and Home Cooks*. New York: Bantam Books, 1995. Print.

Theobald, Mary Miley. *Recipes from the Raleigh Tavern Bakery*. Williamsburg, VA: Colonial Williamsburg Foundation, 1984. Print.

Thurman, Sue Bailey, and Anne Bower. *The Historical Cookbook of the American Negro*. Boston: Beacon Press, 2000. Print.

Tillery, Carolyn Quick. *The African-American Heritage Cookbook: Traditional Recipes & Fond Remembrances from Alabama's Renowned Tuskegee Institute*. Secaucus, NJ: Carol Publishing Group, 1996. Print.

Trager, James. *The Food Chronology: A Food Lover's Compendium of Events and Anecdotes, from Prehistory to the Present*. New York: Henry Holt, 1995. Print.

A Treatise on Cake Making to Assist the Baker in Gaining the Cake Business Which Should Rightfully Be His. New York: Fleischmann Division, Standard Brands, 1933. Print.

Volo, James M., and Dorothy Denneen Volo. *Family Life in 19th-Century America*. Westport, CT: Greenwood, 2007. Print.

Wallace, Lily Haxworth. *The Rumford Complete Cook Book*. Providence, RI: Department of Home Economics of Rumford, 1948. Print.

Ward, Jessica Bemis. *Food to Die For: A Book of Funeral Food, Tips and Tales from the Old City Cemetery, Lynchburg, Virginia*. Lynchburg, VA: Southern Memorial Association, 2004. Print.

Warner, Edith, and Patrick Burns. *In the Shadow of Los Alamos: Selected Writings of Edith Warner*. Albuquerque, NM: University of New Mexico Press, 2008. Print.

Weaver, William Woys. *As American as Shoofly Pie: The Foodlore and Fakelore of Pennsylvania Dutch Cuisine*. Philadelphia: University of Pennsylvania Press, 2013. Print.

Whaley, Emily. *Mrs. Whaley's Charleston Kitchen: Advice, Opinions, and 100 Recipes from a Southern Legend*. New York: Simon & Schuster, 1998. Print.

Wigginton, Eliot. *A Foxfire Christmas*. New York: Doubleday, 1990. Print.

Williams, Elizabeth M. *New Orleans: A Food Biography*. Lanham, MD: AltaMira Press, 2013. Print.

Willigen, John Van. *Kentucky's Cookbook Heritage: Two Hundred Years of Southern Cuisine and Culture*. Lexington, KY: University of Kentucky Press, 2014. Print.

Wilson, Mrs. Henry Lumpkin. *The Atlanta Exposition Cookbook*. Athens, GA: University of Georgia Press, 1984. Print.

Young-Brown, Fiona. *A Culinary History of Kentucky: Burgoo, Beer Cheese & Goetta*. Charleston, SC: History Press, 2014. Print.

Zanger, Mark. *The American History Cookbook*. Westport, CT: Greenwood, 2003. Print.

Credits

Index

Boldface page numbers indicate photographs or illustrations. <u>Underscored</u> references indicate boxed text.

Goodfellow, Elizabeth (cooking teacher), <u>21</u>, <u>43</u>

Goodman, Donald (*The Happy Table of Eugene Walter: Southern Spirits in Food and Drink*), 291

Gooey Butter Cake, 184–86, **185**

Gottlieb, Sadie (Gottlieb's), 200

Gottlieb's bakery (Savannah), 200

Graham, Sylvester (graham crackers), <u>154</u>

Grandma's Mincemeat Cake with Caramel Icing, 122–24, **123**

Grand National Recipe and Baking Contest, 1949 (now Pillsbury Bake-Off®), <u>221</u>

Granny Kellett's Jam Cake, 52–54, **53**

Grapefruit
Brown Derby Grapefruit Cake, 159–61, **160**
Grapefruit Frosting, 159, **160**, 161

"Great Cakes" (colonial fruitcakes), <u>34</u>

Greater Midwest Food Alliance, <u>217</u>

Greene, Gael (food writer), 256

"The Gulf Between Them" (Stephens, 1864), 46

H

Hachten, Harva (*The Flavor of Wisconsin*), 8

Hadassah Society, Minneapolis chapter, <u>229</u>

Hale, Sarah Josepha (*Godey's Lady's Book*), 39

Half Pound Cake, 284, **285**

Halsey, Admiral William, <u>169</u>

Hamblet, Polly, 224

Happ, Gary (Barrington Brewery), 288

Harbury, Katharine (*Colonial Virginia's Cooking Dynasty*), 13

Harper, Mrs. J. D., <u>217</u>

Harriman, Mary (founder, Junior League), <u>182</u>

Harriott Horry's Water Cake, **30**, 31

Harrison, Ruth, 197

Hartford Election Cake, <u>34</u>, <u>37</u>

Hartridge, Emelyn (Vassar fudge), <u>119</u>

Harvey, Betty, 173

Harvey, Fred (hotel and restaurant owner), 154

Harvey, Lucile Plowden, 173

Hatrak, Amy (*The Thirteen Colonies Cookbook*), 84

Haughton, Natalie (food writer), 287

Hawaiian Chantilly Cake, 273–75, **274**

Hawaiian Pineapple Company (now Dole Food Company), 145, <u>147</u>

Hayes, Lucy Webb ("Lemonade Lucy"), 76

Hays, Charlotte (*Being Dead is No Excuse*), 208

Hazelnuts (filberts), <u>49</u>, <u>270</u>
blanching, <u>272</u>
Robert Redford Cake, 270–72, **271**

Head, Thomas (*The Happy Table of Eugene Walter: Southern Spirits in Food and Drink*), 291

Heatter, Maida (*Maida Heatter's New Book of Great Desserts*), 156, 178, 270

Heitzman Bakery (Louisville, Kentucky), <u>54</u>, 184

Helen Corbitt's Coffee Angel Food Cake, **192**, 193

Helfrich, Ella Rita ("the Cake Lady"), 223, 226, <u>228</u>, <u>229</u>, <u>260</u>

Hemings, James (cook, slave), 8

Herbsaint, 284
Half Pound Cake, 284, **285**

Hershey, Milton (chocolate), 68, 197

Hershey Bar Cake, 197–99, **198**

Hess, Karen (food historian), 9, <u>14</u>, <u>24</u>, <u>37</u>

Hesser, Amanda (food writer), 261

Hickory nuts, <u>49</u>
Sarah Polk's Hickory Nut Cake, 50, **51**

Hill, Margaret, <u>117</u>

Hills Brothers Company (Dromedary Gingerbread Mix), 17

Hogue, Jessie (cooking teacher), <u>189</u>

Home demonstration agents, 187, <u>189</u>

Homemaker clubs, <u>189</u>

"Home-Making Helps" (Barton, 1923), <u>183</u>

Honey, 4, <u>6</u>, 138
Robert Redford Cake, 270–72, **271**
Scripture Cake (Bible Cake), 74, **75**
Sister Sadie's Honey Cake, 200, **201**

Hooker, Richard J. (A Colonial Plantation Cookbook), 3, 31

Hooton, Mary, 194, <u>195</u>

Hooton, Sarah, 194

Horry, Harriet Pinckney (*A Colonial Plantation Cookbook*, 1770), 3, 31, 61

Howard, Maria (cookbook author), 88

Huckleberries
James Beard's Huckleberry Cake, 224, **225**

Huguenot Tavern (Charleston, South Carolina), 181

Huguenot Torte, **180**, 181

Humble, Nicola (*Cake: A Global History*), <u>131</u>

Hummingbird Cake, The, 235–37, **236**

Hunt (Hunt's perfect baking products), <u>103</u>

Hurley, Marion, 52

Husted, Marjorie Child (builder of Betty Crocker image and brand), <u>182</u>

Hutchison, Ruth (*The Pennsylvania Dutch Cook Book*), 139

Hutzler's tearoom, <u>112</u>

I

Ice Cream
Ice Cream Sundae Cake, 199

Icings. *See* Frostings and icings; Glazes

Ihrig, Leona Rusk (cooking teacher), <u>189</u>

Ilarraza, Christine (chef), 84

Indian Pound Cake, <u>21</u>

Ingleheart brothers (Swans Down), 4

Ingredients. *See also* specific ingredient
baking powder, 7, <u>24</u>
in early America, 3–7
extracts, <u>50</u>
almond, <u>50</u>
vanilla, <u>50</u>, <u>98</u>
flour, 4–5
for pound cakes, <u>21</u>, <u>28</u>
impact of railroads on, 68
introduction of new in early 20th century, 100
leavenings
in early America, 7, 12
introduction of new, 7, <u>24</u>, 38
shortening and cooking oil, 1, <u>24</u>, 100, <u>124</u>

Inskeep, Mrs. Russell (Mrs. America 1957), 187

Italian Cream Cake, 246–48, **247**